Context and the Attitudes

Context and the Attitudes

Meaning in Context, Volume 1

Mark Richard

OXFORD
UNIVERSITY PRESS

Great Clarendon Street, Oxford, OX2 6DP,
United Kingdom

Oxford University Press is a department of the University of Oxford.
It furthers the University's objective of excellence in research, scholarship,
and education by publishing worldwide. Oxford is a registered trade mark of
Oxford University Press in the UK and in certain other countries

© in this volume Mark Richard 2013

The moral rights of the author have been asserted

First published 2013
First published in paperback 2015

All rights reserved. No part of this publication may be reproduced, stored in
a retrieval system, or transmitted, in any form or by any means, without the
prior permission in writing of Oxford University Press, or as expressly permitted
by law, by licence, or under terms agreed with the appropriate reprographics
rights organization. Enquiries concerning reproduction outside the scope of the
above should be sent to the Rights Department, Oxford University Press, at the
address above

You must not circulate this work in any other form
and you must impose this same condition on any acquirer

Published in the United States of America by Oxford University Press
198 Madison Avenue, New York, NY 10016, United States of America

British Library Cataloguing in Publication Data
Data available

Library of Congress Cataloging in Publication Data
Data available

ISBN 978–0–19–955795–0 (Hbk.)
ISBN 978–0–19–955794–3 (Pbk.)

Links to third party websites are provided by Oxford in good faith and
for information only. Oxford disclaims any responsibility for the materials
contained in any third party website referenced in this work.

For Nancy, *illa sine qua non*

...an art critic having written somewhere that in Vermeer's *View of Delft*...a little patch of yellow wall...was so well painted that it was, if one looked at it by itself, like some priceless specimen of Chinese art, of a beauty sufficient in itself, Bergotte ate a few potatoes, left the house and went to the exhibition.... At last he came to the Vermeer...he noticed...the precious substance of the tiny patch of yellow wall. His dizziness increased; he fixed his gaze, like a child upon a yellow butterfly that it wants to catch, on the precious little patch of wall. "That's how I ought to have written," he said. "My last books are too dry, I ought to have gone over them with a few layers of color, made my language precious in itself, like this little patch of yellow wall." Meanwhile he was not unconscious of the gravity of his situation.

Marcel Proust, *La Prisonnière*

Acknowledgments

Thanks to those who have kindly given me permission to republish the essays collected here. The introduction to this volume is new. First publication of the other essays is as follows.

"Direct Reference and Ascriptions of Belief," *Journal of Philosophical Logic* 12 (1983) 425–47.

"Quantification and Leibniz's Law," *The Philosophical Review* 96 (1987) 555–87.

"Attitude Ascriptions, Semantic Theory, and Pragmatic Evidence," *Proceedings of the Aristotelian Society* 87 (1986/87) 243–62.

"How I Say What You Think," in P. French, T. Uehling, and H. Wettstein (eds), *Midwest Studies in Philosophy i4* (University of Minnesota Press, 1989), pp. 317–37.

"Attitudes in Context," *Linguistics and Philosophy* 16 (1993) 123–48.

"Defective Contexts, Accommodation, and Normalization," *Canadian Journal of Philosophy* 25 (1995) 551–70.

"Propositional Quantification," in J. Copeland (ed.), *Logic and Reality* (Oxford University Press, 1996), pp. 437–60.

"Sense, Necessity, and Belief," *Philosophical Studies* 69 (1993) 243–63.

"Semantic Pretense," in A. Everett and T. Hofweber (eds), *Empty Names, Fiction, and the Puzzles of Nonexistence* (CSLI Publications, 2000), pp. 205–32. (This article appears here with the ending, which was omitted in the published version, restored.)

"Intensional Transitives and Empty Terms," in P. French, T. Uehling, and H. Wettstein (eds), *Midwest Studies in Philosophy* 25 (2002) 103–27. (Originally published under the title "Seeking a Centaur, Adoring Adonis: Intensional Transitives and Empty Terms.")

"Objects of Relief," in A. Jokic and Q. Smith (eds), *Time, Tense, and Reference* (MIT Press, 2003), pp. 157–89.

"Meaning and Attitude Ascriptions," *Philosophical Studies* 128 (2006) 683–709.

"Kripke's Puzzle," in A. Berger (ed.), *Saul Kripke* (Cambridge University Press, 2011), pp. 211–34. (Originally published under the title "Kripke's Puzzle about Belief.")

I have tried my best to correct typographical errors in the original. I have also normalized the syntax of formalizations across papers.

Contents

1. Introduction: Mental States and their Ascription — 1
2. Direct Reference and Ascriptions of Belief — 26
3. Quantification and Leibniz's Law — 48
4. Attitude Ascriptions, Semantic Theory, and Pragmatic Evidence — 65
5. How I Say What You Think — 80
6. Attitudes in Context — 100
7. Defective Contexts, Accommodation, and Normalization — 121
8. Propositional Quantification — 137
9. Sense, Necessity, and Belief — 156
10. Semantic Pretense — 172
11. Intensional Transitives and Empty Terms — 197
12. Objects of Relief — 222
13. Meaning and Attitude Ascriptions — 246
14. Kripke's Puzzle — 263

References — 283
Index — 287

1

Introduction
Mental States and their Ascription

Propositional attitudes—belief, knowledge, desire, and so on—pose tough questions, both for philosophy of mind and philosophy of language. The essays collected here address issues about both mind and language with an emphasis on the latter. This introduction provides an overview, summarizes the approach subsequent essays take, corrects some of their mistakes, and addresses a few topics on which they are silent.

1. The work of Burge, Kaplan, Kripke, and Putnam made belief and other propositional attitudes seem particularly problematic to philosophy of language and mind. That work seemed to have two morals: (1) For the most part, words and mental states don't get their semantic properties from the conceptualizations of speakers and thinkers. Reference—what a name picks out, what a predicate is true of—is instead determined by social and causal relations of which we are by and large innocent. (2) The ways in which we conceptualize objects and properties are typically idiosyncratic and often erroneous. Thus, they are unlikely candidates for publicly accessible meaning.

These morals led many to accept the broadly Russellian thesis that propositions—the objects of thought and contents of sentence uses—are individuated referentially, in terms of the objects and properties they are about. Where Russell went wrong, the many said, was somewhere on the road from *Principles of Mathematics* (in which ordinary names were supposed to be *names*, contributing only their referents to what is said) to the paper "Knowledge by Acquaintance and Knowledge by Description," with its fatal misstep of assimilating ordinary names to descriptions extracted from the contents of consciousness. According to this line of thought, Russell was right to think that what is asserted by "Twain is Twain" is not less, not more, than what is asserted by "Twain is Clemens." Thinking this, many of the many came to think that there could be no difference between believing that Twain is Twain and believing that Twain is Clemens, since the objects of the beliefs are the same.

Morals (1) and (2) have always seemed to me correct. The idea that belief involves a relation to something like one of Russell's propositions seems to me to have considerable merit. The idea that whoever thinks that Twain's Twain thinks that Twain's Clemens seems to me a non-starter. The slide from the meritorious idea to the crazy one, I think, is the result of an overly simple picture of belief and the other attitudes, one shared by Russell and Frege.

Frege and (the early) Russell each present belief, knowledge, and kindred attitudes as simple, unmediated relations to a truth determining object. It is not just that Frege thinks that our "ideas" are idiosyncratic, private objects that (since they can't be shared) can't be thoughts. One gets the impression that Frege's view is that mental representations are close to *irrelevant* to the question, How do we come to believe what we do? My mental representation of redness or of the apple may provide the occasion for my grasping the abstract "ways of thinking" of the color and the fruit that constitute my thought that the apple is red. But my grasp of the thought that the apple is red is apparently a sort of unmediated intercourse between my mind and a "Third Realm" in which representational powers of my ideas play no role. On the contrary: that my mental representation of redness is a representation *of redness* is to be explained by my "grasping" the sense **redness** and associating it with the mental particular.

According to Russell, we are related to the objects of our attitudes by being "acquainted" with them. Whatever acquaintance is, among its hallmarks is that it is a direct, unmediated relation: to be acquainted with an object is to be "given" the object in experience. Indeed, objects of acquaintance are, in some sense, "completely given" to me in experience, so that they are "immediately known to me just as they are."[1] One gets the impression that Russell thinks there is precious little work for the notion of mental representation to do in an account of the attitudes: To entertain a thought is to be ("actively") acquainted with it and its parts; to be acquainted with something is for it—all of it—to be there, given in experience, somewhat as a pile of bricks might be there, lying on the street. To think the thought that x is F, I don't need to have a representation of x or F; to think that thought is (in good part) for x and F to be "directly presented" to me in experience.

I find these views odd. What seems odd to me about Frege's view is not the idea that thought involves ways of thinking of the objects and properties it is about. What is odd is Frege's attempt to divorce these ways of thinking—to divorce representation—from the mind. Frege's "ways of thinking" are abstract objects, out there in the "Third Realm," no more cognitive than a rock, an Aristotelian universal, or the number 72. Surely, however, ways of thinking are, well, ways of *thinking*—they are properties of the medium of thought.

What seems odd to me about Russell's view is not the idea that in our experience or thought we might be "directly aware" of objects and properties. There is a perfectly good sense in which Laura is thinking about Eli directly, when she thinks "Eli's coming" or, seeing him approaching, forms a belief based on her visual presentation that he approaches. The thought is direct because its aboutness is unmediated—it is not about Eli *because* it is in the first instance about something else. When Laura thinks "Eli's coming" or sees him come, her thought is about Eli not because she describes an individual

---

[1] Russell (1912), 47.

in a certain way, a way that as it happens fits Eli and no other. In the latter case, there are two steps in the process of getting from Laura to Eli: We go from Laura's conceptualization to a condition determined thereby, and then from the condition to Eli. In the case in which Laura's belief is realized by a name or visual state, the name or state itself, given Laura's situation in the world, determines Eli.

What is odd about Russell's view is not the idea that thought or experience might in some interesting sense tie us directly to the world. What is odd is the way Russell excises mental representations that are distinct from what they represent from his account of the attitudes. My visual experience and token sentences connect me quite directly, in a perfectly good sense of "direct," with the objects and properties of my world. Laura's visual experience of Eli represents Eli; her tokening *he's here* is a matter of her talking about him. But her experience and sentence are not identical with, constituted by, or very much like the objects and properties they connect her with. And her being cognitively in touch with Eli, in virtue of the experience or sentence tokening, is very much a matter of *relational* properties of those *mental* representations.

We think about—we think, if you like, "directly about"—the objects and properties in our world. We do this by representing them in one way or another. When you or I have a belief, a bit of knowledge, a wish, or another attitude, there are three players: The thinker, the representational state that realizes the attitude, and the state of affairs that that state represents. Belief and the other attitudes are not simple binary relations, as Frege and Russell would have it; they are importantly triadic.[2]

For both Russell and Frege the objects of our attitudes are structured. The Fregean thought that the apple is red has a way of thinking of the apple and a way of thinking of being red as constituents;[3] the Russellian singular proposition that the apple is red has the apple itself (with all its alar) and the property of being red as parts. Both Russell and Frege would say that to think a thought one must be in "cognitive contact" with its constituents. Insofar as representing something is a way of being in cognitive contact with it, I more or less agree. When you or I think that the apple is red, we represent the apple as red, and thus represent the apple and represent being red.

I'm willing to go a step further and nominalize the verbs here: when you or I think that the apple is red, we have a representation of the apple and a representation of the

---

[2] Two qualifications. (1) Of course, we can have representations that are defective in one way or another: sentences with empty names, visual states that purport to present objects but in fact do not. In such cases we have representations that do not represent. For perfectly good reasons we group the states we are in when we have such representations with those we are in when we have non-defective representations. The belief that Satan will greet me when I die is as much a belief as the belief that Laura wrote a song about dying, though what realizes the first belief is defective in a way that what realizes the second is not. Belief and the other attitudes are triadic when not defective. We classify, for very good reason, the defective states with the non-defective.
(2) In Section 5 below, I discuss the attitudes of animals and things like computers. There I will qualify the idea that having an attitude about X requires having a *representation* of X, though I will not retract the claim that (non-defective) attitudes are three-way relations.

[3] I ignore delicate issues about the relation of a Fregean thought to the senses of phrases in sentences expressing that thought.

property of being red. Some find such nominalization noxious. They think it's the crucial first step down the road to a language of thought, the representations introduced by the nominalization of "represents" being something like the lexicon of thought's language. Myself, I don't see all that much of a difference between saying

> John represents the apple and (representing it as red) represents the property of being red

and

> John has a representation of the apple and (representing it as red) a representation of red.

What nominalization buys is compactness of expression, especially when we speak of someone's representing an object in the same or different ways. Instead of having to stumble through

> In thinking that Twain wrote *Huck Finn*, John represented Twain in the same way as he did when he thought that Twain wrote *1609*, but not in the way in which he did when thought that Twain was born in Hartford,

we can say

> The representation of Twain involved in John's thoughts that Twain wrote *Huck Finn* and that he wrote *1609* isn't the same as that involved in his thought that Twain was born in Hartford.

What is crucial is that we are able to speak of identity and diversity of ways of representing. What separates the view I am sketching from the views of Frege and Russell is the idea that when we speak of "ways of representing" we (at least sometimes) are speaking not of the mind independent constituents of our thought, but of aspects of the medium of representation, be those aspects linguistic or mental.

The idea that we represent objects, their properties, and relations in various ways should not be terribly controversial. Neither should it be terribly controversial that different states of belief may involve representing an object in the same way, or that different beliefs may represent one object in different ways. It makes perfectly good sense to say that there is a way Venus is represented in our experience when we look at it in early evening, that there is a different way it is represented in our experience when we look at it at sunrise, and that Venus is represented in the first way, but not the second way, in beliefs we acquired on Monday and Tuesday. What is controversial is how such ways of representing are to be individuated, and how identity and difference of ways of representing are reflected in our knowledge of our thoughts. Suppose, for example, that Venus is represented in the same way in two of my belief states—my beliefs that it rises in the West and that it sets in the East, say. Must I be aware of that identity of representation (in a sense testified to by my being disposed to think that something rises in the East and sets in the West)?

It is tempting to answer "yes." Almost everyone, philosophers and non, thinks meaning and thought are in some sense transparent to the thinker. What this means is obscure, but not *that* obscure. It implies, for example, that if I think that Marty is in the closet, and then think that if Marty is in the closet, Sandra is too, I should be in a position to know more or less immediately that my second thought (as we might put it) involves the content of my first thought. If we agree with the idea about transparency, it will be natural to say that representational identity is transparent to the thinker, and so the answer to the question at the end of the last paragraph is *yes*. That is, it is natural and reasonable to think that token representational states have types (and have token parts that themselves have representational types) that (a) are at least reasonable first candidates for what grounds talk of sameness of thought or meaning, and (b) are transparent to the thinker in the relevant ways.[4]

This is, as I say, a reasonable thought. But it is only roughly right. Imagine that John watched a dog cross the road, and that bits of that experience are now recorded in his long-term memory. One wants to say that the dog was represented in the same way in the perceptual experience as it is in the memory that records it. And one wants to say that the dog is represented in the same way in temporally abutting bits of the perceptual experience. But the memory John has of the start of the dog's journey and the memory he has of its end might not be related in such a way that, when he reflects on them, it is clear to him whether they are memories of the same animal. Of course one can tell stories about mental representation on which this sort of failure of recognitional transitivity cannot arise. I doubt that such stories have a firm grounding in pre-theoretic intuition, or in anything else to which philosophical theorizing about the attitudes need to attend to. I also rather doubt that empirical investigation would really help here.

Suppose that there is something in the phenomena that corresponds to our presuppositions about representations—myself, I think this a reasonable supposition. Whatever that may be, it need not underwrite an *equivalence* relation on aspects of belief states. It might be that there is something *approximating* an equivalence relation between "token parts" of belief states, when we confine our attention to everyday situations and don't try to extend judgments of sameness of representation too far across time or representational mediums. But any such relation can be expected to be a rounding off and averaging up of a collection of relations whose magnitudes can be stronger or weaker. If we look for total determinancy in the relation *is a token of the same representational type*, we should expect to find failures of transitivity.

2. Though Mark Twain is Sam Clemens and Suzy knows that Mark Twain wrote *Huck Finn*, she does not know that Sam Clemens wrote it. How can this be?
According to Frege, when we say what others think we refer not to objects and properties, but to ways of thinking of them. When I utter *Suzy thinks that Twain wrote it*, my use of *Twain* refers to its sense; when I utter *Suzy thinks that Clemens wrote it*, my use of *Clemens* refers to **its** sense.[5] These can be expected to differ, even if I know the identity. So the second utterance can be false when the first is true.

---

[4] To say this is not to say that if I take representations to be the same, they are. Representations are most naturally typed *partially* in terms of what they represent. But representations of different objects may be (in a relevant sense) indistinguishable.

[5] Here and below I use italics as a device for mentioning expressions.

There is an obvious problem with this proposal. As Frege observed, ways of thinking vary across individuals: the sense **Suzy** assigns to "Twain" can be expected to differ from the sense I assign to it. So Suzy usually won't believe the sense of *Twain wrote it*—that is, its sense as I use it—when she believes that Twain wrote it. But when Suzy says, expressing belief, *Twain wrote Huck Finn*, I can ascribe her belief by echoing her, saying *Suzy thinks that Twain wrote Huck Finn*.

Could we say that in the sentence *a believes that S* the words in *S* refer to their sense for the person *a* names? I don't think so, for it's hard to see how, if this is the way the ascription works, arguments like

Everybody knows that Twain wrote pornography.
So, there's something (about Twain) that everybody knows.

It's surprising that Clemens is Twain.
Jim believes that Clemens is Twain.
So, something Jim believes is surprising.

could be (as they certainly are) valid.[6]

In thinking about these issues, it's useful to think about somewhat more complicated examples. Consider the pair of ascriptions:

John said that Flopsy chased Mopsy and then Flopsy chased him.
John said that Flopsy chased Mopsy and then Mopsy chased him.

One feels that the sentences can vary in truth value, even given that Flopsy is Mopsy, since they seem to convey different pieces of information about John. The first sentence tells us that John represents the world as containing a Mopsy then John chaser; the second sentence, one thinks, does not entail that John so represents the world.[7]

Suppose that this is so, and that belief and assertion involve representations in the way discussed in Section 1. Then it is plausible to think that the Flopsy/Mospsy ascriptions differ by implying different things about the **structure** of John's representations of who chased whom. If John utters the sentence *Flopsy chased Mopsy and then Flopsy chased me*, his uses of "Flopsy" are "linked" or connected in a way that his uses of "Flopsy" and "Mopsy" are not: the Flopsy representations are of the same representational type, in the sense of *same type* that I tried to limn in the last section.[8] It is in virtue of this linking that John's utterance represents the world as containing a Mopsy then John chaser. What the

---

[6] I discuss these sorts of issues at length in Richard (1988) and chapter 2 of Richard (1990). Essay 9 discusses some sophisticated versions of Fregeanism that concede the validity of Kripke's criticisms of Frege's Fregeanism.

[7] Likewise, one wants to say that the sentences

There are an x and y such that x = y and John said that x chased y and then x chased John

and

There are an x and y such that x = y and John said that x chased y and then y chased John

can differ in truth value. Such cases are discussed in Essay 3.

[8] Assuming, of course, that John does not stand to Flopsy as does Kripke's Peter to Pederweski.

ascription *John said that Flopsy chased Mopsy and then Flopsy chased him* conveys is that John's assertion was achieved using a representation in which representations are linked as are the *Flopsy's* in *Flopsy chased Mopsy and then Flospy chased me*.

Each Flopsy/Mopsy ascription tells us that John's belief involves *linked representations*;[9] the linking in each case is different. This is not to say that the ascriptions actually *refer* to John's token representations or to their types. What is reported by *John said that Flopsy chased Mopsy and then Flopsy chased him* is something that is made true by John uttering any of

> Flopsy chased Mopsy and then Flopsy chased me.
> Flopsaut a chassé Trotsaut et puis Flopsuat m'a chassé.
> Dieses [point at Flopsy] hat Mopsy gejagt und dann hat dieses [Flopsy] mich gejagt.

The ascriptions convey information about identity and difference of John's ways of thinking of things without actually telling us what those ways of thinking are.

Something similar is true of groups of ascriptions. When I say *Suzy handed Twain a flower because she thought that Twain was sad and she wanted to make him happy*, I imply that there is an identity or at least an intimate cognitive connection between a way of thinking of Twain involved in Suzy's belief and one involved in her desire; if there weren't such a connection, the ascriptions would not explain or rationalize Suzy's behavior.

Ascriptions of attitudes may tell us something about the way in which someone represents the objects and properties he thinks about without actually referring to (or quantifying over) the other's representations. This idea unifies many of the papers that follow. Essays 2 through 4, for example, develop the ideas that

(a) belief, desire, hope, and so on are relations to propositions mediated by representations;

(b) the truth of a belief (desire, hope, etc.) ascription of the form *x believes (hopes, desires, etc.) that S* is a matter not only of *x* believing the (Russellian/Millian/referential) proposition determined by S, but of x's attitude involving a representation that has various properties systematically determined by the meaning of S. For example, *John believes that Flopsy chased Mopsy and then Flopsy chased him* requires one pattern of representational identity in what realizes John's belief; *John believes that Flopsy chased Mopsy and then Mopsy chased him* quite another. Attitude ascription tells us not only *what* another believes, but something about *how* that belief is realized.[10]

---

[9] Being repetitive: that is to say, each ascription tells us that John's belief involves several representations of the same type, in the sense I tried to limn in the last section.

[10] In "Essay 2," I suggest that *de se* ascriptions of attitudes—ones like "Tom expects to win" or (on its most natural reading) "Marie thinks that she is pretty"—convey that the attitude ascribed involves a distinctive *kind* of representation of the person to whom the attitude is ascribed, the kind that an object uses to "represent itself to itself."

The account I give of *de se* thought in Chapter 2 is far too linguistic—it's hard to see how one could take that account seriously, think that dogs had *de se* beliefs, but not think that the canine medium of thought

(c) Collections of attitude ascriptions also convey information not only about what is believed, but how it is believed. This fact can be used to explain many of our intuitions about such ascriptions. For example: uttering both of the ascriptions *Ham believed that Hesperus rose in the west; he believed that Hesperus set in the east* conveys that there is a way of representing Hesperus such that, using it, Ham believed the planet to both rise in the west and set in east. So, uttering the second ascription when the truth of the first is *presupposed* can be expected to convey this too. And this provides an answer to the question, why do we think that Suzy might know that Twain is Twain but not that Twain is Clemens? For we know, and thus presuppose (for example), that Suzy knows that Twain was called "Twain" and that she knows that Clemens was called "Clemens." But then to say that Suzy knows that Twain is Clemens is to commit to Suzy knowing that Twain (and thus someone) was called both "Twain" and "Clemens." But of course Suzy, who denies "Twain is Clemens," didn't know *that*.

3. As Chapters 2 through 4 develop these ideas, a sentence of the form *Cyril believes that John Rs John* entails that Cyril has a belief realized by (as I put it above) linked representations of John. Mark Crimmins objected that a sentence like

Cyril fell for it; he thinks that John is John's father

can ascribe to Cyril something less than a belief that someone fathered himself; we'd say this if we tricked Cyril into thinking that a film of John was a film of John's father.[11] In Essay 6 I replied that (a) the just displayed sentence has the same range of readings as does

Cyril fell for it; he thinks that John is his own father;

and (b) the latter can only be used to ascribe a belief in self-fathering to Cyril.

I continue to think (a) is correct. (b), I am afraid, isn't, though something in the neighborhood is. Say that when an attitude is realized by linked representations, the attitude is *reflexive*. What is correct is that when someone uses either of

John is John's father
John is his own father

---

was very like English—enough so that dogs had representations with the semantic properties of English's pronoun "I."

It would not be difficult to separate the ideas about *de se* ascriptions in that essay from the idea that *de se* attitudes are invariably realized by things with natural language meanings. Rather than say (and here I put things very crudely) that *Rex expects to eat* is true provided Rex has an expectation whose representation has a part with the meaning of *I*, we say that it is true provided one of Rex's expectations involves a representation that plays a certain "*de se* role" for Rex, a role that "I" plays in English speech. (Of course one wants, when one gets around to philosophy of mind, an account of this role.)

I stand behind such an account of the semantics of *de se* ascriptions. One of the advantages of such an account is that it does not require us to posit object language quantification over ways of thinking, something one tends to find in Fregean accounts of *de se* ascriptions.

[11] Crimmins (1992b).

to express a belief, the *user expresses* a reflexive belief.[12] What is wrong is the thought that the sentences *must ascribe* such beliefs.

I continue to think that the Cyril sentences have a reading on which they ascribe reflexive beliefs, and so a reading on which they are true only if Cyril is daft. I thus take attitude ascriptions in which a single name has multiple occurrences in the complement clause to be semantically ambiguous. I argue for this ambiguity as follows. Crimmins is right about his example, and the example strongly suggests that sentences of the form *a believes that...n...n...* have a reading whose truth doesn't require a belief that involves linked representations. The question is whether such ascriptions have *another* reading whose truth requires belief under linked representations.

Surely in *some* cases this is so. Suppose that John thinks [that Suzy wants to help Twain and Suzy believes that if she gives Twain a pen, that will help him].[13] John's belief—in the absence of reason to think that Suzy is a sociopath (or is asleep, or distracted, or...)—warrants John in thinking that Suzy will feel some inclination, if she has a pen handy, to give it to Twain. And so this

> Whenever John is warranted in thinking [that Suzy wants to help Twain and she believes that if she gives Twain a pen that will help him], John is (unless he thinks Suzy is sociopathic, or...) warranted in thinking that she will be inclined to give Twain a pen if she has one handy

is true. But surely this is *not* true unless the antecedent is being used to ascribe a reflexive belief to John. After all, suppose John simply thinks to himself *Suzy wants to help Clemens; she thinks Twain would be helped by getting a pen. Too bad she doesn't realize Clemens is Twain.* Then he has no warrant for thinking that Suzy will be inclined to give Twain a pen. But the unlinked reading of the antecedent is presumably true when John has a belief he'd express with the italicized sentence. Only if the antecedent has a reading on which it entails that John has a linked belief is there reason to think that the just displayed sentence can be used to express a truth.

So sometimes when an ascription has multiple occurrences of a name in its complement, it has a linked reading. It's hard to see why this would only *sometimes* be true. And in any case, variants of the sort of argument just given could be run for any complement clause with multiple occurrences of a name.[14]

This leaves the question of how these readings arise. Let me sketch a proposal. To motivate it, consider for a moment the sort of "mixed quotation" that occurs in ascriptions like

---

[12] In the first case, the user has to mean to use the same name twice over, in a way that does not happen in Paderweski examples.
[13] Brackets here delimit the complement of "John thinks."
[14] Each argument turns on a premise kindred to the claim that a sentence like

> If we have reason to think that John thinks Twain has stepped on Twain's foot,
> we have reason to think that John thinks that someone stepped on their own foot

has a true reading.

> Sarah said that Eric was acting like "a horse's patoot."

In this sentence, it seems that the quoted words are used both to indicate content (*what* was said) and representation (*how* it was said). There is an ambiguity in such sentences that, to my knowledge, has not been discussed in the literature.[15] Consider

> Bernanke said that Greenspan said that his agreement with Reich was "a pleasant surprise."

This sentence is ambiguous. It might be a report that, in saying that Greenspan said that his agreement with Reich was a pleasant surprise, Bernacke used the words "a pleasant surprise." On this reading, the sentence does not imply that Bernanke said that Greenspan used the words in question. But it also has a reading on which it reports that in saying that Greenspan said that his agreement with Reich was a pleasant surprise, Bernacke ascribed to Greenspan a use of the words "a pleasant surprise."

It is hard to credit the idea that the ambiguity here is the result of an ambiguity in one of the words in the sentence. One might try to explain the ambiguity in terms of movement: perhaps when the sentence is interpreted, the quoted words move to the vicinity of the subject to whom they are attributed, somewhat as a quantifier may move to take scope. For various (mostly syntactic) reasons, such an account seems unlikely.[16] The most natural account, I think, is one that involves some sort of indexing of the quoted phrase to the subject to whom its use is attributed.[17] The logical form of the Bernanke sentence on its first reading would then be something along the lines of

> Bernanke$_i$ said that Greenspan said that his agreement with Reich was ("a pleasant surprise")$_i$;

its form on the second would be something like

> Bernanke said that Greenspan$_i$ said that his agreement with Reich was ("a pleasant surprise")$_i$.

Once we acknowledge the existence of such indexing, it is relatively straightforward to give a semantic account of sentences with mixed quotation. Otherwise it is not.

There is thus reason, independent of the question of how to account for the ambiguity of the Cyril sentence, for thinking that expressions in the complement clause of an attitude verb may be indexed to a subject higher in the sentence. If quotations get indexed in this way, why not unquoted phrases as well—especially when such indexing allows a straightforward explanation of the ambiguity of the Cyril sentence? Suppose that there are two logical forms for

> Cyril thinks that John is John's father,

---

[15] This ambiguity and mixed quotation are discussed in "Did I Mention What he Said?," which appears in Volume II of *Meaning In Context*. The next paragraphs borrow from this paper.

[16] Such an account is discussed at length in "Did I Mention What He Said?" Among its problems, as Ray Jackendoff pointed out to me, is that it requires movement of arbitrary constituents out of what linguists call "islands."

[17] Alternatively, the index may be tied to the verb of which the subject is an argument; see "Did I Mention What He Said?"

one unindexed, the other indexed so:

Cyril$_i$ thinks that John$_i$ is (John)$_i$'s father.

Suppose further that one property of such indexes is this: a sentence of the form

x_i Vs that ... n_i ... n_i ...

says something true only if what x names believes the proposition determined by ... n ... n ... under a representation that is linked in the appropriate way.[18] Then we have enough to generate the two readings of the original Cyril sentence. So far as I can see, fairly natural restrictions on this sort of indexing will insure that this proposal doesn't overgenerate readings.

The account of attitudes and their ascription sketched in the papers collected here assumes that attitude ascriptions contain a syntactic reflex of the difference between an attitude toward a claim that is realized by linked representations and an attitude toward the same claim realized by unlinked representations. What objections like Crimmins' show is not that there isn't such a syntactic reflex. Rather, they show that I misidentified it.

4. There is only so much of our practice of ascribing attitudes to be explained by the idea that attitude ascription reflects linking of representations. Consider the following story:

Eleanor Jane (= EJ) is Jane to her friends, Eleanor to others; her friends are well aware of this. You and I are her friends. I see that Bob and Ray, who know EJ but are not her friends, see her leave; I see that only Ray realized that it was EJ. (Of course, what Ray thinks is "there goes Eleanor.") I say to you "Bob and Ray saw Jane leave, but only Ray knew/realized that it was Jane who left."

The way I speak in this example is quite natural. What information, exactly, would I normally convey by speaking in this way? How is it conveyed?

It is surely *not* conveyed then that only Ray knew the Russellian content that Jane left. For Bob, knowing that *that* woman left, knew that too. Appeal to Fregean senses does not seem to be helpful—why think that the sense of my use of "Jane" is involved in any thought known by Ray? Appeal to the idea that I am conversationally implying that Ray's belief is associated by him with the sentence "Jane just left" is no help—it's part of the story that Bob and Ray don't know Jane is so-called.[19]

---

[18] If we suppose, as seems natural, that every representation is linked with itself, there will be no semantic difference between

Cyril thinks that John is a jerk

and

Cyril$_i$ thinks that John$_i$ is a jerk.

[19] Neither will it help to appeal to Kit Fine's idea, developed in Fine (2007), that some content is irreducibly relational. Fine's idea is in some ways analogous to the idea of linked representations discussed in Sections 2 and 3 above and developed in Essays 2 through 4 below. Fine assumes that there may be a "semantic requirement" on tokens that they co-refer, and that assignment of content to sentences must reflect the "strict coreference" that such requirements induce. The content of "Twain is Twain" and "Twain is Clemens" will thus differ, since in the first the name tokens are strictly co-referential, in the second they are not.

It would be natural for me to speak as I do even if I didn't expect you to know whether Bob and Ray are friends of EJ's. So it would be natural for me to speak as I do even if I have no expectations about what you might assume about how they refer to EJ when they recognize her. What I convey in this example, roughly put, is that Bob and Ray saw Jane leave, but only Ray recognized her: Ray had a bit of knowledge realized by something along the lines of *a just left*, where *That's a* would, for Ray, be good answer to the question, *Who's that?*; Bob had no such knowledge.

If that's what I convey, how exactly do I convey it? Essays 5, 6, 7, and 13 develop and defend a particular answer to this question, one that is an extension of the account in Essays 2 through 4. On this account, when we ascribe a belief saying *so and so believes that S*, we offer the sentence *S* as a **representation** or **translation** of what realizes one of so and so's beliefs. Attitude ascription thus presupposes something like a "translation manual," one keyed specifically to the individuals to whom attitudes are ascribed. In our story, I intend—and, if you understand me, you understand me to intend—that my use of "Jane" in ascribing a belief to Ray "translates" or represents representations of Jane that identify her to Ray; likewise, for Bob and "Jane." The semantic rule governing belief ascriptions is something like: *x believes that S*, used in a context *c*, is true just in case *S*, relative to context *c*'s translation manual, translates some belief realizing state of (the referent of) *x*.

In our story, Ray thinks to himself *That's Eleanor who left*; Bob, on the other hand, just thinks *that woman left*. The operative translation manual for my comment is something like this:

> When talking about what Ray thinks, "Jane" represents only Ray's customary representations of Jane.
> When talking about what Bob thinks, "Jane" represents only Bob's customary representations of Jane.
> Otherwise, any translation that preserves referential values is fine.[20]

Given this, it's easy to see why it's true that Ray but not Bob realized that Jane left. Translating Ray's thought *Eleanor left* with *Jane left* doesn't violate the translation rules, as *Eleanor* is one of Ray's customary ways of thinking of EJ, and so the translation rules allow *Jane* to translate it. So it's true that Ray realizes that Eleanor left. But since Bob

---

Something similar is true of the pairs of sentences <"Twain wrote *Huck Finn*", "Twain was born in Missouri">, <"Twain wrote *Huck Finn*", "Clemens was born in Missouri">. It is perhaps not too much of a distortion of Fine's account to say that what it does at the level of content is what the first few essays in this volume try to do by distinguishing between content and representational structure and invoking representational linking.

The idea of relational content is a good one. But it will only carry us so far. In particular, it's hard to see how it can help us understand what is going on in examples like that in the text (or in various essays below), in which we apparently use our words as in some sense representatives of the words or representations of others, even though our words and those of the other don't stand in anything remotely like Fine's relation of "strict coreference."

[20] By *x's customary representations of Jane*, I mean those of *x*'s representations of a type that *x* customarily employs to think about Jane.

doesn't recognize Eleanor, there's no belief state of his that can be translated with "Jane left" without breaking the second translation rule above. So it's not true that Bob realizes that Jane left.

"How I Say What You Think" presents a view of attitude ascription along the above lines. There are some interesting technical details in working out a systematic semantics for this view. Many of them are taken up in that and subsequent essays; others are discussed in Richard (1990). There are a good many objections to and worries about the view.[21] "Attitudes and Contexts," "Defective Contexts, Accommodation, and Normalization," and "Meaning and Attitude Ascriptions" respond to many of them.

Later essays take up general problems raised by attitudes and their ascription. "Propositional Quantification" is an attempt to see whether the semantics of the attitudes can be done with both feet stuck in the mud—that is, without universals, intensions, possible worlds, or any of the other non-extensional gizmos that usually get invoked in philosophical semantics. "Sense, Necessity, and Belief" discusses the prospects for sophisticated Fregean accounts of meanings, ones that acknowledge Kripke's point that names behave as rigid designators in modal contexts. Its primary target is Graeme Forbes' *Languages of Possibility*, but many of its critical points apply to other broadly Fregean accounts of natural language semantics, including various versions of "two-dimensionalism."[22] This essay also discusses Kripke's idea of contingent *a priori* knowledge, distinguishing various senses in which a belief can be *de re*.

"Semantic Pretense" evaluates the idea that attitude ascription and talk about the non-existent involve a kind of pretense or play acting. "Intensional Transitives and Empty Terms" is about the semantics of verbs (like "seeks," "draws," and "worships") that are non-extensional but seem to have the syntax of extensional transitive verbs (like "chase," "catch," and "caress"). These two essays respond to (or at least discuss) a well-known worry about the Russellean semantics that is the departure point for the work collected here: that since it grounds meaning in reference and nothing more, it is unable to explain how empty names or kind terms are meaningful. "Objects of Relief" is a mostly critical, somewhat deflationary discussion of accounts of the role of tensed thought. "Kripke's Puzzle" tries to say what is, and what is not, puzzling about the celebrated Pierre.

5. There are worries about the project of these essays which they do not address. When I say that attitude ascription involves translation or representation of another's token attitudes, this of course suggests that attitudes are realized in a linguistic or quasi-linguistic medium. The way I implement the idea introduced in the last section is by treating the complements of attitude ascriptions—their "*that*-clauses"—as referring to fusions of

---

[21] Scott Soames has generously (I mean that non-sarcastically) and persistently criticized versions of this idea—see, in particular, Soames (1995) and Soames (2002). Other useful (to me, at least) criticisms are those of Jenny Saul (1999) and Ted Sider (1995). Besides the discussion in Chapters 6, 7, and 13, Richard (2006) and Richard (2006a) defend aspects of the view developed here.

[22] Forbes himself has pointed this out, showing how versions of some of the points in this article apply to recent work by David Chalmers and others. See Forbes (2011).

their words with their semantic values. To be specific: identify the Russellian proposition that Mary is a foreman with the pairing of the woman Mary and the property of being a foreman:

<Mary, being a foreman>.

The proposal limned above involves the idea that the complement of

Jane thinks that Mary is a foreman

names

<<Mary, "Mary">, <being a foreman, "is a foreman">>.

So when I utter the Jane sentence, I relate Jane to this. Roughly put: a use of the belief ascription is true when Jane has a token belief b whose Russellean content is <Mary, being a foreman> which involves ways of representing Mary and being a foreman that can themselves be represented or "translated" by "Mary" and "is a foreman" in the context of use.[23]

It will be said that the idea that a belief ascription's truth must be grounded in the ascribee's believing the Russellian content of the ascription's content can't be sustained. Suppose I pretend to throw a ball and Diva the dog runs across the yard. Why did she do that? Well, because she thought that I threw a ball. So much is surely true. But the dog can't think the Russellian content of my use of "I threw a ball." After all, she isn't disposed to group tennis balls, ping pong balls, footballs, and ball bearings together. But she would have to be able to do something like that to have the concept of a ball. And she would have to have the concept *ball*, were she able to think the Russellian content that I threw a ball.

I respond: If it's *true* that the dog believes that S, how can it fail to be true that the dog believes what I say with the sentence S? If we have eliminated a Fregean account of the semantics of my sentence, then the semantic properties of the sentence I use are Russellian. Or at least they are referential. When I use the sentence "I threw a ball," the sentence has a part that refers to me, a part that refers to the property of throwing a ball; its truth involves *me* having *that* property. We may, of course, debate about what the property of throwing a ball is. It might be an abstract entity of some sort, or a function from worlds to sets of ball throwers, or just the set of this worldly throwers of balls. No matter: if the dog believes that I threw the ball, the dog has a belief that can be reported as having the Russellian, or at least referential, content of my use of "I threw the ball." Rather than conclude that the dog can't believe a Russellian content because it lacks our concept, better to say that believing that content doesn't require having anything all that much like our concept.

---

[23] Essay 8 investigates the idea that the complement of an attitude ascription—the *that S* in *Jane believes that S*—names something even more linguistic. Not wholly linguistic, because we want to be able to say that (for example), for every x, there is a proposition that x = x (and to say that if x is not y, the proposition that x is x is not the proposition that y is y). The proposal Essay 8 takes most seriously is one that identifies propositions with sentences combined with their extensional values.

What motivates the original objection, I think, is the idea that the dog's believing that I threw a ball can't be a matter of its being in a state that *independently of and prior to my interpretation of it* has the content of the sentence "I threw a ball." This I concede. But that doesn't mean that that it is incorrect to say that the dog believes that content. To see why, it may help to reflect on the way Hilary Putnam sought to establish that "meanings ain't in the head."[24] Putnam's argument involved three claims: the word *water*'s reference in English in 1975 is not its reference in Twin English in 1975; the word *water*'s reference in English in 1975 is its reference in English in the 18th century; the word *water*'s reference in Twin English in 1975 is its reference in Twin English in the 18th century. The latter two claims tend to be treated as if they go without saying: after all, when an 18th-century Englishman—Boswell or Dr. Johnson, say—uttered the sentence "I want a glass of water," didn't he say that he wanted a glass of water?

Indeed he did. But to agree to this is not to say that the semantic properties of Boswell's utterance, independently of and prior to my interpretation of it, are identical or even all that close to those of the sentence I use to interpret that utterance. It is today determinate that "water" is not true of more or less pure samples of D_2O, aka "heavy water," which though visually indistinguishable from H_2O is lethal in large doses to fish and humans. It is hard to believe that this was *determinate* before the advent of modern chemistry.[25] The semantics of Boswell's words, independently of and prior to my interpreting them with my own words, are just not the same as the semantics that my words have, independently of and prior to my using them to interpret Boswell. We sharpen the content of Boswell and Johnson's utterances when and by saying what they said in our idiom. In ascribing an attitude to them, we are not, or not merely, giving a report of a pre-existing identity of content. We are interpreting them.

The fact that Boswell's words need not, prior to our interpreting him, have the content we ascribe to him does not mean that our ascription of that content is incorrect. Why shouldn't we say the same sort of thing about the dog? Of course, this response raises a question: if the truth of my report *a believes that S* doesn't require a *match* of content between the sentence *S* as I use it and the content that some state of *a*'s has independently of my ascription, what *does* the truth of the ascription require?

Consider again the example of Boswell and the water. There is a certain semantic isomorphism between what is reported and what is used in the report. Boswell says "I want a glass of water;" I report him with "he said that he wanted a glass of water." Ignoring some subtle issues connected with tense, the reporting sentence recapitulates the *term-verb-quantifier* structure of the vehicle of the attitude.[26] The report's accuracy turns on whether there is the right sort of relation between what realizes the attitude

---

[24] In Putnam (1975).

[25] Here I echo the thoughts of Joesph LaPorte; see the discussion in LaPorte (2004). I also take indeterminacy to be reflected by gaps between extensions and anti-extensions, and thus take it to be a semantic matter.

[26] Some think that "wants" is actually taking a sentential complement in both vehicle and report. This doesn't affect the point.

and the sentence in the report: the sentence in the report has to be a "good interpretation" of the vehicle. And as we've seen, considerations that have nothing to do with mismatches of referential content suggest that part of a correct account of attitude ascription will invoke the idea of the words in a report being a "good interpretation" of the vehicle of the attitude being reported. This was the moral of the example of Bob, Ray, and Eleanor Jane above.

The upshot of all this is as follows. It is a fact that the semantic properties of Diva the dog's states, independently of and prior to our interpreting them, are not identical to the semantic properties of the sentence we use to interpret her. This fact simply does not imply that our interpretation of her is incorrect. The dog just doesn't have to have our concept of a ball, or a concept that independent of interpretation has its semantic properties, in order for our words to provide a good representation of her mental state.

Now, I expect that objections will persist. The semantic structure of the complement in the report *Diva the dog believes that I threw a ball* is *term-verb-quantifier*. Are we to suppose, someone will ask, that the dog is in a state with an aspect or part that can be identified as a quantifier? Is the dog a candidate for a logic course?

I have mixed emotions about this challenge. On the one hand, I think we need to acknowledge that there is something out of whack about the epistemology suggested by the picture of attitude ascription as involving a piece-by-piece matching of the content of an attitude ascription's complement with the content of the parts of some state realizing the attitude. Most anyone who watches Diva and me knows that the dog thinks that I threw a ball. We know it without reflection and on the basis of no more evidence than our familiarity with the dog's fetching behavior and our current observation of her. But given the account of attitude ascription I have sketched, it may seem that in order for us to be justified in thinking that the dog thinks I threw a ball, we should be onto some fact that justifies our thinking that the dog has a mental structure that plays a role like that of the indefinite "a ball." But surely observation of the dog justifies no such thing.

In the case of Bob and Ray, we have good reason to think that their beliefs involve representations of EJ and of the property of leaving the room—after all, we have excellent reason to think that those beliefs would be expressed by them with English sentences. In the case of Diva the dog, perhaps we don't have much reason to think that she is quantifying over balls, either those contextually available or otherwise. But we have reason to think that the dog's state has *some* structure, even if it lacks all of the structure of the complement of

A. Diva the dog believes that I threw a ball.

As we usually think of that complement, it has a hierarchical structure, something along the lines of

A'. [[$_{DP}$ I] [$_{VP}$ threw [$_{DP}$ a ball]]].

Surely we have reason to think that the state that realizes Diva's thought has an element M that represents me. Don't we also have reason to think that there is some canine cognitive mechanism—TAB, call it—that is involved in the dog's belief and is reasonably interpreted as representing the property of throwing a ball? The dog, after all, is plausibly thought to recognize my action as being of a kind with your actual throwing of a ball, and as of a kind with young children's underhand ball tosses, etc., etc. She *does*, after all, reliably respond to all these in the same way. If the dog's ability to recognize this sort of action is implicated in her belief, then her belief involves something that is reasonably interpreted as a representation of the property of throwing a ball.

The state that realizes the dog's belief has *some* of the semantic structure of the sentence I use to report the belief. My sentence is a combination of the phrases "I" and "threw a ball," with the latter predicated of the former, so that the whole has a referential content that might be represented so

P. <Mark Richard, the property of having thrown a ball>.

The dog's belief state is composed of the representations M and TAB, with the latter related to the former in a way that is well understood as predicative. Thus, the dog's belief state has a referential content that is reasonably interpreted with my sentence.

When I think to myself "she thinks I threw a ball," I do not have the sort of interests I have when I am focused on the ancients' beliefs about Venus, or on Bob and Ray's thoughts about EJ. I am only interested in the objects and properties she is thinking about, not how she thinks about them. So there are no special constraints, beyond the usual requirement of (loose) match of referential content, on how my words are to represent a belief state of Diva's. So in context the complement of (A) is indeed a "translation" or representation of one of Diva's states of belief—"I" represents M and "threw a ball" represents TAB.

I have been pointing out that understanding attitude ascription as involving a kind of translation doesn't require supposing that the belief states of others recapitulate all the semantic structure of the sentences with which we report their beliefs. It will be said that I haven't addressed the deepest problems with the idea that attitude ascription is a kind of translation. Consider an example of Dan Dennett's.[27] The way a computer plays chess may make it correct to say that it thinks that it needs to get its queen out early. But there need be nothing in the machine that could plausibly be said to represent this belief *by* representing its parts. That the machine has this belief is not something that is true in virtue of its having and appropriately combining representations of itself, the temporal stages of a chess game, and a certain strategy that involves moving the queen up. After all, we would say this sort of thing if the machine just has a pronounced tendency to move the queen out early, even when there's no immediate advantage in doing so.

Let us concede that the computer may have the belief. Let us concede that it has no state that realizes the belief by having proper parts that are adequately interpreted by proper parts of

---

[27] Dennett (1978).

B. One needs to get the queen out early in a chess game.

Still, if the computer *has* the belief, it is in a state that realizes a belief and whose content is adequately rendered by B. If there are states that can have the content of B without recapitulating its structure, those states can be reported—and thus "rendered" or "translated"—using a sentence whose syntactic structure makes explicit the structure of the state's content.

It is no part of the ideas, that content is structured and attitude ascription is a kind of translation or representation, that belief states **must** be structured like sentences. A belief can be realized by a complex of dispositions—at least when those dispositions are embedded in the right sort of cognitive system—and dispositions lack sentential structure. Just as we may choose, in interpreting Dr. Johnson's utterance of "water is tasty," to render it as involving the content of our term "water," so we may choose, in interpreting the dispositions of the computer, to render them with our concepts of chess, the queen, and so forth. In the case of the computer, this is a good rendering because there is a rough parity between belief grounding dispositions of the computer and those that ground the belief of someone with an articulated belief about getting the queen out.[28]

Some will say that beliefs realized by dispositions are properties of the whole organism. They will note that attitudes that are properties of the whole organism need not be recorded by substates of the organism with semantic structure. And they will conclude that the contents of those attitudes are unstructured, and that ascription of those attitudes must be ascription of unstructured content. One argument to this conclusion goes as follows. It is determinate what the computer believes. But the determinacy in its belief does not extend below the level of truth conditions. After all, we can report the computer's belief with B or with

C. It is generally a good thing for a chess player to move out her most powerful piece before the mid-board is crowded.

Each of these is acceptable because each captures what the world must be like for the belief to be correct. There is, in the case of the computer, nothing more to capture about the content of its belief than its truth conditions; differences between B and C due to their semantic structures are irrelevant to saying what the computer believes. Thus, those differences must be irrelevant to capturing the content of its belief. Thus, sometimes an ascription of an attitude is an ascription of something whose content is unstructured; the content is simply the truth conditions of the attitude. But surely we are ascribing the same belief to the computer and to Sandrine when we say

D. Both Sandrine and her opponent the computer think that a player should get its queen out of the back rank early in a chess game.

---

[28] As I say in the coda to this introduction, there are really *two* sorts of translation or interpretation involved in attitude ascription. We first interpret another's state (his belief, assertion, or whatever) as having the content of our words. We (may) then go on to use particular words and phrases of our own as representations of the way the other represents that content.

So even when there is a sentential record of a belief, that doesn't mean that the belief's content is structured. So the argument goes.[29]

It is true that we could use either B or C to ascribe a belief to the computer. It is true that the computer does not have an articulated representation of the semantic structure of either sentence. How does it follow—why is it even *plausible*—that differences between sentences that don't effect their (possible worlds) truth conditions are irrelevant to the content of the belief we report using them? It is not *just* the fact that the computer's behavior is appropriate iff sentence B is true, that makes it true to say that it thinks it ought to get its queen out early. It is also that the computer's dispositions are relevantly similar to the dispositions of people who have articulated beliefs realized by B (and C, and D's complement). Like such people, the computer is disposed to manipulate certain objects (referred to in the sentences) in certain ways (also picked out in the sentences) in certain situations. It is *this* difference between D and

> E. The computer believes that one needs to get one's queen out early in a chess game just in case the number of moves in the game will be equal to the product of some set of powers of primes

which explains why, though D and E's complement are necessarily equivalent, D can be used to ascribe the computer a belief while E's cannot.

It is simply false that if a belief is realized by something that itself lacks semantic structure—a set of dispositions, say—then there is nothing more to the belief's content than what is given by the set of worlds in which it is true. The computer's belief about the queen is a belief *about* the queen and the early parts of the game; it is not a belief about how these relate to arithmetical properties of the number of moves the game might contain. That this is so, of course, is manifest in what realizes the belief in the computer—the computer has dispositions to respond to and manipulate the queen in the early stages of the game; it presumably has none that relate number theoretic calculations of the likely length of the game to getting the queen out. There are more ways for the psychological facts about someone to make a structured content one that he believes then his simply tokening a sentence that articulates that content.

To have a belief is, *inter alia*, to represent a possible state of the world—to represent, that is, a particular distribution of objects, properties, and relations. The content of such a belief is a complex of objects, properties, and relations.[30] To take the content of a belief

---

[29] Something like this argument can be found in the first chapter of Stalnaker (1984).

[30] I am (intentionally) echoing the words of Robert Stalnaker here, who writes at the beginning of a defense of the view that attitude content is unstructured

> What is essential to rational action is that the agent be confronted, or conceive himself as confronted, with a range of possible outcomes of some alternative possible actions.... the primary objects of the attitudes are not propositions [i.e. not what the complements of attitude ascriptions pick out, which Stalnaker identifies with sets of possible worlds] but... alternative possible states of the world. When a person wants a proposition to be true, it is because he has a positive attitude towards certain concrete realizations of that proposition. Propositions [*qua* objects of attitudes like belief and desire]... are simply ways of distinguishing between the elements of the relevant range of alternative possibilities. (Stalnaker (1984), 7)

to be an unstructured set of worlds is in a sense to *deprive* it of content: since contents are representations of states of affairs—of objects having properties and standing in relations—merely to ascribe truth conditions to something is not to ascribe a *determinate* content to it at all, but merely a range of possible contents.

So say I, but the fan of unstructured content is likely at this point to resurrect past arguments. The dog, it will be said, has a perfectly determinate belief. Since the dog's belief is determinate, it must have determinate content. But since the dog lacks a sophisticated representational system, it is not in a position to represent the structured contents associated with sentences we might use to ascribe it beliefs. But if the dog *determinately* believes a structured content, it must represent it—else why think that it believes *that* content, as opposed to one of the many structured contents that are equivalent to it? Why think that it is A that is determinately true, as opposed to

> F. Diva the dog believes that I propelled a ball through the air with a movement of my hand and arm.

As I see it, the question this argument raises is whether sentences like A or F can be determinately true when interpreted as ascribing a structured content to the dog. The answer is: why not? Let us by all means agree that there is a good deal of slack between Diva's states, considered by themselves or in tandem with her everyday interactions with the world, and ascription of one or another concept of ball propulsion to her. Why should this lead us to say that A or F, if ascribing a structured content, is not determinately true? I would say that it is determinately true that Boswell and Johnson believed that water is wet. But I would not say that there is something about them and the relations they had to their environment and society in the 17th century that determines, prior to my interpretation, that the content of one of their beliefs is that *water* is wet. There is a certain amount of courtesy involved in the ascription of the belief that water is wet to Boswell and Johnson. That does not mean that the ascription is not determinately true. Why is it that we cannot say the same thing about the dog?

6. Not everyone who picks up this book is likely to want to read all of it. What would I recommend to such a reader? What are the best bits?

The essay "Kripke's Puzzle" motivates the view of attitudes in the essays collected here. It's better written than some of those essays, more playful and less technical to boot. "How I Say What You Think" gives a summary of what I continue to think is the right story to tell about attitude ascription. The essays "Defective Contexts, Accommodation, and Normalization" and "Meaning and Attitude Ascriptions" fine tune that account. I like the story I tell in the former about conversational context and accommodation of others' speech. I am fond of the account in "Quantification and Leibniz's Law" of (what

---

I could not agree more with the beginning of this passage, or agree less with the conclusion that Stalnaker draws from the idea that attitudinal content is to be understood, first and foremost, in terms of the role of content in rational deliberation and the production of action.

is and is not essential to) objectual quantification and of what "Intensional Transitives and Empty Terms" says about how verbs like "seeks," "worships," and "expects" interact with quantifiers. These two papers, however, get a bit technical at points. And there is a fun argument in the third section of "Direct Reference and Ascriptions of Belief" that purports to show (roughly put) that the argument *a = b and c thinks that a is in danger; so c thinks that b is in danger* is valid. That argument is something to put on the shelf to play with on long winter nights—obviously something is wrong with it, but it's hard to find two people who agree on what that is.

Coda. The remarks in Section 5 raise more questions than they answer. For example, someone familiar with the semantics for attitude ascription in "How I Say What You Think" may ask how to modify it to accommodate what I say there. Or one might ask whether the "interpretationism" I endorsed when speaking about Boswell, Johnson, and Diva is committed to a pernicious sort of relativism about content ascription. In this section, I take up these questions.

To answer the first question, I need to review the semantics given in Essay 5.[31] Take the notion of a representation(al type) to be given. Say that an *annotated proposition* (an *a-proposition*) is what you get from a Russellian proposition if you pair its (simplest) constituents with representations. Intuitively, an a-proposition is a possible content of a belief, assertion, or other propositional attitude **along with** a way of representing that content.

Call the pairings of Russellian propositional constituents with representations *annotations*. A sentence S expressing a Russellian proposition p determines an annotated proposition, obtained by pairing each constituent of p with the constituent of S responsible for it. When q is an a-proposition obtained by adding annotations to the Russellian proposition p, we say that p is the *r-reduction* of q.

Example. Let us suppose that Russellian propositions are ordered tuples: the proposition that John loves Mary is <Loving, <John, Mary>>; the proposition that Mary loves John is <Loving, <Mary, John>>. a-propositions are the results of pairing constituents of such propositions with representations. For example, the a-proposition determined by the sentence "John loves Mary" is <<Loving "loves">, <<John, "John">, <Mary, "Mary">>>.

Suppose I utter something of the form *X believes that S*. My utterance of S determines an a-proposition q with an r-reduction p. If my ascription is true, it's true because: X is in a representational state that is a belief; that state determines an a-proposition q★ whose r-reduction is p; and the a-proposition q is, in the context, a good representation—a "translation"—of q★.

The discussion of Section 5 allows that it may be correct to say that a computer believes that it should decline the Evans Gambit simply because the computer is disposed to play in a way that happens to lead to its not taking the pawn offered in this gambit; the computer needn't have anything in its program that could be said to be a

---

[31] The exposition departs from the terminology used there.

representation of the Evans Gambit. The question is: how much modification of the above is called for, given this acknowledgment?

Quite minimal. The original proposal presupposed that if X has a belief with a certain Russellian content p, X is in a state with parts that represent p constituent by constituent. We continue to assume that when X has a belief with a Russellian content p, it is in *some* belief state s that determines p. State s *may* determine p by representing some or even all of the constituents of p. But it may not. We thus need to allow that in the construction of the a-proposition determined by a representational state, some or even all of its constituents may not be paired with representations. And that's easy enough.

Explanation

Things go most simply if we assume that there is something, ~, that is not a representation. Suppose s is a state of belief with the Russellian content p, but s does not determine p by representing constituent y of p. Then in constructing the a-proposition determined by s, we pair y with ~.

For example, suppose that the computer's overall state makes it the case that it has a belief with the Russellian content that it should decline the Evans Gambit. Then it has a belief with a Russellian content along the lines of

<ought-to-decline, <the computer, the Evans Gambit>>.

If the computer has this belief simply by virtue of dispositions that do not represent any of the constituents of this belief, then the a-proposition determined by the computer's state of belief is

Q. <<ought-to-decline, ~>, <<the computer, ~>, <the Evans Gambit, ~>>>.

We need make almost no changes in the account of translation in Essay 5 in order to explain how, if some state of the computer determines Q, then "The computer thinks that it ought to decline the Evans Gambit" is true. On the story told there:

1. A "translation manual" is a systematic way of going from a-propositions to a-propositions. Specifically, a manual is a rule—a function—that takes an annotation to an annotation, thus projecting one a-proposition onto another. An a-proposition p translates an a-proposition q under translation manual f provided that q is the result of replacing each annotation in p with its image under f.[32]

Change this account simply by allowing translation manuals to map annotations to things of the form <x, ~>, as well as to things of the form <x, r>, r a representation. Then there are obviously translation manuals under which the a-proposition that the computer ought to decline the Evans Gambit translates Q.

2. In context, a speaker may intend to use her words to represent particular representations, or sorts of representations, of the person to whom she's ascribing belief. In saying, "Mary doesn't know that Sam Clemens wrote this book," for example, I may intend to represent Mary's mental tokenings of "Sam Clemens" with my use of "Sam Clemens." When this is the case, there is a contextual restriction on what translation manuals one may use to translate an

---

[32] Since we may translate one person differently from another, such manuals are relativized to individuals. As noted above, translation is required to preserve Russellian content: if f is a translation manual, then for any annotations <a, b> and <a', b'>, if f (<a, b>) = <a',b'>, then a = a'.

individual's a-propositions. If I intend to use "Sam Clemens" to represent Mary's tokenings of "Sam Clemens," then a translation manual f can be used to to translate Mary's a-propositions only if f(<Clemens, "Sam Clemens">) = <Clemens, "Sam Clemens">.

Suppose we ascribe beliefs to the computer in virtue of its dispositions, but not in virtue of representations of the objects and properties its beliefs are about. In this case, we won't intend our (subsentential) phrases to represent X's representations. In such a case ascription of any Russellian content the computer believes is straightforwardly true.[33]

Turn now to the "interpretationism" I endorsed in Section 5. I suggested that I can correctly report Boswell's utterance of "I'd like some water," by saying that Boswell said that he wanted water. I also (in effect) suggested that this report might be false in contexts in which we are focused on diachronic semantics. This may make it appear that I am committed to a pernicious sort of relativism. For you and I mean the same by "Boswell wanted water;" this phrase doesn't change meaning when embedded. So musn't I say that when I utter "Boswell said that he wanted water" and you utter its negation, we contradict each other and yet each speaks truly? I'm thus committed to saying that when we ascribe beliefs and other attitudes, what we say is only relatively, and not absolutely true.

---

[33] Such ascriptions will thus be "Millian"—that is, when an ascription like *The computer thinks that ... a ...* is true, and the names *a* and *b* are coreferential, the ascription *The computer thinks that ... b ...* will be true too. Since substitution failure after "believes" seems to result from the fact that the words after the verb in some way indicate "ways of thinking" or "ways of representing" what is thought about, we would expect this.

There are other quasi-technical questions raised by the discussion in Section 5. One is the question of how to incorporate what we might call "quasi-articulated representation" into the semantics developed in the essays collected here. Consider Diva's belief that I threw a ball. I argued in Section 5 that it was plausible to think that Diva had representations of me and of the property of thowing a ball, even if she didn't have a representation that was at all like our indefinite "a ball." The question is how to combine the idea that

Diva thinks that I threw a ball

ascribes a belief in something with the semantic structure of my use of "I threw a ball" with the idea that the "representational structure" of the state which makes the ascription true might not completely recapitulate that semantic structure.

This really is a *technical* problem, and it has a relatively straightforward technical solution. Sketching in very bold strokes: note that it is plausible that whatever we identify Russellian contents with will have something like the hierarchal structure of the sentences that express them. Thus, there will be "positions" in such propositions that correspond not only to the atomic expressions in a sentence, but to the complex phrases in the sentence. Thus, the Russellian proposition that John loves Mary will have positions that correspond to the positions of "John," "Mary," "loving," *and* the position of "loves Mary" in the sentence "John loves Mary." If we can imagine an annotated proposition in which some but not all of John, Mary, and loving are paired with the non-representation ~, we can also imagine an a-proposition in which John and loving Mary are paired with representations, though neither loving nor Mary are so paired. Likewise, we can imagine an a-proposition obtained from the Russellian proposition that I threw a ball in which I am paired with Diva's representation of me, the property of throwing a ball is paired with Diva's representation of that property, but the throwing relation and the semantic value of "a ball" are paired with ~. An a-proposition like this encodes both the articulated Russellian content of the dog's belief and the partial representational articulation of that content by the dog.

Once we recognize this sort of thing, we may also recognize that in ascribing an attitude we might have "translation rules" that are concerned not only with how individual words translate or represent representations of she who has the attitude, but also rules that dictate how complex phrases can be used to represent the representations of the other. I hope to spell these ideas out in detail elsewhere.

It's not clear to me that such a commitment is a bad thing.[34] But it's certainly not true that a reasonable interpretationism is committed to it.[35] In working up to an explanation of why this is, I begin by noting that the account of attitude ascription in the essays below takes verbs like "believes" to be contextually sensitive, naming different relations in different contexts. The account is one on which such verbs have an implicit argument place for what I called above a translation manual, so that

Boswell thinks that S

has a logical form along the lines of

There's an acceptable translation manual f such that one of Boswell's beliefs [i.e. an a-proposition determined by one of his belief states] is translated, under f, by the a-proposition that S.

Furthermore, what counts as an acceptable translation manual (from the a-propositions determined by English complements to those determined by a particular individual's a-propositions) will vary across contexts with the interests of speakers. So there is already a commitment in the essays that follow to contextual sensitivity in verbs like "believes." This sort of sensitivity doesn't make for relativism about truth. Suppose my context restricts the use of "Jane" in ascribing beliefs to Ray so that it can only represent representations of Jane that Ray used in the past, while your context contains no such restriction. Then "realizes" picks out quite different relations in your context and mine; given the story told in Section 4 above, your use of "Ray realizes that Jane just left" may be true, thought mine will be false. But that is not to say that we contradict each other when you utter "Ray realizes that Jane just left" and I utter its negation.

Turn now to interpretationism, which posits a layer of contextual sensitivity for verbs like "believes" beyond that just noted.[36] For the interpretationist, content ascription involves two steps. It begins with—it *presupposes*—a way of assigning referential content to the states of those of whom we speak. This assignment is often (at least partially) conventionalized, as there are often established conventions for giving a referential interpretation of the thoughts and talk of others in our idiom.[37] Once the assignment of referential content to the states of others has been determined, there is then a further step in content ascription, in which we determine (in a way that is usually *not* conventional) how our words are to represent or otherwise indicate how the ascribee represents referential content.

---

[34] See the discussion in the Introduction to Volume 2 of *Meaning In Context*, as well as the papers "Contextualism and Relativism" and "Relativisms" in that volume.

[35] We need, of course, to distinguish between saying that a claim is only relatively true (and thus denying that "all truth is absolute") and saying that certain sentences express different things relative to different contexts. No one denies the latter sort of "relativism." What follows is the observation that nothing said in this introduction involves a commitment to the first, controversial sort of relativism.

[36] Interpretationism is not a part of the view developed in the essays that follow. They aren't inconsistent with it; it just wasn't something I took seriously when I wrote them.

[37] Discussions of indeterminacy of translation are in good part observations that these conventions are very much *conventions*, insofar as they could in principle, though rarely in practice, be altered.

Make explicit all that is presupposed or otherwise contextually variable about the ascription *Boswell believes that S*; if you do, you'll see that the sentence has a logical form along the lines of

> There's a way i of interpreting (*viz.*, a way of assigning referential content to) Boswell's states and an acceptable translation manual f (*viz.*, a way of representing Boswell's representations) such that under i, one of Boswell's beliefs [i.e. an a-proposition determined by one of his belief states] has the referential content of and is translated, under f, by the a-proposition that S.

It's a mouthful, for sure. But if this is what my claim that Boswell believes that S comes to, it doesn't involve relativism about truth. Rather, the interpretation and representation of Boswell's contentful states is a highly contextual process. This is not a shocking or even particularly surprising thesis.

What perhaps *is* surprising is how little of an attitude ascription's truth conditions is determined independently of and prior to the interpretive enterprise. Most of us come to formal semantics with the assumption that its point is to calculate the relative product of two more or less context-independent factors—how things are out there in the world and what our words and sentences mean. Before we speak, there are, out there in the world, objects with properties, standing in relations; before we speak, our words refer to objects, and express properties and relations. *Wir machen uns Bilder der Tatsachen*, and semantics tells us how the two, *Bilder und Tatsachen*, have to be related to make a truth.

That's the picture, anyway. But though it may be true that the dog thinks that I threw a ball and though it *is* true that for the dog to have that thought is for it to be related to the proposition that I threw a ball—i.e. to what I say, when I say that I threw a ball—that is a relation that in a certain sense gets forged in the moment of my saying that it obtains. It's not magic, and it's not arbitrary: that the dog is correctly described in this way is a function of its dispositions and perceptual state and of my choice of rendering those in the way that I do. Practically speaking, I don't have much a choice in rendering the facts about the dog as I do. But we do well to remember that when we write

> A use of a sentence of the form *x believes that S*, taken relative to a context c, is true iff what *x* names (in c) bears the relation picked out by "believes" in c to the proposition determined (in c) by S

the reference of *x* and of the complement *that S* (in c) are often a heck of a lot more independent of facts about the context than is the relation named by "believes."

Thinking does not normally make it so. Thinking about thinking, though, often comes closer to making it so than we sometimes think.[38]

---

[38] Thanks to David Braun and Peter Momtchiloff for comments. Thanks also to Kit Fine for correspondence about his views which informs the brief remarks about them in Section 4.

2

Direct Reference and Ascriptions of Belief

It is often supposed that demonstratives and indexicals are *devices of direct reference*—that they are, as David Kaplan puts it, terms which "refer directly without the mediation of a Fregean *Sinn* [or individual concept, set of properties, etc.] as meaning."[1] Most of the resistance to this view, I think, arises from the suspicion that it is not possible to give an acceptable treatment of the semantics of belief ascriptions and other so-called propositional attitude contexts which is consistent with the thesis of direct reference. For it seems that a straightforward construal of the thesis (along with some plausible semantical assumptions) requires that demonstratives, when co-referential, be intersubstitutable everywhere, even in belief contexts, *salva veritate*. But many feel that it is *obvious* that such substitutions do not always preserve truth.

The purpose of this paper is to motivate and present a semantics for a first-order treatment of belief ascriptions which is both consistent with the thesis of direct reference and intuitively satisfactory. The paper is structured as follows: In Section I, I discuss semantical consequences of the thesis of direct reference—in particular, what it does and does not require with respect to the overall form of a semantical treatment of belief ascriptions. I also discuss a view about belief, championed by Kaplan and John Perry, which I call the triadic view of belief. Crudely put, it is the view that belief is a triadic relation among a person, a proposition, and a sentential meaning, the latter entity a different sort of thing than a proposition. On this view, to believe a proposition is to do so "under" a sentential meaning.

The champions of the triadic view of belief have shied away from using the view to motivate a semantic account of belief ascriptions.[2] But the triadic view of belief suggests,

---

[1] Kaplan (1989), p. 483. Henceforth, I will use "demonstratives" as shorthand for "demonstratives and indexicals."

[2] Thus, for example, Kaplan, in the section of Kaplan (1989) entitled "Adding 'Says'" suggests truth conditions for (indirect discourse) ascriptions of belief which have the effect of making something of the form ⌜α believes that ϕ⌝ true exactly if α's referent believes (under any meaning whatsoever) the proposition the semantics assigns to ϕ. Elsewhere in Kaplan (1989), Kaplan claims that all (non-quotational) operators of English are "at most intensional"—*viz.*, they all can be construed as operating on (the formal representatives of) propositions.

as I note at the end of Section I, that ascriptions of belief not only imply that a proposition is an object of belief, but that it is believed in a certain way. The purpose of Sections II and III of the paper is to show that an account of belief ascriptions on which they behave in just this way can be formalized rather easily, and that it nicely handles certain cases which, at first blush, seem quite problematic for those who accept the view that demonstratives are directly referential. Section II is concerned with the semantics of ascriptions of belief *de se*: That is, with giving a first-order syntax and semantics which adequately represents (different readings of) ascriptions of the form ⌜*a* believes himself to be *F*⌝ (and of allied forms) and the relations of such ascriptions to *de re* ascriptions of belief. Section III is concerned with semantics for "standard" belief ascriptions in which the sentential complement to "believes that" contains demonstrative and indexical terms.

I

The core of the thesis that demonstratives are directly referential is negative.[3] A somewhat long-winded way of expressing the thesis is this: Associated with well-formed expressions of English (taken relative to a context) is an entity which we may call the expression's *content*. (As will become clear, I am using this expression, as well as the term "proposition," in a very technical and circumscribed way.) Contents play a number of semantic roles. One of the things the content of a singular term does is to determine, relative to a possible circumstance of evaluation, an individual; the individual so determined at a circumstance by the content of a term (taken relative to a context) is the referent of the term (taken relative to the context) at the circumstance.[4] To say that a term is directly referential is to say something about how its content determines an individual: It is to say that it does *not* do this by means of a complex of properties, a Fregean sense, an individual concept, etc. A picturesque way of putting the matter is this: The content of a directly referential expression, taken relative to a context, *is* that thing which the expression, taken relative to the context, has as a referent at any circumstance of evaluation.

What specific semantical consequences we suppose the thesis of direct reference to have depends, of course, upon what sort of semantical assumptions we make beyond the assumption that demonstratives are directly referential. As noted at the beginning of this paper, it is often assumed that one consequence of the thesis of direct reference is that any ascriptions of belief which differ only in that one contains a demonstrative *d* where the other contains a demonstrative *d'* have the same truth value relative to any context in which *d* and *d'* are co-referential.

---

[3] An excellent discussion of what the thesis of direct reference does and does not imply can be found in Salmon (1981).

[4] I am adopting here some of the terminology and semantic assumptions of Kaplan's (1979) and (1989).

Those who think that this is a consequence of the thesis of direct reference seem to reason as follows: The content of a declarative sentence, taken relative to a context—I'll use the term *proposition* for sentential contents—is what determines the truth value of a sentence, relative to the context. Content, however, is determined functionally. More precisely: The content of a sentence in a context—what proposition it expresses—is a function solely of the contents of the parts of the sentence (in the context) and the syntax of the sentence. Now the thesis of direct reference surely requires that demonstratives that denote the same thing have the same content. Hence, given this thesis, one must say that *any* sentences, differing only with respect to co-referential demonstratives, express the same proposition and, therefore, have the same truth value.

An advocate of the view that demonstratives are directly referential *could*, I suppose, deny that co-referential directly referential terms have the same content, where the content of a term is characterized as it was above. But such a denial, I think, makes the claim that a certain sort of expression is directly referential extremely mysterious. For recall that the claim that a term is directly referential is the claim that the term does not have as a content a sense, an individual concept, etc. This, coupled with the fact that such expressions are supposed to behave as rigid designators (*viz.*, a use of such a term has the same referent at every circumstance of evaluation at which it has any referent at all), makes it difficult to see how one could coherently maintain that co-designative directly referential terms can have different contents. How, one wants to know, could they differ?

A more plausible response to the above argument, I think, is to deny that it is invariably the case that the content of a complex expression is a function of the contents of its parts and their syntactic mode of combination. For there is no reason to think that content is the only sort of semantic value which expressions may have. Indeed, those who subscribe to the thesis of direct reference generally recognize at least one other sort of semantic value which expressions have. Thus, for example, Kaplan holds that the linguistic meaning of an expression (meaning in the sense of what is known by one who understands an expression) is to be identified, not with its content, but with what Kaplan calls the expression's *character*, the function which takes a context to the content of the expression therein. If the only sort of semantic value we recognized was content, it would be strange, to say the least, to suppose that the determination of content was not functional across the board. However, once we recognize yet another sort of semantic value, it is far from clear that we should suppose that the content of the whole is invariably a function of the contents of the parts.

This is particularly unobvious when the second semantic value is related to content as is character: In a fairly clear sense, character determines content, not the converse. Should the language contain an operator which is sensitive (not just to content, but) to character, it is at least an open question as to whether content is invariably functional. For suppose there were an operator, O, such that $O(A)$ is true only if the character of A has P. Since expressions with distinct characters may, relative to a context, have the same content, it is at least *a priori* possible that there be expressions B and B' such that the character of B has P, the character of B' does not, but, relative to some context c, B and B' have the same content. In this case, $O(B)$ and $O(B')$ have different contents (*viz.*, express different propositions) relative to c, since they diverge in truth value.[5]

I contend that this is not just an idle possibility: In Section III, I will urge that "believes that" is sensitive to linguistic meaning (construed as character) as well as to content. This, however, is anticipating matters somewhat. For the moment, all we have established is this: The advocate of direct reference need not assent to the view that ⌜a believes that S⌝ and ⌜a believes that S'⌝, taken relative to a context in which S and S' express the same proposition, invariably have the same truth value.

It is worth observing that the above argument is consistent with the claim that, in a circumscribed but nonetheless significant number of cases, the content of an expression is determined as a function of the contents of its parts. In particular, we have given no reason to think that the advocate of direct reference would deny that what proposition is expressed by a sentence which contains at most truth functional or simple intensional operators (*viz.*, temporal or modal operators) is determined functionally by the contents of its parts and their mode of combination. I shall assume, for the purposes of this paper, that an advocate of the view that demonstratives are directly referential would say this.

We are now ready to discuss belief and ascriptions of belief. A fairly "standard" view of belief is that propositions, characterized as above, play the role of objects of belief in two senses: (a) they are objects of belief in the sense that belief is a dyadic relation, the second term of the relation being a proposition; (b) they are objects of "belief," in the sense that an ascription of belief ⌜a believes that S⌝ is true iff what a denotes bears the belief relation to the proposition expressed by S.

Many who are sympathetic to the thesis of direct reference—notably Kaplan and John Perry[6]—have proposed that propositions are objects of belief in some sense, but that the relation between a person and a proposition, when the latter is an object of his belief, is somewhat more complex than the above account suggests. On this view—the triadic view of belief, as I will call it—belief is a triadic relation between a person, a sentential meaning (understood as being a Kaplanesque character), and a proposition; to believe a proposition is to do so under a sentential meaning.[7] I will use the term *acceptance* for the relation which one bears to a sentential meaning when one believes a

---

[5] I have argued in Richard (1982) that tense operators can be given an adequate semantical treatment only on the assumption that they operate on the meanings of, not simply on the propositions expressed by, sentences. Thus, questions about "believes that" to one side, I think the possibility of there being an operator such as O, is not at all idle.

[6] See Kaplan (1989), Perry (1979), and Perry (1989).

[7] This is closer to Kaplan's view than Perry's. On Perry's account, the second term in the relation is what Perry calls a *belief state*, which is a mental state individuated (in part, at least) in terms of the sentence types (or meanings thereof) which an agent in that state accepts, where *acceptance* is a technical term with a meaning related to (but probably not identical with) the meaning the term is accorded below in the text.

I characterize the triadic theory as in the text because I find it easier to motivate the formalism of Sections II and III in terms of such a characterization.

proposition under it; it is to be understood that, on the triadic view, a proposition p is an object of someone's belief if and only if he accepts a meaning which, relative to the context of which he is the agent, has p as value.

It is not my purpose here to defend this view of belief. I will, however, note that a view of belief along these general lines seems mandatory for those who accept the thesis that demonstratives are directly referential and take propositions to be, in some important sense, objects of belief. For, to take an example, on the thesis of direct reference (making, of course, the kind of semantical assumptions we are currently making), someone who expresses something he believes by saying "You [person X is addressed, say, through the telephone] are happy, but she [X, who is standing across the street, is demonstrated] is not happy" expresses belief in the same proposition as does one who addresses X and says "You are happy, but you are not happy." Without invoking a view like the triadic view, it is difficult to explain, or even explain away, the intuition that an irrationality is present in the latter belief which is not present in the former—for the object of belief, in the sense of proposition believed, is the same in both cases. Invoking the view, however, what one can say is this: What is irrational is not to have the proposition in question as an object of belief, but to believe it in the way the second person does. For a rational person who understands English must know that the second meaning cannot yield a truth.[8]

It is worth noting that on such an account of belief, propositions are not (or, at least, need not be) simply vestigial remains of the simpler dyadic view of belief, playing no particularly important or indispensible role in the triadic theory. Propositions are here identified with the *contents* of beliefs; meanings are identified with *manners* in which one may hold beliefs.

Presumably, *what* is believed is just as important as *how* it is believed. Furthermore, it is, presumably, in terms of propositions (or, at least, mostly in terms of propositions) that we

---

[8] I ought to say something here about what these meanings are, and how they differ; what needs to be made clear is what the meaning of terms like "you" and "she" is.

I presume the following (and do not suggest that it is an original view; it is a version of Kaplan's own view). There are what we might call "modes of demonstrating" things and "modes of addressing" things. These modes are such that the same mode can be used in different contexts or several times in one context. It is only when "she" is accompanied by a mode of demonstrating ("you" is accompanied by a mode of addressing) that it refers to an object. Furthermore, although "she" plus mode m of demonstrating ("you" plus mode m' of addressing) may pick out different objects in different contexts, "she" accompanied by one mode of demonstrating picks out the same object every time it is used in a context; analogously for "you."

The meaning (in Kaplan's sense of meaning as character) of "she," then, is roughly this: "she," accompanied by a mode of demonstrating, functions as a directly referential term; it denotes, relative to a context, what its accompanying mode of demonstrating demonstrates.

Thus, in giving formal representatives for sentences such as those mentioned in the text, what we really represent is the sentence type and aspects of the modes of demonstration or address. (For we wish to be able to assign the representatives of propositions to the formal representatives of sentences; the sentences being represented don't express propositions, on the view assumed here, unless accompanied by modes of demonstration or address.) We thus represent two occurrences of "she" (of "you") with the same term if and only if they are accompanied by the same mode of demonstration (or address).

These details will be germane to the view of *de re* belief ascriptions discussed in Section III.

evaluate claims concerning the retention of belief and claims that two people have the same belief.

As I have characterized it, the triadic theory is a (metaphysical) theory about the nature of belief; as such, it is not directly concerned with the semantical problem of truth conditions for ascriptions of belief. Some partisans of the triadic view[9] have suggested that even though belief is to be understood as above, an ascription ⌜*a* believes that *S*⌝, *a* a term, *S* a sentence, is true exactly if *a*'s referent believes (*viz.*, has as the content of a belief) the proposition expressed by *S*. Nonetheless, if we suppose the triadic view of belief to be correct, it is natural to think that the triadic nature of belief might be reflected in ascriptions of belief. One way in which such a reflection might occur is this: Some ascriptions of belief may imply, not only that a particular proposition is an object of belief, but that it is believed in a certain way—that is, that it is believed under a meaning of a certain sort.

It is the task of the remainder of this paper to make it plausible that this indeed *is* true of ascriptions of belief. Of course, the account of belief ascriptions to be developed will be consistent with the thesis of direct reference, as we have characterized it. We will begin by developing, in the next section, a treatment of so-called *de se* ascriptions of belief.

II

A *de se* ascription of belief is one of the form of

(1) *a* believes himself to be *F*

where *a* is a term, and *F* is a predicative expression.[10] It is widely acknowledged that a *de se* ascription of the form of (1) is not implied by the corresponding *de re* ascription, that of the form of

(2) There is an *x* such that *x* is identical with *a* and *x* believes that *x* is *F*.

---

[9] For Kaplan's views, see footnote 2 above. Perry has suggested in conversation that he accepts something along the general lines of the semantical view expressed in the sentence to which this is a footnote.

[10] As a referee pointed out, it is misleading to single out (1) as "the form" of *de se* ascriptions in English. This is, firstly, because sentences of the form ⌜I believe that I am *F*⌝ seem, at least sometimes, to be used to ascribe *de se* belief and sometimes merely *de re* belief. Secondly, some sentences (e.g., "I believe that Edwina will build a house near mine") seem to be used to report belief *de se* but are neither of the form of (1) nor such that they have a colloquial equivalent of the form of (1). (A further worry is whether or not (1) has a reading on which it is equivalent to (2); whatever the answer to this question, I do not think it will affect the points made in this section.)

I will persist in speaking as if (1) gave the canonical form of *de se* ascriptions—a fiction which, I hope, is no more harmful in this context than the common fiction, in discussions of belief *de re*, of pretending that ⌜*a* believes, of that *b* she's *F*⌝ is unambiguously *de re*, while ⌜*a* believes that *b* is *F* *is* unambiguously *de dicto*.

I presume that the reader is acquainted with the standard arguments that sentences of the form of (2) don't imply ones of the form of (1);[11] I will assume here that such an implication does indeed fail. It is initially difficult to see how an advocate of the thesis of direct reference could deny that this implication fails.

The problem is this: Consider a particular *de se* ascription—say, "John believes himself to be wise"—and the corresponding *de re* ascription, "there is an x such that x is John and x believes that x is wise." Under what conditions is the *de se* ascription true? Presumably, it is used to ascribe to John belief in the proposition John would express by saying "I am wise"; thus, one thinks, it will be true iff John believes that proposition. But on the thesis of direct reference, this is the proposition that is expressed by a sentence of the form ⌜d is wise⌝, d a directly referential term denoting John. It seems that the advocate of direct reference ought to hold that John's believing such a proposition is both necessary and sufficient for the truth of the corresponding *de re* ascription. After all, "$(\exists x)$ (x = John and x believes that x is wise)" seems to ascribe to John a belief in what "x is wise" expresses, when John is assigned to "x"; but the free variable under an assignment seems to be the paradigm of a directly referential term.

A straightforward account of why the implication does not go through is motivated by the triadic theory of belief. For one can say that the ascription "John believes himself to be wise" implies that John believes the proposition that he would express by saying "I am wise" in a certain way—roughly, under the meaning of "I am wise." Pretty obviously, given the triadic theory of belief, John can believe this proposition under meanings other than that of "I am wise": perhaps, for example, John sees a reflection of himself, doesn't know that he sees himself, accepts the meaning of "He [John demonstrates his reflection] is wise," but doesn't accept the meaning of "I am wise." As long as John believes the proposition under some meaning, the *de re* ascription is true. Thus, we have an explanation of how it is that the *de re* ascription fails to imply the *de se* ascription.

A general treatment of *de se* ascriptions may be developed along the following lines. First, let us introduce some structure to meanings. Instead of thinking of a meaning as simply a function from contexts to propositions, think of it as a pair $\langle \langle s_1, ..., s_n \rangle, M^n \rangle$ ($n \geq 0$), where each s_i is a (demonstrative) term-meaning—a function from contexts to individuals—and M^n is an n-place predicate-meaning—a function from contexts to n-place properties. (I will, for the sake of expediency, identify n-place properties with functions from n-tuples of possible individuals to sets of possible worlds; propositions with zero-place properties—*viz.*, sets of worlds.) The proposition such a meaning yields in a context c is, of course, the proposition p such that w is in p exactly if w is in $[M^n(c)]$ $(\langle s_1(c), s_2(c), ..., s_n(c) \rangle)$.

---

[11] A sampler of such arguments is to be found in Chisholm (1981). It is not my purpose here to defend any particular argument as showing that the implication fails. Rather, I assume that it is *very* plausible that the implication does fail. Given this assumption, the question arises: How could an advocate of the view that demonstratives and indexicals are directly referential account for this?

Note, now, that we can "partially interpret" such meanings, relative to a context. For example, if we start with a meaning $m = \langle\langle s_1, s_2\rangle, M^2\rangle$ and a context c, we can "plug in" the values of s_1 and M^2 in c to get a "reduced meaning" $m' = \langle\langle s_2\rangle, P^1\rangle$, P^1 the one-place property such that $w \in P^1(u)$ iff $w \in [M^2(c)](\langle s_1(c), u\rangle)$. The reduced meaning m' in turn, corresponds to the function from contexts to propositions which applied to a context c' yields the proposition that the value of s_2 in c' has P^1.

The basic intuition behind the general treatment of *de se* ascriptions we propose is this: a *de se* ascription

(3) *a* believes himself to be *F*

is true exactly if *a*'s referent believes the proposition that he is *F* (*viz.*, the proposition that he has the property which is expressed by ⌜is *F*⌝ relative to the context at which we interpret (3)) under a meaning *m* which has as one of its reduced meanings $\langle\langle\{I\}\rangle, F\rangle$, where $\{I\}$ is the meaning of "*I*." This, in turn, will be true precisely if *a*'s referent accepts a meaning which is the meaning of a sentence of the form ⌜$\phi(I)$⌝, where $\phi(x)$ expresses, relative to his context, the property *F*. When someone believes a proposition under such a meaning, we will say that he self-attributes the property, allowing us to state our view in summary form as: (3) is true exactly if *a*'s referent self-attributes the property expressed by ⌜is *F*⌝.[12]

---

[12] To those familiar with views of *de se* belief in Chisholm (1981) and Lewis (1979), this will sound somewhat familiar. Chisholm introduces a primitive notion *x directly attributes property P to y* which, according to Chisholm, is necessarily reflexive. Chisholm then says that to believe oneself to be *F* is to directly attribute *F* to oneself. Lewis suggests that we understand belief *de se* as the *self-ascription* of property.

There are several important differences between our approach and the approaches of Chisholm and Lewis. We do not hold that properties are the objects of *de se* belief, as do Lewis and Chisholm; we also hold that the objects of all beliefs are of uniform character, unlike Chisholm.

On Chisholm's view, it is somewhat mysterious as to why one can directly attribute properties only to oneself. Indeed, for Chisholm, there is no real correlate of direct attribution, relating distinct individuals and a property: Chisholm's indirect attribution (in terms of which Chisholm defines *de re* belief) is simply a complicated form of direct attribution.

On our view the reflexivity of self-attribution is not mysterious at all: it's reflexive because it involves meanings which contain $\{I\}$. Furthermore, we could define a perfectly analogous notion of indirect attribution, without invoking the notion of self-attribution, if we wished. Indeed, something like this is defined in Section III, below.

We have analogous differences with Lewis, who characterizes belief *de re* in Lewis (1979) as a kind of belief *de se*. (For Lewis, as for us, the objects of belief are of uniform character; but, unlike us, he takes them to be all properties.)

It is worth noting that the formalization introduced in this section could be used, with some alterations, to regiment Lewis' view. (The major alterations would be to drop the "B^r" operator introduced below, translating English sentences of the form of *a believes that S*, where *S* involves no reflexives, as: $aB^s\hat{\alpha}$ ($\alpha = \alpha \wedge \phi$). One would also be required, in a formalization of Lewis's view, to prohibit quantification into "B^s," and to come up with a scheme to represent *de re* ascriptions. This is discussed at the end of Section II.) This should not hide the fact that there are fundamental differences in motivation between Lewis and ourselves. Beyond those mentioned above, we note that this essay and its formalism is intended to function in the defense of the thesis of direct reference, a thesis which—insofar as it is bound up with what Lewis and Kaplan call "haecceitism"—is anathema to Lewis.

The semantical details of a formalization of our approach to *de se* ascriptions are not particularly complex. Syntactical details, however, are slightly subtle.

Consider, to begin with, the behavior of "believes" in *de dicto* and *de re* ascriptions and in *de se* ascriptions. In the first two sorts of ascriptions, the belief operator—use "B^r" to represent it—appears to operate on an *n*-place predicate ($n \geq 0$) to yield an $n + 1$-place predicate. For example, "at the level of logical form," "B^r" combines with "*x* loves *y*" to yield "$zB^r(x$ loves $y)$." The belief operator in *de se* ascriptions, on the other hand—let us use "B^s" to represent it—apparently combines with an *n*-place predicate ($n > 0$) and a specification of an argument place to yield an *n*-place predicate. Thus, for example, applying "B^s" to "*x* loves *y*" and specifying the first argument place seems to yield something along the lines of "zB^s (he himself loves *y*)."

Of course, given that we do not want *de se* ascriptions to be implied by the corresponding *de re* ascriptions, we cannot assume that something like "zB^s (he himself loves *y*)" is reducible to an expression involving "B^r" and other syntactic operations. For example, we would not want to identify "zB^s (he himself loves *y*)" with the result of applying the operation "identifying the first two argument places" to "$zB^r(x$ loves *y*)." For the latter object—"zB^r (z loves y)"—will be true, relative to an assignment f, precisely if $f(z)$ believes *de re*, with respect to $f(z)$ and $f(y)$, that the former loves the latter.

Thus, we will use two distinct belief operators, "B^r" and "B^s," in our formalization. "B^r" will, as is usual, take a sentential complement. We will, however, have "B^s" take as complement a "property abstract" (something of the form ⌜$\hat{x}(\phi)$⌝, ϕ a sentence). The reasons for treating "B^s" in this way have, for the most part, to do with elegance in presentation. We could, in principle, allow "B^s" to take a sentential complement, so long as we introduced apparatus for indicating what argument positions in an embedded sentence are "specified argument places" in the sense indicated above. Such a treatment, however, is messier than need be.

It should be stressed that the decision to treat the *de se* belief operator in this way does *not* constitute surrender of the view that the objects of belief (*viz.*, the contents of belief, in the sense of Section I) are uniformly propositions, nor does it make it at all inappropriate to say that something of the form ⌜$\alpha B^s \hat{x}(\phi)$⌝ is (a representation of) an ascription of *belief*. Our semantics will take a formula of the form of ⌜$\alpha B^s \hat{x}(\phi)$⌝ to be true precisely if α's referent believes a *proposition* under a meaning m which has $\langle\langle\{I\}\rangle, \overline{\hat{x}(\phi)}\rangle$ as a reduced meaning, where $\overline{\hat{x}(\phi)}$ is the property the semantics associates with $\hat{x}(\phi)$. Furthermore, as we will show, a *de se* ascription will, in this treatment, imply its corresponding *de re* ascription (and thus imply that a certain proposition is believed), although the converse implication of course will not hold.

The vocabulary and formation rules for our treatment are as follows. As primitive vocabulary items we have: a denumerable set $V = \{x_1, x_2, \ldots\}$ of variables; denumerable sets $Y = \{y_1, y_2, \ldots\}$ and $T = \{t_1, t_2, \ldots\}$ of demonstrative terms (used to represent, respectively, uses of second person singular "you" and third person singular demonstratives such as "he," "she," "that," etc.); the singular term: *I*; for each *n*, a denumerable set F^n of

n-place predicates; the truth functors: $\neg, \wedge, \vee, \rightarrow, \leftrightarrow$; the belief predicates: B^r, B^s; the abstraction operator: $\wedge$; the quantifiers: $\exists, \forall$; and, as punctuation, "(", ")". We use D to name the set of demonstratives of the language, the set $Y \cup T \cup \{I\}$; $\mathscr{T}$, the set of terms, is $D \cup V$.

The definition of well-formed formula is:

1. If $\Pi \in F^n$ and $\alpha_1, ..., \alpha_n \in \mathscr{T}$, then ⌜$\Pi^n \alpha_1, ..., \alpha_n$⌝ is a formula.
2. If ϕ and Ψ are formulas, then ⌜$\neg\phi$⌝, ⌜$(\phi \wedge \Psi)$⌝, ⌜$(\phi \wedge \Psi)$⌝ ⌜$(\phi \rightarrow \Psi)$⌝ and ⌜$(\phi \leftrightarrow \Psi)$⌝ are formulas.
3. If ϕ is a formula, $\alpha \in V$, then ⌜$\exists \alpha \phi$⌝, ⌜$\forall \alpha \phi$⌝ are formulas.
4. If ϕ is a formula, $\alpha \in \mathscr{T}$ then ⌜$\alpha B^r(\phi)$⌝ is a formula.
5. If $\alpha \in \mathscr{T}$ and Γ is a proper abstract, then ⌜$\alpha B^s \Gamma$⌝ is a formula, where a proper abstract is any expression of the form ⌜$\hat{\alpha}(\phi)$⌝ ϕ a formula and α a member of V which occurs freely in ϕ.
6. These are all the formulas.

Before discussing the semantics, it is perhaps worthwhile to discuss the intuitive readings of those expressions which are formulas in virtue of clauses (4) and (5). Consider the following well-formed expressions of the language:

(4) $IB^r(IB^r(FI))$

(5) $IB^r(IB^s\hat{x}(Fx))$

(6) $IB^s\hat{x}(xB^r(FI))$

(7) $IB^s\hat{x}(IB^r(Fx))$

(8) $IB^s\hat{x}(xB^s\hat{x}(Fx))$

The semantic differences among these can be brought out as follows. Read "Fx" as "x is wise"; imagine me to be standing by a mirror. (4) through (8) can be understood as representing different readings of "I believe that I believe that I am wise," the difference in readings corresponding to different sorts of meanings under which I might hold the belief: (4) will be true simply if I hold a belief under the meaning of "He believes [de re] that he is wise" (occurrences of "he" always accompanied by a demonstration by me of my reflection); (5) corresponds to belief under the meaning of "He believes himself to be wise"; (6) under "I believe that he is wise"; (7) "He believes that I'm wise"; (8) "I believe myself to be wise."[13]

We define an interpretation for the language as a quartet $M = \langle U, W, C, V \rangle$ which obeys the following strictures:[14]

---

[13] It is difficult to come up with natural sounding English sentences which unambiguously capture these readings. I believe that anyone who takes the notion of de se belief seriously will agree that the beliefs represented by (4) through (8) are different beliefs; if the beliefs are different, an adequate treatment of belief ascriptions de se and de re ought to be able to differentiate them, syntactically and semantically.

[14] The semantics presented here is modeled upon that of Kaplan's Logic of Demonstratives; see Kaplan (1979) and (1989) for a detailed exposition.

36 CONTEXT AND THE ATTITUDES

1. U, W, and C are non-empty and disjoint sets (which, intuitively, represent possible individuals, worlds, and contexts, respectively).
2. (a) Associated with each member c of C is four-tuple $\langle c_A, c_W, c_Y, c_T \rangle$,
   (i) $c_A \in U$ (c's agent),
   (ii) $c_W \in W$ (c's world),
   (iii) c_Y and c_T are denumerable sequences of members of U (the potential addressees and demonstrata of c).
   (b) $c = c'$ iff $c_A = c'_A$, $c_W = c'_W$, $c_Y = c'_Y$, and $c_T = c'_T$.
   (c) No world contains distinct contexts with the same agent.
3. V is a function which assigns
   (a) a member of $((\mathcal{P}(W))^{U^n})^C$ to each member of F^n, for each n;
   (b) sets of meanings to each member of C, where a meaning is a pair $\langle \langle s_1, \ldots, s_n \rangle, M^n \rangle$ ($n \geq 0$), each $s_i \in U^C$ and M^n a member of $((\mathcal{P}(W))^{U^n})^C$

A word on the workings of V is perhaps in order here. V's assignments to predicate letters are, intuitively, predicate-meanings (taken to be functions from contexts to properties). V's assignments to contexts are to be understood as representing the class of meanings under which the agent of the context holds beliefs; in the terminology of Section I, $V(c)$ is the set of meanings which c_A accepts. Note that, for each context c, $V(c)$ determines a set of propositions, a proposition p being in the set so determined by $V(c)$ exactly if, for some m in $V(c)$, m, completely interpreted relative to c, yields p. These, of course, are the propositions which are objects of belief of the agent of c.

We must, in order to give a definition of truth, characterize the conditions under which the agent of a context self-attributes a property. This we do using the notion of a reduced meaning, introduced above. Where $M = \langle \langle s_1, \ldots, s_n \rangle, M^n \rangle$ is a meaning, a reduced meaning corresponding to M, relative to a context c, is any function in $\mathcal{P}(W)^C$ which results (in the way indicated above) by interpreting M^n and one or more of the s_i, relative to c. An i-reduced meaning is any reduced meaning such that (a) not all the s_i's are interpreted; (b) the only s_i's not interpreted are $\{I\}$ ($\{I\}$, of course, is the function which yields c_A, when applied to a context c). Where M is a meaning, we denote the set of i-reduced meanings of M, relative to c, by $M^{i,c}$. A member M_1 of $M^{i,c}$ is said to attribute a one-place property P just in case, for any context c' and world w

$$w \in M_1(c') \text{ iff } w \in P(c'_A).$$

When an $M_1 \in M^{i,c}$ and property P are so related, we write: $P \in [M^{i,c}]$. We can now say that the agent of a context c self-attributes the property P precisely if there is an M in V_c such that $P \in [M^{i,c}]$.

To define truth and denotation in an interpretation (reference to which is continually suppressed), we proceed as follows. The denotation of a term α, relative to a context c, assignment (member of U^V) f, and world w (write: $|\alpha|_{cfw}$) is defined: $f(\alpha)$, if $\alpha \in V$; c_A, if $\alpha = I$; C_{T_i}, if α is t_i; C_{Y_i}, if α is y_i. We begin the definition of ϕ, taken relative to c and f, is true at w (write: $cf[\phi]w$) as follows:

1. $f[\Pi^n\alpha_1...\alpha_n]w$ iff $w \in [V(\Pi^n)(c)] (<|\alpha_1|_{cfw},...,|\alpha_n|_{cfw}>)$

2. $f[(\emptyset \wedge \Psi)]w$ iff $f[\emptyset]w$ and $f[\Psi]w$.

And so on, for the other truth functors.

3. $f[\exists \alpha \emptyset]w$ iff $\exists u(u \in U$ and $f_u^\alpha[\emptyset]w)$.

Analogously for $\forall \alpha \emptyset$.

4. $f[\alpha B^r(\emptyset)]w$ iff $\exists c'(c'_A = |\alpha|_{cfw}$ & $c'_w = w$ &
   $\exists m(m \in V(c')$ & $m(c') = \{w' | f[\emptyset]w'\}))$.

$m(c')$ here is the proposition yielded by m in c', defined as above.

The intuitive content of clause (4) is this. $\alpha B^r(\emptyset)$, taken relative to c and f, is true exactly if: there is a meaning m such that α's denotatum accepts it (formally: $m \in V(c')$, c' the context of α's denotatum), and m yields relative to c' the proposition expressed by $\emptyset$ relative to c'. Note that this clause has the result (given that a person believes a proposition p if he accepts a meaning which yields p relative to his context) that $\alpha B^r(\emptyset)$ is true iff what α denotes believes the proposition expressed by $\emptyset$.

Let $\hat{\alpha}(\emptyset)$ be a proper abstract. We say that P is the implied property of $\hat{\alpha}(\emptyset)$, taken relative to c and f, if and only if P is the one-place property such that, for all u and w,

$w \in P(u)$ iff $f_u^\alpha[\emptyset]w$.

We use $\overline{\hat{\alpha}(\emptyset)^{cf}}$ to denote the implied property of $\hat{\alpha}(\emptyset)$, taken relative to c and f. We may complete our definition of truth by saying that a *de se* ascription $\alpha B^s \hat{\beta}(\emptyset)$, taken relative to c and f, is true at w precisely if: α's denotatum believes a proposition under a meaning which has, as one of its *i*-reduced meanings, one which attributes $\overline{\hat{\beta}(\emptyset)^{cf}}$ - that is, just in case α's denotatum self-attributes $\overline{\hat{\beta}(\emptyset)^{cf}}$. Formally, we have

5. $f[\alpha B^s \hat{\beta}(\emptyset)]w$ iff $\exists c'(c'_A = |\alpha|_{cfw}$ & $c'_w = w$ &
   $\exists m(m \in V(c')$ & $\overline{\hat{\beta}(\emptyset)^{cf}} \in [M^{i,c'}]))$.

These semantics adequately capture the view of the truth conditions of *de se* ascriptions discussed at the beginning of this section. In particular, they have the consequence that a *de se* ascription implies (what we will presently define as) its corresponding *de re* ascription, although the converse implication does not hold. Thus, something of the form $\alpha B^s \hat{x}(\emptyset)$ involves an ascription of *belief*: the ascription is true only if α's denotatum believes the proposition $\emptyset$ expresses, when the denotatum of α is assigned to x.

We define the *de re* ascription corresponding to a *de se* ascription $\Psi = \alpha B^s \hat{x}(\phi)$ as follows. Let v be the least (i.e., with smallest subscript) variable not occurring in $\alpha B^s \hat{x}(\phi)$. The *de re* ascription corresponding to Ψ is then

$$\exists v (v = \alpha \wedge v B^r \phi'),$$

where ϕ'' is ϕ with all free occurrences of x replaced by v. (We of course understand the expression $\hat{\alpha}$ to bind free occurrences of α within its scope.) Thus, for example, corresponding to

$$I B^s \hat{x}_1 (x_1 B^s \hat{x}_1 (F x_1)).$$

is

$$\exists x_2 (x_2 = I \wedge x_2 B^r (x_2 B^s \hat{x}_1 (F x_1))).$$

It follows fairly directly from the above definitions that whenever a *de se* ascription, taken relative to c and f, is true at w, then so is its corresponding *de re* ascription. Of course, the converse does not hold. For example, if $V(c')$ consists solely of the meaning of "Ft_5", "t_5" denotes c'_A relative to c', then

$$\exists x_1 (x_1 = I \wedge x_1 B^r (F x_1))$$

will be true, relative to c' and an assignment f, at c_w, but

$$I B^s x (Fx)$$

will not.

There is a sense in which the semantics allows us to dispense with "B^r" and make do with only "B^s" as a belief predicate. For we can define "B^r" using a schema along the lines of

$$\alpha B^r \phi =_{df} \alpha B^s \hat{\beta} (\beta = \beta \wedge \phi)$$

With some minor tinkering, this would be an adequate definition. (The tinkering required is this: as it stands, it's not the case that

$$\alpha B^r \phi$$

and

$$\alpha B^s \hat{\beta} (\beta = \beta \wedge \phi)$$

always agree in truth value, since (speaking very loosely) the latter's truth requires that the believer believe under the meaning of ⌜$I = I \wedge \phi$⌝, while the former requires simply belief under the meaning of ϕ. Now, although these meanings are identical when *conceived as functions* from contexts to propositions, they are not identical when conceived, as in our semantical system, as ordered n-tuples of the meanings of constituent expressions. Thus, to implement the above definition, we'd need to impose a requirement on the function V in our models to the effect that $\{I = I \wedge \phi\} \in V(c)$, if $\{\phi\} \in V(c)$.)

However, such a definition has little, philosophically, to recommend it. The possibility of such a definition does not show that in our regimentation belief *de dicto* and *de re* are kinds of or are reducuble to belief *de se*. (What it shows, I think, is that our system is committed to the thesis that anyone who believes a proposition *p* believes that he's himself and *p*, and the converse.) And it is certainly not the case that such a definition is what authors like Lewis (1979) and Chisholm (1981) have in mind when they suggest that belief *de re* is a kind of belief *de se*.

To take Lewis as an example: his view is that to believe *de re* of *u* that she's *F* is to self-ascribe the property *bearing R to one and only one thing, a thing that's F*, where *R* is an "suitable" relation and one indeed bears *R* to *u* and *u* alone. On such a view, *de re* belief isn't to be represented via quantification into the belief context (as we have represented it), nor will someone with such a view be sympathetic with our treatment of belief ascriptions involving demonstratives other than "I" (which is, in part, designed to represent such ascriptions as ascriptions of belief in propositions "singular" with respect to the referents of the demonstratives). What is critical to regimenting Lewis' view is not eliminating "B^r" in favor of "B^s" (although that's involved), but giving a procedure for representing ascriptions, which appear to involve quantifying in, as not involving it.

Thus, we will preserve the operator "B^r" devoting the next section to a discussion of its semantics.[15]

III

Our approach to *de se* ascriptions of belief is consistent with the view that the contents of *de dicto, de re*, and *de se* beliefs are all of the same category: They are all propositions. On the view just formalized, a (use of a) *de se* ascription of belief ascribes belief in a proposition. That is, for any such use *u*, there is a proposition *p* such that *u* is true only if whomever belief is ascribed to, by *u*, believes *p*. But, on the approach we have suggested, that is not all such an ascription does; it also tells us something about (it implies that there is a particular) way in which belief is held.

Why should this be true only of *de se* ascriptions? Why, indeed: I believe that this is also true of *de re* ascriptions of belief.[16] I will argue in this section that there are pairs of *de re* ascriptions which ascribe to a person belief in the same proposition (given the theory of direct reference), but diverge in truth value. I will then discuss how a generalization of the semantics developed above can help the advocate of direct reference to account for this.

Consider *A*—a man stipulated to be intelligent, rational, a competent speaker of English, etc.—who both sees a woman across the street in a phone booth, and is speaking to a woman through a phone. He does not realize that the woman to whom he is speaking—*B*, to give her a name—is the woman he sees. He perceives her to be in some danger—a run-away steamroller, say, is bearing down upon her phone booth. *A* waves at the woman; he says nothing into the phone.

---

[15] I now think the account of *de se* attitudes in this section is not quite right, since it makes having a *de se* attitude depend on being related to a natural language meaning. But I think the semantics given here can be easily modified to avoid this. See the discussion in Essay 1. (Note added in 2012.)

[16] As will become clear below, I consider any ascription of the form ⌜α believes that ϕ⌝, which is such that ϕ has explicit occurrences of demonstratives, a *de re* ascription of belief.

If *A* stopped and quizzed himself concerning what he believes, he might well say

(1) I believe that I can inform you of her danger via the telephone.

(It is understood here, and in the sequel, that uses of "she" are accompanied by demonstrations of the woman across the street; uses of "you" are addressed to the woman through the telephone.) *A* would deny the truth of an utterance by himself of

(2) I believe that I can inform her of her danger via the telephone.

The embedded sentences in (1) and (2) differ only with respect to demonstratives co-referential in the context. Hence (since the embedded sentences do not themselves contain any epistemological operators), if we accept the view that demonstratives are directly referential, we must say the embedded sentences express, relative to the context, the same proposition. Thus, (1) and (2), taken relative to the context, ascribe to *A* belief in the same proposition.

Surely, however, (1) and (2) diverge in truth value here, (1) being true and (2) being false. One can muster convincing evidence for both these claims. To argue for the truth of (1), for example, we may first note that *A* surely knows what proposition he expresses when uttering its embedded sentence. For he knows the meaning of the sentence, he is perceiving the referents of the demonstratives therein, and may be said to know of each demonstrative that it denotes the thing perceived. (To forestall one sort of objection, suppose *B* to be speaking into the phone throughout the example.) Furthermore, the embedded sentence in (1) certainly seems to express something that *A* believes, namely "I can tell *this* of the danger of *that* via the phone." Given all of this, and the fact that *A* would, sincerely and after reflection, attest to the truth of (1), it seems that we ought to allow that (1) is true.

It does not follow, however, that (2) is true; indeed, it would seem that (2) is certainly not true. One argument one could advance in favor of this claim is this: (2) is true only if *A* believes that there is someone in danger with whom he can converse via the phone. As the case is set up, there's every reason to think that *A* does not have this belief. Hence, there's every reason to think that (2) isn't true.

Presently, I will discuss what an advocate of the view that demonstratives are directly referential ought to say regarding cases like the one I've just presented. Before doing so, I will digress in order to consider a case which, superficially, appears similar to one I've just outlined.

Consider again the situation of *A* and *B*. If *A* stopped and quizzed himself concerning what he believes, he might well sincerely utter

(3) I believe that she is in danger,

but not

(4) I believe that you are in danger.

Many people, I think, suppose that here, again, we have a case in which sentences which ascribe belief to *A* in the same proposition (given that demonstratives are directly referential) clearly diverge in truth value, (3) being true and (4) being false.

It's clear that if we accept the thesis of direct reference, we must say that the embedded sentences in (3) and (4) express, relative to A's context, the same proposition. But the view—that (3) is true in the context and (4) is not—is, I believe, demonstrably false. In order to simplify the statement of the argument which shows that the truth of (4) follows from the truth of (3), allow me to assume that A is the unique man watching B. Then we may argue as follows: suppose that (3) is true, relative to A's context. Then B can truly say that the man watching her—A, of course—believes that she is in danger. Thus, if B were to utter

(5) The man watching me believes that I'm in danger

(even through the telephone) she'd speak truly. But if B's utterance of (5) through the telephone, heard by A, would be true, then A would speak truly, were he to utter, through the phone

(6) The man watching you believes that you are in danger.

Thus, (6) is true, taken relative to A's context. But, of course,

(7) I am the man watching you

is true, relative to A's context. But (4) is deducible from (6) and (7).

Hence,[17] (4) is true, relative to A's context.

Note that a similar argument can't be used to show that from the claim that (1) is true in A's context, it follows that (2) is true. Consider how we might attempt to construct such an argument. We would have to argue that if A can truly utter (1), then B can truly say that the man watching her believes that he can inform her of her danger via the phone. That is, we would have to claim that if A can truly utter (1), then B can truly utter

(8) The man watching me believes that he can inform me of my danger via the phone.

Here, I think, the new argument goes awry. For it follows, from the claims that B can truly utter (8) and that A is the man watching B, that A believes that there is someone in danger who's such that he can tell her of her danger via the phone. But, as the case is set up, this is not so. Hence, there's no reason to think that an utterance of (8) by B would be true. (I will discuss this further below.)

Let us now return to the original case. It is clear what we will say about this case, if we accept the view of belief above labeled the triadic view. We will say that A believes the proposition—that B can be informed of her danger via the phone—under the meaning of the embedded sentence of

---

[17] I assume a definition of validity such as that which Kaplan gives for his Logic of Demonstratives. (See Kaplan (1979).) I also assume (what is true in that logic) that if A follows from B and B is true in context c, then A is true in c.

(1) I believe that I can inform you of her danger via the telephone.

but not under the meaning of the embedded sentence of

(2) I believe that I can inform her of her danger via the telephone.

This analysis shouldn't be terribly puzzling, even given that A understands both sentences and knows of each, and the proposition it expresses, that the former expresses the latter. For, as A doesn't know that his uses of "she" and "you" are co-referential, he can hardly be expected to know that the embedded sentences express the same proposition.

Compare, now, the position of A with that of a person X, who is in the same situation as A, but who knows that the woman he sees is the woman to whom he is speaking. X will hold a belief about B under both the meanings mentioned above. He will also differ from A in the following way: there will be a woman whom X believes to have the property *being such that she can be informed of her danger via the phone*. It seems that we cannot explain this difference between A and X in terms of proposition believed, since both of them believe the proposition that B can be informed of her danger via the phone. In order to explain the difference, we must appeal to *how* A and X hold their beliefs. It would seem that to believe the proposition expressed (relative to a context c) by a sentence in which demonstratives occur is to have a *de re* belief with respect to the objects denoted in c by the demonstratives in the sentence. If one has a *de re* belief with respect to an object, then one may be said to *attribute* certain properties to the object. However, it does not follow, from the fact that x and y each believe the proposition p expressed in c by a sentence $S(d)$, d a demonstrative occuring in S and denoting u in c, that every property which x attributes to u, in virtue of his believing p, is one which y attributes to u, in virtue of this belief. For which properties one attributes to an object is determined by the meaning under which one's belief is held: X, for example, who believes the proposition that he can inform B of her danger via the phone under the meaning of "I can inform her of her danger via the phone," will attribute to B the property *being a thing that can be informed of its danger via the phone*: A, who doesn't believe the proposition under the meaning just mentioned, will not attribute this property to B.

If this much be accepted, we have the basis of an answer to the question: how can

(1) I believe that I can inform you of her danger via the telephone.

and

(2) I believe that I can inform her of her danger via the telephone.

diverge in truth value in a context in which their embedded sentences express the same proposition? For we may say: an ascription of belief ⌜a believes that S⌝, S a sentence in which demonstratives occur, not only implies that the proposition expressed by S is believed, but that certain properties are attributed to the referents of the demonstratives in S. What properties the ascription implies are attributed depends in turn upon the meaning of S. In the case in question, ascription (2) implies that a property (that associated with a use in this context of "I can inform x of x's danger by phone") is attributed which (1) does not imply is attributed. Hence, (1) may true be while (2) is not.

Let us consider how we might give a systematic development of this proposal. In order to simplify matters, we will do this for a language with only a *de re* belief operator; it will be obvious how the treatment would be generalized to a language including a *de se* operator such as that discussed in Section II.

We assume, then, that our language has the same primitive vocabulary as the language of Section II, minus the B^s operator and the abstraction operator; the formation rules are identical to those of Section II, save the omission of the clause for the *de se* operator. We preserve the definitions of interpretation, denotation, and the clauses for the truth definition for atomic, truth functional, and quantified sentences. We now need to characterize, in terms of the formal structure, two things: when an individual, in believing a proposition under a meaning, attributes a property, and when a belief ascription, taken relative to a context, implies the attribution of a property.

Let $m = \langle \langle s_1, \ldots, s_n \rangle, M^n \rangle$ be a meaning. The intuitive answer to the question—When does the agent of a context c attribute a property P, in virtue of believing under m?—is as follows. Consider, first of all, what one "gets" if one (a) replaces M^n with $M^n(c)$ (*viz.*, replaces the meaning M^n with the property which is its value in c); (b) replaces each s_i either with its value in c or with a variable; (c) doesn't replace distinct s_i's with the same variable. Call such entities the *proto-properties* associated with m in c.

(For example, proto-properties associated with

$$m_1 = \langle \langle \{t_1\}, \{y_1\}, \{F_1^2\} \rangle \rangle$$

—which could be identified with the meaning of "$F_1^2 t_1 y_1$"—in a context in which "t_1" denotes u, "y_1" denotes u' and "F_1^2" denotes P are

(i) $\langle \langle u, x \rangle, P \rangle$,
(ii) $\langle \langle x, u' \rangle, P \rangle$,
(iii) $\langle \langle x, x' \rangle, P \rangle$.

Proto-properties associated with

$$M_2 = \langle \langle \{t_1\}, \{t_1\}, \{F_1^2\} \rangle \rangle$$

in such a context are all of the above and

(iv) $\langle \langle x, x \rangle, P \rangle$.)

To each proto-property there corresponds, in a rather obvious way, a property. For example: to (ii) corresponds the one-place property P^1 such that $w \in P^1(u_1)$ iff $w \in P(\langle u_1, u' \rangle)$; to (iii) corresponds the two-place property P^2 such that $w \in P^2(\langle u_1, u_2 \rangle)$ iff $w \in P(\langle u_1, u_2 \rangle)$; to (iv) corresponds the one-place property P^3 such that $w \in P^3(u_1)$ iff $w \in P(\langle u_1, u_1 \rangle)$.

We can now answer our initial question thus: an agent attributes a property P in virtue of holding a belief under a meaning m iff P corresponds to one of the proto-properties associated with m relative to the agent's context. We will write

$$P \quad P \in P(m,c)$$

for: the agent of c attributes P, in virtue of holding a belief under m.

A fully rigorous characterization of the above notion would disperse with the notion of a variable in the construction of proto-properties. It is easy enough to give such a characterization; we henceforth assume that the predicate $P(m,c)$ has been so defined in terms of our model structure. We now need a way to get from a sentence (taken relative to a context and an assignment) used to ascribe belief to the set of properties it implies the believer attributes. One way of doing this is as follows. Consider a sentence ϕ; let $\alpha_1, \ldots, \alpha_n$ be a complete enumeration of those demonstratives and variables (which occur freely) in ϕ. Let $v_1, \ldots, v_n$ be distinct variables which do not occur in ϕ. We say that Ψ is a frame of ϕ just in case ϕ is the result of replacing one or more of the α_i's with v_i's, subject to the restriction that distinct α_i's are replaced with distinct v_i's.

Thus, for example, consider the sentences

(i) $F_2^2 t_1 y_1$,

(ii) $F_2^2 t_1 t_1$.

Frames of (i) are: $F_2^2 t_1 x_1$, $F_2^2 x_1 y_1$, $F_2^2 x_1 x_2$; frames of (ii) are the above and $F_2^2 x_1 x_1$. Note that this last is not a frame of (i).

We say that a sentence ϕ implies the attribution of the property P^n, relative to c and f, just in case there is a frame ψ of ϕ, obtained by substituting the n distinct variables $v_1, \ldots, v_n$ for terms in ϕ and, for every w and $u_1, u_2, \ldots, u_n$:

$$\mathit{cf}^{u_1,u_2,\ldots,u_n}_{v_1,v_2,\ldots,v_n}[\Psi]_w \text{ iff } w \in P^n(\langle u_1, u_2, \ldots, u_n \rangle)$$

We define the attribution class of a sentence ϕ relative to c and f as the set of those properties such that ϕ implies their attribution relative to c and f; we denote this class with $A(\phi, c, f)$.

We now define truth for *de re* ascriptions of belief:

$$\mathit{cf}[\alpha B^r \phi] w \text{ iff } \exists c'(|\alpha|_{\mathit{cfw}} = c'_A \& c'_W = w \& \exists m(m \in V'_c \&$$
$$m(c') = \{w' \mid \mathit{cf}[\phi]w'\} \& (f)(f \in A(\phi, c, f) \to f \in P(m, c'))))),$$

where $m(c')$ is the proposition expressed by m relative to c'. Verbally, these truth conditions amount to this: $\alpha B^r \phi$, relative to c and f, is true exactly if there is a meaning m such that (i) $|\alpha|_{\mathit{cfw}}$ believes a proposition under m; (ii) m yields, relative to $|\alpha|_{\mathit{cfw}}$'s context, whatever ϕ expresses, relative to c and f, and (iii) whatever properties ϕ implies are attributed are such that belief under m requires their attribution.

It is easy to show that, given this semantics, representatives of sentences (1) and (2) can diverge in truth value relative to a context in which their embedded sentences express the same proposition.[18] On the other hand, the semantics validates the claim, for which we argued above, that in any context in which the uses of "she" and "you" in

(3) I believe that she is in danger,

and

(4) I believe that you are in danger.

are co-referential, the truth of (4) is implied by the truth of (3).

It is, perhaps, worth discussing sentences (3) and (4) again. Many people, even after a rehearsal of the argument given above—that (4) is implied by (3)—are still uncomfortable with the claim that both (3) and (4) are true. A virtue of the semantics just presented, I think, is that it can be used to motivate an explanation of why the intuition, that (3) and (4) diverge in truth value, is so persistent.

Take a finite set of sentences and conjoin them; form what we called a frame of the result. (For example, if you start with {that$_2$ is sad, you$_3$ will make that$_4$ happy if that$_2$ helps you$_3$}, you will end up with something along the lines of "x_2 is sad $\wedge x_3$ will make x_4 happy if x_2 helps x_3.") Call the property associated with such a sentence a *picture*; if all the members of the initial set are sentences, the meanings of which are accepted by an agent u, say that the resulting property is a picture *held by u*.[19]

The intuition motivating our semantical account is that an ascription is true provided it ascribes belief in a proposition which is believed and the ascription doesn't imply anything false about what pictures are held by the believer. Since sentence (4), as used by A,

---

[18] We can also show that the semantics validates certain forms of "quantifying in." Precisely, given our semantics, we have:

If β is a member of D which occurs in ϕ, then if $cf[\alpha B^r(\phi)]w$, then
$cf[\exists v(\alpha B^r(\phi[\beta/v]))w$, provided that β is free for v in ϕ.

(If our semantics had allowed for the possibility that members of D failed to denote in some contexts, this rule would have to be weakened. For simplicity's sake, we have not allowed for this possibility.) That such a rule is sound justifies, in part, the claim that something of the form of ⌜$\alpha B^r \phi$⌝ is a *de re* ascription, provided that ϕ contains a member of D.

Note that not very "way of quantifying in" is permitted by our semantics. In particular, from

(i) $t_1 = t_2 \wedge IB^r(F^2 t_1 t_2)$

the formula

(ii) $\exists x_1 \exists x_2 (x_1 = x_2 \wedge IB^r(F^2 x_1 x_2)$

follows, but

(iii) $\exists x_1 (x_1 = x_1 \wedge IB^r(F^2 x_1 x_1))$

does *not* follow. Given our reasons for adopting the treatment we have adopted, of course, one would not want (iii) to follow from (i).

[19] Strictly speaking, of course, we can associate properties with open sentences possibly containing demonstratives only relative to a context. My ignoring that here does not affect the point.

does not *when taken by itself* imply anything false about what picture A holds, (4) so taken is true, since A believes B to be in danger.

Note, now, that a set of belief ascriptions may (conventionally) imply things about the pictures a believer holds that the conjunction of the members of the set does not (strictly) imply.[20] For example, the use of the ascription "A believes that you are unhappy because she$_2$ spurned you!" in a context in which the ascription "A believes that she$_2$ loves a Greek" has been used (and no one has disputed the truth of the latter ascription) will imply that A holds the picture associated with y loves a Greek and x is unhappy because y spurned x." Both ascriptions can be true, even if A doesn't hold this picture; however, their joint use, in such a case, would be very misleading.

In general, we tend to avoid using an ascription ⌜α believes that ϕ⌝, if an ascription ⌜α believes that ψ⌝ is assumed by all the parties to the conversation to be true (and we know this), and we think that the person to whom belief is being ascribed does not hold pictures associated with frames of ⌜ϕ and ψ⌝. Likewise, we will find an ascription ⌜α believes that ϕ⌝ bizarre or objectionable if it is assumed by those conversing that the ascription ⌜α believes that ψ⌝ is true and we have good reason to think that the believer doesn't hold all the pictures associated with ⌜ϕ and ψ⌝.

All of this, I believe, helps to explain why some find the assertion that A's use of

(4)   I believe that you are in danger.

is true counter-intuitive, even after a rehearsal of the argument that A's use of (4) cannot be false if his use of (3) is not. For as we have just seen, without qualification and explanation the claim that (4) is true relative to A's context is very misleading. For obviously, in the case under consideration

(9)   I believe that I am talking to you.

is true relative to A's context. Thus, without further qualification, the claim that (4) is true implies that

(10) I believe that I am talking to someone who is in danger.

is true, relative to A's context. But, obviously (10) is not thus true.

I close with some observations on the semantical theory suggested in this paper. According to this theory, ascriptions of belief are primarily, but not exclusively, vehicles for making reports about the content, as opposed to the manner, of belief. That ascriptions are primarily used to make reports about content ought not be surprising. For, first of all, we are very often not in a position to say how a belief is held, although we know that it is held. (For example, one may know that Hank believes that Will spies, but not

---

[20] I must stress that "implies" is being used in two senses in this sentence. The first use of "implies" is quite weak (certainly not the sort of implication which preserves truth). Roughly, the use I intend here is the sort present in (typical) uses of "His saying that the movie was boring implies that he did not like it."

whether he accepts the meaning of "that spies" or "Will spies.") Furthermore, it is often quite irrelevant to our purposes to specify how a proposition is believed.[21] Finally, we often cannot say how belief is held in any perspicuous way, even though we know. (Consider: Hank, Bernie, and Sally all believe that I am a spy.)

None the less, ascriptions of belief are, to a limited extent, used to report how belief is held. Indeed, in the semantics for ascriptions of belief suggested in this paper, the belief operator is construed as operating on sentential meanings, and not simply as an operator on the propositions which meanings, relative to a context, have as values. I have focused here upon relatively simple aspects of sentential meaning, in an attempt to make a case for the claim that by construing the belief operator as an operator on meanings, as opposed to propositions, we can generate plausible solutions to semantical puzzles associated with the (quite plausible, I believe) theory of direct reference. If the approach taken here strikes the reader as not without merit, he or she will, I hope, consider the question of how it is to be given the extensions and refinements it requires in order to yield a fully satisfactory theory.[22]

---

[21] Note, however, that it *is* very often important to us to get across that belief is held under a meaning involving $\{I\}$. One reason for this is that we seem to presuppose the truth of a psychological theory which predicts how people will behave when they so believe (and when they have certain desires, etc.). To effectively make use of such a theory in everyday affairs—in particular, to justify predictions of behavior via the theory—we need a way to say that a person believes in the relevant way. It is for reasons such as this that English has a *de se* belief operator like that discussed in Section II. That we have no very general need, as we do for beliefs held under meanings involving $\{I\}$, to say that someone holds a belief under the meaning of a sentence involving $\{that\}$ or $\{you\}$ explains, I think, the absence of belief operators in English which single out beliefs held under such meanings.

[22] I am indebted to David Auerbach, Edmund Gettier, Richard Grandy, and Harold Levin for comments on my syntax and these semantics. An anonymous referee for this journal also made useful comments on an earlier draft, for which I thank him or her. Part of the work on this paper was done while I held NEH grant FX-28919; I am grateful for this support.

3

Quantification and Leibniz's Law

I

Fix a language; Leibniz's Law for that language is the principle

(L) Any universal closure of a sentence of the form of
    if x is identical with y, then, if S, then S'
    (where S' differs from S only in having one or more occurrences of y free, where S has free occurrences of x) is true.

It is held by most logicians and philosophers of language that (L) is a principle fundamental to the intent of objectual quantification. It is widely believed, furthermore, that quantificational devices of English involving "all," "every," and analogous universal quantifiers, as well as English devices of existential quantification, are objectual quantifiers. And thus, it is widely believed that (L), or at least a somewhat more carefully formulated analogue, in which talk of variables is replaced or supplemented by talk of pronominal reference, is true of English.

In this essay, I argue that (L) is not in any way fundamental to objectual quantification. All of the quantifiers of a language may be objectual, and yet sentences of the language which are instances of (L) may be false. I argue further that there are reasons for thinking that English is a language whose quantifiers are objectual, but for which (L) fails.[1]

I will begin by presenting a putative counter-example to (L) in English. Suppose that John says to you:

Last night, I observed the planet Hesperus and then the planet Phosphorus. I was disappointed; I wanted to observe Phosphorus and then Hesperus.

---

[1] The Indiscernibility of Identicals—the principle that for any x, y, and z, if x is identical with y, then z is a property of x only if z is a property of y—is also, sometimes, called Leibniz's Law. I have NO quarrel with the Indiscernibility of Identicals. In suggesting that (L) is not a truth of quantification theory, I do NOT impugn the trivial truth that things which are one share their properties.

The next day, you want to tell me what John told you about his astronomical exploits and desires, but you have forgotten the names of the two planets. Certainly, you would speak truly if you reported:

(1) There are planets, x and y: John said that he observed x and then y, and he wanted to observe y and then x.

But it seems that you would not speak truly, if you were to say:

(2) There are planets, x and y: John said that he observed x and then y, and he wanted to observe x and then y.

Suppose that John has never spoken about planets save during your conversation. It seems to follow, given the fact that the quantifier "there are planets" is objectual, that the assignment of Hesperus to "x" and to "y" makes the sentence

John said that he observed x and then y, and he wanted to observe y and then x

true, but that no assignment to the variables of

John said that he observed x and then y, and he wanted to observe x and then y

makes that sentence true. But this means that

(3) If x = y, then: if (John said that he observed x and then y, and he wanted to observe y and then x), then (John said that he observed x and then y and he wanted to observe x and then y)

is false, if we assign Hesperus to "x" and Phosphorus to "y." So the universal closure of (3) is false. This certainly seems to be a counter-example to (L).

One response to this example would give up the view that English quantification is objectual. Let us suppose that we are resolved, come what may, to treat English quantifiers as objectual. If we think that this resolve requires that (L) be true of English, how might we respond to the preceding argument?

First of all, we might resort to syntactic ingenuity. We might argue that although (3) appears to have the syntactic form described in the statement of (L), in reality it does not; thus, its falsity is no threat to (L). Such a response is suggested by Quine's "Quantifiers and Propositional Attitudes."[2] On this view, even though the open sentences

John said that he observed x and then y, and he wanted to observe y and then x

and

John said that he observed x and then y, and he wanted to observe x and then y

appear to differ only by a permutation of variables, their logical syntax differs much more radically. Because of this, sentence (3) is not *really* of the form

---

[2] Quine (1956); reprinted as Quine (1966).

if x = y, then, if S, then S'

mentioned in the statement of (L). Such a response is reminiscent of Russell's analysis of sentences containing definite descriptions. For Russell, that the sentences "The author of this paper is a genius" and "I am a genius" have the same logical syntax is only appearance, not reality.[3]

A second kind of response chooses to ignore the speaker's intuitions in these situations. To respond in this way is to insist that a speaker who thinks that sentence (2) is false is simply wrong: believe it or not, there are things x and y such that John said that he saw x and then y, and he wanted to observe x and then y. On this response, as on the first, that (3) is false follows from the fact that (1) is true and (2) is false (and the facts of the case). Unlike the first response, this response holds that the falsity of (3) would constitute a counter-example to (L). But now it is said that this is not a problem, since (2) is true, if (1) is.

Neither of these responses is particularly attractive. The first requires a certain high-handedness with syntactic intuitions; the second a disregard for semantic ones. Both responses assume that, once we grant the objectuality of the quantifiers, we must explain away the appearance of a violation of (L). As I said, I want to argue that this last assumption is false. The idea that (L) is fundamental to the intent of objectual quantification is, I think, completely mistaken.

I will try to establish this piece of apostasy in the next section. Following that, I sketch a third response to the example presented above, one which sticks to the resolve to treat English quantification as objectual, but does not do violence to syntactic or semantic intuitions; this I compare in some detail with Quine's response. In the fourth and final section, I compare the merits of some of these responses.

II

What determines whether a quantifier is objectual? Of course the answer is this: An objectual quantifier is one which accommodates a Tarski-style definition of satisfaction. For example, what makes Q an objectual universal quantifier is that an analogue

---

[3] A Fregean view which parses, for example,

    There is an x such that John says that x is happy

as

    There is an x and an s such that s is a sense which presents x and John says "s is happy"
(with the double quotes acting as sense quotes) may also validate the intuition that (3) is false. If one accepts the Fregean view, that expressions embedded within "that" refer to senses, it seems that one can motivate the introduction of elements which are unrealized in surface structure in a way in which Quine cannot.

I do not intend to discuss the Fregean view in this chapter; this discussion can be seen as an attempt to deal with the problem sketched above, without resorting to the introduction of Fregean senses. In any case, I think there are compelling reasons for supposing that attitude ascriptions do not involve explicit or implicit reference to senses; see Richard (1988) and Richard (1990), chapter 2.

of the following principle gives satisfaction conditions for sentences of which Q is the main operator:

(S) A sequence s satisfies QvS iff every sequence s' which differs from s at most in what it assigns to v satisfies S.

This criterion of objectuality can be expressed in a number of ways. Here is one which will figure in subsequent arguments.

Associated with each open sentence of a(n interpreted) language is what we may call a condition. The notion of a condition can be cashed out in a number of ways. Often, conditions are identified with extensions, or with constructions from extensions and entities such as times and/or possible worlds. Sometimes, they are taken to be creatures of darkness such as properties. For now I will remain coy as to what a condition might be. But no matter how we understand the notion, a condition will be something which determines, or is even identical with, an extension (which is a set of sequences). To say that a sequence s satisfies a sentence is to say that it is in the extension of the condition determined by the sentence.

Our first criterion of objectuality may thus be rephrased in terms of the contribution which the quantifier makes to determining a condition. We could, for example, say that for Q to be an existential objectual quantifier is for it to determine a condition in accord with this rule: The condition determined by QvS has a sequence s in its extension just in case some sequence like s (except perhaps in what it does to the variable v) is in the extension of the condition determined by S.

This way of characterizing objectuality is in keeping with the intuitive underpinning of the notion of objectuality. For Q to be objectual is for it to be the case that the only thing relevant to whether s satisfies QvS (or to whether QvS is true) is what sequences satisfy S. Each of our characterizations of objectuality makes it a necessary and sufficient condition, for the objectuality of Q, that the satisfaction conditions of QvS depend only on the satisfaction conditions of S itself.[4]

---

[4] As is well known, some languages whose quantifiers are substitutional turn out to have Tarskian quantification, as we have characterized it. Take, for example, a language whose syntax is that of first-order logic with constants and identity. Suppose we defined an interpretation I for the language as something which assigns truth-values to all atomic sentences for the language, subject to the restriction that if I(t = t') is true, and B = A(t'/t) for atomic A, then I treats A and B in the same way. Go on to define truth in an interpretation in the obvious, substitutional way.

If we suppose that all of the constants of the language already name things, then we may say that, relative to the domain consisting of the things named by the constants, the quantifiers of the language are Tarskian. For, in the case under consideration, it is trivial to specify a way in which an interpretation assigns an extension to each open sentence of the language. If we limit our attention in constructing sequences to the things named by the constants of the language, the quantifiers of the language satisfy the conditions given in the text.

None of this affects the argument of this chapter. My goal is to show that possessing a Tarskian semantics does not require adherence to (L). The counter-examples below consist of languages for which truth is defined in a natural, Tarskian way, by direct assignment of satisfaction conditions to sentences, and not in the "accidental" way of the substitutional example above.

52 CONTEXT AND THE ATTITUDES

What is the role of the variables in languages with objectual quantifiers? Clearly, one purpose of the variables in objectual quantification is to supply an object, relative to an assignment: as rehearsed above, a(n open) sentence is satisfied by a sequence just in the case the relevant tuple, of the objects supplied by the variables, is in the extension of the condition determined by the sentence. This task is, I take it, familiar enough.

What is not always noticed about the variables is that they have another task, at least in familiar first-order languages. One who has noticed this is Quine, who writes:

> Basically, the variable is best seen as an abstractive pronoun: a device for marking positions in a sentence, with a view to abstracting the rest of the sentence as predicate. Thus consider... "Some number x is such that $x^3 = 3x$".... The variable can be eliminated:... we could say "Some number gives the same result when cubed as when trebled", thus torturing the desired complex predicate out of "$x^3 = 3x$" with a modicum of verbal ingenuity. In more complex examples... use of "x" is the only easy way of abstracting the jagged sort of predicate which we are [interested in]. Where the variable pays off is as a device for segregating or abstracting a desired predicate by exhibiting the predicate sentence wise with the variable for blanks.[5]

According to Quine, one syntactic role for variables (along with connectives and quantifiers, and, perhaps, even closed terms) is to expand the stock of predicates of a language beyond the primitive or "simple" predicates. Put another way, variables encode operations which map predicates to predicates. Semantically speaking, a role of the variables (along with the quantifiers and connectives) is to encode a set of operations on the conditions which are associated with primitive predicates or sentences of the language in which they occur.[6]

This idea shouldn't be terribly foreign. What, after all, makes "x loves y" and "x loves x" different, semantically? Put somewhat simply, Quine's answer is that the sentences determine different conditions (roughly, those of loving and self-loving, respectively); it is one of the roles of the variables to get us from simple predicates, such as "loves" and "kisses," and the conditions they determine, to complex predicates and the conditions which they determine.

It is not implausible to think that a complete explanation of the role of the variables in first-order languages is given thus: Variables are used both to help determine what condition is associated with a sentence, and to supply individuals relative to an assignment.[7] On this view of the variables, a sentence of ordinary first-order logic such as

---

[5] Quine (1966b), 228.

[6] Quine posits four operations, which he characterizes in terms of satisfaction conditions for the output predicates. It is worth noting that Quine's choice of operations is not the only possible choice, nor is it the best possible: see the discussion in Chapter 1 of Levin (1982).

[7] This ought, perhaps, to be put more cautiously. There may be some semantically relevant function which the first-order variables perform which I have not mentioned. If so, that does not affect the argument which I am about to present: that any language whose variables and quantifiers behave as just characterized is a language with objectual quantification; but not every such language obeys (L).

As will become apparent, I do not assume that predicate abstraction is the only possible way in which variables might help to determine a condition.

(1) Ayxy

might be more explicitly written as

(2) Ident(A)[x,y].

Here, Ident is an operation which maps a three-place condition A (*viz.*, a condition whose extension can be represented as a set of triples) to a two-place condition B.[8] In (2) we have one syntactic device, the operator "Ident," playing the role of predicate abstractor; another syntactic device, the variables and brackets, serves to supply objects. In (1), economy triumphs, with one device, the variables, doing both jobs.

We have an account of what makes the quantifiers and variables of a language objectual. As we will now see, it does not follow from the fact that a language's quantifiers and variables behave as just characterized that (L) is true of the language. This, I think, makes it dubious that (L) is fundamental to objectual quantification. In fact, consideration of our description of the role of the variables not only makes it obvious that (L) is not a tenet of objectual quantification theory; it suggests a number of ways in which a language with objectual quantifiers and variables might come to violate (L).

Whether (L) is true of a language depends upon how conditions are associated with the sentences of the language. For example: (L) strongly suggests, although it doesn't require, that open sentences which are alphabetic variants determine the same condition; (L) requires that open sentences which are alphabetic variants have the same extension. Of course, we are used to thinking of open sentences and conditions in this way: how, it might be asked, could "A(x)" be true of things of which "A(y)" wasn't true? Mere relettering of an open sentence couldn't change what it is true of!

I disagree. Why is it a fact about objectual quantification, as opposed to a fact about the first-order languages with which we are familiar, that "Fx_1" and "Fx_2" determine the same condition? One can give a Tarski-style definition of truth for a language in which "$\exists x_1 Fx_1$" and "$\exists x_2 Fx_2$" may differ in truth value, the quantifiers and the connectives receiving their usual satisfaction conditions.

To give such a definition, one needs first to explain, for each simple predicate, the conditions under which a sequence satisfies atomic sentences in which the predicate occurs. Suppose we think of "F" as by itself determining the same condition as the English predicate "prime." Then the *usual* way to begin a definition of truth for a language with the predicate "F" will include a clause to the effect that

A sequence s satisfies "F" followed by the ith variable iff what s assigns to that variable is prime.

The truth definition goes on to treat truth-functional and quantified sentences in the familiar Tarskian way.

---

[8] The mapping is subject to the restriction that <a,b> is in the extension of B iff <a,b,a> is in the extension of A. Since I am being coy about the nature of conditions, I do not say which of the many operations on conditions which satisfy this stricture Ident is.

But there are *many* other ways to assign conditions to the atomic sentences of a language which allow a Tarskian treatment of connectives and quantifiers. Here's one: Let G be a set of some, but not all, of the integers. Then, instead of the above clause, use

A sequence s satisfies "F" followed by the ith variable iff [what s assigns to the ith variable is prime and i is in G].

This assigns a determinate condition (taken as a set of sequences) to each atomic sentence involving "F." One can now go on, without incoherence, paradox, or any particular problem, to define truth for the language as a whole *exactly* as one would in the usual case. In particular, the quantifiers may be treated in the Tarskian way described above. Of course many of the usual quantificational meta-theorems cannot be proven for such a language. But this, it can be said, shows that these meta-theorems are not true of every language containing objectual quantifiers.

Many will claim to find the closed sentences of the resulting language incomprehensible. It is clear why, in such a language, "$(Ex_1)(Fx_1)$" and "$(Ex_2)(Fx_2)$" can diverge in truth value: the formulas cash out, respectively, to something like "$\exists x_1([C("Fx_1")](x_1))$" and "$\exists x_2([C("Fx_2")](x_2))$," where the bracketed predicates are stipulated to express the conditions determined by the object language sentences. This, some might argue, militates against understanding the object language "E" as an existential quantifier: "$\exists x_1 Fx_1$" doesn't seem to say ⌜something is an F⌝.

But this is because "$\exists x_1 Fx_1$" *doesn't* say ⌜something is an F⌝ in this language; rather, it says something more complex, depending upon the nature of G, the set involved in the clause assigning conditions to sentences in which "F" occurs. In the language under consideration, the "x_1" in "Fx_1" helps to determine what condition is determined by the open sentence, in a way unlike it does in first-order logic. It does not follow that the quantifiers (or the variables) are non-objectual. In a sense, the variables here behave just as they do in familiar first-order languages: They provide objects, relative to an assignment, and they help to determine conditions. It is just that their contribution, to determining a condition, is somewhat different than the contribution they make in the familiar first-order case.[9]

This, it seems to me, settles the matter of whether (L) is fundamental to objectual quantification. Admittedly, languages which violate (L) in *this* way are of little, if any, interest, as vehicles for representing natural language. For it seems obvious that natural languages do not violate (L) in just this way.

There are other ways of violating (L) which are, I think, of considerably greater theoretical interest. To see this, observe first of all that pairs of sentences such as

(3) Teaches (x,y)
(4) Teaches (x,x)

will generally determine distinct conditions, no matter what notion of condition we adopt. Let conditions be extensions—that is, sets of sequences. (3) determines the

---

[9] I am indebted to correspondence with Scott Soames about this argument.

condition consisting of those sequences which assign to "x" a teacher of what's assigned to "y." (4), on the other hand, determines the set of sequences which assign self-teachers to "x." Neither of these sets will, in general, include the other. (Of course, there is a relation between the two conditions: A sequence <... u ...u ...> is in the condition determined by (3) iff every sequence <... u ...v ...> is in the condition determined by (4).) Let us say that conditions related as (4)'s is to (3)'s are such that the latter condition *reduces* the former.

Observe now that each connective of a(n interpreted) language has associated with it a function from conditions to conditions. This is particularly obvious in the case of familiar first-order languages, given the identification of conditions with extensions: That each connective of such a language maps tuples of extensions to extensions in a reliable way is what makes a Tarskian truth definition possible.

These two facts together point to a substantive restriction on the semantics of languages which conform to (L), a restriction which seems to have nothing to do with the question of whether the language's quantificational apparatus is objectual. The restriction is one on the kind of sentence connectives which the language can contain: If the language is to conform to (L), all of its connectives must operate in such way that if condition C reduces condition C', then the condition a connective maps C to reduces the condition to which the connective maps C'.[10] Many easily specifiable functions on conditions will violate this restriction; one example is exhibited in the next section.

This restriction has nothing to do with whether the quantifiers of the language are objectual. A language can contain operators which contravene the restriction and yet it may be true that for any sentence of the form ⌜(v)A⌝ of the language, a sequence satisfies the sentence exactly if all the sequences which vary with respect to v satisfy A. Thus, the presence or absence of operators which violate the above restriction doesn't have the first thing to do with whether the quantifiers of a language are objectual. (L) is not fundamental to the objectuality of quantifiers.

III

Let us return to the putative counter-example to (L). In the first section, we resolved to treat English quantification as objectual, come what may. In the last section, we argued

---

[10] It is not very difficult to show this. Intuitively, here is why it is true. Suppose that O is a connective which doesn't obey the restriction. Then there can be some pairs of sentences which vary by a free variable—let's say

Teaches(x,y)
Teaches(x,x)
—for which the condition expressed by
O[Teaches(x,y)]
doesn't reduce the condition expressed by
O[Teaches(x,x)].

But this means that there's some individual—u, call her—who's such that, when she's assigned to "x" and "y," she makes one sentence true and the other false.

that such a resolution doesn't require us to assume that English conforms to (L). In particular, we argued that a language might have objectual quantifiers and still, because of the way in which some of its sentence connectives map conditions to conditions, violate (L). Is this last point at all relevant to the putative counter-example to (L)? Very much so: We can treat expressions such as "John said that" as operators which force English to violate (L). This section begins by sketching one way in which this might be done. It then outlines a response to the counter-example along the lines suggested by Quine in "Quantifiers and Propositional Attitudes."

Think of saying as the ascribing of a condition to an individual or individuals. For example, when John utters "You are svelte" and thereby says that I am svelte, he ascribes a condition—being svelte—to me. When John utters "Hesperus is smaller than Phosphorus" he says that Hesperus is smaller than Phosphorus, ascribing the condition—being smaller than—to the pair <Hesperus, Phosphorus>.

How do we get from the sentence which someone utters to the condition which he ascribes? Here is one suggestion. Assume, for simplicity, that the sentence contains no ambiguous names. Take the sentence uttered; take exactly as many variables as there are distinct names (that is, proper names, demonstratives, and indexicals) in the sentence. (The variables should all be new to the sentence.) Now, systematically replace names with variables—assign each name a distinct variable from your set of variables, and replace all occurrences of the name with the variable assigned. The resulting sentence determines the condition the speaker ascribed to the object or objects he named.

For example, suppose John is regaling us with tales of two animals he observed, named "Flopsy" and "Mopsy." If John says

(1)   Flopsy chased Mopsy and then Mopsy chased me

he ascribes the condition determined by "x chased y and then y chased z" to the trio: Flopsy, Mopsy, John. On the other hand, if John says

(2)   Flopsy chased Mopsy and then Flopsy chased me

he ascribes the condition determined by "x chased y and then x chased z" to the same trio. This is so, it should be noted, even if Flopsy is identical with Mopsy.

Now, consider a sentence of the form

(3)   John said that S

where S may contain free variables.[11] Under what conditions is such a sentence true, relative to an assignment f to the variables? Given the above, the natural answer is this. Suppose that S contains just the variables $v_1, \ldots, v_n$ free, in that order. Then (3) is true just

---

[11] I am suppressing a great many technical details in what follows, as well as ignoring complications which the possible presence of names in S would occasion. The analysis suggested below is a streamlined and somewhat altered version of that proposed in Chapter 2. Suggestions by David Kaplan have helped in the streamlining.

in case John ascribed the condition determined by S to the n-tuple: <what f assigns to v_1,..., what f assigns to v_n>.

Here are two examples of how this proposal works. First, consider

(4) John said that x chased y and then y chased z

and suppose that we assign Flopsy to "x," Mopsy to "y," and John to "z." Then, (2) is true, under this assignment, if John ascribed the condition determined by "x chased y and then y chased z" to <Flopsy, Mopsy, John>. Thus, if John uttered (1), then (4) comes out true under this assignment. So an existential closure of (4) would be true, *simpliciter*. Consider now

(5) John said that x chased y and then x chased z.

Suppose the same assignments to the variables. Relative thereto, (5) is true just in case John ascribed the condition determined by "x chased y and then x chased z" to our trio. In this case, if John uttered (2), an existential closure of (5) is true.[12]

Note that the conditions expressed by the open sentences within (4) and (5) are, on most ways of understanding the notion of a condition, distinct conditions. For example, think of a condition as a function from possible worlds to extensions. "x chased y and then y chased z" determines the condition which takes us from a world to those trios <a,b,c> such that (in that world) a chased b and then b chased c. The embedded sentence in (5) determines a different function—one which, given a world w, returns the collection of trios <a,b,c> such that a chased b and then a chased c.

In fact, even thinking of a condition purely extensionally, the conditions are distinct. Identifying the condition determined by a sentence as the collection of assignments which satisfy it, the conditions determined by the sentences embedded in (4) and (5) are distinct. For there is a trio <a,b,c> such that a chased b and then b chased c, although it's not true that a chased b and then a chased c.

This means that (4) can be true (relative to an assignment), even though (5) is not (relative to the very same assignment). John might ascribe the condition relevant to (4) to the trio—Flopsy, Mopsy, John—even though he didn't ascribe the other condition to the trio. This may be so, even though Flopsy is identical with Mopsy.

This proposal for understanding the semantics of "says that" is simple, not at all unnatural, and one which is completely consistent with treating the quantifiers as objectual. We may easily define truth for the language by assigning conditions (which may be completely extensional) to atomic sentences, functions from conditions to conditions to the connectives (including 'John said that'), and treating the quantifiers in the usual Tarskian way.

In general, (L) fails on this proposal. Suppose that John did utter (1), and did not utter (2). Suppose, in fact, that (1) is the sum of all John ever said, and that Flopsy is Mopsy.

---

[12] I haven't explicitly stated what the function from conditions to conditions associated with John said that' is. In part, this is because I am being coy about the nature of conditions (and the nature of the function depends upon what conditions are); in part, this is because I am suppressing *technicalia* whenever possible. It's pretty easy to say what the function in question must be, given an identification of conditions with either sets of sequences or with functions from worlds to extensions.

Then, assigning Flopsy, Mopsy, and John to "x," "y," and "z" respectively makes "x = y" and (4) true. In fact, this is the only assignment which makes (4) true. But no assignment makes (5) true. Hence, the universal closure of

(6) If x = y, then if John said that x chased y and then y chased z, then John said that x chased y and then x chased z

is false. (L) forbids this.

Call this response to the putative counter-example of Section I *R*. Let us contrast it with one suggested by Quine's "Quantifiers and Propositional Attitudes," which we will call *Q*. Quine suggests that sentences of the form of

(7) a V's that $A(v_1, \ldots, v_n)$

V a verb of propositional attitude, *A* a sentence which contains the variables $v_1, \ldots, v_n$ free, be treated as being of the form

V[a, I, s]

where *I* is the name of an intension and *S* names a sequence. On this recommendation, we treat

(8) (∃x) (Ralph says that x is a spy)

as having the form

(8') (∃x) (Says [Ralph, $\hat{x}$ (x is a spy), <x>])

where "$\hat{x}$" is an operator, which turns a predicate into the name of an intension. (Note that this operator binds the variables in its scope: The "x" in "x is a spy" is bound by the capped variable.) (8') is true, presumably, just in case Ralph ascribed the intension named by "$\hat{x}$ (x is a spy)" to something. Indentifying intensions with conditions, this seems to attribute pretty much the same truth conditions to sentence (8) as would proposal R.

Quine would treat

(∃x) (∃y) (Ralph says that x denounced y)

as having the form of

(∃x) (∃y) (Says [Ralph, $\hat{x}\hat{y}$(x denounced y), <x,y>]).

Here, "$\hat{x}\hat{y}$ (x denounced y)" names the intension or condition *denouncing*; again, the "x" and "y" in the name of the intension are bound by the capped variables. The sentence as a whole says that Ralph ascribed the condition, *denouncing*, to some pair of things. Once again, the truth conditions accorded the sentence agree with those of proposal R. In general, one might suppose, Quine's view is that a sentence with the surface form of (7) has the underlying form

(9) $V[a, \hat{v}_1 \ldots \hat{v}_n (A(v_1 \ldots v_n)), < v_1 \ldots v_n >]$.

On this view, the sentences

(4) John said that x chased y and then y chased z

and

(5) John said that x chased y and then x chased z

are regimented, respectively, as

(4') Said [John, x̂ŷẑ (x chased y and then y chased z), <x,y,z>]
(5') Said [John, x̂ŷẑ (x chased y and then x chased z), <x,y,z>].

Each sentence is true, relative to an assignment, just if John ascribed the appropriate intension, that named in the sentence's regimentation, to the trio assigned to the variables.[13]

As we observed above, the conditions named in (4') and (5') are distinct; it is perfectly possible that a person ascribe the first condition to a trio without ascribing the second condition to the trio. On Quine's position, then, it is possible that the assignment of Flopsy, Mopsy (= Flopsy), and John to "x," "y," and "z" makes (4') true, even though no assignment makes (5') true. This means that for Quine the universal closure of

(10) if x = y, then if (4'), then (5')

(with (4') and (5') used instead of mentioned, of course) may be

---

[13] In Kaplan (1986), David Kaplan agrees that Quine intended to regiment (7) along the lines of (9). Kaplan criticizes Quine for this. Instead, Kaplan makes the following proposal. Let $B = A(w_1,..., w_n)$ be the result of replacing each free *recurrence* of each v_1 in $A = A(v_1,..., v_n)$ with the first variable new to A. Let $t_1,..., t_m$ be such that replacing each w_1 in B with t_1 yields A. Now, regiment the likes of (7) as

(K) $V[a, ŵ...ŵ(B), < t_1,...t_m >]$.

Some comments ought to be made here. First of all, regimenting (7) via (K) does not by itself solve the problem presented by the putative counter-examples to (L). (K) regiments pairs of sentences such as

For some x and y: x = y and (John said that he saw x chase y and then y chase x) and it's not the case that John said that he saw x chase y and then x chase y
For some x and y: x = y and (John said that he saw x chase y and then y chase x) and it's not the case that John said that he saw x chase y and then y chase x

in such a way that they turn out to be logically equivalent. The puzzle which such pairs of sentences present, of course, is that they would seem to fail to be equivalent.

The burden of this essay is to argue that such pairs of sentences are not *logically* equivalent, even if equivalent, since (L) is not a principle of quantification theory. Putting this sort of apostasy to one side, it's not altogether clear that Kaplan's criticism of Quine is justified.

Kaplan's criticism of Quine is, essentially, that Quine regiments pairs of sentences such as the above in such a way that they turn out to be logically inequivalent. But Quine accepts the validity of (L). So *how* could such pairs of sentences turn out to be inequivalent?

However, it was Quine's position that sentences such as the above, which *appear* to involve quantification into opaque position, simply could not involve it, since quantification into opaque position is impossible. Now pairs of sentences such as the above pair are obviously logically equivalent only if these sentences are, in reality, what they appear to be—that is, they are obviously equivalent only if they really do involve quantification into opaque position. Since Quine denies this, I can see no obligation on his part to regiment such sentences so that they come out logically equivalent.

false. This does not imply a violation of (L). (4') and (5') do not differ only by free occurrences of "x" and "y." In the names of the conditions which occur in (4') and (5'), the interior variables are bound (by the capped variables); in fact, (4') and (5') differ in containing names of quite different intensions or conditions.

Now, the universal closure of (10) would, for Quine, be the proper way of regimenting the universal closure of the English

(6) if x = y, then if John said that x chased y and then y chased z, then John said that x chased y and then x chased z.

Thus, for Quine, a closure of (6) may full well be *false*; likewise, the problem sentence of Section I, whose surface form appeared to make its falsity incompatible with the truth of (L), may be false on Quine's view. On Quine's strategy, the proper understanding of sentences such as (the closure of) (6) is given by a regimentation. In asking whether the falsity of (6) violates (L), we are asking whether the falsity of (6)'s regimentation violates (L). We just saw that no such violation was to be found. Hence, the fact that the universal closure of (6) is false doesn't show that English fails to conform to (L), at least according to Quine.

IV

Is there a reason to prefer Q to R, or vice versa? In this section, I discuss this question. I argue that there is some reason to prefer R to Q, and, thus, some reason to think that English is a language for which (L) does not hold. It turns out that the reasons there are for preferring R to Q have more to do with matters of syntax than with matters of semantics.

If we confine our attention only to semantical matters, it is difficult to see a reason for preferring one of the two proposals to the other. The two proposals attribute the same truth conditions to ascriptions of assertion. On a more fine-grained level, they also make very similar assignments of semantic values to expressions of English. R assigns conditions to sentences of English, and a function from (n-place) conditions to (n + 1-place) conditions to "says." Q assigns conditions to the names which it manufactures out of the content sentences of ascriptions, and so could be seen as at least implicitly making the same assignments to these sentences as does R. And Q's assignment to "says" is, from a set-theoretic viewpoint, equivalent to R's.

This might tempt one to see the two proposals as notational variants; taken merely as proposals about truth conditions, they probably are. Taken as outlines of proposals about both the syntax and semantics of English, however, they do not appear to be equivalent.

To see this, we must consider the status of the "forms" which the proposals ascribe to sentences of English. Observe, first of all, that there is a *prima facie* difference between the theories with regard to structural matters. For there is a *prima facie* difference between a theory, like R, which assigns the form

(1) Sentence connective + sentence

to a sentence such as

(2) John said that y is chasing z

and one, like Q, which assigns to this sentence the form

(3) Predicate + name + name.

(I have let "says" here absorb the argument 'John'.) For one thing, the two theories make different judgments about identity of structure. For example, consider the sentence

(4) It is not the case that y is chasing z.

The natural treatment of this sentence is one which ascribes to it the form (1); it borders on the perverse to ascribe it the form (3). So, presumably, Q and R will differ as to whether (2) and (4) have the same structure—R will say they do, Q will say that they do not. So far as we have intuitions about identity of structure, intuition seems to favor R here. There are other structural differences between Q and R. In particular, Q posits elements—the variable binders "x̂" and so on—which are not realized in surface structure, while R does not.

Of what importance, if any, are these differences? Note that when we theorize about natural language, we are faced with two important tasks.[14] The first is to characterize the sentences and, more generally, the well-formed expressions of the language, as well as such grammatical relations as "is a constituent of." The second task is to characterize semantic notions such as truth. We often think of each task as being completed by a theory which assigns what are usually called structures or forms to (a subset of) the (possible) vocalizations and inscriptions of the speakers of the language. (In the case of the semantic task, we envision the theory assigning the forms and then recursively defining truth in terms of the assigned forms.) We may call the forms which are assigned, in completing the first task, syntactic forms (SF's); those assigned in the second case, logical forms (LF's). This way of characterizing the two tasks leaves it open as to what the relation between SF's and LF's is to be. They might be more or less identical (with LF's being "interpreted SF's"), or they might be quite different (as they would appear to be in a system like that proposed by Montague.)

We're now in a position to see why R might be preferable to Q. Suppose that we think of Q and R as consisting of the relevant parts of fuller accounts of both the syntax and semantics of English. Thinking of Q and R in this way, we will then think of the forms which the proposals ascribe to English sentences as playing the role of syntactic forms as well as the role of logical forms.

We might now argue as follows. *All else being equal*, we ought to prefer (a) theories (about the syntax and semantics of natural languages) which conform to pre-theoretic intuitions about the sameness and difference of syntactic structure of sentences to those

---

[14] Of course, I don't mean that these are the only important tasks to which to attend.

which do not; (b) theories which refrain from postulating underlying syntactic elements which are not apparent on the surface, to theories which involve such postulation. R is to be preferred to Q on both of these counts. Furthermore, there is no apparent reason to prefer Q to R, as a (part of) a theory of the syntax and semantics of English. Thus, R is *prima facie* preferrable to Q.

Note that the first premise is really quite modest, since it is fully consistent with the claim that conformity to intuitions and "respect for the surface" are easily defeasible reasons for preferring one theory to another. In particular, the premise is consistent with the claim that we may postulate "invisible" constituents, or disregard intuitions, whenever this would, for example, enable us to capture an important generalization, or simplify the overall theory. What the first premise of the argument demands is that such postulation or disregard for intuitions have an appropriate motivation.

The second premise surely needs no defense; the comparison of Q and R above brought out just this point. The critical premise here is that there is no reason to prefer Q to R. It is important to realize that the fact that Q preserves (L) while R doesn't is *not* a good reason for preferring Q, as a theory of the syntax and semantics of English. Certainly there is no salient fact about quantification in English which requires that the language conform to (L); in particular, the fact that English enjoys objectual quantification is not such a reason, since objectual quantification doesn't require (L).[15] Furthermore, it can't be said that we complicate our account of the semantics of English by adopting R over Q. R is different from what we are accustomed to: It forsakes a familiar law. We should be careful not to confuse novelty with complication.

The argument I have just given requires us to take Q and R as theories which do not posit distinct levels of form, one syntactic and one logical, for natural language. They aspire, as I have represented them, to what Kaplan has called logical perfection,[16] where logical form recapitulates syntactic form. It is then syntactic considerations which require a departure from (L). Of course, there are traditions in which different levels of form are attributed to natural language expressions: One thinks, for example, of Russell's analysis of descriptions, Davidson's account of action sentences, as well as of recent extensions of transformational grammar.

But even supposing that we will eventually endorse such a theory, I think the above argument establishes a *prima facie* case for R over Q. For surely we should prefer theories in which there is as little departure as possible, between the two levels of form postulated. R, in itself, requires no reworking of syntax whatsoever, before we give the semantics.[17]

---

[15] A referee for *The Philosophical Review* suggests that we may be drawn to Q as a result of a tendency to over-generalize: We notice that (L) holds for a goodly segment of English, and thus suppose that it holds for all of it.

[16] See Kaplan (1964) and Kaplan (1975).

[17] Commenting on an earlier draft, a referee for *The Philosophical Review* suggested that Q might be preferrable to R, *qua* theory of logical form, since it makes explicit the abstraction of conditions involved in attitude ascriptions in a way in which R does not.

I do not see this as a virtue, since I do not see that attitude ascriptions involve abstraction of conditions in any sense which doesn't beg the question at issue between Q and R. When spelled out in complete detail,

I most probably have not canvassed all the relevant considerations. Thus, the above argument may be taken as a challenge: Given that there are some syntactic grounds on which a preference for R over Q can be justified, and that we have uncovered no obvious semantic reason for preferring Q to R, why shouldn't we prefer R?

Even if Quine's response to the putative counter-examples to (L) is rejected, it doesn't follow that (L) isn't true of English. For there remains the other response to these examples mentioned in Section I. This response, it will be recalled, required us to say that if John uttered

(5) I saw Hesperus and then Phosphorus; I wanted to see Phosphorus and then Hesperus

then, for some x and y, John really *did* say that he saw x and then y and he wanted to see x and then y. This response seems to strike many people as so obviously outlandish as not to merit serious consideration.

I think it does indeed merit serious consideration; but it is not my intention here to give it its due.[18] What I have tried to do here is to clear away some of the meta-logical debris surrounding (L), so that we will be in a position to evaluate views which require us to say that such reports are true. Some may have thought that the very logic of our language requires the truth of

(6) There are planets x and y such that: x = y and John said that he saw x and then y and wanted to see x and then y

---

R will explicitly state the function from conditions to conditions associated with "says," and will require an explicit assignment of conditions to sentences. But then R will give an explicit account of the relations among semantic values which make attitude ascriptions true or false. I don't see what is gained by going from this account to one in which we allow names of conditions to enter into logical forms.

Perhaps the point, as well as the position for which I argue in the text, will be clearer if we consider a parallel situation in the treatment of modality. Let us assume that something of the surface form

(a) It is possible that A

is true iff A's intension takes some world to the true. Then a parallel problem can be raised, concerning the choice between a theory—T, call it—which treats "it is possible that," at the level of logical form, as a sentence connective or predicate, and one—T★, call it—which, in effect, takes some version of world theory as a theory of logical form, assimilating "it is possible that" to a quantifier over worlds.

To take the position concerning the choice between Q and R which I am taking is very much like holding that T is to be preferred, all else being equal, to T★. I would argue that this is the correct position. It is one thing to say that "possibly" behaves semantically in a way analogous to an existential quantifier over worlds in a language such as that of world theory. This does not entail that in any interesting sense it is a quantifier. Of course, from a purely syntactical perspective, it seems reasonable to say that it is not. Since there is no semantic motivation for treating it as a quantifier—nothing is lost, in terms of truth conditions, by taking it to be a predicate or sentence connective—there seems to be some reason not to treat it as a quantifier.

It might be said that I am simply exhibiting a prejudice for theories which "recurse" directly on syntactic structure, over those which do this by proxy, as does semantics for (a) via a translation into world theory. ("Semantics by Proxy" is Mark Sainsbury's term; see Sainsbury (1977).) The sort of considerations brought forth in the text, I hope, suggests that this is more than mere prejudice.

[18] Nathan Salmon argues for the virtues of such a response (to similar problems) in Salmon (1986).

given the truth of

(7) There are planets x and y such that: x = y and John said that he saw x and then y and wanted to see y and then x.

Hence, it was thought, there is simply no alternative in accounting for contrary intuitions, but to chalk them up to confusion, or to consign them to the garbage dump of informal pragmatics.[19] This, I have argued, is wrong. There is nothing, from a logical point of view, which is incoherent about the view that (7) is true while (6) is false; for there is nothing, from a logical point of view, which requires objectual quantification to conform to (L).[20]

---

[19] I have appropriated this wonderful phrase from Anil Gupta; see Gupta (1982).

[20] I am indebted to David Austin, Jody Azzouni, Harold Hodes, Ernest LePore, Nathan Salmon, and Scott Soames for comments.

4

Attitude Ascriptions, Semantic Theory, and Pragmatic Evidence

Traditional Fregeanism takes the truth value of a propositional attitude ascription to depend upon whether the subject of the ascription is appropriately related to a sense picked out by its "that"-clause. The virtues of this view are supposed to be threefold: It is responsive to our intuitions about the truth conditions of such ascriptions; it makes it plausible that what appear to be explanations of behavior via the ascription of attitudes are truly explanatory; it explains the validity and invalidity of certain inferences involving ascriptions, especially the failure of substitutivity. In short, Fregeanism is supposed to account for the pragmatic evidence, that concerning our practice of ascribing attitudes and our intuitions about this practice.

A Russellian approach to ascriptions takes them to be ascriptions of relations to entities individuated in terms of the Russellian referents—individuals and attributes—of the constituents of the ascription's "that"-clause. Particularly when Russellianism treats ordinary proper names as having their referents as semantic values, it is thought to suffer from vices corresponding to the virtues of Fregeanism. That is to say, it is thought that Russellianism gives an inadequate account of the truth conditions of ascriptions; makes impossible the explanation of behavior via the ascription of attitudes; is unable adequately to account for the validity and invalidity of inferences involving ascriptions. Russellianism does not seem to explain the pragmatic evidence. Insofar as this is the primary data for semantic theory, Russellianism seems an inadequate semantic theory.

I argue for two theses in this essay: First, that Fregean accounts of the truth conditions of attitude ascriptions do not have the virtues enumerated at the beginning of this paper; secondly, that Russellianism, when properly formulated, is able to give a systematic, theoretically satisfying account of the phenomena its critics claim it is unable to explain.

I argue for the first claim in the first section of the essay. My argument starts from the observation, due to Frege, that the sense of a sentence varies intersubjectively. I try to show that once this claim is accepted, it is not possible to give a Fregean account of truth conditions of ascriptions of attitudes which has the virtues Fregeanism is supposed to have.

I argue for the second claim in the second section of the essay. I do this by sketching a formulation of Russellianism which has the virtues in question. I suggest that ascriptions of attitude are used to convey different "levels" of information about relations to a number of Russellian entities. Simplifying somewhat: Taken in isolation, an ascription conveys the information that a certain Russellian proposition is an object of attitude. Taken within a conversation, along with other ascriptions of attitude, an ascription is used to convey information about the relation of the ascribee to a more complex Russellian entity, one constructed out of propositional functions. The first sort of information, I argue, determines the strict truth conditions of an ascription. The second kind of information, while it is regularly and systematically conveyed, does not determine the strict truth conditions of the ascription. It is no less important for that, since by appeal to it an explanation of our seeming success in explaining behavior by attitude ascription, and of failures of substitutivity, can be given.

I

It is not clear that the appeal to senses can do the semantic work it is supposed to. A problem appears when one asks *which* sense a "that"-clause in an attitude ascription refers to. It is common coin among Fregeans that expressions typically vary in sense (without a corresponding variation in reference) among speakers. Frege's example was of the proper name "Aristotle," but there is no reason that predicates should not suffer in such intersubjective variations of sense as well.

Probably the sense which you associate with "Frege was a logician" is distinct from that which I associate therewith. This quite obviously does not stop me from being able truly to ascribe to you the belief that Frege was a logician by saying "You believe that Frege was a logician." This seems to imply that on Fregean terms that a "that"-clause does not name the sense I associate with its sentence. So what does a "that"-clause name in an attitude ascription?[1]

I believe that there are four sort of answers which a Fregean might offer.

(1) He might yet say that a "that"-clause names its sense for the person using it, by carefully explaining what relations are named by verbs such as "believes." Call the relation we would normally take the verb "believes" to name capital-"B" Believes. The Fregean might claim that a use of a sentence of the form of

x believes that S

is true if and only if x Believes a sense which bears some relation R to the sense of S for the user. One can imagine different candidates for R—similarity relations are perhaps

---

[1] This point seems to have been first made in Kripke (1979). Some of the arguments in this section are developed at greater length in Richard (1987).

the most plausible.[2] But no matter what relation one picks, the following problem arises: either agreement in reference between the corresponding constituents of two thoughts is sufficient, for those thoughts to bear R to one another, or it is not. If it is sufficient, then it would seem that the notion of sense does no semantic work. If identity of reference is sufficient for the relation R, whatever bears R to the thought I express with ⌐Hesperus is F⌐ bears it to that I express with ⌐Phosphorus is F⌐. And so, if I can say ⌐He believes that Hesperus is F⌐, I can say ⌐He believes that Phosphorus is F⌐. What point, then, in appealing to senses?

But if referential agreement is not enough, for one sense to bear R to another, then surely we will be obliged to deny what was suggested above: That if A can express a belief with "Frege was a logician," then B can ascribe it to him with this sentence. Just suppose (as on this alternative must be possible) that A and B use the constituents of this sentence to refer to the same things, but their senses for the sentence vary enough, so that B's do not bear the relation R to A's.

There is a version of this objection to which the use of a similarity relation for the relation R is especially vulnerable. We all assume that we may unproblematically ascribe attitudes to those who do not speak our language by using translations of their sentences into our language. We can ascribe, for example, belief to the mono-lingual Frenchman who expresses belief with "Londres est grande" by saying "He believes that London is large." It is not at all obvious that the senses that these aliens associate with their sentences are at all similar to those of our translations; in fact, it seems likely that they associate dissimilar senses. Thus, on this view, it is not at all obvious that we can successfully ascribe attitudes in this way. This seems quite clearly wrong.

(2) One might say that a "that"-clause names its sense for the person to whom the attitude is ascribed. To this there is the obvious objection, that we can successfully ascribe attitudes to those who do not speak our language. Just as seriously, it makes "that"-clauses flaccid in an unacceptable way. On this proposal, "that Russell is a logician" changes its reference, as it migrates from "Ramsey believes that" to "Moore believes that," rendering invalid the argument: Ramsey believes that Russell is a logician; Moore believes everything Ramsey does; hence, Moore believes that Russell is a logician.

One might try to evade the second objection by claiming that propositional quantification is substitutional. If the quantifier in the second premiss is substitutional, the argument is indeed valid. This seems somewhat disingenuous. The Fregean is committed to the claim that there are (objectual quantifier) senses, and that attitude ascription involves genuine reference to them. It seems somewhat *ad hoc*, on such a view, to say that what appears to be a straightforward quantification over the objects of attitudes, as objectual as any quantification, is not objectual.

---

[2] Graeme Forbes has argued for the similarity view in an unpublished manuscript. The text confuses use and mention in an easily correctable way. I do this, here and below, to avoid needless prolixity.

(3) Thus far I have argued against views on which "that"-clauses function as names of senses. I wish now to consider the view that in attitude ascriptions senses are specified quantificationally. On such views, some or all of the expressions within a "that"-clause are, or at least function as if they were, variables over senses, ones which are bound by implicit quantifiers. I will consider two such views.

The simplest version of such a view is this. Let us for simplicity ignore the existence of demonstratives and free variables within the content sentences of ascriptions. Use the parameter in things such as $A(t)$ to indicate a (non-repetitive) sequence of precisely the proper names in the sentence A, ordered by first appearance, left to right; let us then use $A(v)$ to indicate systematic substitution of a sequence v of variables new to A for the parameter t. Then, one might suggest that an ascription of attitude of the form of

> a V's that A(t)

is really (or at least has the same truth conditions as) the ascription

>   For some v, such that v_1 presents t_1 and… and v_n presents t_n:
>
> a V's "A(v)"

(Here, and in the sequel, double quotes function as "sense quotes." The v_i and t_i are of course elements of the parameters.) On such a view, for example, the sentence

>   John wishes that Twain visit Clemens

is treated as

>   There are senses s and s' such that s presents Twain and s' presents Clemens and John wishes "s visits s'."

I have an objection and an observation. The objection is that the view makes senses more or less otiose, semantically. Such an account doesn't block most of the inferences that the appeal to senses is supposed to block in the first place. For example, on this account, the inference: John thinks that Twain is here; Twain is Clemens; thus, John thinks that Clemens is here—is valid. Those inferences it does block—for example: John believes that Twain visited Clemens; Twain is Clemens; thus, John believes that Twain visited Twain—can also be blocked by the Russellian. The Russellian might say the ascription

> a V's that A(t)

ascribes a relation to the Russellian proposition whose constituents are the propositional function $\hat{v}(A(v))$ and the sequence of individuals named by t. This makes the propositions picked out by "Twain visited Clemens" and "Twain visited Twain" distinct propositions, identified respectively with

> $<\hat{x}\hat{y}(x$ visited $y)$, $<$Twain, Twain$>>$
> $<\hat{x}(x$ visited $x)$, $<$Twain$>>$.

Although the truth conditions the Russellian and Fregean account offer are different, there appears to be little, if any, difference in the way they would distribute truth values to ascriptions. Thus my suggestion, that on this account sense is in danger of becoming semantically otiose. (I will return to such Russellian views in the next section.)

The observation concerns the widespread belief that we can explain behavior by the ascription of attitudes. An account of attitude ascriptions ought to be compatible with this intuition. It ought, for example, to be compatible with the view that instances of the schema

(A) If (a believes that (if Ab, then Bb) and a wishes that Bb),
then a will make it the case that Ab
a believes that if Ab, then Bb
a wishes that Bb
Thus, a will make it the case that Ab

give genuine explanations. ((A) is oversimplified; this does not affect the point I will make.) This is not to say that semantics must somehow validate this intuition. Perhaps folk psychology is idle folklore, as some insist. But an account of attitude ascription ought not to make the widespread belief an unreasonable one. The straightforward way of doing this would be to treat the first premiss so that its instances gave plausible candidates for psychological laws—and, of course to make the schema a valid one.

Suppose we segregate the major premiss of such an explanation, treating it as a universal quantification:

For any sense s such that s presents b: If (a believes "if As, then Bs" and a wishes "Bs") then a will make it the case that Ab.

This is plausible enough. But the schema is not valid, since the second and third premisses become

For some s such that s presents b: a believes "if As, then Bs"
For some s such that s presents b: a desires "Bs."

(4) There is a second quantificational strategy open to the Fregean which merits consideration. As an account of truth conditions, I will argue, it is inadequate. But it bears some relation to parts of the Russellian account I shall propose in the next section. Thus, I shall spend some time explaining it.

Within the context of a Fregean account of attitude ascriptions, for an instance of schema (A) to be valid it is necessary that the embedded sentences in its second and third premisses name the same sense; at least, they must behave as if they named the same sense. One way in which we could get them to behave in this way is to treat their constituents as if they were variables over senses, and allow that variables in distinct sentences may be bound by one (existential) quantifier. On such a treatment, argument (A) might be assimilated to

For some s, such that s presents b:

For any sense s' such that s' presents b: If (a believes "if As', then Bs'" and a wishes "Bs'"), then a will make it the case that Ab.

a believes "if As, then Bs"

a desires "As"

Hence, a will make it the case that Ab.

Such an argument can be "given" by several people in the course of a conversation, one uttering one premiss, another another, the major premiss being perhaps suppressed. Thus, it is natural to take the quantifiers binding the sense variables to be "implicit to the conversation." Let us call this sort of account of the truth conditions of attitude ascriptions an implicit quantifier account.

There is a way of motivating this account which gives it considerable intuitive appeal. Let us suppose that we are attracted by the idea that belief, desire, and the rest of the attitudes are relations to Fregean senses. If the preceding arguments have merit, this should not incline us to the view that ascriptions of these attitudes are straightforward ascriptions of relations to such senses. What, then, are we doing, when we ascribe attitudes? One not unnatural answer would be this: We use the sentences of such ascriptions as a sort of a model of the cognitive structure of the ascribee. If we say, for example

(B) Twain believes that Hesperus is hot
Twain wishes that Hesperus was wet

we commit ourselves to a model of Twain's mental life which might be written thus:

Twain:	Belief	Desire
	Hesperus is hot	Hesperus is wet

The model is accurate, just in case there is a way of assigning senses to the expressions in the model so that (i) the sense assigned to an expression is a sense of the ordinary referent of the expression, and (ii) the assignment results in listing only thoughts Twain believes under "Belief," ones he desires under "Desire," and so on.

Two aspects of the proposal must be spelled out if it is to be definite enough to evaluate. First of all, we need an account of how truth is to be defined for the implicit quantifications. I think the only solution is to treat sentences with the same variable as if they were conjuncts in a "conversationally extended" conjunction closed by the implicit quantifiers. Then, a use of a sentence S with the implicitly bound variables v is true iff some assignment makes all preceding uses of sentences in the conversation which contain members of v true (when taken individually), and does the same for S. So, for example, the second member of conversation (B) comes out true iff there is a way of assigning senses to "Hesperus," "is hot," and "is wet" which yields beliefs and desires of Twain for all the ascriptions in (B). Only such a dependence upon earlier sentences makes the embedded expressions behave as co-bound variables. I return to this feature below.

Secondly, there is what might be called the variable identification problem—when are different occurrences of embedded expressions to be taken as proxies for the same variable?

To make vivid the range of possible solutions to the problem, consider the conversation (C):

a: Clemens believes that Hesperus is hot.
b: Twain believes that Hesperus is wet.
c: Melville wishes that Hesperus were wet.
d: Twain believes that Hesperus is not hot.

Let us talk of two occurrences of a term being co-relativized, when they are treated as if they were occurrences of the same existentially bound variable. One strategy co-relativizes all occurrences of the same term in ascriptions. (I am supposing, for simplicity, that orthography indicates identity of terms.) This strategy treats even the occurrences of "Hesperus" in (b) and (c) as proxies for the same variable. Given what we said above about intersubjective variation of sense, it is difficult to see how this could be justified.

A strategy at the other extreme co-relativizes occurrences only when they are occurrences of the same term in ascriptions with the same subject term. This strategy would co-relativize the occurrences of "Hesperus" in (b) and (d), but not those in (a) and (b).

This strategy makes the subject position of attitude ascriptions opaque. Suppose, for simplicity, that Twain has only the three beliefs he expresses with "Hesperus is hot," "Phosphorus is not hot," "Phosphorus is wet." If we continue the above conversation thus:

e: Twain is Clemens
f: Clemens believes Hesperus is not hot

each contribution to the conversation is true, up to (f), the relevant parts of the conversation being parsed:

For some senses s and t such that s presents Hesperus and t presents Hesperus:

a: Clemens believes "s is hot"
b: Twain believes "t is wet"
d: Twain believes "t is not hot"
e: Twain is Clemens
f: Clemens believes "s is not hot."

But (f) will not be true. I take it that this result is undesirable, and that we ought therefore consider some intermediate course. Let us then consider co-relativizing occurrences of terms just when they are occurrences of the same term within ascriptions with subject terms which name the same thing. Thus, the occurrences of "Hesperus" in (a), (b), and (d) in conversation (C) are all to be co-relativized. This account, it might be noted, has as a bonus a lack of commitment to interpersonal identity of sense.

Compared to the first quantificational account, this account of attitude ascriptions has at least two virtues. First of all, it seems to give an acceptable account of explanation of behavior by attitude ascription. Arguments such as (A) turn out valid, and their major premises are not altogether unreasonable candidates for psychological laws. Secondly, the account does not make embedded positions of terms, such as that of "Twain" in "John thinks that Twain is dead" transparent, as should be clear from the above discussion.

However, this strategy has an unacceptable consequence. Suppose that early on in a conversation, someone says

> John believes that Twain wrote *Moby Dick*.

Suppose that there is no sense s which presents Twain such that John accepts "*s* wrote *Moby Dick*." Then the ascription is false. This is not objectionable. But now *any* later contribution to the conversation beginning "John believes that" in which the name "Twain" is embedded is false. This is because the truth definition we have proposed treats such latter contributions as if they were conjoined to the false contribution. As noted above, it seems it must do this, if it is to treat expressions in different ascriptions as co-relativized variables. Surely an early falsehood like the above does not keep later ascriptions of belief to John using "Twain" in the content sentence from being true. As an account of truth conditions, then, this account seems unacceptable.

II

I will now sketch a proposal on which attitude ascriptions convey information about relations to Russellian propositions (RPs) and other Russellian entities. I assume that attitudes are relations to RP's had in virtue of relations to natural language sentences. On this view, belief, desire, and so on are three-place relations between an individual, a sentence (which he may, so to speak, believe-true, desire-true, etc.), and a Russellian entity.

The basic idea is that embedded sentences in ascriptions, or series of ascriptions within conversations, are used both to convey what RPs are objects of attitude, as well as something about the structure of the sentence in virtue of which this is so. For example, consider the two series of ascriptions

(1) He believes that Twain is dead. He desires that Twain come.
(2) He believes that Twain is dead. He desires that Clemens come.

Each series ascribes attitudes towards the same RPs. However, I suggest, the two series convey different information as to overall structure of the sentences believed and desired-true. Roughly, (1) conveys the information that there is some one name n of Twain, such that the individual believes-true ⌜n is dead⌝ and desires-true ⌜n comes⌝; (2) conveys the information that there are names n and n' of Twain such that the individual believes true ⌜n is dead⌝ and desires true ⌜n' comes⌝.

I thus associate several "levels" of informations with ascriptions. A first level, which the ascription conveys when taken in isolation, is information about the Russellian proposition which is the object of an attitude. A second level, which the ascription conveys relative to a conversation, may be characterized as information that an individual is related to a certain complex object, constructed from Russellian propositions.

Here, in outline, is how this occurs: Let f and g be the propositional functions associated with "is dead" and "comes," respectively. Observe that there are two different ways in which one can believe f(Twain) and wish g(Twain). The first might be verbalized: of him (Twain is indicated), I believe f and wish g. The second might be verbalized: of this and that (Twain is indicated twice), I think f of the first and wish g of the second.

The first system of belief and desire could be said to be captured by a certain function, from (1-termed) sequences of individuals to sequences of propositions, along with a sequence of individuals (namely, the sequence whose sole member is Twain). This function and argument might be aptly represented by

(1') $<\hat{x}(f(x), g(x)), \text{Twain}>$

The second system of belief and desire could be said to be captured by a different function from sequences of individuals to propositions, and a different sequence of arguments:

(2') $<\hat{x}\hat{y}(f(x), g(y)) <\text{Twain}, \text{Twain}>>$.

Overall, then, the series of ascriptions (1) conveys that the individual has a system of attitudes characterized by (1'); (2), one characterized by (2').

The two sorts of information I have suggested ascriptions convey are obviously similar to the sorts of information ascriptions are said to convey, on the two Fregean quantificational accounts of attitude ascriptions discussed in the last section. But the account I am proposing does not make use of anything very much like traditional Fregean senses, either for its motivation or as semantic values. I will argue presently that this account can give a satisfying explanation of the phenomenon often thought to be most favorable to Fregean accounts—explanation of behavior by ascription of attitudes and failures of substitutivity. I will first be a bit more specific about the way I propose attitudes convey information.[3]

We treat the parameters t and v as before.[4] I will call the Russellian entities about which ascriptions convey information R-structures. These structures are associated both with single sentences and with sequences thereof. The R-structure of a single sentence $S(t)$ is the pair of the propositional function corresponding to $S(v)$ and the sequence of referents of t, which we indicate as $<\hat{v}S(v), t^\star>$. The R-structure of a single sentence, then, is a Russellian proposition, separated into a propositional function and its arguments.

---

[3] In this sketch I am simplifying considerably. In particular, I do not extend the treatment to predicates in ascriptions, but discuss only singular terms. I ignore the qualifications necessary to treat context sensitive expressions. And I do not discuss the complications involved in treating ascriptions with free variables in the content sentence.

[4] The conventions are those introduced in the discussion of the third view in Section I.

The notion of R-structure generalizes to sequences of sentences in a fairly obvious way. Let S be a sequence $S_1(t_1), \ldots, S_n(t_n)$ of sentences.[5] The sequence S may be rewritten $\hat{v}_1 S_1(v_1)t_1, \ldots, \hat{v}_n Sn(v_n)t_n$, explicitly indicating the R-structure of each of its members. Suppose t to be a non-repetitious sequence of exactly the terms in the parameters t_i in order of first occurrence, left to right; w to be an equinumerous sequence of distinct variables, new to the sentences in S. Then the R-structure of the original sequence of sentences is indicated by

$$<\hat{w}(\hat{v}_1 S_1(v_1)w_1, \ldots, \hat{v}_n S_n(v_n)w_n), t^\star>$$

where the w_i' s are what result from replacing the members of t in the t_i' s with the corresponding members of w.

Two examples of this process: consider the two sequences indicated schematically by

$A(t,c); B(t)$
$A(c,t); B(t)$

Rewriting to make individual R-structure explicit, we obtain

$\hat{x}\hat{y}(A(xy))tc; \hat{x}(B(x))t$
$\hat{x}\hat{y}(A(xy))ct; \hat{x}(B(x))t$

respectively. The R-structures of the sequences are then, respectively,

$<\hat{x}_1\hat{y}_1[\hat{x}\hat{y}(A(xy))x_1 y_1, \hat{x}(B(x)) x_1], <t,c,>>$
$<\hat{x}_1\hat{y}_1[\hat{x}\hat{y}(A(xy))x_1 y_1, \hat{x}(B(x)) y_1], <c,t,>>$

Recall the motivation suggested for the implicit quantifier approach: that attitude ascription within a conversation involves something along the lines of building a model of the cognitive structure of an individual. The idea was that, for example, a conversation in which the ascriptions

(3)   *a* believes that if Twain is hit, then Twain will fall
(4)   *a* desires that Twain fall
(5)   *a* believes that if Smith comes, Twain is hit

occur generates the model:

a: *Belief*   *Desire*
     (3')   If Twain is hit, then Twain falls   (4')   Twain falls
     (5')   If Smith comes, Twain is hit.

Call such models cognitive models, or CMs. Such models may be thought of as sequences of sentences, each member of the sequence being a conjunction of the sentences under one of the attitude headings.

---

[5] The distinct parameters may contain some of the same terms, though the same term does not recur within a parameter; each parameter contains, as before, all the terms of a sentence.

We can now say that the first level of information conveyed by an ascription

a V's that S(*t*)

is that its subject has the attitude indicated by V to the R-structure of its embedded sentence. The second level conveyed by the ascription is that is subject has a system of attitudes which is correctly characterized by the R-structure of model M, where M is the model obtained by taking the CM for the ascription's subject and extending it by adding S(*t*) in the appropriate column.[6]

In ascribing attitudes and evaluating ascriptions, we proceed by extracting R-structure, both of content sentences taken in isolation, and the more global sort of R-structure just characterized. I do not propose that both of these levels of information should be taken as determining the truth conditions of an ascription. The argument against the claim that the implicit quantifier approach gives an adequate account of truth conditions can be used to show that the conversational level of information is not truth conditional: If someone makes an utterly incorrect ascription to an individual in a conversation, no extension of the CM for that individual will be accurate. This makes it inappropriate to say that this sort of information determines the strict truth or falsity of an ascription. Engaging in conversation with a misinformed individual doesn't render one incapable of saying things which are true.

I do not mean to imply, in denying such information truth conditional status, that it is somehow of merely subsidiary importance. By appeal to this second level of information, it seems possible to explain how ascription of attitudes can be explanatory of behavior. Consider the schema:

(A) If (a believes that (if A*b*, then B*b*) and *a* desires B*b*),
then *a* will make it the case that A*b*.
a believes that if A*b*, then B*b*.
a desires that B*b*.
Hence, a will make the case that Ab.

Taken together, the second and third premisses of the explanation convey the information that a is characterized by the R-structure $<\hat{y}(\hat{x}(\text{if}Ax, \text{then } Bx)y, \hat{x}(Bx)y), b>$. It is not implausible to suggest that the major premiss may be understood as a conditional whose antecedent is that a is so characterized, and whose consequent is that he will make it the case that Ab. So interpreted, the information which the premisses jointly convey does entail the conclusion of the explanation. And the major premiss is not a wildly implausible claim. Roughly speaking, a person is characterized by the above R-structure just in case they accept a sentence of the form ⌜if A*t*, then B*t*⌝ and wish true a sentence of the form ⌜B*t*⌝, for some name *t* of *b*.[7]

---

[6] I am suppressing some details here. In particular, the definition of *model M characterizes u* is suppressed.

[7] This is not quite true, since I have ignored predicates in characterizing R-structure. Once they are included, the "laws" associated with the first premises of instances of (A) appear to be as plausible as Fregean equivalents.

Whether such sentential attitudes really do make it likely that one will behave in a certain way is a difficult question. But it is not necessary for the project I am engaged in, that I show that the Russellian can associate genuine laws with folk psychological generalizations. All that is required is that I show that the Russellian is able to make sense on his own terms of our practice of trying to explain behavior by attitude ascription. For this, it suffices that I show that the information conveyed by the premises of such ascriptions on a Russellian view is as plausible a candidate for being explanatory, as is the information which the Fregean would say was associated with the premises.

I wish to propose a third level of information which may be conveyed by an ascription, one which is in some sense a generalization of the second level. We often come to a conversation with convictions about the attitudes of others, ones which we would express to ourselves in certain ways. For example, most of us come to philosophical discussions about attitude ascription with convictions which we would express with

(7) The ancients believed that Hesperus rose in the west.
(8) The ancients believed that Phosphorus rose in the east.

Such convictions are often matters of mutual belief among participants in a conversation. That is, those conversing not only would express beliefs using them, but believe that others have beliefs they would so express, that those others believe that they have such beliefs, and so on, up a familiar hierarchy.

When such convictions are present, it is plausible to think that they are used to construct what I have called the CM of an individual. Thus, an ascription will convey not only the two levels of information I have just discussed, but a third, which is obtained by using the content sentences of such tacit ascriptions, as well as the content sentence of the explicitly made ascription, to form the CM.

For example, if someone utters

(9) The ancients believed that Phosphorus rose in the west

we will evaluate it in terms of the model

The ancients:	Belief
	Hesperus rose in the west
	Phosphorus rose in the east.

We do this by adding the content sentence of (9) to this model, to get a model with three sentences in the belief column:

(M) The ancients:	Belief
	Hesperus rose in the west
	Phosphorus rose in the east
	Phosphorus rose in the west.

We find the ascription (9) accurate only if we think that the R-structure of (M) characterized the ancients.

I have already observed that some failures of substitutivity are explained by appeal to the first level of information conveyed by an ascription, which I have suggested is semantic. Clearly, not every such failure is so explained. Looking at this level, there is no difference, in terms of the information conveyed, between (7) and (9). More failures of substitutivity are explained by appeal to the second level. But not all such failures are explained. And neither is the dogged intuition that it is simply wrong to say "The ancients believed that Phosphorus rose in the west."

Most failures of substitutivity, as well as intuitions such as the one I have just mentioned, do receive a satisfactory explanation when appeal to all three levels of information is made. For example, although we would not put it in just this way, it seems plausible to think that we share the belief that the cognitive structure of the ancients was not characterized by the R-structure of M. This model, after all, requires that the ancients had some way of picking out Venus, relative to which they could identify it as both an east riser and a west riser.

We come to discussions of attitude ascriptions with the beliefs expressed by (7) and (8) in the forefront of our minds. Now, if we begin with those beliefs, what does the hypothesis, that we evaluate ascriptions by looking at the information about R-structure which they convey, predict? That we evaluate (7) by asking whether a model such as the above is accurate. Since we think such a model is inaccurate, we are led to predict that we will find ascription (9) incorrect—just the fact which was to be explained.

In general, substituting co-referential expressions in attitude ascriptions alters the information which they convey. Of course, it does not always do this at the level of truth conditions. But it will generally distort information at "higher" levels, ones no less important than the level of truth conditions, if the picture I have been sketching is correct. Our focus, in evaluating ascriptions, is on the information we are transmitting and receiving with them, both truth conditional and otherwise. And so we have the (quite accurate) intuition that substitutivity fails in such ascriptions—that is to say, that such substitution may lead us to make inaccurate reports about the attitudes of others.

It is not uncommon for Russellians to insist that many of our intuitions about attitude ascriptions are to be accounted for in terms of pragmatic factors, and not in terms of the strict truth conditions of these ascriptions.[8] Of course, I endorse such a view, since I have tried to explain most of the intuitions most troubling for the Russellian in just such terms.

The above account offers a better explanation than that offered by what seems to be the most common pragmatic explanation offered by Russellians, that an ascription generally conveys the information that its subject believes (desires, etc.) the proposition its content sentence expresses by believing (desiring, etc.) true its content sentence. The

---

[8] See, for example, Salmon (1986). Scott Soames (1987) also argues for a pragmatic explanation of some of the pragmatic evidence. The accounts which Salmon, Soames, and I offer differ a good deal, both with respect to truth conditions we ascribe to ascriptions, as well as with respect to the pragmatic component of our explanation.

primary problem with this latter explanation is that it does not apply to a very large number of cases. For example, ascriptions involving demonstratives and indexicals, like "Smith believes that I am tired," obviously carry no such implication. So appeal to such an implication cannot explain failures of substitutivity, or the explanation of behavior by attitude ascription, for such cases. A similar point can be made concerning ascriptions involving quantifying in.[9]

Furthermore, the proposed explanation does not seem adequate to the following sort of case. Suppose that it is common knowledge between us that Smith does not know the name "Hesperus," but that he constantly refers to Hesperus with "Phosphorus." Suppose further that he accepts "If there is waving, then Phosphorus will be happy" and wishes true "Phosphorus is happy." So smith waves at Hesperus and you ask me why he is waving at Hesperus. I might well say that he is doing so because he thinks that if there is waving, Hesperus will be happy, and he wants Hesperus to be happy. I would, I believe, be conveying an accurate explanation of why Smith waved, if folk psychological explanations are indeed explanations. The pragmatic principle mentioned above cannot explain how this is so; the account I have suggested can.

Philosophers are often bothered by appeals to pragmatics to explain intuitions about uses of language. Two reasons for this seem to be as follows: (1) pragmatic phenomena are often characterized in a way which makes it difficult to tell when a particular pragmatic implication obtains; (2) the decision to classify a particular phenomenon as pragmatic often seems arbitrary.

I think the proposal I have made is not liable to either of these objections. The account I have offered associates information conveyed by utterances with utterances in as systematic a way as does a traditional definition of truth for utterances. And I believe I can point to an acceptable principle, for sorting the truth conditional from the pragmatic, which justifies the way in which I have done it. Loosely formulated, the principle is that information conveyed by a number of conversational contributions instead of a single contribution, is a matter of pragmatic implicature, not truth conditions.

I have only sketched a view here, and I ought to indicate where it needs to be supplemented. The two primary lacunae are these. First, something more systematic about the construction of models of the attitudes of others needs to be said. The problems here are very much like those of what I called the variable identification problem for the implicit quantifier view.

The second lacuna is the absence of a discussion of how higher level information is conveyed by truth functionally and quantificationally complex sentences involving ascriptions, such as "Jones doesn't believe that Smith has come," "If it is Tuesday, then Jones thinks that it is Smith's birthday," and "Anyone who Jones thinks is married is married." I believe that natural generalizations of the mechanism I have presented can be given which do this.

---

[9] I discuss the behavior of variables, within and without attitude ascriptions, in Essay 3.

Take, for example, the negation of an ascription, like "Jones doesn't believe that Smith has come." We might plausibly suppose that such an ascription conveys second level information, to the effect that the current model of Jones cannot be correctly extended in a certain way—namely, by adding its content sentence to the belief column. I think a relatively straightforward extension of the notion of R-structure can be used here, but I will not go into it.

The view which I have sketched suggests that in interpreting attitude ascriptions, we have one basic strategy—extracting R-structure—which we apply in a number of ways. It eschews senses, save for the ersatz level of sense introduced by the picture of attitudes as relations to (constructions from) individuals and attributes mediated by a "more direct" relation to sentences. But this ersatz level of sense is not very threatening, and does not seem liable to many traditional objections to the doctrine of sense. For example, there seem to be no problems on this view about interpersonal identifications of sense. The view, I have argued, has all the virtues, in terms of accounting for pragmatic evidence, that traditional Fregeanism is thought to have.

I do not take the argument of this essay to refute Fregeanism as a semantic doctrine. The Fregean may help himself to a pragmatic account of attitude ascriptions, perhaps arriving at an account which is as adequate to the data as is the account I have suggested. My intent has been to incline you towards the view that Russellianism is no worse off in its ability to explain the data than is Fregeanism.

If this is correct, the choice between the views would have to be made on the basis of other considerations. Overall simplicity of theory and ontological cost are two criteria which come to mind. I am inclined to think that Russellianism may have the advantage in these regards. But I cannot argue for that here.[10]

---

[10] I am grateful to Harold Levin for conversations and corrections, and to Jody Azzouni for detailed comments on an earlier draft. I have a more general debt to Nathan Salmon and Scott Soames for conversations and correspondence on the topics of this essay.

5

How I Say What You Think

Mutt and Jeff agree on what sentences Odile accepts. They agree about her dispositions to behavior. They agree on just about everything which seems relevant to the question, does Odile believe that Twain is dead?

They don't agree on the answer. When Mutt was asked, it was because someone wanted to know whether Odile would list Twain under dead Americans. Mutt knew she accepted "Twain is dead" and thus said "yes." Jeff was asked by someone who couldn't understand why Odile, who's pointing to Twain's picture, wants to meet him. Doesn't she realize that Twain is dead? Jeff knew she rejected "he's dead." He answered that, no, Odile didn't believe that Twain was dead.

What are we to make of this? This essay investigates a way of saying that they're both right. Not because

(1)   Odile believes that Twain is dead

is syntactically ambiguous. Not because there is a semantic ambiguity in the sentence. At least, (1) is not semantically ambiguous in the way that, say,

(2)   Odile dropped Marie Bernard

is.

I propose that "believes" and other verbs of propositional attitude are indexical. The truth of (1) varies across Mutt's and Jeff's contexts. There is not a change in reference in expressions other than "believes," nor any change in Odile. And in some important sense "believes" remains constant in meaning. If we accept all this then we will say that "believes" is an indexical.

What varies across contexts that is relevant to the interpretation of "believes"? I think that it's what counts as an acceptable translation of the sentences (in a *very* broad sense of "sentence") Odile accepts; what varies is what functions are acceptable translation or correlation functions. (1) is true in a context iff its content sentence is an acceptable translation of some sentence Odile accepts. In Mutt's context, we may suppose, there are no substantive restrictions on translation at work: If Odile accepts ⌜a is dead⌝ for some name *a* of Twain, that makes (1) true, since "Twain is dead" here translates any such sentence. In Jeff's context, something more stringent is required. Perhaps it's required that Odile accept ⌜I am pointing at *a*⌝ before "Twain" can translate *a*.

I sketch some of the details of this view in Section I. The claim that attitude ascription involves translation will remind *cognoscenti* of Church's objections to Carnap's and other translational accounts of such sentences. In Section II, I turn to consider how the view fares in the face of some Church-style objections. Section III discusses Kripke's Pierre-London and Peter-Paderewski cases. I conclude with a discussion of some broadly logical issues.

I

I'm going to make a somewhat controversial assumption: that belief and the other attitudes are had in virtue of relations to sentence-like entities, whose constituents determine (relative to a context) Russellian referents. That is, when I have a belief, I'm related to a "sentence" which typically contains things which function like natural language proper names and demonstratives (in determining an individual), predicates (in determining properties or relations), as well as constituents which have the semantic roles of natural language connectives, quantifiers, and so on.

In fact, for simplicity, I am going to assume that attitudes like belief are realized by relations to natural language sentences. The account I'll give could get by with a *considerably* weaker assumption than this—for one thing, the mediators of belief needn't be sentences of a natural language. But I'll leave a discussion and defense of this assumption for another occasion.[1]

I thus assume a picture of the attitudes much like that assumed by many contemporary Russellians, who see belief as a relation to a Russellian entity, a relation mediated by relations to sentences or sentence-like entities.[2] I think this picture is a good first approximation to the truth about belief. But I am now unsatisfied with the account of belief *ascription* which the Russellian offers, on which "Odile believes that Twain is dead" and "Odile believes that Clemens is dead" must agree in truth value, since their "that"-clauses name the same Russellian proposition.

What shall we offer in its place? Consider the example of Hammurabi, who reputedly believed that Hesperus was Hesperus, but not that Hesperus was Phosphorus. If we allow ourselves to talk about belief blackboards and such, we can describe what the

---

[1] I defend this assumption in chapter 1 of Richard (1990).
[2] Such a view is strongly suggested, for example, by some passages in Kaplan (1989). Nathan Salmon invokes a more general notion, that of being acquainted with a proposition under a *guise* or *way of apprehending* such. (See Salmon (1986).) Salmon's guises are sententially structured at least to the extent of having parts corresponding to constituents of the proposition: "The means by which one is acquainted with a singular proposition includes as a part the means by which one is familiar with the individual constituent(s) of the proposition" (108).

relevant facts are: There are two possible mediators of Hammurabi's belief—pretend that they are

(1) $H = H$

and

(2) $H = P.$

Here, "*H*" is doing duty for the Babylonian word canonically translated "Hesperus"; "*P*," for that canonically translated "Phosphorus," and "=" goes proxy for a Babylonian identity predicate. Hammurabi, presumably, had (1) written on his blackboard, but not (2). It is this fact, or one like it, that someone who utters

(3) Hammurabi believes that Hesperus is Hesperus; but
(4) Hammurabi doesn't believe that Hesperus is Phosphorus

is trying to get across. The question is, how do (3) and (4) get this across?

In some way or other, in uttering (3) and (4) the speaker uses "Hesperus" to represent "*H*," "Phosphorus" to represent "*P*," and "is" to represent "=." And thus, the "that"-clause "that Hesperus is Hesperus" represents (1), while the "that"-clause "that Hesperus is Phosphorus" represents (2). (3) is true just in case what its t-clause represents is on Hammurabi's belief blackboard; likewise for (4). Since what (3)'s "that"-clause represents is on the board, while what (4)'s represents isn't, (3) is true while (4) is not.

It will be said, perhaps, that this is correct, but that it leaves unanswered the most important question: How does "Hesperus" come to represent "*H*"?

A popular answer is that "Hesperus" and "*H*" have the same or similar non-referential, cognitive content: they have the same or similar Fregean senses or conceptual roles (for the speaker and Hammurabi, respectively).

I've argued elsewhere that this sort of answer is untenable.[3] It is untenable because the sense (conceptual role, etc.) of a sentence will, on any reasonable account, vary intersubjectively. Here's a hint of the sort of problems which arise because of intersubjective variation. Observe that it's obvious that, if x can use sentence S to express a belief, and I can use S without altering the references of its expressions, then I can use S to ascribe to x the belief she expresses with S. If, for example, Odile can express a belief about Twain with "Twain is dead," then I could echo her words, and use "Odile believes that Twain is dead" to ascribe a belief to her.

Now this is so, even if Odile and I associate wildly divergent senses with the sentence "Twain is dead." Odile needn't *grasp* my sense for the sentence, for my ascription to be true. And what's more, when I echo someone's words to ascribe belief or assertion to them, I never seem to worry about identity or similarity of sense between their words and mine.

These facts refute Frege's account of attitude ascription. He held that in "Odile thinks that Twain is dead," the "that"-clause names a sense, my sense for "Twain is dead"; the

---

[3] I have argued for this in Richard (1988) and chapter 2 of Richard (1990).

sentence as a whole says that Odile believes the sense named. But as we saw, the ascription may be true even though Odile doesn't believe my sense for "Twain is dead."

We were wondering how "Hesperus" in "Ham believes that Hesperus is Hesperus" comes to represent one or another of the expressions in Ham's belief mediators. If we reject Fregean and allied accounts of attitude ascription, we will agree that the right answer to the question is *not*: "Hesperus" has for us the same sense, or cognitive role, as "*H*" for Hammurabi. Is, perhaps, the fact that one of the expressions conventionally translates the other relevant here?

Well, of course it's relevant. But it is also something which is an accidental feature of the example. Recall the case of Mutt, Jeff, and Odile. Jeff is asked if Odile believes that Twain is dead. His inquisitor wonders whether Odile, pointing at Twain's picture, realizes that Twain's dead. Jeff knows that she does not accept "that one is dead"; he says "Odile doesn't believe that Twain is dead." Jeff's use of "Twain" represents Odile's use of "he" or "that one." So *t* can represent *t'* without *t* being a conventional translation of *t'*, or vice versa.

In this case there doesn't seem to be any interesting connection—beyond sameness of Russellian referent—between Jeff's use of "Twain" and the part of Odile's belief mediator it represents. Beyond the identity of Russellian interpretation of "Twain" and "that one," there doesn't seem to be anything about the content of "Twain"—in an intuitive sense of "content"—which makes it an apt representative of Odile's use of "that one." The two needn't have the same cognitive content; neither need the one be a translation, in some meaty sense of "translation," of the other, etc.

The idea that there is something intrinsic to the content of Jeff's sentence, which would make it represent one but not another of the mediators of Odile's belief, is a mistake. "Twain" can in principle represent any name, demonstrative or indexical, which Odile uses to refer to Twain. Of course, given contextual factors, there may be something which makes "Twain" a more apt representative of "that one" than other expressions the speaker might have used. Given the context of Jeff's remark, it's clear to all—that is, to Jeff and the inquisitor—that what's at issue is whether or not Odile accepts "that one [Odile points at the picture] is dead." Given that the question the inquisitor asked was "Doesn't she realize that Twain's dead?" it is quite appropriate to use "Twain" as a representative of "that one."

The right answer to the question—How does *e* in

Odile believes that...*e*....

come to represent some expression (or class thereof) in Odile's belief mediators?—seems to go something like this. The interests and intentions of a speaker (and, to some extent his audience) determine how expressions in a "that"-clause may be and are used to represent mediators of belief. Sometimes, for example, the speaker and audience are focusing on a specific name or term or other way of representing something. This is what is going on in the case of Mutt and Jeff. This produces a restriction on what the expressions in a "that"-clause can represent. In Mutt's case, a restriction like—use "Twain" to represent "Twain"—

is operative. In Jeff's, something like—"Twain" is to represent only terms Odile associates with her current perceptual experience of Twain('s picture)—is operative.

Of course, in some situations we are not focusing on how someone thinks about the objects and properties about which they have beliefs. In some contexts, as the Russellian is fond of pointing out, we just don't care about the how of Odile's belief—that is, about the sentences whose acceptance constitute her beliefs—but only the Russellian what. In these situations there's no restriction operative on what "Twain" may represent—as long as it represents a name of Twain.

Let's see if we can parley these remarks into an account of the overall semantics of belief ascription. Perhaps the most straightforward way to proceed makes use of hybrids which come from fusing sentences and Russellian referents. Think of a sentence as being a set-theoretic entity. Identify, for example, "Twain is dead" with

(4)   <"is dead," "Twain">.

A pure Russellian can identify the proposition a sentence expresses (in a context) with the result of replacing the expressions in a sentence with their Russellian referents. In the case of (4), this yields

(5)   <being dead, Twain>.[4]

Consider what we get if we pair off the constituents of a sentence with their Russellian interpretations. If we do this with (4), for example, we get

(6)   <<"is dead," being dead>, <"Twain," Twain>>.

Such hybrids are not Russellian propositions. They are not Fregean thoughts. They are fusions of things which represent—in this case, the expressions in a "that"-clause—with their Russellian interpretations. Perhaps we should give them a new name, since they are somewhat different from run-of-the-mill propositions. Since they are obtained by annotating the matrix provided by a sentence with the Russellian interpretations of its parts, we call them RAMs, for Russellian Annotated Matrices.

In general, one gets RAMs by fusing English sentences and Russellian referents, German sentences and such referents, indeed, from fusing arbitrary things which could be words or representations with Russellian referents. Take an arbitrary set of objects which could play the roles of parts of a language or system of representations. Pair off these "vocabulary" items with the parts of a Russellian proposition, and you have a RAM. The RAM represents, in a somewhat crude way, what it is for a sentence made out of the "vocabulary" to express the proposition.

---

[4] I ignore, here and elsewhere, complications introduced by tense.
The identification of Russellian propositions (and RAMs) with interpreted sentence structures must of course be made with some care. The structures cannot invariably be surface structures, if only because of the existence of idioms. So I assume some assignment of "logical forms" to sentences, which will yield Russellian propositions when their linguistic constituents are replaced with interpretations.

Think now of the believer. She accepts various sentences, each of which has a Russellian interpretation. Just as we can fuse the content sentence of a t-clause with its Russellian interpretation, mating (4) and (5) to get (6), so can we do this to each of the mediators of the believer's belief. If we do this for all of the mediators of her beliefs, we end up with a set of RAMs. This set encodes all of the facts about the believer which are relevant to the truth and falsity of belief ascriptions to her. Let's call this set the believer's representational system, or RS.

When we ascribe an attitude, using, say

(7) Odile believes that Twain is dead

we seem to be saying something about the believer's RS, and not something simply about the collection of Russellian propositions believed. The remarks we made above suggest that what we are doing is saying (roughly) that the RAM our "that"-clause determines represents one of the believer's RAMs.

For our RAM to represent one of the believer's RAMs, it seems necessary (but not always sufficient) that our RAM be related to the believer's in a certain straightforward way. Putting the matter crudely, the necessary condition is that, stripped of their linguistic parts, the two RAMs amount to the same Russellian proposition.

Let's not rest with a crude statement of the condition. Call the pairs of things in RAMs, consisting of a vocabulary item and an interpretation, annotations. So <"Twain," Twain> is an annotation, <"he," Twain> is an annotation, <"is dead," being dead> is an annotation, and so forth.

Say that a correlation is a rule (a function) which maps annotations to annotations and preserves reference: that is, if a correlation takes $<a,b>$ to $<a',b'>$, then b is b'. It's often convenient to speak as if correlations just mapped expressions to expressions, leaving the fact that annotations contain references as understood. Thus, for example, I'll sometimes say things like such and such a correlation takes "Twain" to "Clemens" and "Clemens" to "Clemens."

Take a RAM p, and a correlation f (assume f is defined for all the annotations in p). Consider what we get if we systematically replace what's in p with its image under f. For example, if we begin with the RAM p determined by

Hesperus is Phosphorus

and use the correlation

f: "Hesperus" → "H"; "Phosphorus" → "P"; "is" → "="

we obtain the RAM—call it q—determined by

$H = P$.

When p, q, and f are related in this way—q comes from p via the correlation f—I say that p represents q under f.

The relation I mentioned above, the one that is necessary for the truth of a belief ascription

Odile believes that S

is that the RAM determined by the "that"-clause represent, under some correlation or another, a RAM in Odile's RS. So, for example, our old friend

(7) Odile believes that Twain is dead

is true only if the RAM determined by the "that"-clause

(6) <<"is dead," being dead>, <"Twain,"Twain>>

represents, under some correlation, a RAM in Odile's RS. As I remarked above, this is roughly equivalent to what the Russellian thinks to be necessary and sufficient for the truth of (6).

But we don't think it to be *sufficient* for the truth of a use of (7). As remarked above, sometimes we impose restrictions on the way an expression can be used to represent parts of the mediators of someone's belief. Some contexts contain restrictions on the functions we may use to correlate our RAM (the one determined by the "that"-clause in an attitude ascription) and the RAMs in the subject's RS. When Mutt uttered (7), it was understood that "Twain" was to represent "Twain" and nothing else. So in evaluating Mutt's claim for truth, we are restricted in what correlations we can use. We can only use ones which map "Twain" to "Twain." What Mutt said was true provided that his RAM ((6) above) represents one of Odile's RAMs under a "Twain" to "Twain" correlation.

A context, then, provides a collection of restrictions on correlations. We can think of each restriction provided by a context as containing three things: A person u, an annotation a, and a collection of annotations S. For example, Mutt's context provides the restriction

Odile; <"Twain,"Twain>; {<"Twain,"Twain>}

A restriction involving u, a, and S tells us that, in evaluating an ascription of attitude to u, we are restricted to using correlations which map a to something in S. Mutt's restriction, for example, tells us that in evaluating an ascription to Odile, we are restricted to using correlations which map "Twain" to "Twain."

Our remarks above may now be codified as follows: Taken in a context, call it c, an ascription of the form of

a believes that S

is true if and only if the RAM determined (in c) by S represents a RAM in the representational system of what a names (in c), under a correlation which obeys all the restrictions operative in c. Or, a bit more loosely: the ascription is true iff the

RAM *that S* represents one of *a*'s RAMs, given the context's restrictions on correlations.[5]

It should be tolerably clear how this proposal works in the case of Mutt, Jeff, and Odile. In the case of Hammurabi, too, matters seem relatively straightforward. Suppose we have heard the story of the ancient Babylonians, and say that Hammurabi believes that Hesperus is Hesperus, but not that Hesperus is Phosphorus. Given our focus on the way Hammurabi thought about the planets, it is natural to suppose that we are operating under the restrictions

Ham; <"Hesperus," Hesperus>; {<the Babylonian word which "Hesperus" conventionally translates,Venus>}

Ham; <"Phosphorus," Phosphorus>; {<the Babylonian word which "Phosphorus" conventionally translates,Venus>}.

We can abbreviate here, and represent the restrictions thus:

Ham: "Hesperus" → the Babylonian it conventionally translates

Ham: "Phosphorus" → the Babylonian it conventionally translates.

Given these restrictions, as well as the non-controversial assumptions— "Hesperus" conventionally translates "H," and not "P"; "Phosphorus" conventionally translates "P," and not "H"; the facts about what Ham accepted as given at the beginning of this section—it is clear that the RAM determined by "Hesperus is Hesperus" represents one of Ham's RAMs, relative to the context's restrictions, but that determined by "Hesperus is Phosphorus" does not. If we are ascribing belief to Hammurabi, the latter RAM

---

[5] It is probably not obvious what the semantic value of the verb "believes" is supposed to be. Simplifying somewhat: "Believes" and its ilk are to be treated as indexicals. They have a constant meaning, or, to use Kaplan's term, character; their interpretation, or content, varies from context to context. The character of "believes" is a rule which, given a collection of restrictions, returns an appropriate intension. Since "believes" looks at a person and a RAM—it acts as a dyadic predicate which joins a term like "Odile" with something that names a RAM, like "that Twain is dead"—appropriate intensions for "believes" will be functions from pairs, of individuals and RAMs, to sets of worlds. Write

Rep (p, q, f)

for "*p* represents *q* under *f* ". Write

Obey (r, f, u)

for *f* obeys all the restrictions in *r* which are relevant to *u*'. (A restriction $<x, a, S>$ is revelant to *u* iff $x = u$; *f* obeys the restriction if $f(a)$ is in S.) Then, if *r* is the collection of restrictions operative in *c*, "believes" takes as value in *c* the function which maps $<u,p>$ to the set X of worlds such that *w* is in X iff, at *w*, *u* has a RAM in her RS such that, for some *f*, Obey (r, f, u) and Rep (p, q, f).

The simplification here is that of making "believes" two-placed. In Richard (1990), the proposal of this essay is given an alternative development, in which the verb is made three-place, with the extra argument place one for correlations. This allows the nicest formalization of the treatment of Kripke's puzzles which is given in Section III of this essay. The resulting system retains the virtues of the system of this essay—e.g., it avoids Church-style objections and allows the sorts of generalizations discussed in Section IV.

<<"is," Identity>, <<"Hesperus,"Venus>, <"Phosphorus,"Venus>>>

can, given the restrictions, *only* represent a RAM of the form

<<*e*, Identity>, <<"*H*," Venus>, <"*P*," Venus>>>

where *H* and *P* are fixed as above. (Since there are no restrictions on "is," *e* can be any piece of vocabulary.) Since such a RAM is clearly not in Hammurabi's RS, the claim that he believes that Hesperus is Phosphorus is false.

Isn't this a sort of closet Fregeanism, with expressions in "that"-clauses doing duty for the senses of expressions for those to whom we ascribe attitudes? I don't want to quibble about the epithet (or honorific, depending on your perspective) "Fregean." If you're willing to accept this account, and it makes you feel better about things to call it Fregean, by all means do so. But we have wandered quite far from any *traditional* sort of Fregeanism. For example, as I observed above, this view abandons the Fregean view, that attitude ascription involves a match of non-referential, cognitive content between a t-clause and some state of, or sentence accepted by, the subject of the ascription. Whether or not Mutt and Odile associate similar ways of thinking of Twain with their uses of "Twain" is wholly irrelevant to the question, "Does, or could, Mutt use 'Twain' to represent Odile's uses of 'Twain'?" In fact, one can comfortably hold the sort of view I am urging and insist that, in general, interpersonal comparisons of a sentence's sense or cognitive role cannot be made. One could say, for instance, that such comparisons presuppose an isomorphism of the subjective probability functions users associate with their sentences, a sort of isomorphism which, practically speaking, is never to be found.

Furthermore, there is nothing in this view which suggests that associated with a use of an expression, as a matter of the expression's meaning or otherwise, is a descriptive condition which determines the expression's reference. This view does not retain even the shade of the idea that sense determines reference.

It is also worth comparing the way this and Fregean views treat quantification into attitude ascriptions. For Fregeans, quantification into an attitude ascription, as in

(8)   There's an x such that Odile believes that x is dead

involves implicit quantification over senses, with (8) being glossed as

For some x and s: s is a sense which presents x and Odile believes $^s s$ is dead^s,

the "*s*"s here being "sense quotes." The view I've glossed allows a straightforward, objectual treatment of quantification in. Relative to an assignment v to the variables, the sentence "x is dead," "x" a variable, determines the RAM

<<"is dead," being dead>, <"x," v ("x")>>.

For example, if v("x") is Twain, then "x is dead" determines the RAM

<<"is dead," being dead>, <"x", Twain>>.

This can represent one of Odile's RAMs just as well as the RAM that Twain is dead. So quantification in is treated quite straightforwardly, with (8) true just in case "Odile believes that x is dead" is true for some assignment to "x."[6]

It would be misleading to say that the view of attitude ascriptions I am sketching has nothing in common with Fregean views. Like the Fregean, I see the truth of an attitude ascription as being sensitive to facts about the way an individual represents objects and properties. But I reject the mechanism the Fregean proposes to explain this sensitivity. I also would prefer to be committed to as "thin" an account of ways of thinking as possible. I am somewhat dubious of the significance of comparisons of non-referential content across speakers, and am trying to offer an account which avoids them. In fact, so far I've said nothing that commits us to a very interesting notion of *intra*personal identity of non-referential content, between different expressions or "modes of thought."

My account also has a good deal in common with Russellian accounts of attitude ascription. It rejects the idea that senses or non-referential, cognitive "contents" like conceptual roles are apt semantic values for "that"-clauses. It is compatible with views about reference—for example, that names and demonstratives are directly referential—which partially motivate Russellianism. My view honors the intuitive evidence for Russellianism—for example, that the truth of an attitude ascription is often unaffected by substituting one directly referential expression for another which names the same thing. It gives a natural, objectual account of quantifying in. But unlike Russellian-ism, this account is consistent with the idea that, for example, someone might know that Clark Kent is Clark Kent, but not know that Clark Kent is Superman.

II

On my view, a "that"-clause of English names is something quite different from its natural translation into German. "that Twain is dead" names something in which the expression "is dead" occurs; its German translation, "*dass Twain tot ist*" names something in which the German expression "*ist tot*" occurs. You might anticipate that this would make English belief ascriptions and their natural German translations diverge in truth conditions in an objectionable way.

This, in essence, was Church's complaint against Carnap.[7] I do not think that any version of this objection has force against the account I've given. Consider first

(1)   Odile believes that Twain is dead

---

[6] I assume that a context cannot provide restrictions on how free variables are treated by correlations. This is necessary (and sufficient) to validate arguments like

   Odile thinks that Twain is dead.
   Thus, for some x, Odile thinks that x is dead.

I think this account of quantification in escapes the objections which Scott Soames made to the account I proposed in Chapter 3. Soames' objections are in Soames (1987).

[7] Church (1950).

and its German translation

(1')   Odile glaubt, dass Twain tot ist.

If a sentence has indexical elements, we can speak of its truth conditions only relative to a particular context or use. We are treating "believes" as an indexical, and would give its German translation "glaubt" a perfectly parallel treatment. So both (1) and (1') can be assigned truth conditions only relative to a context.

Now, there are a number of worries you might have about the way in which truth conditions are assigned to uses of (1) and (1') on this theory. For example, you might complain that a use of (1) in one context and a use of (1') in some other context could have different truth conditions. And this, you might say, is unacceptable, (1) and (1') being translations of one another.

Of course (1) and (1') can be used, so that they have different truth conditions. But this is no objection: One of the *motivations* for this view, you will recall, is that sentence (1) *itself* can be used in such a way that it says different things in different contexts. One reason for adopting the view is that a sentence like (1) is used some, but not all, of the time to say something quite specific about the how of Odile's belief. The same is true of (1'). So the observation that (1) and (1') might be used to say different things is not an objection to the theory.

For another thing, you might worry that no use of (1) can have precisely the truth conditions of a use of (1'). *If* this were true it would be a serious objection.

However, consider "believes" and "glaubt." There is no reason that they can't have exactly the same meaning. (To use Kaplan's terminology: They have the same character.) The verbs' common meaning is something which given a contextually supplied "translation manual" (i.e., a set of restrictions) pairs off people and RAMs: Person P is paired with a RAM R, provided R represents, under the manual, a RAM that P has in his RS. Of course, the manuals the English verb is given are usually different from those the German verb gets. So in context the verbs typically have different contents. But this is consistent with their having the same meaning. (The situation is to *some* extent parallel to that of "I" and "*ich*"—in contexts they may refer to different things; the two still have the same meaning.)

Thus it is perfectly possible for uses of (1) and (1') to have the same truth conditions. (I suppose truth conditions to be sets of worlds.) If (1) is used in a context in which no restrictions are operative, then (speaking roughly) (1) says that Odile accepts some sentence of the form $D(t)$, where D refers to being dead, and t refers to Twain. Used in a context without restrictions, (1') says exactly the same thing.

Even when restrictions are operative, (1) and (1') may have the same truth conditions. For example, suppose (1) is used in a context c in which the restrictions require that "is dead" be mapped to "is dead" (and no other restriction is operative). A use of (1') in a context in which just the restriction Map "*ist tot*" to "is dead" is operative will be one in which (1') is assigned the same truth conditions as is (1) in c.

Here is another issue raised by Church's objections to Carnap's account of attitude ascriptions. Church himself noted that his objection to Carnap was really only forceful for the case of iterated attitude ascriptions like

(2) John believes that Hammurabi believes that Hes is hot

and their natural translations into foreign languages.[8]

What will we assign a "that"-clause in which "believes" occurs, like "that Hammurabi believes that Hes is hot"? What we need to know is whether, in constructing a RAM for this, we pair off "believes" with its meaning (the rule for getting from context to content) or with its content in a particular context. It's clear that for most indexicals we should pair the indexical off with its content. Thus, for example, in a context where I am speaking, the "that"-clause in

(3) Peter believes that I am fat

should name the RAM

(3') <<"is fat," being fat>, <"I," Mark Richard>>.

The exception to this rule is the verbs of attitude. In constructing the RAM that Hammurabi believes that Hes is hot, "believes" is paired with its (context-independent) meaning. We also think of the RAMs in the believer's representational system, which

---

[8] Ascriptions like (2) raise the following problem. Consider an ascription like (2) in the context of a pure Russellian account. The Russellian assigns a relation to "believes" and a structured entity to the "that"-clause. The assignment to the "that"-clause contains the semantic values of the expressions in the "that"-clause. So if the "that"-clause contains "believes"—as it does in (2)—we have the relation assigned to the main verb—the belief relation—trying to relate something which contains that very relation. Besides sounding like the opening of a book by Kierkegaard, this is more or less like a function taking itself as an argument, something which on the normal set-theoretic understanding of a function is impossible.

I have investigated what happens, in a system like the one I have been sketching, if we stratify the belief predicate, more or less in the way Tarski stratified the truth predicate, by introducing a series of languages. (This requires that RAMs come in levels, as well.) I have found nothing untoward in the system, save that it requires fragmenting "believes" (as Tarski's approach, adapted to natural language, would require fragmenting "true").

I am aware that many people object to this way of treating "true" in natural languages. I believe that other treatments of "believes" would also work here—in particular, I think that modeling propositions and the semantic values of expressions like "believes" in a set theory like that of Peter Aczel's, in which sets can be members of themselves, would mesh quite well with the approach I am sketching, and would yield a more satisfactory treatment of "believes." (Aczel (1988).) But at present I have not fully investigated this.

In the text, I suppress all reference to this complication. This essay is about the way expressions—in particular, singular terms and garden variety predicates—function within the scope of attitude verbs. It is not about the semantical paradoxes or paradoxes like the knower. While the latter are of course important, I think it is fair to ignore them in discussing the current problems. One insoluble problem at a time, please.

In Section IV, when I discuss the introduction of a truth predicate, I again ignore the fact that some method to forestall paradox is needed. Again, I have investigated a series of languages approach here, each with a truth predicate for the languages below, in the context of implementing the proposal of this paper. Other than objections to the levels approach, which are not relevant to the issues this paper is concerned with, I do not see any problems with the resulting system.

correspond to sentences in which "believes" occurs, as being constructed out of the meaning of "believes," not out of its content in the believer's context.

If we proceed in this way, there's nothing particularly puzzling about iterations of "believes." Consider, for example, (2) and its natural German translation. The only difference between what the English

> that Hammurabi believes that Hes is hot

names and what its natural German translation names is in the vocabulary items in the RAMs. There's no difference in the semantic values paired with the vocabulary.

So what we will say here will be exactly parallel with what we would say about (1) and (1'). For example, suppose that we use (2) in a context without restrictions. Suppose further that John accepts the sentence "Hammurabi believes that Hes is hot." Then what we say is true. It's easy to work out that a use of the natural German translation of (2) ("*John glaubt, dass Hammurabi glaubt, dass Hes heiss ist*," or something of the sort), used in a context with no restrictions, will be true in the same circumstance. In fact, it will have the same truth conditions.

A last, related objection. Ali Kazmi pointed out to me that on my view, a sentence like "Odile believes that Cologne is large" and its translation into a foreign language (say, "*Odile glaubt, dass Köln gross ist*") may differ in truth value taken relative to one context. For the context may provide restrictions which deal only with English vocabulary, not with foreign language vocabulary. Kazmi suggested that this was a problem.

If it is a problem, it is because of the truth of a principle like:

> (I) If a sentence type *S* of one language is naturally and correctly translated by a sentence type *T* of a second language, then there is no context relative to which *S* and *T* do not have the same truth values.

I doubt that (I) is true. As I understand it, there is a sort of animal, the woodchuck, for which English has two expressions ("woodchuck" and "groundhog"), where French has but one ("la marmotte"). The French "*Louis croit que Chuck est une marmotte*" is thus correctly and naturally translated by both "Louis believes that Chuck is a woodchuck" and "Louis believes that Chuck is a groundhog." But presumably, the latter two sentences can diverge in truth value relative to some context. So the French and a natural and correct translation thereof will diverge in truth value relative to some context.

III

I want to discuss Kripke's puzzle about belief, both in its version involving Pierre, "London," and "Londres," and that involving Peter and "Paderewski." I assume familiarity with the case of Pierre. Kripke writes "This is the puzzle: Does Pierre, or does he not, believe that London is pretty?" Kripke argues successively that

> (1) Pierre believes that London is pretty

is (or at least seems) true (focusing, of course, on Pierre's "French beliefs"); that

(2)   Pierre believes that London is not pretty

is (or at least seems) true (focusing now on Pierre's "English beliefs"); but that they can't both be true, because Pierre, a leading logician, "would *never* let contradictory beliefs pass. And surely anyone, leading logician or no, is in principle in a position to notice and correct contradictory beliefs if he has them."[9]

What counts as a solution to the puzzle? Certainly, all else being equal, we want to preserve as much of our pre-theoretic intuitions about sentences (1) and (2) as possible. This suggests that in the ideal, a solution to the puzzle will provide a way of saying that both sentences are true—that is, the uses Kripke makes of them, when he ascribes truth to them, are true uses; and yet (1) and (2) together can't be true, for more or less the very reason Kripke gives.

One nice thing about the view I've been sketching is that it does allow us to say something like this. One way in which restrictions on correlations should come to be operative is this: If the speaker is focusing on how someone expresses his beliefs, thinks that his audience is so focusing (and thinks his audience thinks he knows that they are so focusing), then the appropriate restrictions tend to come into play. So when Kripke begins walking us through the puzzle, focusing on Pierre's French beliefs, we might expect the restriction

(3)   "London" → "*Londres*"

to be operative. This will make (1) true. Then Kripke asks us to focus on Pierre's English language beliefs. The old restriction is no longer operative, and a new one

(4)   "London" → "London"

comes into play. So (2) is true. Then Kripke asks us, in effect, to answer the question: Can (1) and (2) be true together? And he observes that they seem to imply that Pierre is in some sense irrational.

And this is quite correct. Any natural way of evaluating (1) and (2) in the context of one conversation will use a single correlation function. It would be unnatural to adopt a completely new correlation each time we reascribe belief (or desire or another attitude) to an individual within the course of a single discourse.[10] So any natural way of evaluating

---

[9] Kripke (1979), 257.
[10] Conversational principles ("Don't be confusing") alone dictate this much. Furthermore, only if we assume that sets of ascriptions are to be so interpreted does the widespread belief—that explanations of action in terms of beliefs and desires are at least candidates for true explanations—even make sense. For example, the claims
   Randi thought that if there were waving, Ann would smile
   Randi wished that Ann smile
evaluated together, instead of separately, are true only if (roughly speaking) part of Randi's overall text (the family of sets of sentences believed-true, wished-true, and so on) looked thus:

the conjunction of (1) and (2) makes it false.[11] And it is false for just the reason Kripke suggests: It suggests that Pierre is irrational, accepting some sentence and its negation. It is (roughly) in this sense that anyone with contradictory beliefs is in a position to recognize such and correct it.

The case of Peter and "Paderewski" may appear to present something of a problem for my view. The case seems like that of Pierre and "London"—"*Londres*": Peter hears one day of a famous musician, Paderewski, and thinks to himself "Paderewski had musical talent." He hears on some other day of a Polish statesman, Paderewski. Thinking that politicians are poor musicians, he thinks to himself "Paderewski did not have musical talent." We have, Kripke urges, exactly the same sort of puzzle about

(5) Peter believes that Paderewski had musical talent
(6) Peter believes that Paderewski did not have musical talent

as we did concerning the Pierre sentences.

I suggested that on any natural reading of the Pierre sentences they wouldn't be true in the same context. It would seem that I can't say this sort of thing about this case. For here there seems to be but one sentence (type), that of

Paderewski had musical talent

one such that Peter accepts both it and its negation. So it seems that no matter what restrictions are operative, if (5) is true, so is (6). So, it appears, I have to treat like cases (Pierre and Peter) in unlike ways.

Belief: $W \to Sa$; Desire: Sa

where W, Sa, and a are expressions determining the set of worlds in which there's waving, the property of smiling, and Ann, respectively. But it is plausible to think that this being true is a reason for thinking that Randi waved. So the explanation which goes "Randi waved, because he thought that if there were waving, Ann would smile, and he wanted Ann to smile" can plausibly be said, in a very straightforward sense, to be a genuine explanation. If, on the other hand, we switch correlations in midstream, then the truth of the belief and desire ascriptions gives us no reason to think that Randi will wave.

The fact that on this view we can make sense of the *idea* that action could be explained by attitude ascription is surely a strong reason to prefer this approach to Russellianism. For on Russellian grounds the truth of the premises of a belief-desire explanation gives one *absolutely no reason whatsoever* to think its conclusion true.

It is not trivial to systematically assign truth conditions to complex sentences (i.e., ones containing truth functional and temporal operators, as well as quantifiers), once we allow that sentences of the form *he believes that S, and he believes that T* can have truth conditions on which they imply that *that S* and *that T* represent RAMs under a single correlation, especially if we want to preserve the validity of classical logical principles. I try to characterize one way of assigning truth conditions, while preserving classical logic, in chapter 4 of Richard (1990).

[11] I do have to say that there is a way of interpreting the conjunction of (2) and (3) so that it is true. If we are in a context in which no restrictions are operative, and we interpret the ascriptions singly, and not jointly, then both (2) and (3) will be true. I don't think that this is a disaster. First of all, as I argued above, this is a very unnatural way to evaluate multiple ascriptions. So, I think, I may fairly say that the account I've been presenting leads us to expect that there will be at best a weak inclination among speakers to say that (2) and (3) are both true, if they are presented together. And this is what we do seem to find.

And we do have *some* inclination to say that in the case of Pierre that both are true. Most of us are inclined to reason as follows: Well, (2) *is* true. And, gosh, (3) *is* true. (Notice one does this by evaluating (2) and (3) individually.) So I guess (gulp) their conjunction is true.

I do not think I do. I could say that the expression "Paderewski" in Peter's spoken dialect is ambiguous: appearances to the contrary, Peter does not accept some natural language sentence and its negation. I think this somewhat *ad hoc*, so I will try to get by without saying it.

Let's go back to the picture of belief that we are working with. Think of the believer as having sentence tokens written inside of his head, on a blackboard next to the pineal gland. Think of his representational system, the set of RAMs we quantify over in giving truth conditions for attitude ascriptions, as being determined somehow by what's written on the blackboard.

Up to now, I have been pretending that the way the blackboard determined the RAMs was as follows. Suppose a token of "Twain is dead" is on Odile's blackboard. Then a RAM that looks thus:

<<"is dead," being dead>, <"Twain," Twain>>

is in Odile's RS. Here, the quoted items are the types of the relevant tokens. On this picture, we would have in the case of Peter a RAM and its negation in Peter's representational system. (I haven't defined a negation of operation for RAMs, but it's obvious, I think, how to go about it.)

I want now to distinguish between the sentence tokens on the blackboard and representations. I think of the sentences on the believer's blackboard as determining representations; in constructing RAMs to put in the believer's RS, we form them from the representations which the sentences on the blackboard determine. Instead of putting *expression* and referent in the RAM, we pair the *representation* determined by the expression with the expression's referent.

To return to the example above: If Odile tokens "Twain is dead," then her RS contains the RAM

<<R1, being dead>, <R2, Twain>>

where R1 and R2 are the representations determined by her tokens of "is dead" and "Twain," respectively.

We could identify representations with sets of tokens on the blackboard. Then we have only the problem of saying when two inscriptions on the blackboard determine the same representation. I won't give a full-blown theory about this. But I think such a theory is possible, and I think its broad outlines are fairly clear.

As I see it, there will be two sorts of conditions which together will be necessary and sufficient for two tokens to determine the same representation. Intuitively, the two sorts of conditions are what we could call "outside" and "inside" conditions. The outside conditions will be broadly causal in nature. If we have two proper name tokens written on the blackboard, for example, they will have to be residues of the same causal or historical chain (and thus refer to the same thing) in order to satisfy the outside condition. I take it that this will result, if we make the outside condition (in the case of proper name tokens) that two proper name tokens determine the same representation only if they are tokens of the same name (type). Let us do this. Observe that this rules out, for example, "Hesperus" and "Phosphorus" determining the same representation.

The interior condition should be a "recognition" condition. Let me speak rather intuitively about this. Usually, when we hear someone talking about someone, we think we know who is being talked about. We *hear* someone say "Reagan is going to bomb Nicaragua," and assume that it's Reagan the president who is being discussed, not the Regan the animal rights philosopher. When this happens, we somehow "file" the token of "Reagan" we are hearing with certain other tokens ("presidential tokens") on our blackboard, and segregate if from others. In such a case, the new token of "Reagan" has the interior relation to the presidential tokens. Our segregating the new token with the older ones is a sort of "recognition." Suppose that it was the president that was being talked about, and that outside conditions were satisfied. Then, with both outside and inside conditions satisfied, the new token of "Reagan" and the older presidential tokens will all determine the same representation.[12]

I haven't given a theory of representations here, of course. At the least, before I have even the vague outlines of a theory, I need to talk about demonstratives and sensuous experiences. It's a lacuna, but for now I have to live with it.

In the case of Peter, we have a token of "Paderewski has talent" on one place on the blackboard, a token "Paderewski has no talent" somewhere else. It is quite clear, I hope, that on any way of spelling them out, the interior conditions will not be satisfied with respect to the two tokens of "Paderewski." So they determine different representations.

This means that, in principle, we can treat the Paderewski case just as we treated the case of Pierre.

IV

I close by mentioning some issues of a broadly logical nature. First of all, we can introduce propositional quantifiers and variables, letting them range over the class of all RAMs. These are treated as one would expect, with

For all p: a believes $p \rightarrow b$ believes p

being true just in case any assignment of a RAM to "p" makes the matrix sentence true.

---

[12] I assume that all the old presidential tokens are tokens which refer to Reagan the president. Incidentally, I take the interior, "recognition," condition to be such that terms which do not name the same thing may satisfy it. For example, suppose I hear "Reagan will bomb Nicaragua," and see someone point at a man and say "he is president." If I "group" "Reagan" and "he" together (I take the same person to be spoken of and ostended), the terms satisfy the interior condition, even if the man pointed at was not Reagan.

I should say here that, while none of what I say can be attributed to David Kaplan, much of it is influenced by various remarks he has made about identity of words, recognition, and other matters.

A second issue is that of RAMs and truth bearers. Traditional Russellian propositions are both the objects of attitudes and the bearers of truth. Many RAMs are indistinguishable, *qua* truth bearers, from such. The RAM of "Hesperus is hot," for example, is more or less the Russellian proposition that Hesperus is hot with some extra material in it, material we can ignore for the purposes of assigning truth conditions.

But RAMs corresponding to sentences in which belief predicates occur are in a certain sense incomplete. For these RAMs contain the (context constant) meaning of "believes," not one of its contextually varying contents. If we appoint RAMs to the office of official bearers of truth, then we will have some truth bearers—e.g., that Odile believes that Twain is dead—which are true in some contexts and false in others.

This means I'm committed to either (a) contextual variation in the truth value of the bearers of truth, or (b) uses of a sentence like "It's true that Odile believes that Twain is dead" ascribing a property not to the RAM that Odile believes that Twain is dead, but to a supplemented RAM, a pair consisting of the RAM and the restrictions operative in the context of use.

There's nothing objectionable *per se* about either (a) or (b). There is, after all, a long tradition which sees the object of belief as changing truth value across contexts. Some have wanted to say, for example, that the proposition that Reagan is president is true now, but—patience—won't always be true. I happen to disagree that the objects of belief change truth value in response to change of time. But just because objects of belief don't change truth value in response to some contextual variations doesn't mean that they don't respond to others. And there is evidence that certain objects of belief have their truth value relativized, in one way or another, to context. When Mutt and Jeff say "Odile thinks that Twain is dead," we agree that, within the confines of their respective conversations, one may speak truly, the other falsely. But they both believe that Odile believes that Twain is dead. So it looks as if one thing, their common belief, is true at one place, false at another.

In any case, we evaluate beliefs for truth, as well as tie the truth of beliefs to the truth of the sentences which express them. So we should give some account of how truth and RAMs are related. A natural way to do this is as follows. Let us say that a supplemented RAM is a pair consisting of a regular RAM and a set of restrictions. Note that a sentence taken in a context determines a unique supplemented RAM: pair the RAM the sentence determines with the contextual restrictions.

A supplemented RAM will determine truth conditions, and thus a truth value at the actual world, in a straightforward way. If the RAM corresponds to a sentence with no belief operator, the supplemented RAM has the truth conditions of the corresponding Russellian proposition. If the RAM corresponds to a sentence with a belief operator, one uses the set of restrictions in the supplemented RAM to turn the meaning of the "believes" operator into a content, and then assigns truth conditions in the way suggested by the truth definition for belief ascriptions.

We can thus introduce a predicate "is true" which combines with "that"-terms to form sentences. ⌜That S is true⌝ is itself true in a context c iff the supplemented RAM consisting of the RAM named by ⌜that S⌝ in c and the set of restrictions in c is true. The predicate behaves nicely enough. We have such intuitively satisfying results as the validity of the argument schema:

For all p: a believes p → p is true

a believes that S

Thus, that S is true.[13]

Finally, I'll say something about reference to, and individuation of, propositions. We ought to treat ⌜that S⌝ and ⌜the proposition that S⌝ in the same way. So let terms of the latter form name what those of the former do.

People will object that this cuts propositions far too finely. I can't answer every objection to the fineness of the cut here, so I'll address only the one I think most serious.

Objection: Surely the sentences "snow is white" and "la neige est blanche" say the same thing, a thing which Odile believes. So there's something, p, such that Odile believes p, "snow is white" says p, and "la neige est blanche" says p. You have to deny this, because you say that the proposition that snow is white is distinct from that named by "que la neige est blanche."

Response: Well, this depends upon the exact semantics of "say" as it is used in "'snow is white' says that snow is white," doesn't it?

Note, in working up to an account of this use of "says," that it does not make sense to assess what a sentence says, unless we imagine the sentence taken relative to some context or other. After all, "London is pretty" says one thing at noon (that London is pretty then), and quite another at six o'clock.

Suppose we take a sentence relative to a context c. The sentence will determine a RAM p in the context. We can ask whether p represents, relative to the restrictions of the context, various other RAMs. Call the set of RAMs so represented p's profile in the context. (Strictly, the profile of a RAM is a function from worlds to pairs of an individual and a RAM, since restrictions are keyed to individuals.) Then we might say that

"S" in context d says that T

is true in a context c iff the profile in c of the RAM determined by T in c is identical with the profile in d of the RAM determined by S in d.

If we suppose that we are working in a context in which no restrictions are operative, and that "la neige est blanche" and "snow is white" are to be taken relative to that context, then it will be true that "snow is white" says (in the context) that snow is white, and "la neige est blanche" (in the context) says that snow is white. And so it will be true

---

[13] I suppose consequence to be defined as follows: Sentence A is a consequence of a set S of sentences (in a model M, relative to a context c thereof) iff for any w in the model, if w is in the intension of each member S, taken relative to c, then w is in the intension of A, taken relative to c. (Intuitively, this amounts to: A is a consequence of S iff, taken in any context, what S's members say jointly entails what A says.) Logical consequence is a relation between sets of sentence types defined by the obvious generalization of the above.

(assuming Odile's beliefs are rightly arranged) that there's a p such that Odile believes p, "snow is white" says p, and "la neige est blanche" says p.[14]

---

[14] I assume, of course, that "*la neige*" is a syntactical unit.

I am indebted to Ed Gettier for a discussion of an earlier draft of this essay, as well as for conversations over the years on the topics of this paper. David Austin, Jody Azzouni, Harold Levin, Graeme Forbes, and Ali Kazmi made helpful editorial and philosophical comments on versions of the paper, for which I thank them as well. I acknowledge a general debt to Richard Grandy, who tried many years ago to convince me that attitude ascription had something to do with translation.

6

Attitudes in Context

Why has the semantics of attitude ascription proven so difficult? Some say the fault lies in a contextual shiftiness of sentences like

(P) Pierre believes that London is expensive,

a shiftiness not evident from surface structure, and thus liable to be overlooked. On this view, different uses of (P) convey different information about Pierre's representations of London. But though the information is semantically conveyed, conveyance is not via a sentential constituent whose role is to refer to or otherwise pick out representations about which information is imparted.

I have offered a version of this view on which attitude ascription involves something like translation.[1] In (P), "that London is expensive" is offered as a representation or translation of one of Pierre's thoughts; a use of (P) is true provided its "that"-clause is an acceptable translation of such a thought, according to currently prevailing (and contextually shifting) standards of translation. Such standards are keyed to and shift because of our varying interests in agents' differing ways of representing the world to themselves. Thus, in context, (P) will typically be true only if Pierre holds belief using a particular kind of representation.

Another version of the view is offered by Mark Crimmins and John Perry in Crimmins and Perry (1989); it is further developed in Crimmins (1992a). According to Crimmins and Perry, a use of (P) may involve "tacit reference" to Pierre's representations, the reference tacit because it is not made via constituents of (P). The representation of Pierre's referred to in a use of (P) varies as do our interests in his representations.

The accounts are different, but, one might think, not all that different. What Crimmins and Perry achieve by positing a tacit reference to a representation, one might say, Richard can achieve by positing a standard of translation involving the type of representation at issue. And vice versa. Is there a reason to prefer my translational account to the

---

[1] See Richard (1990). A brief sketch of the view is given in Essay 5. Further references to these and other works occur parenthetically in the text.

referential account, or vice versa? In Crimmins (1992b), Crimmins offers two arguments which he thinks show his account to be preferable to mine. One is that a better account of iterated attitude ascriptions is given by taking them as involving reference to representations. The other is that, construing translation (as I do) as a relation between the sentence *type* of a "that"-clause and the representational *types* of a believer produces mistakes about truth conditions. This objection is related to a difference between myself and Perry/Crimmins about the proper treatment of contextual sensitivity in natural language. Perry and Crimmins, in the tradition of situation semantics, see the object of semantic evaluation as a sentence token or concrete utterance; working in the tradition of Kaplan's *Demonstratives*, I take the object of semantic evaluation to be a sentence type, evaluated relative to a Kaplanesque context.

In this essay I respond to Crimmins' objections, and offer reasons to prefer my account of attitude ascriptions to Perry and Crimmins' account. Section I quickly reviews the semantics I gave in Richard (1990); Sections II and III respond to Crimmins' arguments. Section IV sketches a modification to the framework of Richard (1990) occasioned by the complexities of iterated attitude ascriptions. Finally, Section V offers some reasons, having to do with the logical properties of sentences like (P), for preferring the kind of account given here and in Richard (1990) to an account like Crimmins and Perry's.

I

I take beliefs—the psychological states belief ascriptions are about—to involve sentence-like mental representations. Among the ways in which representations are sentence-like is that their parts have the sort of content that Russellians are wont to ascribe to natural lanugage terms, predicates, and the like. If we take a (token) belief-making mental representation and pair off (the types of) its parts with their contents, the result is something along the lines of a Russellian proposition, each constituent of which is paired up with something that (in the proper context) represents it. Such interpreted representations seem good candidates for objects of belief. In Richard (1990) I called such representation/content pairings "RAMs"; a RAM that is the object of someone's belief I'll refer to as one of the person's *thoughts*.[2]

The point of a belief ascription is to tell us something about a person's thoughts. It always tells us about Russellian content, and it often tells us something about the representations the believer uses to get at this content. How does an ascription do this? I think it's done by letting the words in the ascription's "that"-clause play two roles. One role is to pick out a Russellian content: One of the things "Tom" does in "Jenny believes that Tom is tired" is to pick out Tom. But we also use the words in a "that"-clause to translate or represent the representations the believer uses to realize his belief. In some uses of "Jenny thinks that Tom is tired," "Tom" stands proxy for one of Jenny's representations

---

[2] Crimmins and Perry use *thoughts* for mental representations, not for pairings of these with their (contextually established) interpretations. "RAM" is acronymous for "Russellian annotated matrix."

of Tom. When it does, "Tom" functions as a name of Tom *and* as a translational proxy for one of Jenny's representations of Tom.

Given an ascription of attitude, we can form a RAM from its content sentence, pairing the word (types) in the sentence with their interpretations. In ascribing an attitude, I suggested in Richard (1990), we offer the RAM provided by the ascription's "that"-clause as a "translation" of one of the believer's thoughts; the ascription is true provided the proffered RAM adequately represents or translates one of the believer's thoughts. The standards for translation shift from occasion to occasion. This explains how it is that sometimes we can truly say that Pierre thinks that London is pretty, and sometimes we cannot, though nothing about Pierre's thoughts has altered.

How does the contextual shifting of standards of translation get reflected in the semantics of attitude ascriptions? On my view, the reflection is in the meaning of the attitude verbs, which are indexical. What's said by "Jenny believes that Tom is tired" might be made more explicit by saying "Jenny has-a-thought-that-for-present-purposes-may-be-rendered-as-the-RAM that Tom is tired." The hyphenated material gives a rough gloss of the attitude verb, and indicates that the content of the verb will shift, as what counts as an acceptable rendering shifts.

Context, on this view, offers constraints on translation or representation. These act as input to the meaning of "believes." Given such input, the verb's value in context is a relation $B_c(u,f,p)$ that a believer u bears to a RAM p and a "translation manual" f just in case f conforms to whatever restrictions on translation the context offers and p translates under f one of u's thoughts. If $B_c(u,f,p)$ is the content of the verb in c, then our running example is true in c iff for some f, B_c(Jenny, f, the RAM that Tom is tired).

"Translation manuals" aren't anything more in the formalism than functions that map word/content pairs (which go to make up the RAMs named by "that"-clauses) to representation/content pairs (which make up thoughts). p translates q under f if we can obtain q from p by replacing parts of p with their image under f. Thus the RAM

⟨⟨"is tired," being tired⟩, ⟨"Tom," Tom⟩⟩

translates the thought

⟨⟨Jenny's representation j_1, being tired⟩, ⟨Jenny's representation j_2, Tom⟩⟩

under the manual f_1 that maps ⟨"is tired," being tired⟩ to ⟨j_1, being tired⟩ and ⟨"Tom," Tom⟩ to ⟨j_2, Tom⟩. Given that e translates r only if they have the same Russellian content, we can cheat in describing the manuals, for example describing f_1 as mapping "is tired" to j_1 and "Tom" to j_2.

What of the restrictions on translation offered by context? They are, I assume, keyed to individuals, and arise (in part) as a result of our interests in and attention to the ways believers represent individuals in thought and express thoughts in public. An example of such a restriction would be that an ascription to Jenny can use ⟨"Tom," Tom⟩ only to represent something of the form ⟨r, Tom⟩, where r is the natural language name "Tom." Such a restriction might arise if we were trying to convey the way in which Jenny's thought is or would be expressed in her public language. For brevity I will sometimes compress the statement of such restrictions by writing things like

Jenny: "Tom" → "Tom."[3]

II

To this account, Crimmins objects that

> Since what context provides is sensitive only to name-types, any two uses of the same nametype in a that-clause must be mapped to the same representation if the report is true.... [I]n normal contexts this seems right. But I think there are cases in which this result conflicts with strong intuitions. Consider the natural use of
>
> (R) He's falling for it; Cyril believes that John is John's father.
>
> On Richard's account, unless Cyril is cognitively deficient or a believer in science fiction this statement is false.... Richard would hold that (R) is strictly speaking false, but pragmatically okay.... this kind of move is mistaken for the same reason Richard rejects similar moves in the naive Russellian approach... if we do not need to abandon truth intuitions, we should hang onto them. (Crimmins (1992), 192; Crimmins' numbering has been altered)

---

[3] The fact that restrictions are keyed to individuals is of course reflected in the semantic values of attitude verbs. In context c, the semantic value of "believes" is a function that takes u, p, and f to the set of worlds w such that at w: there's a RAM q that is a thought of u's, and p represents q under f, and f conforms to every restriction c offers that is concerned with u. See Richard (1990), p. 142.

I suggested in the text that translation always preserves Russellian content (qua what is picked out by a meaningful expression in context), but this is not quite correct. In particular, when it comes to indexical expressions, there seems to be a continuum, as to whether preserving Russellian content in translation for attitude ascription is obligatory, optional, or at best accidental.

In some cases—terms like first person pronouns are paradigmatic—we are required to preserve content. If Lauben thinks to herself "Ich bin eine Artz," I cannot report her as thinking that *I* am a doctor. I must in this case preserve reference. Here, preservation of content is mandatory, and thus preservation of meaning, in Kaplan's sense of meaning as function from context to content (*character*, as Kaplan calls it), is usually impossible—save in the relatively unusual case where the speaker is the subject of the ascription.

In other cases, however, preservation of content seems optional; preservation of character instead is apparently permissible. Relatively non-controversial examples are provided by the adjectives "domestic" and "foreign," as well as the adjectival "the local." Suppose, for example, that I am in America, Martin is in England, and we are on the phone. Martin says "I had some domestic plonk last night; it made me dreadfully sick." I can, I think, report what Martin said by uttering either "Martin said that he had some domestic wine" or by saying "Martin said that he had some English wine." Here, we can preserve character or content, though not, in this situation, both.

Finally, there are cases in which preservation of character is mandatory, and preservation of content is generally barred (save in unusual circumstances when character and content coincide across contexts). Examples are the verbs of propositional attitude. Clearly, if Lauben thinks to herself "*Gottlob glaubt, dass ich ein Mann bin*," I can generally correctly report her as believing that Gottlob believes that she is a man. This is so even if her context and mine provide different restrictions on translation, and thus the verb "believes" has in my context a quite different content from that of "*glaubt*" in hers. The difference in content is no bar to the truth of my report if the sort of translation involved in attitude ascription requires that "believes" translates r when the two share their *character*, not their Russellian content.

In Crimmins (1992), Crimmins calls this aspect of my account *ad hoc*. In Richard (1990), I failed to make the point that there is this sort of continuum of options for translating indexicals.

My view is that (R) is on all fours with things like "Cyril believes that John is his own father," that would also be naturally used in the sort of situations Crimins has in mind. As I see it, "his own" is a "reflexivizer," and the proposition that John is his own father *is* one that only the cognitively deficient or believers in science fiction believe. If this is right, then the sort of case that Crimmins' objection plays upon is one in which *everyone* is forced to "abandon truth intuitions," since the intuition that Cyril believes that John is his own father will be at least as strong as the intuition that he believes that John is John's father. And as a matter of fact, intuitions about the two beliefs seem to run roughly in tandem—if you think Cyril has (or doesn't have) one of the beliefs, you are pretty likely to think he has (does not have) the other.[4]

Crimmins suggested (in correspondence) that the truth of "Cyril believes that John is his own father" in the sort of case at issue could be explained by granting "his own" the power to reflexivize, but (speaking very loosely) letting the domain of the reflexive be the entire sentence, instead of just "John is his own father." The reading of "Cyril believes that John is his own father" which Crimmins has in mind is suggested thus

(R1) $\hat{x}$ (Cyril believes that x is x's father) John;

the reading I have in mind is suggested thus

(R2) Cyril believes that $\hat{x}$ (x is x's father) John.[5]

Crimmins claims that by appealing to (R1), one might explain why we take "Cyril believes that John is his own father" to be true in a case in which we would not, on reflection, think that Cyril has a reflexive belief. This is because on Crimmins' view, although to believe (R1) is to have a reflexive belief, the belief in question is not that *Cyril* has a reflexive belief.

The problem with this response is that it does not generalize to cases that seem perfectly parallel to the sort of case Crimmins has in mind. Consider this variation on Crimmins' example. We have pointed out John to Cyril and said "that's John's father." Cyril accepts this, and says things like "that is John father" while demonstrating John. We now have the following dialogue with a third party:

- Ha! Cyril was taken in. He actually believes it.
- What exactly does he believe?
- That John is his own father.

The last response is in no way strained. And it could be replaced by "That John is John's father" without effecting the acceptability of the exchange. But by separating the

---

[4] It may seem puzzling that we so naturally say something that we so obviously know is false. I have offered an account of how this comes about in this sort of case in section 4.2 of Richard (1990).

[5] For present purposes I don't dispute that the sentence has two different readings along the lines of (R1) and (R2), the difference residing in (as it's put in the text) the domain of the reflexive. But I would not ascribe a difference in truth conditions to the readings, since I take the reading suggested by (R1) to be one that is true only if Cyril has a reflexive belief.

propositional name from the attitude verb as the dialogue does, we block the reading Crimmins has in mind. The obvious and natural—and I think only correct—way to understand this dialogue is to see it as involving the claim that Cyril believes what's expressed by an unembedded use of "John is his own father." So the point made above goes though.

The upshot is that saying that (R) would be literally false in a case in which Cyril has a belief he would express by saying "that [pointing unbeknownst to John] is John's father" doesn't force us to abandon some intuition that there wasn't reason to abandon *quite independently* of whether we adopt my theory, Perry and Crimmins' theory, or some other theory. The issue raised by (R) is whether embedding multiple occurrences of a singular term within the scope of an attitude verb forces the ascription of a "reflexive belief," a belief like that (relatively uncontroversially) ascribed using sentences in which "self" or "his own" occurs. So far as I can see, Crimmins does not give us a good reason for thinking that to believe that John is John's father is not to have a reflexive belief.[6]

III

Imagine that Tom knows of Pierre's confusion about London.[7] He knows that Pierre has a sort of representation of London he acquired in France—let us call it *FR*—and another, *ER*, acquired in England; he knows that Pierre fails to connect these appropriately. Tom himself is not confused about London. My account was designed in part to explain how different uses of

(1) Pierre believes that London is pretty

by Tom might have different truth values, without any shift in Pierre's mental state. Suppose Pierre thinks London pretty using FR but not ER. A use of (1) by Tom when the restriction on translation

(R1) Pierre: "London" → FR

is in effect is true, since the RAM that London is pretty then represents one of Pierre's thoughts under an acceptable translation manual. But a use of (1) in a context in which the restriction

(R2) Pierre: "London" → ER

is in force would not be true, since Pierre doesn't have a thought of the form $\langle\langle r, being\ pretty\rangle, \langle ER, London\rangle\rangle$.

Crimmins claims that when we turn to talking about Tom's beliefs about Pierre's beliefs, we run into problems. Crimmins thinks that if Pierre and Tom are as I've described them, there should be two readings of

---

[6] I would now respond somewhat differently to Crimmins' objection. See Essay 1 for discussion. (Note added in 2012.)

[7] See Kripke (1979) for details.

(2) Tom believes that Pierre believes that London is pretty.

The readings correspond to the two readings just accorded to (1). One of the readings says something that is (roughly) conveyed thus:

(3) Tom thinks that among Pierre's thoughts is one like this: ⟨⟨one or another representation of beauty, being beautiful⟩, ⟨FR, London⟩⟩.

The other reading says something roughly conveyed so:

(4) Tom thinks that among Pierre's thoughts is one like this: ⟨⟨one or another representation of beauty, being beautiful⟩, ⟨ER, London⟩⟩.

Crimmins' second objection involves the two readings just suggested:

Assume that Tom knows that Pierre has two representations of London, and that Tom himself, not being confused, has only a single representation of London. Corresponding to *Pierre's* two representations of London there should be two readings of...2.: I may mean that Tom's belief is about...[FR], or about...[ER]. But there is no way for Richard's contextual machinery to distinguish these claims, because there is no constituent in the RAM [that Pierre believes that London is pretty]...of which Tom has two representations. (Crimmins 1992, 193; numbering altered to conform to present essay)

The passage raises two questions. The first is whether the "machinery" sketched in Section I can distinguish between the claims (3) and (4)—that is, can it provide the two readings of sentence (2)? The second question is whether on my account both readings of the sentence could be true if Tom had but one (type of) representation of London, and, if so, whether this is undesirable.

The brief answer to the first question is that of course the account can provide both readings. Varying contextual restrictions on translation changes what (2)'s complement may represent, and thus varies the truth conditions of uses of (2) in the way in which Crimmins thinks they should vary. Achieving this sort of variation in truth conditions is part of the point of making "believes" indexical. Since this may not be completely clear, I will supply a few details.

What would it be like, for Tom to have the belief conveyed by (3)? As I see it, it would be for Tom to be in a mental state in which he thinks of Pierre more or less as follows:

(H) Hmmh. Pierre has a way of thinking of London—he associates it with "Londres"—and when he thinks that way of London, he thinks that London is pretty.

If this is the way that Tom thinks about Pierre when he thinks the thought that (3) conveys, then when he thinks the sort of thought that (3) conveys certain restrictions on translation are operative in his context. In particular, the restriction (R1) is operative.

Tom is Crimmins' example, and for all I know, Tom thinks in French. So a more precise statement of the last point is this: If Tom has the belief in question, he has it in virtue of *his* using *some* representation, TR1, of London—perhaps "London," perhaps "Londres," perhaps "dieses Burgstadt"—to pick out London *and* to function as a representative in Tom's thought of Pierre's representation FR. If, for example, Tom has the belief in virtue of tokening (H), a particular token of "London," the last one appearing in (H), does this job. In any event, if Tom has the belief in question, the restriction

Pierre:TR1 → FR

is operative in Tom's context. Analagously, if Tom has the other belief, then there must be some representation of Tom's, TR2, such that the restriction

Pierre:TR2 → ER

is operative in Tom's context.[8]

Different readings of (2), corresponding to (3) and (4), presuppose differences in how Tom represents Pierre's beliefs. If I am trying to convey that Tom has one or the other of the beliefs in question, this can only be because I am focusing on one of Tom's putative representations of Pierre's representations, as opposed to the other. If I utter (2) trying to convey (3), I have a picture of Tom on which he has some way, TR, of thinking of London as he thinks of Pierre's thoughts about London. Tom uses TR not just to think of London but to represent Pierre's French representation, FR, of London. Thus making use of TR, Tom thinks that Pierre thinks that London is pretty. Of course, this last representation of Tom's thought processes lets "London" go proxy for TR—and has it name London, as it always does. That is, in uttering (2) to convey (3), the restriction

Tom: "London" → a way of thinking of London, TR, of Tom's such that in Tom's situation the restriction *Pierre TR → FR* is operative

is operative. But if this is so, then my use of (2) is true only if Tom has the sort of belief mentioned in (3). A corresponding restriction will assign to a use of (2) truth conditions suggested by (4). The upshot is that the account sketched in Section I provides readings of (2) corresponding to (3) and (4).[9]

---

[8] Actually, I think that restrictions are almost always non-specific about what representations are in their range. The last mentioned restriction, for example, should be replaced by something suggested by

Pierre: TR2 → representations that would naturally find expression by Pierre with the English "London."

(What this indicates is that in ascriptions to Pierre, TR2 can only represent representations in the class picked out by what follows the arrow.) I think this because I think an adequate account of representations will individuate them so finely that direct—as opposed to quantificational—reference to them will turn out to be (practically) impossible. But this difference with Crimmins and Perry is not relevant here, so I have suppressed it.

[9] I suppose someone might say that my story lacks a certain "psychological reality." Of course I don't mean to suggest that a user of (2) goes through any of the above rigmarol consciously, or even unconsciously. But I do think that it is plausible to think that if (2) has the sorts of readings Crimmins alleges it has, then (a) he who uses (2) to convey one of the readings is in some sense cognitively focused upon how Tom thinks Pierre thinks of London, and (b) the use of (2) involves some sort of "cognitive co-ordination" between the focus in (a) and the embedded use of "London." If (a) and (b) are plausible, then, I think, it is not implausible that my psychological state, when using (2) to convey (3), is one that ties my use of "London" to Tom's representations in a way that induces the last mentioned restriction.

Let's turn to the second question Crimmins' objection raises: Suppose Tom expresses a belief with

(1) Pierre believes that London is pretty

while restriction (R1) is in place (so the belief expressed is focused on Pierre's French representations); next he expresses a belief using (1) while restriction (R2) is in place (so the expressed belief focuses on an English representation). Could Tom have these beliefs *simultaneously* if he had but one way of representing London?

There is, in fact, nothing about the account of Richard (1990) that rules this out. Richard (1990) treats "believes" as an indexical. The relation "believes" picks out with (R1) in place is quite different from that it picks out with (R2) in place. The first relates Pierre and the RAM that London is pretty to one of Pierre's "French thoughts," but not to an English one; the second relates the RAM to an English thought but not a French one. This variation in what "believes" picks out allows a single word, "London," to go proxy for different representations of Pierre's in different uses of (1). So long as Tom can simultaneously represent belief relations that differ as these do, he can have both beliefs with only one representation of London. Nothing in Richard (1990) bars this. Call this the *multiple relation solution*.

While the multiple relation solution is an option for the theory of Richard (1990), it is an option I would prefer to avoid. Here's why. If Tom represents different belief relations—i.e., different possible semantic values of "believes"—he presumably does so using "believes." Thus, for Tom to simultaneously represent different belief relations, different mental tokenings of "believes" by Tom will have to pick out different relations. But this implies that simultaneous mental tokenings of the verb by Tom occur in different contexts. For if they occurred in the same context, they would have the same semantic value. At least this is true on the Kaplanesque view of indexicals and contexts presupposed by Richard (1990).

Because the multiple relation response requires this sort of multiplication of contexts, it sits somewhat uneasily with the overall view of context sensitivity which Kaplan suggested in Kaplan (1989) and which (I will suggest below) we have good reason to wish to hold on to. A Kaplanesque context is determined by an agent, a time, a place, and a world. It is supposed to provide the resources for interpreting arbitrary sentences of its language; generally speaking, sentences which are supposed to be "interpreted together" (for example, premises and conclusions of arguments) are to be interpreted within a single context. Switching contexts in the middle of interpreting a sentence is clearly contrary to the spirit, not to speak of the letter, of Kaplan's approach to indexicals. But the multiple relation response employs a notion of a context on which many contexts will correspond to an agent, time, place, and world. These contexts seem destined to interpret only specific sentences (or sentence tokens!) of a language; it thus seems that several contexts might be needed to provide the interpretation of an argument's premises and conclusion. And the multiple relation response positively invites us to switch contexts in mid-sentence.

So I fear that the multiple relation response would force us to either abandon a Kaplanesque account of context sensitivity, or to provide two accounts of how sentences receive semantic values, when they are used privately to think and when they are used publically to air thought: A multiple context account for private use, a Kaplanesque one for the public. While I have no reason to think that such a bifurcated account is impossible,[10] such accounts strike me as awkward and as something which, all else being equal, are to be avoided. And they *can* be avoided, since there are straightforward responses to the question we are considering besides the multiple relation response.[11]

Couldn't Tom have both of the beliefs mentioned in (3) and (4), though he had only one way of thinking of, or kind of representation, of London? To answer, we need some illumination as to how we are to individuate representational types, since there are many ways of sorting token representations to come up with types. One account identifies ways of thinking or representational types with what correspond to mental files, mental dossiers, or vivid names. On such a view one who accepts an identity—say "Twain is Clemens"—and thus directs information tagged with either name to a single file, associates the same way of thinking with each name in the identity. This makes for a relatively coarse-grained concept of representation. Much finer grained accounts are, however, quite natural. For example, it is quite natural to think that tokens of distinct, though co-referential, natural language name types—for example, tokens of "Clemens" and "Twain"—determine different ways of thinking even for one who understands the terms and knows that the relevant identity is true. That they function as different representations, even for someone who knows that Twain is Clemens, is witnessed by the difference in their function when embedded within "believes" and other attitude verbs: To think that John doubts that Twain is asleep is not to think that John doubts that Clemens is asleep. That "Twain" and "Clemens" can play different roles in thoughts about the beliefs of others while continuing to name Twain makes them different representations of Twain in some (fairly important) sense of "representation."

Certainly there is *a* sense of "representation" in which, provided Tom is not confused, all of Tom's tokenings of "London" are tokenings of the same type of representation. In this sense of "representation," Tom doesn't need multiple representations of London to have the two beliefs at issue. But there is no reason that every (singular) representation I have must directly correspond to a natural language term naming what it represents. In particular, to think about what others think when they are confused may require minting new representations of the objects of their thought in order to keep track of

---

[10] We can of course fragment a Kaplanesque context $c = \langle a,t,p,w \rangle$ into a family $c_i = \langle a, t, p, w, v_i \rangle$ for any family of values V; we may then use the fragmented context to interpret sentences in thought, the unfragmented to interpret sentences in public. One would need, if one adopted such a course, some assurance of uniformity of interpretation of a sentence, when it is used privately to think and publicly express what is so thought. I see no reason why one couldn't construct such an account. But it is horribly redundant.

[11] I am grateful to a referee and an editor of *Linguistics and Philosophy* for urging me to explain why I do not avail myself of the multiple relation response.

their confusion. A natural way to manufacture new representations is to ambiguate existing ones. This is something we clearly do consciously in thinking about puzzle cases—we say that Peter thinks Paderweski-the-musician plays the piano, but not that Paderweski-the-politician does.

To say that Tom has multiple representations of London, in the quasi-technical sense being suggested, is *not* to say what is informally suggested by saying that he has "different ways of conceptualizing" the town. Tokens of different natural language name types of the same thing are, in my view, tokens of different representational types. For example, "Twain" and "Clemens" are of different representational types for reasons just rehearsed. But this difference need not and typically is not accompanied by multiple "ways of conceptualizing" Twain.

Let's apply all this to Tom, London, and "London." Suppose that Tom thinks that when Pierre thinks of London as he did as a child, he thinks that London is pretty, but that when Pierre thinks of London as he does in adult mode, he doesn't think that London is pretty. Tom has a number of token representations of London that perform different functions in his thoughts about London and Pierre: Some of them represent Pierre's representation FR, others his representation ER. Of course, they are all names of—and therefore representations of—London. It seems not inappropriate to assimilate the difference among these tokens of "London" to the difference between tokens of "Twain" and "Clemens" in my thought. If we do, we will say that these tokens are, in one sense of "representation," of different representational types. So Tom has different representations of London. We may look upon routines like (H) above—or "mental models" of the belief systems of others which would be partially rehearsed by the likes of (H)—as among other things introducing new representations, or ambiguating old ones. This would have the effect of allowing "London" to function in one way in its last appearance in (H), and in a different way in its last appearance in

(H') Hmmh. Pierre has a way of thinking of London—he associates it with "London"—and when he thinks that way of London, he thinks that London is not pretty.

The suggestion I've just made is, in effect, that (i) there is a way of partitioning a person's token representations of an object *o* that tends to generate finer divisions among representations—i.e., more sets of representations—as the person comes to recognize that others have multiple representations of *o*. Furthermore, (ii) the way we ascribe beliefs and other attitudes is sensitive to the divisions induced by this way of partitioning representations.

For reasons just rehearsed, it seems appropriate to think of the collections of representations so generated as constituting different ways of thinking of *o*, and thus as different representations of *o*. You may find this way of using "representation" offensive. Then we have a difference about the semantics of "representation". But this is merely a difference about the semantics of "representation." It does not bear on claims (i) and (ii) in the above paragraph, and thus doesn't constitute an objection to Richard's (1990) view of the semantics of "believes."

IV

Let us pretend that Tom's language of thought is some extension of English, differing from English only by explicitly ambiguating terms (say by subscripting) in a manner along the lines discussed in the last section. Thus Tom, under the impression that Pierre has two representations of London, extends his language of thought to include terms "London$_1$" and "London$_2$" that go proxy for the representations in ascriptions of attitude to Pierre. Suppose Tom thinks that Marie-Bernard is also confused about London, though her confusions differ in various ways from Pierre's. So Tom has further ambiguated, and uses "London$_3$" and "London$_4$" to think about Marie-Bernard's thoughts.

Consider

(5) Tom thinks that Pierre thinks that London is ugly, and Marie-Bernard thinks that London (or: it) is ugly.

(The scope of the second "thinks" extends to the comma, of the first to the period.) This would normally be taken to be true if Tom could voice a belief using

(6) Pierre thinks that London is ugly; Marie-Bernard thinks that London is ugly, too.

Given the position I took in Richard (1990), one would expect that I would hold that a use of (5) would be true only if Tom accepted a sentence of the form of (6). But it is hard to see how I can hold that, given what I suggested in the last section. For the suggestion seems to require that the thought Tom gives voice to, when he utters (6), is of a form different from (6), because it does not involve multiple occurrences of one name or representation of London; what Tom is giving voice to is really of the form

(6') Pierre thinks that London$_1$ is ugly; Marie Bernard thinks that London$_3$ is ugly, too.

If you combine this example with Crimmins' example, you have the following problem: Crimmins' example seems to point to the necessity, in the context of my account, of assigning different representations to different occurrences of "London" in Tom's thought; this example seems to show that one must generally assign a single representation to different occurrences.

Things are not as bad as they appear. After sketching a way of modeling the mental structures underlying beliefs about beliefs, I will use the model to solve the problem.

When I have beliefs about what Pierre believes, I have a mental structure which can be modeled by a table headed by a representation of Pierre—say, "Pierre"—and then a list of beliefs. Part of the model might look like this:

Pierre: *Beliefs*
    that Paris is lovely
    that London is not lovely
    that PA's consistency is provable in ZFC

The table contributes a number of "sentences" that go to make up my thoughts. Minimally, it contributes "Pierre believes that Paris is lovely" and two other simple belief ascriptions; perhaps it also contributes sentences ascribing conjunctive beliefs. In combination with other sentences, it will contribute still more. Suppose I have opinions that some of Pierre's beliefs are, or are not, held in a certain way, or tied to certain ways of thinking of or talking about things. That is, suppose I have a mental structure that would be naturally rehearsed by the likes of (H) or (H'). To model this we need something that will encode the information that I believe that Pierre has multiple ways of thinking of one or another object. And we need something that will encode whatever opinions I may have about the multiples.

The first job can be done simply by subscripting. (Subscripting applies to all expressions with a semantic value, but let's keep things simple and just subscript singular terms.) When different subscripts appear upon a term in my table of Pierre's beliefs, as in

Pierre: *Beliefs*
  that Paris is lovely
  that $London_1$ is not lovely
  that $London_2$ is expensive
  that $London_2$ is 425 km from Paris

— this indicates that I do not presuppose that the representations corresponding to the distinct subscripts are "merged" by the subject. Thus, if the above models my opinions of Pierre, I don't believe that Pierre believes that London is 425 km from Paris and not lovely. But I do believe that he believes that London is 425 km from Paris. And I (probably) believe that he believes that London is expensive and 425 km from Paris.[12]

The second job mentioned above can be done by devoting a separate section of the table to information, comments, conjectures, and such about the modes of thought and speech that the subscripts track. A full blown Pierre-table might thus contain a section that would be fairly represented with something like

$London_1$: proxy for a way of thinking of London acquired in London
$London_2$: proxy for a way of thinking of London acquired in France
$London_3$: proxy for a way of thinking Martin had in mind yesterday; probably identical with one of the above.

I may have opinions about what opinions Pierre has about Marie-Bernard's opinions. We might extend the subscript notation to deal with multiple iterations, generating things like

Pierre: *Beliefs*:
  that $London_1$ is not lovely

---

[12] Probably only because I hesitate to say that one always believes some conjunction corresponding to each pair of beliefs one has.

I should stress that I see the subscripting and the resulting syntactic distinction among names of London as an artifact of the model. I am suggesting a way of modeling mental states that would naturally be voiced by things like (H) and (H') in the last section. Such structures might be realized in the mind by tokenings of English sentences in which only occurrences of the natural language "London" were to be found.

....

Marie-Bernard: *Beliefs:*
   that London$_{1,1}$ is pretty,
   that London$_{1,2}$ is not pretty.

The mental structure modeled by such a table accurately represents Pierre's system of beliefs only if Pierre has a representation of London, L_1, such that (a) he uses it to believe that London is not lovely; (b) he has used it to go proxy for what he takes to be potentially different representations of London of Marie-Bernard's, in the way the user of (H) and (H') uses "London" as proxy for two of Pierre's representations; (c) analoguously to the user of (H) and (H'), using L_1, Pierre takes Marie-Bernard to think that London is pretty, and he takes her to think that London isn't pretty.

I have been spelling out a way of modeling the sort of mental structures underlying our thoughts of others' thoughts. Using this model, we can solve the problem posed by the iteration examples in a straightforward way.

Let us henceforth use *representational type* in a fairly narrow sense, so that, for instance, all my thought tokens of "London" are of a single representational type, given that they are all names of London and that I "take" them to all name the same thing. Call the collection of sentence tokens, table tokens, and so forth that realize my beliefs my *belief text*. The RAMs of Richard's (1990) semantics for attitude ascriptions are constructions based upon the belief text. They are formed by taking a sentence token from the text and pairing the types of its parts with the referents of the token's parts. If the sort of type used in the construction is representational type, we will have trouble with iteration. What we need in this construction is something reflecting not only sameness and difference of representational type, but also the structure, due to opinions about sameness and difference of representational type in the texts of others, reflected by subscripting. Let's call the replacements for representational types *representational paths*, or paths for short.

To construct a path, pick a representation (type)—say, "London"—and, for each table T in which something of that type occurs, a subscript. If a table T' is embedded in T, as the Marie-Bernard table is embedded in the Pierre table, we pick for T' a subscript that extends the subscript chosen for T, as 1,2 extends 1. The result defines a *representational path* through a system of beliefs. A token *t* is part of such a path if it is of the representational type on which the path is based, and (a) *t* occurs in the belief text outside of any belief table (so, *t* is part of a "zero level" belief, like the belief that snow is lovely), or (b) *t* occurs in a belief table and has the subscript picked for that table.

A representational path is a way of collecting token representations. It collects only representations that are of the same representational type. It also respects the way in which a thinker takes others to represent the world to themselves: If I take *you* to have two representations of London that you fail to connect to one another, a representational path consisting of tokens of "London" from *my* thought does not contain tokens that go proxy for both of your putative representations.

Suppose we have a sentence S from Tom's belief text, perhaps one formed by "conjoining" various sentences that go to make up the text. For each assignment of representational paths to S's token parts, there will be a RAM among Tom's thoughts. Suppose, for example, that Tom's belief text looks (partially) like this:

(Zero level) London is lovely

Pierre: *Beliefs*
    that London$_2$ is ugly
    that London$_1$ is lovely
    that London$_2$ is not lovely
    that London$_1$ is expensive
    that London$_2$ is expensive
      London$_1$: proxy for a French representation
      London$_2$: proxy for an English representation

Marie-Bernard: *Beliefs*
    that London$_3$ is ugly
    that London$_4$ is not ugly

There are a number of paths through this text. One path collects all occurrences of "London" in the zero level text, all the proxies for the English representation—i.e., the "London's" subscripted with "2"—in the Pierre table, plus all the occurrences of "London$_3$" in the Marie-Bernard table; another collects all the "London's" in the zero level, all the proxies for a French representation in the Pierre table, and all the "London$_3$'s" for Marie-Bernard. There are yet more. Call the two paths described p_1 and p_2, respectively.

To construct Tom's thoughts, we take a sentence (possibly a conjunction of subsentences) from his belief text. We then select paths $p_1, \ldots, p_n$ such that for each (atomic) expression (with a semantic value) in the sentence, there is exactly one path in which it occurs. Then, letting the paths play the role of types, we construct a thought by pairing the type of an expression token with the token's Russellian referent.[13] So among the thoughts that Tom has is one corresponding to the sentence "Pierre believes that London$_2$ is ugly; Marie Bernard believes that London$_3$ is ugly," constructed using p_1, and thus constructed so that the two names of "London" are like-typed. A use of (5) (with no restrictions accompanying it) is true in virtue of the fact that Tom has such a thought.

In Crimmins' example, we need to show that there is a reading of "Tom believes that Pierre believes that London is expensive" that is true only in virtue of a thought constructed from a path like p_1—and so is true only in virtue of a belief focused on Pierre's representation ER—and another reading of the sentence that is true only in virtue of a thought constructed with a path like p_2. But that is straightforward, once we say, as we shall henceforth, that the restrictions that a context provides for evaluating uses of natural language attitude ascriptions map the word types in a "that"-clause to ways of thinking that are given by paths. Thus, the first reading of the sentence is induced by a restriction along the lines of

---

[13] The construction will make the relation between sentences accepted and thoughts one many. In Richard (1990) (section 4.3) I argue that this will generally be the case; in particular, the proper treatment of puzzles concerning the retention of belief over time requires this.

Tom: "London" → ways of representing London that, *inter alia*, go proxy in Tom's thought for one of Pierre's English ways of thinking of the town.

The other reading is secured by a corresponding restriction.[14]

There is a faint echo of Frege's hierarchy of indirect senses in all this. Frege is often thought to have held that with each new embedding of "London" in a sequence such as

Pierre thinks that London stinks
Tom thinks that Pierre thinks that London stinks
Marie-Bernard thinks that Tom thinks that Pierre thinks that London stinks

"London" shifts its reference, referring to its sense at the previous level, and expressing a new sense to present the new reference. It is natural to understand such a view as one on which "London" in the above sequence first names Pierre's way of thinking of London, then Tom's way of thinking of Pierre's way of thinking of London, and then Marie-Bernard's way of thinking of Tom's way of thinking of Pierre's way of thinking of London.

"London," on the view I've outlined, functions as a proxy for different sorts of representations in a way somewhat reminiscent of this progression. Representational paths are ways of following shifts in the proxy function within the belief text of an individual. But there are rather significant differences between Frege's position and the position sketched here. In particular, in natural language attitude ascriptions, I take "London," no matter how deeply embedded, to refer to London, while Frege does not. In the progression just displayed I see no variation in the reference or semantic value of "London." The contribution of "London" is always the same, namely the pair ⟨the natural language name type "London," the city London⟩.

Unlike Frege, I do not see attitude ascription as involving reference to the object that the believer has in her "psychological ken" in belief. This is a good part of the point of describing my position as one on which an attitude ascription involves a *translation* of the object of the target's belief: In translating another's words, we wind up with something that refers, not to their words, but to what they referred to therewith. Analogously, for translating their thoughts.

V

The most salient difference between my account and that of Crimmins and Perry is that they take run of the mill attitude ascriptions to involve reference to representations,

---

[14] To complete the picture just sketched, we need an account of when an individual's thoughts are true. The account of section 4.4 of Richard (1990) can be adapted. In generating the appropriate restrictions for evaluating someone's thoughts for truth, we use the appropriate material (for example, things like

London$_1$: proxy for one of Pierre's English representations)

from the tables in which the parts of the path making up the RAM occur. The restrictions in this case must be ones that map paths to paths. (I hope to expand on these cryptic remarks elsewhere.)

while I do not.[15] A (quite simplified) version of their account runs as follows: A speaker who uses a sentence of the form *a believes that T* typically makes "tacit reference" to representations. The tacit reference is tacit, because there is no expression in the sentence uttered which can be identified as the expression with which the reference is made; the tacit reference is reference, since the representations in question are constituents of the proposition expressed by the utterance as a whole. Roughly speaking, and ignoring for the moment iteration of "believes," the semantic value of an utterance of "believes that T" on which the representation R is the object of tacit reference is: *believes the Russellian proposition that T using the representation R*.

Crimmins and Perry account for the multiple readings of (2) by holding that Tom's beliefs about Pierre's beliefs are in part about Pierre's representations; in reporting these by using (2) we may make differing references to Pierre's representations. One reading involves reference to FR, the other to ER. If we adopt the Perrry/Crimmins account, we can get both readings of (2) without multiplying *Tom's* modes of representing London, or introducing the extra complexity of the notion of a representational path. Why not simply accept the idea that when Tom thinks about Pierre, he refers to Pierre's representations of London, and when we think about Tom, *we* refer to *Pierre's* multiple representations, too?

I think there is a very good reason to resist this idea. This reason is best appreciated, I think, when one appreciates what is perhaps the other major difference between the Crimmins/Perry account and my own. This is not a difference about the semantics of attitude verbs, but about the best way to treat contextual shiftiness in natural language. This difference is marked, though not exhausted, by our choices of objects of semantic evaluation and our accounts of the structure of such evaluation. I have couched my account within the framework suggested by Kaplan (1989), in which the objects that get evaluated semantically are sentence types taken in a context, with contexts being abstractions from and idealizations of actual and possible types of speech situations. Such contexts are conceived as typically supplying (in the way in which a function "supplies" its values) the sorts of parameters and determinants necessary for interpreting any sentence of the language; thus one typically (though not invariably) can interpret arbitrary sets of sentences of the language under study relative to such contexts.

Crimmins and Perry's account, on the other hand, is one that semantically evaluates utterances. It allows for a notion of *context of an utterance*, of course. But the Crimmins/Perry view seems to be one on which contexts should be identified with things that would "really be found in a speech situation." (These are my words, not theirs.) A context of use, on this view, need not provide the material necessary to interpret more than whatever sentence or sentences are in fact used therein. This notion of context is not one designed to accommodate the interpretation of arbitrary collections of sentences of

---

[15] Crimmins and Perry suggest that some attitude ascriptions involve (more or less direct) reference to representations, while other attitude ascriptions may make claims involving quantificational reference to or description of representations. This subtlety doesn't affect the argument of this section, so I propose henceforth to ignore it.

the language of study. And in fact Perry and Crimmins disparage the sort of contexts I employ. Crimmins calls them "donut contexts" (because they are unhealthy? because he and Perry donut use them?); Perry and Crimmins suggest that "[o]ne way of taking our claims would be as denying the general usefulness in semantics of" such a notion of context (Crimmins and Perry 1989, 710).

As Crimmins quite correctly suggests, my treatment of the example in Section II flows naturally from my decision to make expression types the objects whose semantically relevant properties shift across context. Crimmins, in suggesting alterations of my account, proposes taking utterance parts—uses of expressions—to be objects whose representational properties shift across contexts. He observes (putting things roughly) that if context makes *uses* of expressions representatives of the mental representations of others, then in an utterance of (R) the first use of "John" can represent one (type) of Cyril's representations of John, the second quite another.

If our only interest were in assigning truth conditions or propositions to the uses of sentences, a case could be made that the Crimmins/Perry approach to the matter must be superior to mine. Suppose a satisfactory semantic account of a certain class of sentences uses can be given by assigning types to the sentences used, inventing a collection of contexts relative to which to endow the *types* with semantic properties, and then evaluating the types-as-taken-in-a-context for truth. Certainly we give an equally satisfactory treatment of the class by assigning semantic properties to the *uses*, assigning property p to a use u iff for some t and c, the first approach assigned u to type t, identified c as u's context, and assigned p to t in c. So anything my approach can do, the Crimmins/Perry approach can do as well. But conversions in the opposite direction are not always possible, simply because a token utterance may be made out of tokens of like type.

The point of this argument is not, of course, that sentence types are irrelevant to semantics. Systematic semantics is impossible without a systematic assignment of types to token utterances, if only because there seems no hope of a comprehensive assignment of semantic values unless the assignment is made *via* types. Rather, the point of the argument is that nothing is lost, and apparently some flexibility is gained, if we identify the things to which we are assigning semantic values as the type-bearing tokens, rather than the types-in-a-context.

The argument, however, is conditional upon the assumption that our only interest is the assignment of truth conditions and propositions to sentence uses. Traditionally we have hoped for more from a semantic account of a language. We have also hoped to extract an account of validity from an account of a language's semantics. Such accounts traditionally proceed by ferreting out types whose tokens are invariably valid: Argument types whose premise tokens guarantee the truth of their conclusion tokens, or sentence types whose tokens enjoy an immunity from falsity or guarantee of truth. Traditionally, it was assumed that logic's types would be identical with or at least parasitic upon the types semantics uses.

Approaching contextual shiftiness *via* the assignment of semantic properties to types in a Kaplanesque context can be thought of as being partially motivated by the desire to cast semantic theory so that it will deliver an account of validity in a form as close to the traditional one as the contextual shiftiness of the language under study will allow. (Certainly this was a primary motivation for the author of *Demonstratives* when he developed the framework to begin with.) In this framework, we can continue to identify the bearers of formal validity with (parasites upon) the syntactic types of the language under study. Validity itself can be identified with the guarantee of being true when taken in any context (Kaplan's definition) or with the guarantee of expressing a necessary truth in any context (an alternative to which I am partial). It is the demands upon the formalism imposed by this approach to validity that require the idealization noted above, on which a context turns out (typically, if not inevitably) to supply the material necessary for interpreting arbitrary sentences of the language.

If the flexibility of assigning semantic values to tokens instead of types is one of which we must avail ourselves, in doing the semantics for a portion of a language, then we will expect the semantic theory for that portion of the language to tell us relatively little about logical properties. For insofar as the assignment of semantic values, and thus truth conditions and propositions, must advert to tokens and not just to types and context, it will not be possible to predict whether the truth of premises guarantees that of a conclusion just by looking at the types of the premises and conclusion. Insofar as semantics is the story of tokens and not types, language has no logic, at least as logic is normally conceived.

Insofar as we have strong intuitions about the logical properties of some portion of a language, we will want our semantic theory to validate these intuitions. When these intuitions are intuitions about formal validity—and surely we do have such intuitions—we shall want our semantic theory, all else being equal, to validate our intuitions by showing that the validity of certain arguments can be seen as a formal matter. What a semantic account says about validity is, in any case, an important test of the theory. One reason for rejecting a semantic theory, after all, is that it sits poorly with, or is outright inconsistent with, particular intuitions of speakers concerning validity and invalidity, or more general logical intuitions, like the intuition that utterances in English that have the form

> whatever a Rs is a thing that b Rs, and aRc

commit the utterer to the truth of one of the form of bRc.

How does all this bear on a choice between the account of attitude ascriptions I've offered and that offered by Perry and Crimmins? The idea that Kaplanesque contexts are somehow unfit for doing natural language semantics seems to me unsubstantiated by any argument Crimmins or Perry gives. As I have suggested, one reason for employing a framework in which such contexts figure is to enable us to give straightforward accounts of validity. The account of attitude ascriptions I have given is in part shaped by common intuitions about logical properties of sentences ascribing attitudes. For instance, I see it as a desideratum of a semantics for attitude verbs that it validate our intuition that inferences such as

Whatever Tom doubts Pierre doubts
Tom doubts that London is lovely
So Pierre doubts that London is lovely.

are valid. To this end, my account assigns a semantic value to the predicate type "doubts that London is lovely" relative to a context, allowing the predicate to be univocal within a context. The initial premise is treated in what seems the most natural way in my framework, as the claim that for any RAM p, if there is an f such that D(Tom, f, p), then there is an f such that D(Pierre, f, p). ("D," of course, names an analogue of the relation B from Section I.) The argument is thus valid in virtue of the principles governing the treatment of the quantifier "whatever."[16]

Among the morals Crimmins and Perry draw from their discussion of the attitudes is that "there is little possibility of an interesting logic of belief sentences" (Crimmins and Perry (1987), 711). Their pessimism results from what I have suggested is a primary difference between us: They eschew the kind of account of indexicality I employ because they think that "such things as the words used in a statement can affect the semantically relevant parts of the statement's context."[17]

Even the simplest sorts of apparently valid arguments are rendered invalid on their account. Recall that on their account a speaker who uses a sentence of the form *a believes that T* typically makes "tacit reference" to representations of a's; the semantic value of an utterance of "believes that T" on which the representation R is the object of tacit reference is: *believes the Russellian proposition that T using the representation R*. Analagous treatment is of course accorded verbs like "doubts." On such a treatment, "doubts that London is lovely" is typically *not* univocal, even within a single context of actual utterance, such as an utterance of "Tom doubts that London is lovely and Pierre doubts that London is lovely." For the predicate uses involve tacit reference to token representations. So the predicate involves, when fronted by "Tom," reference to Tom's representations, not Pierre's; it involves reference to Pierre's representations, not Tom's, when fronted by "Pierre."

How would Crimmins and Perry treat quantifications like "whatever Tom doubts Pierre doubts"? What they say doesn't allow one to confidently generalize.[18] The most natural treatment of "whatever a doubts b doubts" in their framework is arguably one on which it reads so: for any Russellian p, if there is an r such that a doubts p using r, then there is an $r^\star$ such that b doubts p using $r^\star$. But if this is how we should read the initial premise of the argument above, there is apparently no sense in which the argument is

---

[16] See the discussion in Richard (1990), 141–50.

[17] I do not deny that this is so. For example, salience is effected by an utterance and salience is (probably) a semantically relevant "part" of context. What I deny is that the best accounts of the interaction of utterance and context are incompatible with the types-in-a-context method of semantics.

[18] While Crimmins (1992a) discusses some plural attitude reports—for example, "The Egyptians believed that Tut was divine" and "Ann and Tom believe that Max has fleas," the discussion is fairly tentative. So far as I can see, the approach taken in Crimmins (1992a) does not sit easily with the idea that the argument in the text is valid, much less formally so.

valid. Even if we confine our attention to how the premises and conclusion of the argument are interpreted in a single context of utterance, Crimmins and Perry's view seems to commit them to the view that there will be contexts in which uses of the relevant sentences come to something like

>(p)($\exists r$Tom doubts p under $r \to \exists r'$ Pierre doubts p under r')
>Tom doubts the proposition that London is pretty under r_1
>So, Pierre doubts the proposition that London is pretty under r_2

with r_1 and r_2 tacitly referred-to representations. This isn't valid. In fact, since one can presumably say that someone doubts a proposition under r when he doesn't (because, say, he in fact believes it under r), there is every reason to think that there will be cases in which the premises are all true while the conclusion is false.

Perhaps there is some way to render the argument in question valid without violating the spirit of the Crimmins/Perry account, but it is not easy to see what it might be. I am inclined to think that the argument in question is valid. In fact, I am inclined to think that there must be some sense in which the argument *form*

>Whatever Tom doubts Pierre doubts
>Tom doubts that A
>So, Pierre doubts that A

is a valid one. It is not as if one is faced with a choice between honoring the intuition about validity and incorporating contextual shiftiness into an account of the semantics of attitude ascriptions: One can do both by giving an account of the sort suggested in Richard (1990).[19]

---

[19] Mark Crimmins gave useful comments on an earlier version of this, for which I'm grateful. This chapter was written during my tenure as an NEH Fellow; I'm most grateful for the support.

7

Defective Contexts, Accommodation, and Normalization

Propositional Attitudes defends an account of "believes" on which the verb is contextually sensitive.[1] *x believes that S* says (quite roughly) that x has a belief which is "well rendered" or acceptably translated by S; since contextually variable information about what makes for a good translation helps determine the extension of "believes," the verb is contextually sensitive.[2] Sider and Soames criticize this account.[3] They say it has unacceptable consequences in cases in which we make multiple ascriptions of belief to a single individual—as happens, for example, when we say that Odile believes such and such, that the woman in the corner believes so and so, but are ignorant of the identity of Odile and the woman in the corner. I will distinguish two objections along these lines, and argue that neither is forceful. The objections differ as to whether or not the speaker mistakenly presupposes that the believers under discussion are distinct. Against the first sort of objection, I argue that if it were cogent, we would have to reject well-motivated and well-nigh established accounts of contextually sensitive expressions like "tall." For if it were cogent, parallel objections could be raised against the idea that the extension of "tall" is determined by a contextually supplied reference class. The second objection, I argue, is mistaken about what PA requires of an account of an acceptable translation of a belief.

At issue in both objections are the status of general principles governing the interpretation of context sensitive expressions. I hope what I say about such principles makes what follows of interest independently of whatever light it sheds on the semantics of "believes."

It will clarify both the objections and my response if I begin with a brief and informal review of PA's account of the truth conditions of

---

[1] Richard (1990). Henceforth, I use "PA" to refer to that book.
An ancestor of the first third of the present essay was read at the APA symposium on PA in Los Angles in April 1994; Scott Soames and Mark Crimmins were the other symposiasts. I thank Soames and Crimmins for their comments. I'm indebted to Ed Gettier and Terry Parsons for discussion of a draft of the current essay.
[2] PA's account thus presupposes a weak version of the view that our beliefs are realized by psychological states which "are sententially structured." The book's first chapter argues that the psychological sententialism presupposed is quite benign.
[3] Sider (1995); Soames (1995).

(1) Odile believes that Twain is tall.

My idea is that in (1), "Twain is tall" is offered as *a representation or translation* of a "mental sentence" which realizes a belief. (1) is true if the content sentence is an *acceptable* translation of something realizing one of Odile's beliefs, with acceptability varying across contexts. Always required for good translation is preservation of Russellian content; conversants' focus and interests may impose extra restrictions on what can translate what.

Suppose, for example, we are focused on how Odile expresses her beliefs. In ascriptions to Odile, we might then use "Twain" to represent Odile's mental tokenings of "Twain" and nothing else. Suppose we are also interested in the beliefs of the woman in corner, who is looking at Twain. In ascriptions to this woman, we might then use "Twain" to represent her tokenings of "that man there," and nothing else. Our context thus provides a (quite partial) "translation manual." We may for the moment imagine that the manual looks something like this:

(2) A) Odile: "Twain" → "Twain"
    B) the woman in the corner: "Twain" → "that man there."

This is abbreviated, since the sort of translation involved has to preserve Russellian content. (2B), for example, should read "For the woman in the corner, 'Twain' used as a name of Twain can translate only 'that man there' used as a Twain-name." Because this is pretty verbose, I use abbreviated translation manuals in what follows.

Tables like (2) encode what I call a context's *restrictions on translation*. What makes a translation of a mental sentence of Odile's into a public language *acceptable* is that it conforms to all the contextual restrictions which apply to Odile. In our example, acceptable translations of Odile's thought use "Twain" to translate her mental tokenings of "Twain" and nothing else. If under this restriction "Twain is tall" translates one of Odile's thoughts, then (1) is true; otherwise, it's not. So, in a nutshell, runs the account I gave in Chapter 3 of PA.

In its simplest form, the objection Sider and Soames raise to this account is that when a belief *ascriber* is confused, the translation table in the belief ascriber's context will typically inherit the confusion. This in turn may prevent the content sentences in belief ascriptions from translating *anything*. And this induces a counter-intuitive distribution of truth values. For example, suppose that we are confused about Odile's identity. Unbeknownst to us, she is the woman in the corner. In our wretched ignorance, we place incompatible demands on how "Twain" is to be used in translation. We demand that it translate one expression ("Twain") when we speak about Odile's beliefs, and quite another ("that man there") when we speak of the beliefs of the woman in the corner—who *is* Odile.

Our contextual instructions for translation may include (2) even in the unhappy situation in which Odile is the woman in the corner. But then (1) will be false;

(3) Odile believes that Twain is Twain

will be false; *every* sentence of the form

(4) Odile believes that ϕ (Twain)

will be false in our context. For the truth of (4) requires that φ (*Twain*) translate something realizing one of Odile's beliefs. But this sentence can't translate any such thing, if it has to obey the instructions in (2). For these instructions require us to use "Twain" only as a translation of "Twain" *and* to use it only as a translation of "that man there."

The first point I want to make in response is this. If this objection to PA's account were forceful, then objections cognate to it should be telling against quite plausible accounts of the semantics of a large number of "contextually shifty" expressions. Since we should agree these cognate objections are not telling, we should also agree that this objection is not.

To make this point, I leave the attitudes for a moment to consider adjectives, such as "tall," "warm," and "sleazy," whose hallmark is that their simultaneous application to one object may result in claims with different truth values. Suppose I utter

(5) Nancy is tall,

meaning she is tall for a Kerrigan; you utter (5) meaning she is tall for a skater. She is, let us suppose, tall for a Kerrigan but not for a skater. So I speak truly and you do not.

How shall we explain this? A popular account is that the adjectives in question demand a contextually supplied reference class before they can be applied to an object with the expectation that the application is true or false. Typically, the reference class is determined by the interests and focus of the speaker, or of the speaker and others in the conversational context. In our example, I intend to compare Nancy to the Kerrigans, and thus my intentions determine them as the reference class; you mean to compare her to the skaters, and thus your intentions determine them.[4] On this account of "tall" a use of (5) is true in a context c iff c associates a reference class T with "tall" and Nancy's height bears an appropriate relation to the heights of the members of T. Call fleshings out of this idea *implicit reference class theories* (or IRTs) of adjectives like "tall."

Even when the members of a context are self-conscious about providing a reference class, misidentification may block determination of a reference class. Suppose I utter (5), intending to compare Nancy's height with that of the grandchildren of, as I put it to myself, "that gentleman there, Grandpa Kerrigan." Suppose the elderly gentleman is not Nancy's paternal Grandpa Kerrigan, but her maternal Grandpa. Nothing about me, or my conversational partners, we may presume, favors the choice of the maternals over the paternals as class of comparison. Neither need there be a reason to say that the sum, intersection, or any other set-theoretic deconstruction of these collections is the reference class. And so, if we accept one or another IRT, we will have to say that my utterance was not true, *even if* (as we may suppose) Nancy *towers* over all the other grandchildren, maternal or paternal. Let us call this sort of example, in which a speaker's mis-identification prevents his intentions from making a proper contribution to the determination of a semantic value, a *Kerrigan example*.

---

[4] Factors besides the current intentions of speaker and audience may provide the class in question: Prior conversation, for example.

That what I say is false, even if Nancy towers over the grandchildren, seems somewhat counter-intuitive to many, myself included. But surely this counter-intuitive consequence of otherwise well-motivated IRTs does not provide a reason to throw them out and start from scratch on an account of "tall." After all, we can explain our reaction to the Kerrigan example by observing that, however we correct for the speaker's error, we make (5) true. Even if we decide that the intuition that (5) is true, if Nancy towers over all the grandchildren, is correct, what Kerrigan examples show, at most, is that IRTs must be complicated to deal with contexts in which the specification of a reference class is defective. Such examples do not show that IRTs are not approximately correct.

Whenever a semantic value is determined (in whole or in part) by speaker intentions, Kerrigan examples are bound to arise. So we should not be deterred by Kerrigan examples from accepting a theory that sees certain semantic values as being so determined. At least such examples shouldn't deter us, provided there is, Kerrigan examples to one side, strong motivation to think that speaker intentions do contribute to determining the value in question, and a satisfactory account of Kerrigan examples can be given on the theory in question.[5]

Now I think that Sider and Soames agree that there are fairly good reasons for saying that speaker intentions contribute to determining the semantic value of "believes." (They just don't find the reasons conclusive.) If they do, and they agree with the methodological point, then the issue turns on how plausible an account one can give, if one accepts my account, of Kerrigan examples.

Let me give a preliminary account of Kerrigan examples; being preliminary, it ignores some of Soames' more subtle points.[6] Let us first ask what we should say about the Kerrigan example involving "tall." This is a case in which (a) speaker and audience wrongly presuppose that A is the paternal grandpa; (b) partially on the basis of this presupposition, the sets

S_1: A's grandchildren
S_2: the paternal grandpa's children

are both "best candidates" for the reference class for "tall." An extremely natural thing to say is that in this sort of case, whether (5) is true, false, or neither depends on whether it makes any difference, as to whether we choose S_1 or S_2 as reference class. If (5) would

---

[5] Many examples make this point. Some predicates—"heap" "dirty" "round" for example—shift extensions across contexts depending, in part, on what count as good or acceptable examples of satisfiers of the predicate. The contextual provision of exemplars for such predicates may be defective. Misidentifications, as in the Kerrigan case, may cause this. Or conversants may be committed to using a single "paradigm" for a predicate (or a set of paradigms that closely resemble each other relevant respects), but, unknown to one another, have quite different paradigms in mind. (My paradigm for "cooked" may resemble your paradigm for "raw" more than it does your paradigm for "cooked.") Surely this does not speak against the view that such expressions have contextually varying extensions which are determined in good part by the intentions, interests, and focus of conversants.

[6] In fact, I will ignore the modal dimensions of Soames' objection, to keep this response to a manageable length. How to generalize what I say to give modal truth conditions is in any event fairly obvious.

come out true on either choice, it's true; if it would come out true on neither, it's false; otherwise it is without truth value.

I propose that we say exactly the same thing about Kerrigan examples involving "believes." On the account of attitude ascription I propose, a context in which attitudes are ascribed is a context in which speaker and audience are engaged in constructing a "translation manual" for reporting beliefs. Their construction of this manual will be guided in part by their beliefs and presuppositions about the identities of the believers under discussion. If speaker and audience, for example, consider ascriptions with the terms "Smith," "Jones," and "Robinson" as subjects, context will often (though not inevitably) contain a presupposition about the truth of the identities "Smith is Jones" "Smith is Robinson," and "Jones is Robinson."

The Sider/Soames objection involves an example in which the contextual construction of a translation manual goes awry because of defects in these sorts of presuppositions: (Mis)identifying A as different from B, speakers contribute one "translation rule" for A and an incompatible one for B. Such errors are easily resolvable, however. Suppose we have presupposed falsely that A is B, and introduced two incompatible translation rules on this basis. To resolve the error, we delete one or the other rule. To evaluate an attitude ascription for truth in such a context, we consider all the "resolutions" of errors in the translation manual which depend upon mistaken contextual presuppositions: If the ascription is true on all resolutions, it is true *simpliciter*; if false on all, it's false *simpliciter*; otherwise neither.

Slightly more precisely (but still ignoring Soames' subtle points about quantification and modality), the proposal is this. Part of what goes to make up a context is a set of presuppositions. For the moment, I identify presuppositions with sentences-interpreted-as-if-uttered by one or another member of the context.[7] In the examples on which the current objection rests, the context's presuppositions include a sentence of the form *a is not b* (as spoken by one or another of the context's participants). In the particular example given above, "Odile is not the woman in the corner," interpreted as if spoken by me, is presupposed.

The restrictions on translation which a context contains may depend upon one (or more) of these presuppositions, where a restriction depends upon a non-identity a is not b, if the restriction would find natural expression in the context by using one of the two terms therein (and the non-identity is a contextual presupposition). Let us say that a context's restrictions are *defective* if (i) for some individuals u and v, sets S and S', and expression α, the restrictions include

(6)   (*)   For u: α represents only members of set S
      (**) For v: α represents only members of set S'

---

[7] If we identify sentences as uttered by a person with the articulated propositions (the RAMs, in the jargon I used in PA), such utterances would determine, we may then say that what is presupposed is a set of (articulated) propositions, thus achieving a unification of the objects of belief with the objects of presupposition.

where u = v but S is not S', and; (ii) (*) or (**) depends upon a non-identity, that a is not b, which is a false contextual presupposition. In our examples above, "Odile is not the woman in the corner," as spoken by me, is presupposed though false; thus the contextual restrictions given in (2) were defective. If we are discussing what Twain believes but suppose that Twain is not Clemens, then, should we ascribe belief in accord with the manual

(6') (a) Twain: "Hawthorne" → "Hawthorne"
     (b) Clemens: "Hawthorne" → "that fella there"

our context provides defective restrictions. Extending this terminology, I sometimes call contexts defective when they have defective restrictions.

In a defective context the speaker attempts to follow the rules for ascribing beliefs, but the attempt involves an error engendered by one of the context's mistaken presuppositions. The errors in question are always easily resolvable. If we have, for example, imposed both of the restrictions in (6'), we can render the context non-defective simply by withdrawing one of the two restrictions. *Any* defective context can be made coherent by deleting some restrictions. There will typically be several *resolutions* of the set of restrictions of c, if c is defective. Such resolutions are sets of restrictions just like c's, except that, if c's set is defective, just enough restrictions have been removed to render the result non-defective. A defective context does not, of course, tell us which of its resolutions to use, in evaluating an ascription of attitude. But surely the obvious, and the obviously correct, procedure for evaluating an ascription in such a context, is to see whether it makes any difference, as to how we resolve the error. If an ascription would come out true no matter how we resolved the error—if it's true on all the resolutions of the context's restrictions—it's true in the context; if it would come out false, no matter how we resolve, it's false. Otherwise it suffers from what is, alas, a common defect of our assertive stabs at the truth—it's not true, and it's not false.

There is no need to make defective contexts a special case. We can simply say that for any context c and attitude ascription A, if A is evaluated as true (using the account from PA) in all the resolutions of c, it is true in c *simpliciter*; likewise for falsity. Since a non-defective context has only one resolution (itself), this does not effect what PA's account says about non-defective contexts.

To this, Soames responds that *non*-defective contexts may contain incompatible restrictions; the objection re-emerges for such contexts. Suppose, for example, that we are discussing the beliefs of the author of *Gravity's Rainbow* and of the man in the corner. Surely we needn't presuppose that the first is the second or presuppose that they are distinct in order to do this. Suppose I say

(7) The author of *Gravity's Rainbow* thinks that Twain wrote *Huck Finn*.
     The man in the corner thinks that Twain wrote *The Mysterious Stranger*.

My intention is that "Twain" in the first ascription represent or translate the author's use of "Twain"; that it, in the second, represent or translate the man in the corner's use of "Clemens."

Suppose Pynchon, the book's author, is the man in the corner. Soames claims that PA's semantics then make it impossible for both ascriptions to be true. The ascriptions are false, because the context contains restrictions

(8) the author of *Gravity's Rainbow*: "Twain" → "Twain"
the man in the corner: "Twain" → "Clemens."

which are (because the author of the book is the man in the corner) incompatible. But we may suppose that Pynchon accepts "Twain wrote *Huck Finn*" and "Clemens wrote *The Mysterious Stranger*," and that my intention in uttering (7) is to convey that Pynchon believed the propositions these sentences express under these very sentences. PA's semantics is supposed to insure that when I speak with such intentions, my ascriptions are true just in case the beliefs are held using the sentences in question. But it does not. So the view doesn't do what it's supposed to. Call this the *Pynchon objection*.[8]

In fact, it does not follow from what's said in PA that in the Pynchon objection, the context's restrictions include (8). To fix ideas, let us pretend that each time a person ascribes a belief or other attitude using a sentence

a believes that S,

she has a particular set of "directions for translation" in mind, where by "directions for translation" I mean a collection of sentences of the form

In talking about a, e is to represent expressions such that…

where e is some expression in S. According to PA, a context's restrictions depend upon the interests and focus of speaker and audience. Ignoring the audience for the nonce, and working within the current pretense, the suggestion is that a context's restrictions are determined by the directions for translation which accompany the ascriptions made in the context.[9]

The Pynchon objection interprets this as the claim that each direction for translation in a context is a restriction. But this need not be so. It's perfectly consistent with the above, and with PA's semantics, to say that if (i) a conversation involves ascriptions of attitude of the surface forms

a believes that S
b believes that T,

(ii) "a" and "b" pick out the same thing, and (iii) that a is not b is *not* presupposed, then, in constructing the restrictions for the conversation, we *merge* the directions for translation accompanying each ascription. Here, to merge the directions

---

[8] "Supervaluating" in such cases (that is, adapting the procedure suggested above for dealing with defective contexts) is not sufficient to guarantee that both sentences in (7) are true. For Pynchon could fail to accept "Twain is Clemens." If so, he might accept "Twain wrote *Huck Finn*" but not "Clemens wrote *Huck Finn*." In such a case, if the context's restrictions include (8), "Pynchon believes that Twain wrote *Huck Finn*" comes out false on a "supervaluational" approach.

[9] I do not, in fact, think that this is the only factor determining what restrictions are in play. What is presupposed in the context also may contribute to determining restrictions. I ignore this for simplicity's sake.

(D1) In talking about a, e is to represent expressions in S
(D2) In talking about b, e is to represent expressions in T

is to replace them with the direction

(D3) In talking about someone who is identical with a and identical with b, e represents expressions which are in S or T.

Suppose that this is (a first and rough approximation to) the relation which a context's restrictions have to the intentions of its participants. Then in the Pynchon objection the context does not contain the restrictions in (8) but rather

(9) the author of *Huck Finn* and the author of *The Mysterious Stranger:* "Twain" → {"Twain" "Clemens"}.

The core of this response is that in a situation like that in the Pynchon objection—in which the context contains directions like (D1) and (D2), "a is b" is true, and "a is not b" is not presupposed—e may represent either members of S or of T in acceptable representations of a's thoughts. Call an account which allows this an *agglomerative account* of contextual restrictions. My response to the Pynchon objection is that the correct account of contextual restrictions is agglomerative.

The idea that attitude ascription proceeds by agglomeration is in some sense just the idea that it is governed by the rule: If you are using expression e to translate the expressions in a set S, and you decide to use e to translate the expression t as well, then, henceforth, you will use e to translate the expressions in the set consisting of all of S and of T. It is natural (to say the least) to think that if attitude ascription is a kind of translation, then it conforms to such a rule, at least when the attitude ascriber knows whether the ascriptions she makes are ascriptions of attitude to the same or different people.[10] In claiming that restrictions are generally constructed *via* agglomeration, I am only claiming that this rule always applies, unless the sort of confusion found in a defective context is present.

One might object that an agglomerative account has counter-intuitive consequences. Here is a bit of stage setting for such an objection. Suppose I read "Kripke was raised in Nebraska." As a result, I remark

(A) The author believes that he was raised in the Midwest

while demonstrating Kripke, making this remark with an eye to conveying that the author accepts "Kripke raised in the Midwest." Shortly thereafter, I notice Kripke demonstrated while someone says to your mother "he is a metaphysician." Demonstrating Kripke, I remark

(B) Your mother believes that he is a philosopher,

---

[10] Examples which are naturally interpreted in terms of agglomeration are easy to construct. For example When I read your book, I thought you were at least as talented as Jones. And the first time I heard you speak, I thought that you were more talented than he. I also thought, when I read your book, that you'd be a boring speaker. But after having heard you, I know that you aren't.

assuming that she accepts "he is a philosopher" and trying to convey that. Suppose, finally, that your mother is the author of what I am reading, but I am oblivious to this (and so don't suppose that she wrote it, and don't suppose she didn't).

(A) was accompanied by a direction to use "he," when speaking of the author, to represent "Kripke"; (B) with a direction to use "he," when speaking of your mother, to represent "he." An agglomerative account allows (B) to be true should your mother accepts "Kripke is a philosopher" while she rejects "he is a philosopher." One might object to the agglomerative account thus: I would, in this sort of situation, *retract* (B), if I were to learn that your mother rejected "he is a philosopher" (say, because she thought the person demonstrated to her was not a metaphysician but an insurance agent). Thus, the agglomerative account is not supported by our intuitions about truth conditions.

It is true that I would retract (B) if told *only* that your mother failed to accept its content sentence. But it is also true that I would confidently assent to claims such as

(C) If the author is your mother and the author believes that he is a philosopher, then your mother believes that he's a philosopher too.

Indeed, if I took "the author believes that he is a philosopher" as obvious, I would confidently assent to

(D) Your mother believes that he's a philosopher, if your mother's the author.

In the sort of case at issue, there are thus (at least) two pieces of information which may be expected to effect the speaker's intuitions about truth: Information about what sentences your mother accepts, and information about your mother's identity. The objection on the table observes that if you give a speaker *some* of this information, he will deny that (B) is true. The problem with the objection is that it's not at all clear that this denial would occur if you were to give the speaker *all* the relevant information. My own intuitions tell me that speakers reminded of (D) and given both pieces of information would judge (B) true.

It is surely our propensities in these more complicated cases, in which we are given all (or more) of the relevant information, which are relevant to evaluating the agglomerative account, not our propensities in cases in which we reason from an incomplete (and probably misleading) set of assumptions. And I am fairly sure that our judgments in and about these more complex cases do not generate evidence against the agglomerative account.[11]

---

[11] To a response akin to (but somewhat different from) that I give to the Pynchon objection, Soames objects that it "create[s] ... a Russell-like problem for every apparently non-Russellian example" which motivates the account of PA. If we merge restrictions, he suggests, then in a situation in which (i) I utter

(E) Thomas believes that Twain is dead

intending it to be interpreted in a Russellian fashion; (ii) utter

(F) Pynchon believes that Twain is happy

intending "Twain" to translate Pynchon's use of "Twain," and (iii) the subjects of (E) and (F) name the same person, merging requires us to say that both restrictions must be given a Russellian interpretation.

Soames apparently draws this conclusion because he assumes that if (E) has Russellian truth conditions, this is because it is accompanied by a restriction.

To complete my response to the Pynchon objection, I need to do two things. First, I need to convince you that an agglomerative account of how translation manuals are constructed is not just an *ad hoc* patch up job of PA's semantics. Secondly, I need to spell out some of the details of the agglomerative account I propose to adopt.

First things first. It is a commonplace that conversational contributions in which a contextually sensitive expression is used can produce a shift in the expression's semantic value. David Lewis, for example, suggests that the extensions and intensions of some expressions depend in part on what he calls the *conversational score*, an entity which evolves in a (quasi-) rule governed way in the course of a conversation. Incorporating, for example, "standards of precision" conversational score contributes importantly to determining the extensions of vague predicates. One way such standards can shift is simply by someone making an (unchallenged) comment whose truth requires a shift in the standards:

> One way to change the standards is to say something that would be unacceptable [or untrue] if the standards remain unchanged. If you say "Italy is boot-shaped" and get away with it, low standards are required and the standards fall if need be. ....[12]

Lewis suggests that there is a general principle of accommodation at work here, one which might be formulated roughly so: If at time t in a conversation something is said which can be true only if the conversation's score has property P, then, *ceteris paribus* (and supposing certain conditions to hold, such as its being possible for the score to have P), at t the score has P.[13]

I think we should accept the idea that such a principle contributes to the correct interpretation of our everyday discourse. It ought and can be sharpened in various ways, of course. For instance accommodation has to be *conservative*: If there are two ways, A and B, to accommodate a conversational contribution, then, if A, applied retroactively, does a worse job than B in keeping earlier contributions to the conversation true, we cannot (all else being equal) use A to accommodate.

I assume we accept

(a) something along the lines of a principle of accommodation is true of many contextually sensitive predicates
(b) accommodation must be conservative.

If accommodation applies to "believes," then its conservative nature will insure that in the Pynchon example, the context's restrictions will be given by (9); thus, both sentences

---

For Thomas, "Twain" may translate absolutely any name of Twain.

But this is not how the system of PA works: In the sort of case of Soames apparently has in mind, (E) should be understood as having no restrictions on translation accompanying it.

Furthermore, the force of the intuitions Soames is attempting to marshal with this comment are, I suspect, mitigated by the fact that sentences such as (E) and (F) will, in the sort of case Soames has in mind, occur in both a local and a global context. (See the discussion below for an explanation.) Space limitations prevent me from pursuing this last point.

[12] Lewis (1979), 245.
[13] See Lewis (1979), 240, for a more precise formulation.

in (7) will be true.[14] Thus if accommodation applies to "believes," the Pynchon objection fails.

However, even given

(c) "believes" is contextually sensitive because it relies on something like a contextually supplied translation manual,

we can't yet infer that accommodation applies to "believes." For there are contextually sensitive predicates to which accommodation apparently doesn't apply, or at least to which it doesn't usually apply. For example, it doesn't, or at least needn't, apply to "tall" and other predicates which need a contextually supplied reference class. If you say that Nancy is tall, meaning that she is tall for a skater, and I say that Sidney isn't tall, meaning he isn't tall for a basketball player, we surely aren't supposed to evaluate my contribution by considering Sidney's height in relation to the class, skaters or basketball players.

What we need is a test which will help determine whether accommodation applies to a predicate. I think I can supply such (though the test will be much rougher than many would want). Applying it shows, I believe, that, given that "believes" is context sensitive, accommodation applies to it.

Put abstractly, Lewis's observation about "square" was that its use at a time t in a conversation can shape the semantic properties of sentences being uttered at t and thereafter in the conversation. If you reflect on it, you'll see that a use of "square" at a time t in a conversation may also effect the interpretation of sentences uttered *before* t within the conversation. Since this does not seem to have been widely noticed, and since it is, if true, of some importance, I will briefly develop this point. Then I will use it to motivate the test, for whether accommodation applies to a predicate.

Consider the following dialogue.

A. We need to teach the children geography. How are we going to do it?
B. We could talk about the shapes of states. Iowa and Kansas are rectangular, for example.
A. Well, I had in mind European geography, so that won't help. France isn't square or round or hexagonal, and neither are Italy or the rest.
B. Right. Maybe we could put little pictures on the map of native costumes of each country.

If we apply Lewis's proposal to this dialogue, we will say that at its end, the extensions of "square," "round," "hexagonal" and the rest exclude the countries of Europe, in virtue of A's second contribution: His remark, since it goes unchallenged, sets the standards of precision high enough to exclude Italy and so on. As a result, A's claim that France is not hexagonal is true.

Suppose the dialogue continues as follows.

C. What's wrong with the shape idea? Italy's shaped like a cowboy boot; England is shaped like a bishop's hat. And Spain is shaped like a square, for that matter.

---

[14] We should expect accommodation to apply only *ceteris paribus*. In particular, if a context is defective, containing a false presupposition about the identity of those under discussion, it will not apply.

A. Good point. In fact, France is hexagonal, and I shouldn't have said it wasn't. Still, what are we going to do about countries like Greece and Switzerland?

Again applying Lewis's ideas about accommodation, we will say that when A accedes to C, the extensions of "hexagonal," "square," and so forth shift, so that some European countries find themselves in some such extensions.

But now note. (1) It would seem that *simply* by saying what she does, C is not able to shift the standards of precision applying to the shape words, since C is *disagreeing* with something A said. It is only because C says what she does *and* A accedes thereto that the standards shift. But looking at the conversation as a whole, one wants to say that C's contribution was correct. Certainly A and C may be expected to tell us that C was right, when she made her comments. But if C's comments were correct, it seems that something which occurs within the conversation *after* the time at which a sentence S is uttered may affect the conversational score *during* the utterance of S, thereby effecting the interpretation of expressions in S.

(2) A cognate point can be made about A's second and third contributions to the conversation. In his third contribution, A takes back what he said in the second. This is a perfectly natural concession to make in a situation of the sort we're considering. And it is never the case that in such a situation one says things like "Well, Spain *wasn't* square when I was speaking before, but I guess it is now." If we take A's contribution at face value, we will interpret it thus: (i) A (correctly) reports what he earlier said with "France isn't hexagonal" by saying "I said that France wasn't hexagonal"; (ii) in saying that he shouldn't have said it, A (correctly) observes that the claim in question is false. I think we should take A's contribution at face value. We can do this, if we allow that what happens in the course of the conversation effects the semantic value of "hexagonal" at earlier points therein, thereby effecting what was said by earlier uses of sentences in which the predicate occurred. It is not easy to see how else we might be able to take A's contribution at face value.

This again shows, I think, that our conversational behavior presupposes that what transpires in a conversation at a time t may effect the interpretation of predicates used in contributions to the conversation completed (long) before t. It would not be difficult to multiply examples of this sort of *contextual normalization*, in which the interpretation of a predicate within a conversation is determined, in part, by global considerations concerning (intentions connected with) uses of the predicate throughout the conversation.

The idea that there is such contextual normalization may strike some as problematic. After all, given accommodation, A's first contribution to the dialogue above is true, at least when he makes it. By the end of the conversation, it's false—at least it is if there's contextual normalization. But if it's false, it is then false when he makes it. But it can't be both true and false when he makes it.

It's impossible for A's utterance to have two truth values when he makes it only if it occurs in only one context. But there is every reason to say that in the sort of case we are considering, the utterance occurs in at least two contexts. For it occurs within the context established by his utterance at the time he makes it (we might call this the utterance's *local* context), and it occurs within the global context determined by the conversation taken as a whole. The most notable difference between these two contexts, for present purposes, is their difference regarding what it is, to be square, hexagonal, and so forth. This difference determines different extensions for predicates such as "square" and "hexagonal," and thus different truth values for A's utterance.[15]

If there is such a phenomenon as contextual normalization—and it seems to me that examples such as the dialogue above make it plausible that there is—there are a number of questions we need to answer concerning it. Obviously, not every contextually sensitive expression is a candidate for normalization. We do not re-interpret uses of "that" or "you" to achieve univocality of interpretation across a conversation. So what triggers normalization?

A reasonable hypothesis is that the possibility of normalization is decided on a word by word basis, with some expressions ("square," perhaps) marked for mandatory normalization, some ("you") marked as unnormalizable, and perhaps others ("tall"?) cases where normalization is optional.[16] If we suppose this is roughly correct, then a rough test, for whether an expression requires normalization, will be our intuitions about its logical properties. Suppose we find arguments in which expression e enjoys multiple occurrences to be valid in virtue of general logical principles (and not because of special facts about e's meaning.[17]) Then we must take multiple uses of e within an argument to be univocal. This indicates that we take e to be an expression which may safely be taken to preserve its interpretation within a context.[18] If e is also a contextually sensitive expression, we should then suppose that it requires normalization. For otherwise it would not be guaranteed to preserve its interpretation in context. But if it wasn't so guaranteed, then we would not, I presume, have the relevant logical intuitions.

Let us now return to the question, "How do we determine whether accommodation applies to a contextually sensitive expression?" Our examples of predicates to which normalization applies were predicates (of shapes) to which accommodation applied. That accommodation applies to them is no accident. Normalization is a process by which what happens in the course of a conversation fixes the extension of a predicate as

---

[15] Part of the argument for the existence of semantic normalization above required that A's utterance u_2 of "I shouldn't have said that France wasn't hexagonal" at the end of the conversation, says (*inter alia*) that A said p, where p is the proposition he expressed at the beginning of the conversation with the utterance u_1 of "France isn't hexagonal." What I intend in the argument is that u_2, taken relative to the global context of the conversation, is a correct report of what u_1 says, taken relative to the global context.

[16] When I wrote this, I did not clearly distinguish between the two sorts of contextual sensitivity that words like "tall" enjoy. "tall" requires a reference class or property (things aren't tall simpliciter, but tall for a modern building or for a basketball player from Dubrovnik, or...). Once modified with a property, there may still be contextual variation as to where the "cut off" for tallness lies. Arguably, once "tall" is modified by a property, it will behave like "square" as far as normalization goes.

The discussion of gradeable adjectives in "Contextualism and Relativism" (in Vol. II of *Meaning in Context*) is relevant here. (Note added in 2012.)

[17] As, for instance, in the case of the argument "Mary has a brother, so she has a sibling."

[18] I assume a definition of validity along the lines of Kaplan's—on which validity is a matter of (at least) transmission of truth from premisses to conclusion within any context—is correct.

it is used throughout the conversation. A predicate which is normalizable must be one whose extension may be affected by the way in which it is used in the course of a conversation. This strongly suggests that any normalizable predicate will be subject to accommodation. So a test (i.e., sufficient condition) for whether a predicate is normalizable is also as a test for whether a predicate is subject to accommodation.

Now, a broad spectrum of arguments in which "believes" occurs seem to be valid in virtue of quite general logical principles. Schematic examples are

a believes that S
a = b
So b believes that S

and

a believes whatever b does
b believes that S
So a believes that S.

One motivation of PA's semantics, in fact, was to accommodate such logical intuitions while acknowledging the context sensitivity of "believes." Since "believes" is reasonably taken as contextually sensitive, we may conclude that it requires normalization, and thus that it is subject to accommodation. For our logical intuitions and our test for the applicability of accommodation imply that, if the predicate is context sensitive, then accommodation applies to it.

The upshot is that plausible general principles concerning the proper interpretation of conversation imply that if "believes" is context sensitive, it is subject to (conservative) accommodation. If so, then the Pynchon objection doesn't show that there's a problem with PA's account of the semantics of "believes."

Having now convinced you that the agglomerative account of translation is not ad hoc (by showing it's implied by general principles of conversational interpretation), I turn to spelling out some of its details.

Soames quite correctly observes that what I say in PA needs some fine tuning, in order to provide an adequate account of attitude ascriptions with quantified subjects. PA's restrictions on translation are in effect triples, of the form of

(T1) A believer, an expression, a set of expressions.

One modification of PA (which Soames discusses) instead identifies restrictions with triples of the form of

(T2) A property (of believers), an expression, a set of expressions,

where a restriction <F, e, S> tells us that in ascribing belief to an F, e can only represent expressions in S. This strategy turns the restriction <Odile, e, S> into <the property of being identical with Odile, e, S>. It allows for the restriction <being a critic, e, S>, which may be invoked for an ascription like "some critic believes that Kaplan and Quine admire one another."

The modification whose implementation I will sketch here continues to identify restrictions with trios of the form of (T1), but identifies what I called above directions for translation (which are supposed to correspond to the "translational intentions" of conversants) with triples of the form of (T2).

Consider a context c in which attitudes are being ascribed. The speaker's intentions determine, I assume, directions for translation of the form of (T2). Call the set of these D_c.[19] c also provides a collection of presuppositions. Some of what is presupposed will be that various pairs of properties are disjointly instantiated. If, for example, "a is not b" and "no F is a G" are presupposed, then it's presupposed that <being a, being b> are disjointly instantiated, and that <being an F, being a G> are, too. Call the set of all such pairs DP_c. What we want is an explanation of how speakers' intentions and contextual presuppositions interact to determine the context's translation manual. What we want, that is, a recipe for getting from D_c and DP_c to restrictions on translation.

The recipe is simple. D_c can be thought of a collection of lists:

List 1	List 2	......	List n
$F_1: e_1 \to S_{11}$	$G_1: e_2 \to S_{21}$	......	$P_1: e_n \to S_{n1}$
$F_2: e_1 \to S_{12}$	$G_2: e_2 \to S_{22}$	......	$P_2: e_n \to S_{n2}$
......	......	......	......
$F_m: e_1 \to S_{1m}$	$G_m: e_2 \to S_{2m'}$	......	$P_m: e_n \to S_{nm'}$

Each list gives us instructions about a particular expression. For example, List 1 tells us that e_1 is to represent members of S_{11} when we're speaking of things that are F_1's, that it's to represent members of S_{12} when we're speaking of things which are F_2's, and so on. An agglomerative account of restrictions tells us that, for example, if something has the properties F_i and F_j from List 1, we may, when speaking of its beliefs, use e_1 to represent expressions from either S_{1i} or S_{1j}, *so long* as it's not presupposed that no F_i is an F_j.

Generalizing: Define the merge, M_c, of D_c relative to DP_c, thus:

1) if <F,e,S> is in D_c, <{F},e,S> is in M_c;
2) if <Γ,e,S> is in M_c and <F,e,T> is in D_c, then <Γ∪{F},e, S∪T> is in M_c, unless <F,G> is in DP_c, for some G in Γ.[20]

Let i = <Γ,e,S> be in M_c. i applies (in c) to an individual u provided u has F, for each F in Γ, and there's no i = <Γ',e,S'> in M_c such that Γ' properly extends Γ and u has each member of Γ'. We say that r is a restriction on translation in c provided r = <u,e,S> (for some individual u, expression e, and set thereof S) and r is such that for some set of

---

[19] Actually, D_c will typically contain elements determined by intentions and beliefs of the audience, by earlier remarks in the conversation, and so on. I ignore this.
[20] I assume that D_c and DP_c are always finite.

properties $\Gamma, i = <\Gamma,e,S>$ is in M_c and i applies to u in c. A context is *coherent* provided that for any u and e, it yields at most one restriction of the form $<u,e,S>$.

We say, as in PA, that an individual u satisfies a sentence of the form x *believes that* S, taken relative to a context c, at the world of c, just in case there's some articulated proposition q such that u believes q,[21] and such that q can be translated by the articulated proposition that S, without violating any of the restrictions on translation which c provides which are relevant to u.

Summarizing: *Propositional Attitudes* defends a relatively simple account, of the semantics of attitude ascriptions. According to it, a use of an ascription such as

Ralph believes that Margaret lives

presupposes the existence of a contextually generated "translation manual." The ascription is true if (the articulated proposition corresponding to) "Margaret lives" translates (something realizing) one of Ralph's beliefs *modulo* the manual. The Pynchon objection shows that the process by which the manual is generated is more complex than anticipated in PA. The earlier Kerrigan objection shows that the manual, like other contextually generated parameters dependent on speaker intentions, may suffer from defects that call for (relatively routine) adjustments when we go to evaluate an attitude ascription for truth. Neither objection shows that there is anything amiss with PA's account of attitude ascriptions. Neither casts doubt on the claim that attitude ascription, because it involves a sort of translation, goes considerably beyond the ascription of a relation to singular propositions.

---

[21] More precisely: which is, in the jargon of PA, in its representational system.

8

Propositional Quantification

The argument

(A) Katya touched John
     Blair touched John
   So, there is something that Katya and Blair touched

is valid. So, apparently, is

(B) Katya said that John described a map
     Blair said that John described a map
   So, there is something that Katya and Blair said.

Since validity requires preservation of truth, (B)'s conclusion is thus true if its premises are. We explain the truth-conditions of (A)'s conclusion, and thus explain (A)'s validity, by giving an objectual account of its quantifier. We do not have a generally accepted account of these matters for (B).

There seem to be four options: (1) We can extend the objectual account, taking "that"-clauses to be names and invoking a domain of propositions for "something" to range over. (2) We can treat "believes" and its friends as sentence operators, and treat "something" in (B) as a substitutional quantifier. (3) We can treat "believes" as an operator but despair, as does Quine (1960), ruling (B)'s conclusion never true, (B) itself invalid. (4) With Prior we can treat "believes" as an operator, explain (B)'s validity in terms of the logical principles governing quantifiers, but eschew explaining the truth-conditions of arbitrary quantifications: According to Prior, a "formal definition of 'something' is neither necessary or possible" (Prior 1971: 35).

In this essay, I assess the relative merits of approaches to this problem which do not invoke "intensional" entities—possible worlds intensions, properties, Fregean senses, or propositions whose individuation rely on such. I begin with Prior's account. I argue that in refusing to give a systematic account of the semantics of propositional quantifications, Prior makes them unduly mysterious. In fact, it is difficult to see why we ought to prefer Prior's view to an instrumentalism about (B)'s conclusion, on which it is neither true nor false.

I turn next to the substitutional account. I observe that to deal with ambiguity, the substitutionalist will have to individuate sentences in terms of an intra-linguistic relation of *having the same sense as*. I argue that quantification over what is said by foreign-language speakers, requires importing every language into the quantifier's substitution class, at which point the substitution class begins to look somewhat like a domain of propositions.

Finally, I discuss an objectual account of propositional quantification which identifies propositions with the sort of sentences the substitutionalist requires. I argue that the account can meet all the standard objections to the view that sentences play the role of propositions.

I. Prior's view

For Prior, propositional quantifiers (PQs) are neither objectual nor substitutional. This view is a by-product of his insistence that intensionality be explained without appeal to intensions. A typical expression of this view is in this comment on Russell's multiple relation theory of belief:

> I would put [Russell's theory] thus: 1. "Othello ascribes infidelity to Desdemona" = 2. "Othello believes that Desdemona is unfaithful"; but if we are to *explain* anything by adverting to this identity of meaning, we explain 1 by saying that it simply means 2, rather than vice versa, since it is precisely the apparent reference to an abstract object called Infidelity which *needs* explaining. Propositions aren't the *only* logical constructions that need to be shown to be such by being paraphrased away... (Prior 1971: 9)

Thus ruled out is any standard account of PQs, on which they are objectual quantifiers with a domain of Fregean senses, Russellian propositions, Meinongian *objektiven*, or the like.

PQs could still be objectual if "that"-clauses named something extensional—sentences, say, or some other linguistic item. PQs would then range over the class of possible nominata for "that"-clauses. Prior thought this "an obvious error." His most telling point, I think, was the observation that one might fear that there will be war even if the sentence "There will be a war" did not exist—an observation which makes it difficult to explain the truth of "Khrushchev might have feared there would be a war, even though there were no English sentences."

Prior concludes in *Objects of Thought* that PQs are not nominal quantifiers. That is, their substitutends are not names; the variables they bind are not nominal. A Quinean would here infer that natural language PQs are somehow illegitimate, since only first-order, nominal quantification is legitimate. Prior would have none of this, and instead concluded that PQs are sentential quantifiers.

But PQs are not, in Prior's view, substitutional: James might believe something, though it is not within the expressive power of English to say what he believes. That is, "James believes something" might be true though it has no true substitution-instances. But if PQs are neither objectual nor substitutional, what are they? Prior writes

I do not think that any formal definition of "something" is either necessary or possible, but certain observations can usefully be made concerning the truth conditions of statements [involving it]. "Something is red-haired" is clearly true if any specification of it is true... I do not say that "Something is red-haired" or "For some x, x is red-haired" is true *only* if there is some true sentence which specifies it, since its truth may be due to the red-hairedness of some object for which our language has no name or which no one is in a position to point to... If we want to bring an "only if" into it the best we can do, ultimately, is to say that "For some x, x is red-haired" is true if and only if there is some red-haired object or person, but this is only to say it is true if and only if for some x, x is red-haired... All this can be carried over, *mutatis mutandis*, into the discussion of quantifications over variables of other categories, and there isn't the least need to equate them with name-variables in order to see what is going on... "For some p, James believes that p"... is clearly true if any specification of it is... In all this, I cannot see anything mysterious, or anything that need compel us to treat variables that do *not* stand for names of objects as if they did. (Prior 1971: 35–6)

There is something of a mystery here. An account which holds that an infinitely large class of sentences has truth-conditions (and that members of the class are often enough true), but which provides us no hope of finding a systematic account of their truth-conditions, makes the relevant class of sentences mysterious. Prior's account seems to do just this to the class of prepositional quantifications.

Compare Prior's account of PQs with objectual and substitutional accounts of nominal quantifiers. Prior's remarks suggest that even in the case of nominal quantifiers, he rejected Tarskian accounts of truth-conditions or found them unilluminating. Correct or not, accounts of quantification in terms of satisfaction are attempts to provide something most think central to any complete account of language. They are attempts to explain how things have to be in the non-linguistic world, in order for an arbitary sentence to be true. In saying that "something' is F' true just in case something satisfies the predicate, we are assuming something determines satisfaction-conditions for the appropriate range of predicates—tying such quantifications to the situations that make them true, not simply stating the obvious. Minimally, such an account manages to assign with finite means truth-values to (what are typically) an infinite lot of sentences.[1] The substitutional account also systematically assigns determinate truth-values or truth-conditions to quantified sentences—provided, of course, that the instances of the quantification are assigned determinate truth-values or truth-conditions to begin with.

Prior attempts no such thing for propositional quantification. He denies that there is a property or extension associated with "James believes" and an operation on such associated with PQs, whose interaction determines the truth-conditions of "James believes something." Such an approach is completely wrong-headed to someone who thinks, as did Prior, that "James believes that" is a sentence operator. A substitutional account fits well enough with this view of syntax, but Prior rejected it as not fitting with the facts.

---

[1] Sometimes it is possible to see the account as not merely assigning truth-values to sentences, but as implicitly or explicitly assigning "states of affairs" to sentences. The same is true for some semantical characterizations employing a substitutional account of the quantifiers, provided we think of the class of states of affairs as being closed under infinitary Boolean operations.

One could keep Prior's view of syntax, reject the objectual and substitutional accounts of PQs, but preserve a compositional approach by assigning sentences semantic values and sentence operators operations on such. But to do that is thoroughly un-Priorian. It is a hallmark of Prior's views that where we have intensionality in language, we have expressions that *do not have* semantic values sufficient to a compositional account of truth-conditions. When we have intensionality without intensions, and the intensionality is not explained in terms of covert reference to expressions, we have language for which there is no compositional semantics—at least none of a traditional sort. There is in this case no explanation to be had of how the semantic properties of complex expressions are determined by their syntax and their semantic values, since there is nothing to play the roles of semantic values.

What determines the semantic properties of propositional quantifications on such a view? Prior, to my knowledge, had nothing to say about this. But one can imagine how an answer might go. The loose pressure of usage, collective tendencies to affirm and deny, all of these and other factors besides, might suffice to assign propositional quantifications a somewhat vaguely defined collection of situations in which they count as true. On such a view, there is probably very little of a perfectly general nature to be said about the truth-conditions of such quantifications, beyond saying how their truth or falsity is connected to that of their instances, and giving an account of whatever logical principles might apply to them.

Those of us sympathetic to compositional approaches to natural language find this view something of a disappointment, even if we are somewhat sympathetic to the anti-intensionalism that powers it. For this reason alone, I think it worth re-examining the approaches Prior rejects. A further reason is that Prior's position seems inherently unstable: arguably, there is no compelling reason to prefer Prior's view to a Quinean instrumentalism about propositional quantification.

Compare quantifications which are incontestably nominal, such as "James touched something," with more controversial ones, such as "James said something." It is quite plausible to think that all non-controversially nominal quantification in natural language is either objectual or substitutional. And it is difficult to see much of an ambiguity in "something," as we pass from "James touched something" to "James said something." If we agree that nominal quantification is invariably objectual or substitutional, Prior's view forces us to posit a significant and counter-intuitive shift between the two sentences. Not only do we pass from a nominal to a sentential quantifier; we pass from an expression whose semantics is compositional to one whose semantics is—well—not compositional.

If we recognize the similarity of the "somethings," but refuse to counterance propositions, and decline to give a substitutional account of PQs, why count propositional quantifications true to begin with? There are, after all, "bad theories." If there are no propositions, we seem to have enshrined a bad theory in our syntax. Being thus canonized does not make it less bad, or any of its pronouncements true.

Surely preferable to Prior's view is an instrumentalism about propositional quantification according to which the instances of the quantifications generally have truth-value and truth-conditions but the quantifications themselves are without truth-value, there being no domain to quantify over to begin with. It does not follow that we ought to eschew such quantifications. They are useful as a convenient shorthand, as a device for performing something akin to semantic ascent, "useful... in heralding more tangible information" (Quine 1960: 215). One might go so far as to advocate that we adopt a distinctive notation for such quantifications—say, to treat them as sentential, not nominal. Such an instrumentalist might end up talking much as Prior did—except when it came round to talking about semantics.

One might object that most of us think that propositional quantifications are true. We do, but we also think that they imply there are, in some interesting sense, objects of belief. If we need not accede to the second claim, as Prior insisted, why must we accede to the first?

Such instrumentalism leads to the conclusion that it is not really true that there is anything that you and I believe. This would have been only slightly less horrifying to Prior than the idea that our apparent references to abstract objects are genuine. He who wishes to maintain both Prior's respect for intensionality as a linguistic phenomenon and his rejection of intensions would do well to reconsider the anti-intensionalist accounts of propositional quantification Prior rejects.

II. Substitutionalism

Let us reconsider the idea that propositional quantifiers are substitutional. I assume the substitutionalist treats PQs along the lines outlined by Kripke (1976). He claims that we can isolate a substitution class of expression-types for these quantifiers. Presumably it contains English sentences, or, perhaps, "that"-clauses of English. In the latter case, propositional names like "Fermat's last theorem" might be included. Perhaps the substitution class is to include some expressions that do not occur in English, in order to deal with unspeakable thoughts. I discuss this below.

Making reference to the substitution class, one defines a notion of an instance of a propositional quantification. The definition makes precise the intuitive idea that the instances of a propositional quantification are the results of removing an initial propositional quantifier and "replacing the variable it bound" with some member of the substitution class. Existential propositional quantifications are true in a context provided they have an instance true in the context; universals are true in a context provided all their instances are.

Before we can evaluate the substitutionalist view, we need to get somewhat clearer on the nature of the substitution class. Observe that not every inference of the surface form of

(C)   Katya believes that S
          Blair believes that S
          So, there is something Katya and Blair both believe

is valid.[2] (C) may fail if S is syntactically or semantically ambiguous, or contains demonstratives. According to the substitutionalist, instances of (C) are valid only if the substituends for S are of the same sentence type. In what does identity of type consist?

A natural answer is that it consists in identity of logical type or form, in a sense in which sharing a logical form requires containing the same words. Most accounts of logical notions like formal validity presuppose a notion of word- or sentence-identity, since on most accounts validity is in part a result of multiple appearances of expressions. Linking the propositional quantifier's substitution class to the sort of form studied in logic, the substitutionalist might say that the kinds of consideration which determine whether the same words reappear in premises and conclusion of an instance of

(D) If John described a map, he had fun
     John described a map
     So, John had fun

(and thus determine whether the argument is logically valid) determine whether the occurrences of "John described a map" in

(B) Katya said that John described a map
     Blair said that John described a map
     So, there is something Katya and Blair said

are occurrences of the same sentence.

On this view, the substitution class of the PQ is the set of logical forms of English sentence, or some superset thereof. To handle complications introduced by demonstratives, we might weaken the view to hold that identity of logical form is necessary, but not quite sufficient, for identity of substitutional type. Instances of

(E) Smiley believes that he is hungry
     James believes that he is hungry
     So, there is something Smiley and James believe

can fail to be valid because of different demonstrata. But many would not wish to say that meant that "he is hungry" differed in logical type from use to use. A solution pairs logical forms with (possible) extensional semantic values of their parts, identifying the substitution class of the PQs with the set of results. (E) is therefore not invariably valid.

The logical form thesis is the thesis that the substitution class for the PQ is determined along these last lines. Well advised to endorse the thesis is she who allows substitutional quantifiers to bind sentential variables in arbitrary sentential positions, or who endorses the validity and non-vacuity of inferences like

(F) It is not the case that pigs fly, although he believes that pigs fly.
     So, for some p it is not the case that p, although he believes that p.

[2] When I speak here of surface form, I intend a sort of form individuated in terms of morphophonetics. Below, I also use "orthographic form" for this sort of form.

(G) Marta said that John went to the movies
Herman said that John did not go to the movies
So, Marta said something which contradicted something Herman said.

The thesis gives what seems the best non-propositional explanation of the validity of these and allied inferences, which seem (obviously) valid just when the sentences generalized upon have (intuitively) the same logical form (for (F)), or stand in the right logical relation to one another (as in the case of (G)). There is a good reason, as Prior (1971) observed, for those who do not see "that"-clauses as naming propositions to accept the validity of these inferences. Following Prior, the anti-propositionalist can gloss "He has a false belief" by the conclusion of (F), and thus explain how we arrive at the conclusion that someone has a false belief given the argument's premiss. Something analogous is true of talk of one person contradicting another. It is not clear how else someone who does not countenance objects of belief can explain what we are saying when we speak of false beliefs or contradiction.

What determines logical form in the requisite sense? For one thing, a structure not betrayed by morphophonetics. To explain why it sometimes does not follow from

(1) Katya said that a chicken is in each pot
(2) Blair said that a chicken is in each pot

that there is something both Katya and Blair said, we will employ a notion of underlying structure, borrowed from linguistic theory. Recognizing structure in sentences, we might as well identify them with sets built up from expression-types. These we might identify, following Quine, with collections of tokens. What principle of word construction shall we employ, in grouping together tokens to form expression-types? Semantic ambiguity seems to block an appeal to surface orthography or to similarity of morphophonetics. Some instances of (B) are invalid, since "map" has a cartographic and a mathematical sense.

In an invalid instance of (B), the substitutionalist must recognize one word-type "map" consisting of, or at least corresponding to, cartographic "map" tokens, another of mathematical "map" tokens.[3] In a valid instance, she recognizes the same word-type used twice. Even if she resists the identification of types with sets of tokens, a substitutionalist must thus recognize some principle for segregating orthographically identical tokens into types.[4] Presumably the principle will not make reference to possible worlds intensions or Fregean senses. To what, then will it make reference?

One strategy identifies words with pairs of an orthographic type and an extension. An utterance of "David sleeps" about David Kaplan would have as its type something like

---

[3] One could say that the ambiguity does not arise with the word "map," but with some larger unit: a noun phrase or whole sentence. Such an approach seems to miss a significant generalization.
[4] If the substitutionalist accepts the logical form thesis and is moderately realistic about logical relations among sentences uttered at different times by different speakers, she is already committed to fairly strong principles of this sort.

⟨⟨"sleeps," its extensional value⟩, ⟨"David," Kaplan⟩⟩.

(Here quotation names orthographic type, such a type being the set of all like shaped or sounded tokens.) An utterance of "David sleeps" involving reference to Hume is of a type obtained from the above by replacing Kaplan with Hume. On this view, sentence-tokens are of the same type just in case they are isomorphic in structure, and contain, pointwise, expressions of the same orthographic type and extension. Call such sentences *E-sentences*; call the proposed identity of form relation *E-isomorphism*. Admittedly, this stretches the notions of word and sentence somewhat. But the substitutionalist is required to stretch the notion of a sentence anyway, to deal with demonstratives.

Do sentences individuated in terms of E-isomorphism give an adequate substitution class for PQs? I think not. Two questions are relevant. Is E-isomorphism sufficient for identity of logical form? Should we identify sentences within the scope of attitude verbs by appeal to E-isomorphism—as it were, to individuate attitudes in terms of E-isomorphism?

It is wrong to individuate attitudes in terms of E-isomorphism. Suppose that the amused and rubbed senses of "tickled" had been coextensive. If Blair were ignorant of the coextensiveness of uses of the different senses of "tickled," he might sincerely say "I think that Jones tickled Smith when she told her joke, though I do not think that Jones tickled Smith when she told her joke." If we individuate beliefs in terms of E-isomorphism, then what Blair says cannot be true. This seems clearly wrong.

Can one cogently grant this point but say that logical form is determined by E-isomorphism, thereby denying the logical form thesis? It is difficult to know what to make of such a position, especially when combined with the substitutionalist's commitment to the validity of inferences like (F) and (G).[5]

One might posit a shift in logical form when a sentence is embedded, saying that (F) is not valid, but this is:

(F')   It is not true that S, although he believes that S.
So, for some p, it is not true that p, although he believes p.

The claim here is that logical form shifts between the scope of negation and the scope of an attitude verb, although a (an orthographically individuated) sentence can have the same form in the scope of the truth operator and of an attitude verb.

This is pretty desperate. Accounts on which logical form shift under embedding are nearly all Fregean accounts, on which the explanation of the shift in form is that

---

[5] It is somewhat difficult to see how such a view would be spelled out. Suppose Blair says: Jones tickled Smith and Katya believes that Jones tickled Smith; and Jones tickled Smith and Katya doubts that Jones tickled Smith. Suppose the first two uses of "tickled" are intended to be rubbing uses, the last two amusing ones. What existential generalizations are permitted on Blair's utterance? One would think that the first two occurrences of "Jones tickled Smith" ought be existentially generalizable with a single variable; likewise for the last two. This presumably means that the two occurrences of the sentence outside the scope of attitude verbs are not so generalizable, even though they have, according to this view, the same logical form. One wonders exactly what property it is, on this view, that allows valid sentential generalization and specification.

when embedded expressions come to name propositional constituents: This is what the substitutionalist usually aspires to avoid. If a Fregean explanation of the shift in form is incorrect, what does explain it? And why doesn't form *always* shift under embedding?

Exchanging E-isomorphs in the scope of attitude verbs need not preserve truth. So if embedding expressions in the scope of such verbs doesn't affect logical form, neither logical form nor word-identity can be individuated in terms of E-isomorphism. Since it is implausible that a substitutionalist can hold that embedding affects logical form, he seems committed to a finer-grained way of individuating words and thus sentences than that provided by E-isomorphism.[6]

The obvious alternative is to appeal to the different senses an expression has, for a person or within a given population. Such an appeal is not to primitive Fregean senses. Rather, the requisite notion of sense can, one hopes, be explained in terms of regularities of use among speakers, which can in turn be explained in terms of the psychological states of users. Alternatively or additionally, one might try to appeal to differing "mechanisms of reference"—for example, causal histories—associated with an orthographic type.[7]

The words in E-sentences were pairs, or sets, of orthographically like tokens with an extensional semantic value. *S-sentences* are like E-sentences, save their words are pairs of orthographically like tokens with the same sense in a population, along with an extensional semantic value. What identities of sense there are among S-sentences are confined to sentences with the same words; thus all such identities are *intra*-linguistic. If not benign, this notion of sense is at least anaemic.

I suspect that the substitutionalist will be uncomfortable with an appeal to intra-linguistic sense. So far as I can see, it is unavoidable. One might try to avoid it by a "local individuation" of words, appealing to a (single) speaker's psychological states to justify the identification of different tokens as tokens of the same type. Thus, one might say that if in giving an argument, I intend that certain expression-tokens be taken in the same way throughout, then that is how they *ought* to be taken. It does not follow that it is in general possible to identify the senses of tokens used by different speakers, or by the same speaker at different times.

For demonstratives, a principle of word individuation on these lines is probably necessary. But I do not think this proposal suffices in general. Imagine Amanda, Bob, Cathy, and Paul all utter "Someone is tickling David." Amanda and Bob have the rubbing sense in mind, Cathy and Paul the amusing sense. Then both

(3) There is something that Amanda and Bob are saying
(4) There is something that Cathy and Paul are saying

are true. So is

---

[6] This argument applies not just to the substitutionalist, but to those who see the semantic objects of belief—i.e. the referents of "that"-clauses—as being sentences.

[7] The suggestion that word-identity is to be thus individuated in terms of mechanisms of reference is broached by Devitt (1981). Kaplan (1990) investigated this. Some discussion occurs in Richard (1990).

(5) There is nothing that both Bob and Cathy are saying.

Suppose someone utters these sentences. They speak truly, even if they have no idea what the four were saying, just as I can truly say that there is a dog in North America that is rabid, without having the least idea what dogs satisfy "x is rabid," or what terms when substituted for "x" therein yield a true sentence.

On a substitutionalist account, (3) and (4) are true (in a context) only if there are sentences s_1 and s_2 such that

(6) Amanda and Bob are saying that s_1
(7) Cathy and Paul are saying that s_2

are true (in the context). Furthermore, since (5) is true in the relevant context, s_1 and s_2 must be such that neither of

(8) Bob and Cathy are saying s_1
(9) Amanda and Bob are saying s_2

is true in the context. We cannot appeal to the intentions and beliefs of the speaker, with respect to certain expression-tokens or expression-types, in order to explain how s_1 and s_2 come to have these properties. The speaker, *ex hypothesi*, does not know what it is that Amanda and company are saying. He need not even be capable of understanding the sentences they are uttering, in order to be able to use (3) to (5) truly.

The substitutionalist is thus committed to the existence of sentences which disambiguate ambiguous sentences like "Someone is tickling David" in the way s_1 and s_2 do. However these sentences do their disambiguating, they cannot do it in the local way envisioned above. In the present case, the speaker need not have any intentions towards instances. Generalizing on this argument suggests that if an English sentence is n ways ambiguous, then the substitutionalist ought to admit the existence of n distinct sentences in the substitution class of the quantifier, which disambiguate it in the way s_1 and s_2 disambiguate "Someone is tickling David."

Consider now an inter-linguistic version of the last case. Suppose that Katya speaks a foreign language L and assertively utters an existential quantification of some L–predicate P. Sometimes we will be able to say what she said, sometimes we won't. But we can certainly say

(10) Katya said something.

But if the quantifier is substitutional, its substitution class consisting only of sentences of unadorned English, then we must be able to go on in English to report what she said.

Prior was dubious that this might be so: he thought it obvious that the existence of a true specification of an existential quantification was not necessary for its truth. I sympathize with Prior. The only plausible candidates in unadorned English for the role of a specifier of (10) will be of the form of *There are Fs* in which *F* has the same extension (in our context) as does *P* in Katya's. I see no reason to think that English has, for each extension characterizable in some foreign language, a predicate which characterizes that extension. Furthermore, we usually require semantic isomorphism in an attitude report: If Heinz says "Es gibt Dreiecke," it will not usually do to report him as having said that there are closed planar three-sided figures whose angles sum to 180 degrees. Neither English nor other idioms able to quantify over what is said always have the resources to thus ape foreign patterns of description.

The substitutionalist might deny that extensional agreement is necessary for the truth of an attitude report, suggesting that a rough translation of what is said can go proxy for an exact one in an attitude ascription. I disagree. Suppose that Katya utters in *L* "glug lixit," "glug" a demonstrative referring to us, "lixit" a predicate applying roughly but not exactly to treacherous things, there being some few things which are lixit but are not treacherous. Katya did not say that we are treacherous, since something can be what she said we are but not be treacherous. We might *say* that Katya said this. But, if pushed, we would admit that this was not exactly correct—strictly speaking, she did not say we were treacherous. The hedge shows that what we said was only approximately true. But if all the instances of *X said something* we can construct are only approximately true, that is, if they are all false, then construing the quantifier substitutionally we must say that "*X* said something" is only approximately correct, that is, strictly speaking false. And this seems wrong. It can be true that *X* said something, even if we cannot say what it is that he said.

The substitutionalist might deny that the substitution class for the propositional quantifier consists only of English sentences, or only of English sentences supplemented with their extensional semantic values. We must consider, he says, substitution-instances in various possible extensions of English.[8]

This is cheating, if the appeal is to languages which do not actually exist. Part of the point of substitutionalism is to avoid appeal to the sorts of entity from which propositions are traditionally constructed, such as possibilia. Given that the substitutionalist eschews possibilia, it would appear that to say that *X believes something* is true provided it has a true substitution-instance in some possible, but non-actual, extension of English, is to say not that "*X* believes something" is true, but that it might have been.

Perhaps the extensions of English exist, could have been spoken, but are not. If we took words to be pairs of orthographically individuated expressions and extensional semantic values, there are many possible extensions of English, construed as set-theoretic constructions involving words which are not actually a part of English.

This does not work. We have agreed that *X said that S* is not true simply because *X* assertively uttered an E-isomorph of *S*: recall the case where all senses of "tickle" turn

---

[8] Many advocates of substitutional interpretations of first-order nominal quantifiers have proposed that the semantics of the quantifier be given in terms of extensions of the (substitution class provided by the quantifier's) language. To the extent that these advocates are concerned with quantification in languages without failures of extensionality, the objections in the text are not relevant to their projects.

out coextensive. If the extensions of English in question are formed simply by adding a bit of new orthography to English and fixing its extensional semantic value, what determines the truth-values of sentences of the form *John said that S*, when *S* contains some of the new vocabulary? From an intuitive standpoint there is no saying whether such a sentence is true, since there is no saying whether or not *S* captures the *content* of anything which *X* said.

One might consider extensions of English which, instead of just fixing extensional semantic values of a piece of the new vocabulary, go on to fix its *intension* or its *sense* or whatever. But if it makes sense to do this, if such extensions exist, even though no one speaks them, do we really need to resist the appeal to propositions to begin with?

Finally, one might import foreign sentences into the substitution class, assuming they preserve their sense when added thereto. The substitution class of the English propositional quantifier would thus be constructed as follows. One collects all the sentences of all the languages which have been, are, or will be spoken. These sentences are our S-sentences, elaborate sets whose word-types are sets of tokens paired off with extensional semantic values. The substitution class of the quantifier now contains the (type of the) very sentence (token) Katya uttered. So there should be no problem about how (10) can be true, even though unadorned English lacks the resources to say what Katya said.

This could be done. But. this defence of substitutional quantification is somewhat extreme and without point. It makes English semantics include the semantics of every language there is, was, or will be: On this view, English semantics involves reference to the truth-conditions of *Katya said that S* where *S* is an arbitrary sentence of an arbitrary language. Here *S* is *used*, not mentioned. And with propositional quantification into arbitrary sentential position, as in "For some p, p," the semantics involves reference to the truth-conditions of arbitrary sentences of arbitrary languages.

Besides being extreme, this move is without point, since the sentences in question can play the role of traditional propositions.

III. Sententialism

Sententialism is the view that S-sentences can play the role of propositions, serving as the nominata of "that"-clauses and as range for propositional variables. This section partially assesses its prospects.

Many think sentences are obviously non-starters as propositions. Perhaps the standard objection to sententialism is that it is defeated by inter-linguistic ambiguity. Let *L* be a language like English, but possessing a sentence, orthographized as "Pigs fly," which means in *L* that dogs bark. If "believes" in *L* functions as in English, and an English-speaker and an *L*-speaker simultaneously utter "Richard believes that pigs fly," then the English-speaker speaks falsely, since I do not think pigs fly; the *L*-speaker speaks truly, since he says I believe that dogs bark, and I do. But according to sententialism, each ascription is true iff I have the "believes" relation to the sentence "Pigs fly." Since one ascription is true and the other false, I seem to be and not to be related to the sentence.

When we individuate sentences in the way suggested above, this objection has no force. The English sentence-type "Pigs fly" is identical with the L sentence-type "Pigs fly" only if the English word-type "pig" is identical to the L word-type "pig." The English word-type involves a certain set of tokens of the orthographic type "pig," ones produced by me and my fellow English-speakers in the course of communicating in English. Analogously for the L word-type. These sets are not identical. In fact, they would seem to be disjoint. So the English sentence is not identical with the L sentence.

A proposal that "that"-clauses name sentences must eventually be joined to a proposal about the relation named by verbs like "believes" and "says." Confronted with such a package—which amounts to a theory of propositions and our cognitive relations to them—we might have two sorts of worry. On the one hand, we might worry that the package doesn't get the relations right. For example, the proposal might have it that believing that p is carrying around a micro-token of a sentence which expresses p. We, for one reason or another, worry that this is not what belief is.

A quite different sort of worry is that the proposed propositions are inadequate for some logical, semantic, or allied reason. The objection involving inter-linguistic ambiguity is of this sort. Church's objections to Carnap's and allied sententialist accounts of propositions are of this sort. Most objections to the idea that sentences are the semantic objects of belief—i.e. what "that"-clauses name and what the propositional quantifiers range over—are of this sort.

My purpose here is to defuse this sort of objection. But I must also endorse some proposal about the belief relation. Otherwise, the suggestion that sentences can provide a range for the propositional quantifier is empty: How could we evaluate the claim that sentences are the possible values of "p" in "Prior believed p," with no account of what it would be for something to satisfy "Prior believed p"? So I will sketch a sententialist approach to "believes" that seems promising. I shall then return to defending the view that sentences are propositions against various logico-semantic objections.[9]

We want to identify propositions with the S-sentences of the last section: sets whose structure encodes syntactic relations, and whose constituents consist of orthographic expression-types (identified with sets of tokens) paired with their extensional semantic values. Using quotemarks to form names of expression-types, the proposal is to identify the sentence-type of a use of "Richard incites" with something like

⟨⟨"incites," its extensional value⟩, ⟨"Richard," me⟩⟩.[10]

---

[9] An intensional sententialism, on which the view discussed in the text is loosely based, is presented at length in Richard (1990). The extensional version is inspired by Grandy (1986). I am not sure that Grandy would endorse it. Neither is Grandy.

[10] We shouldn't confine the S-sentences simply to those which correspond to actually uttered sentences. Using a notion like that of a sentence-taken-in-a-context, we can talk about the S-sentence determined by a sentence-type in a context. We may thus allow, for example, that for each object x, there's an S-sentence corresponding to "that is identical to that," in which the pair ⟨"that," x⟩ appears in the positions corresponding to "that" in the original sentence.

For the purposes at hand, I simply assume that attitudes like belief are realized by relations to sentences or sententially structured entities. I assume that the constituents of such sentences determine, in context, extensional semantic values, as do natural language sentence constituents. Thus, for each believer, there is a set of sentences, or sentence-like entities, whose constituents have interpretations of the same sort as natural language sentence constituents. Just as a natural language sentence in a context determines an S-sentence, then, so do each of the sentences which serve to establish a believer's beliefs. Thus each believer has a B-set, that set of S-sentences which realize his beliefs.[11]

Suppose that in a context a "that"-clause names the SE-sentence it determines. The sententialist says, at a somewhat airy level of generality, that

(11) John believes that S

is true provided what its "that"-clause names—the S-sentence S—translates some member of John's B-set.

What is translation? Extensional isomorphism is necessary for translation. Obviously it is not sufficient, for (11)'s truth, that S be extensionally isomorphic to a sentence John uses to express a belief. Even intensional isomorphism is not sufficient. "Phil is a groundhog" is intensionally isomorphic to "Phil is a woodchuck." Presumably John can think to himself "Phil is a woodchuck" without its being true that John thinks that Phil is a groundhog. Even if "Phil is a groundhog" sometimes translates "Phil is a woodchuck," it doesn't always do so. So what is necessary for translation?

A plausible answer, I think, is that it depends. In some circumstances we may want to know whether John realizes that Phil is a *groundhog*. We won't count "John thinks that Phil is a groundhog" true unless John accepts a sentence of the form "So and so is a groundhog." In this case, we seem to be using "groundhog" to represent a specific "way of thinking" of being a groundhog: There is, one might say, a restriction on how we translate from John's idiom into our own. So far as translating from John's idiom into ours goes, "is a groundhog" translates only itself.

Such restrictions are not always present. Sometimes we may want only to observe that John has the species right. The kind of contextually imposed restriction on translation just mentioned is not present, and "is a groundhog" may translate John's "is a groundhog" or his "is a woodchuck." All else being equal, "John thinks that Phil is a groundhog" will be true in this case, given only that John accepts "Phil is a woodchuck."

This implies that a sentence such as "John believes that Phil is a woodchuck" or "Pierre believes that London is pretty" may be true in one context, but false in another, simultaneous context. This may happen because of contextual variation in restrictions on translation. I think this a virtue of the proposal. There is a pronounced intuition that the truth of "Pierre believes that London is pretty" does change from context to con-

---

[11] The beginnings of a defence of the psychological sententialism assumed here can be found in Richard (1990).

text, as our interests and attention move from Pierre's "French-language beliefs" to his English ones.

The general picture is this. When an attitude is ascribed, there is the language in which the ascription occurs and there is a language in which the attitude is realized. Sometimes the latter is a natural language, sometimes it is a more rudimentary system of representation. There will exist various schemes of translation from one language to another, sanctioned by custom, explicit convention, or *ad hoc* considerations. Context provides restrictions on translation of the sort just mentioned: restrictions to the effect that, with regard to subject X, an occurrence of an expression e in an ascription can translate only such-and-such expressions. And (11) will be true in a context c just in case (what) S (names), taken in c, translates a sentence in John's B-set, using a "translation manual" which obeys c's restrictions on translation.

Such an approach must invoke canonical or customary schemes of translation. When I say that Gorbachev said that Russia spends too much on arms, I speak truly, but not in virtue of my intentions with respect to the Russian language. Having forgone intensions, senses, and the like, only appeal to canonical or customary schemes of translation can explain why the ascription I actually made, but not others that I might have made, is true.

Such schemes need not be unique. To say that S translates T in context c is to say that S does so under some scheme or other. Presumably, we should not assume that for *any* two languages there is such a scheme. This would be difficult to justify without appeal to linguistically neutral senses or intensions. We may assume the existence of schemes of translation for languages whose users have been in contact with one another, and have actually established such. Of course, every language translates, homophonically, into itself.

On this account, propositional quantifiers are objectual. They range over arbitrary S-sentences. Making the obvious generalization from "believes" to "says," we will say that "Katya said something" is true in a context c exactly in case some S-sentence—not necessarily one of English—satisfies "Katya said p." Something satisfies the open sentence just in case it translates, relative to contextual strictures on translation, an S-sentence determined by one of Katya's assertive uses of a sentence.

If contextual restrictions arise mostly because of our focus on how people express their beliefs or sayings, they will be absent when we are not thinking about someone or their ways of expressing themselves, or when we have no opinion on the subject. In general, if Katya uttered a sentence which determines an S-sentence X, X itself will satisfy "Katya said p" relative to our context, even if what Katya said is unsayable in English. For, as we remarked above, each language translates homophonically into itself. Propositional quantifiers on this account behave much as they do on more traditional accounts of propositions.

Let us return to objections to the idea that sentences are the semantic objects of belief. I will speak briefly to when I take to be the three most important such objections.

There is first this worry: What is said by an English sentence S is what is named by "that S;" what is said by a French sentence is what is named by the corresponding "que"-clause. But if these clauses name S-sentences, they name different ones, since S-sentences contain expressions. So "Snow is white" and "La neige est blanche" say different things.

The sententialist owes us an account of

(12) Sentence S in this context says the same thing as sentence T in that context.

The proper account is roughly that (12) is true iff the sentences, in their respective contexts, translate precisely the same sentences. More precisely: Given a context c and a sentence S, consider the pairs $\langle u, T \rangle$, u a potential believer, T a sentence, for which there is a translation manual, acceptable in c, under which T translates from u's idiom as S. Call this S's saying potential in c. (12) is true provided the sentences it mentions have, in their respective contexts, the same saying potential. There is no reason to think that the English "Snow is white" and the French "La neige est blanche" might not have the same saying potential in some contexts. After all, they do translate one another. So normally it will be true to say that the two sentences say the same thing. And when it is not true, this is because of the existence of someone who satisfies but one of

x believes that snow is white
x croit que la neige est blanche.

A second objection to sententialism is that it makes attitude ascriptions and their translations into foreign languages diverge in truth-conditions, because of the divergent references of the ascription's complements. This, in effect, was Church's most telling objection to Carnap. Now, the fact that

(13) Katya said that John is ill

and its translations might have different truth-conditions or truth-values in simultaneous contexts is no objection to the view. Recall our agreement that an ascription like "Pierre believes that London is hot" may itself have distinct truth-values in distinct, simultaneous contexts.

One might say that the problem is not that uses of (13) and

(14) Katya sagte, dass John krank ist

might have differing truth-conditions, but that they *cannot* have the same truth-conditions, since (13) involves reference to English expressions, (14) to German ones. If the sentences cannot have the same truth-conditions, they cannot be correct translations of one another. Since they are, the view is refuted.

A short response observes that translation does not invariably preserve truth-conditions. Observe that

(15) Robert croit que Phil est une marmotte

can be translated by either of

(16) Robert believes that Phil is a woodchuck
(17) Robert believes that Phil is a groundhog.

The English sentences need not agree in truth-value, even when taken relative to one context. So some French sentence and a natural, correct English translation will diverge in truth-value relative to some context, and thus diverge, relative thereto, in truth-conditions. Thus, since literal translation need not preserve truth-conditions, there would be nothing untoward about saying, of a class of sentences, that in translating them we never preserve truth-conditions.

This response leaves open the possibility that (15) and its translations have nothing in common semantically. A more elaborate response begins by considering how the extensionalist interprets talk of truth-conditions. Given the luxury of possible worlds, we can identify truth-conditions with sets of worlds or structured intensions. The extensionalist can at least avail himself of times. Identifying truth-conditions with sets of times is not tenable, but perhaps a version of the structured intension characterization, employing functions from times to extensions, can be made to work. One identifies the truth-conditions of "John sleeps now" relative to time t_1 with the likes of

⟨John, the function which takes a time t to that which sleeps at t, the time t_1⟩.

(13) and (14) do not have the same truth-conditions in this sense, since they have parts (their complements) which refer to different things. However, there is no reason why the function from times to extensions determined by

(18) said that John is ill

and

(19) *sagte, dass John krank ist*

cannot be the same. One would expect these normally to be the same function, since normally "John is ill" and "*John ist krank*" will have the same saying potential. So, one might say, we *almost* have identity of truth conditions. If we were to treat (18) and (19) as atomic we in fact would have such an identity. This, along with the observation about translation and preservation of truth-conditions made above, seems to me sufficient to respond to the original objection.[12]

Let us finally consider Prior's objection: Whoever fears that there will be nuclear war "does stand in *a* relation to ['there will be a nuclear war'] . . . But his fear does not *consist in* this relation to this sentence . . . a man could have this fear if no such sentence existed, or if it meant something quite different from what it does" (Prior 1971: 16). Prior challenges the sententialist to explain how something like

---

[12] Further improvements on the response can be gleaned from Richard (1990, section 3.3).

(20) Khrushchev might have feared that there would be a nuclear war, although there were no English sentences

could be true on her view. I will make some remarks about how to begin such an explanation.

Sententialist truth-conditions for

(21) It is possible that Khrushchev fears that there will be a nuclear war

might be given either using the idiom of possible worlds (with an extensionalist reduction to follow) or by giving an illuminating completion of the schema

Necessarily, Khrushchev fears that there will be a nuclear war if and only if...

(and, again, following with an extensionalist account of the "necessarily..." idiom). In the possible worlds idiom, we might say (21) is true at w just in case at w there is a sentence S which realizes, at w, one of Khrushchev's fears, and "there will be a nuclear war" as we actually use it translates S as it is used at w. If S is a sentence of a language actually spoken (S is, say, a Russian sentence), there would seem to be no problem in principle in thinking that S as used at w is translatable by some English sentence as it is actually used.

One might object, appealing to the fact that translation requires extensional isomorphism, that the proposal makes it impossible for Khrushchev to fear a nuclear war in situations in which the set of such wars is different from A, the set of actually occurring nuclear wars. For the proposal says that the fear occurs only if some sentence S realizing the fear is translated by the English "there will be a nuclear war" and is thus extensionally isomorphic to it. But if S and the English are extensionally isomorphic, then a predicate in S corresponding to "is a nuclear war" has A as its extension. And the fact that the English translates S means that the predicate means what "is a nuclear war" does, and so has in any situation the set of nuclear wars as its extension. So, in any situation in which Khrushchev has the fear, A is the set of nuclear wars.

In effect, this objection moves from:

(22) "there will be a nuclear war", as we actually use it, can translate some sentence of S as Khrushchev *actually* uses it only if S contains a predicate with extension A (the actual extension of "is a nuclear war")

to

(23) "there will be a nuclear war" as we actually use it, can translate some sentence S as used by Khrushchev in some *counterfactual situation* only if S contains a predicate with extension A.

But there is no reason why the sententialist has to accept this move. She can justly hold that, just as facts about my actual use of "nuclear war" make it true, relative to counterfactual situations, of the nuclear wars in those situations, so facts about my actual use of the English sentence make it a translation of *counterfactual* sentence uses that *counterfactu-*

ally have different extensional semantic properties from the actual extensional semantic properties of the English.[13]

Suppose the details of this treatment can be worked out. What do we say to the worry that the sententialist can say that (20) is true only by allowing the possibility of Khrushchev's being related to something which does not exist?

It helps to reflect on what, according to the sententialist, a sentence like (21) says. A rough gloss of (21) goes thus: Khrushchev could be in a state involving a sentence S which has the following property: S, as used by Khrushchev, is representable by "there will be a nuclear war" as used by us. In (21), a possible state of Khrushchev's is characterized in terms of the actual use of a sentence. *This* kind of relation to a non-existent does not seem like very much of a threat to actualism. The counterfactual properties of Khrushchev's state and the actual properties of the English sentence might make this true, even though the English sentence did not exist in the counterfactual situation. This might be so, for example, if Khrushchev's state involved a sentence with the semantical and conceptual properties of the English sentence.

I do not pretend to have shown sententialism to be viable. As I have developed it, sententialism implies that the attitudes are states realized by relations to sententially structured entities. While I have elsewhere ventured the beginnings of a defence of this view, I would be the first to admit that it is not obviously true. A viable sententialism must deal with the problems for sentential accounts of necessity and the attitudes uncovered by Montague and Kaplan. I have not attempted to do so.

A substitutional account is not (necessarily) liable to either of these problems. But substitutionalism has its own problems. The substitutionalist's sentences bear a striking resemblance to propositions. And a substitutional quantifier lives off its instances—but we have no account of the truth-conditions of belief sentences which does not appeal to some sort of semantic object of belief.

One could say that there is no *account* to be had of the truth-conditions of attitude ascriptions, there being no propositions. I have tried here to block *this* response by showing that certain sorts of extensionally acceptable entities are perfectably serviceable propositions. I conclude, guardedly, that of the views surveyed at the beginning of the chapter, the view of the propositional quantifier as simply one more objectual quantifier is, on balance, the view we ought to accept.[14]

---

[13] Here is a somewhat different way of making the point. If we took the possible worlds idiom seriously, we would want to assign a denotation to the term "that there is a nuclear war" at each world. The objection in the text in effect assumes that the term will be a rigid designator, picking out at an arbitrary world something involving the collection of actual nuclear wars. But this assumption is perfectly gratuitous. The term could be a flaccid designator, in the sense that it picked out, at each world, something which involved the extension of "nuclear wars" at that world. (The final objection to sententialism in Schiffer (1990) can be responded to along these lines.)

In discussing Prior's objection, I try only to show how one might explain (21)'s truth-conditions without having it refer to or quantify over intensional entities. I here ignore the question how one who wishes to make do with only extensional entities is to make sense of talk of necessity or possible worlds. I do not mean to minimize the difficulties involved in an extensionally acceptable account of necessity. I only mean to set this problem to one side, as (I hope) distinct from those this chapter addresses.

[14] I am grateful to Jody Azzouni, Richard Grandy, and the participants at the A.N. Prior memorial Conference for their comments.

9

Sense, Necessity, and Belief*

Of what use is sense to semantics? A standard answer has been that sense provides the key to an account of opaque constructions, such as *it's necessary that S* and *Michael believes that T*. Many would say this answer has been thoroughly discredited. Kripke and Kaplan's arguments that necessity is not a property of Fregean sense are widely seen as conclusive. Russellians and Millians have laid siege to the idea that to ascribe a belief is to talk about sense. Though few have embraced the extremes of direct reference, many have come to agree that the orthodox Fregean's idea—a belief ascription implies a similarity in way of thinking, between ascriber and ascribee—simply doesn't get the facts right.[1]

Will sense go the way of Basic Law Vb? The second half of Graeme Forbes' *Languages of Possibility*, coupled with several of his recent papers, gives a sustained defense of the importance of sense for semantics.[2] While Forbes' account is at points reformed, not orthodox, it aspires to be recognizably Fregean. It seems to me the best sustained contemporary defense of Frege's views in philosophical semantics.

But it is not, I think, entirely successful. In this essay, I present the outlines of Forbes' account of the semantics of necessity, of propositional attitudes, and of their intersection in (putative) examples of *a priori* yet contingent knowledge. In each case I raise objections to Forbes' account. The account of necessity, I argue, is either unFregean or unsuccessful. The account of attitudes, I will suggest, is Fregean and not successful. And the account of the contingent *a priori*, I think, cannot be accepted as it stands.

---

* Contribution to the symposium *Author Meets Critics: Graeme Forbes' Languages of Possibility*, APA Pacific Division Meetings, Portland, March, 1992. Forbes and Mark Crimmins were co-symposiasts. I'm indebted to Forbes for comments on an earlier version of the first section. Work on this paper was supported by an NEH grant; I'm grateful for the support.

[1] See Kripke (1980). See also Almog et al (1989), especially Kaplan's contributions; Salmon (1986), Richard (1990).

[2] Forbes (1989), (1987), (1990). References to the first are indicated parenthetically in the text.

I. The bearer of truth, the bearer of necessity, and the object of belief

In *Naming and Necessity,* Kripke assumes that the sense of a proper name is usually that of a definite description contingently true of the referent. For example, the sense of "Frege" might be that of "the student of Lotze and teacher of Carnap." On Fregean principles it follows that

1. Frege is a student of Lotze and teacher of Carnap
2. The student of Lotze and teacher of Carnap is a student of Lotze and teacher of Carnap

have identical senses. Kripke observes that as sense determines epistemic properties, 1 and 2 would thus have identical epistemic properties. But 2 is (nearly enough) epistemically necessary, while 1 is not. And the Fregean is wrong about modal properties of the sentences, given that sense determines a sentence's modal properties. For example, the necessitation of 1 and 2's biconditional would be true on a Fregean view, when obviously it is not.

Responding to the first objection, Forbes suggests that the cognitive significance of a name N for x is identified with that of "the subject of this body of information," where the information is that which x has "stored" in his "mental file" labeled with the name N. Forbes argues that the thought that Frege is a mathematician and the thought that the subject of *this* body of information is one (where the body of information is "my Frege file") in fact *do* have the same cognitive significance for me.

To meet the modal objection Forbes abandons the Fregean idea that a sentence's reference is a truth value. He identifies sentential referents with states of affairs— congries of individuals, their properties and relations, and properties and relations corresponding to quantifiers and modalities. 1 names a state of affairs with Frege as a constituent. 2's nominatum, on the other hand, doesn't have Frege as a constituent, since definite descriptions are given a quantificational treatment. The state of affairs 2 names has constituents corresponding to the quantifier "the" and the predicate "student of Lotze and teacher of Carnap," but not Frege. Forbes treats *It is necessary that S* as an *extensional* context—i.e., one sensitive to the referent of the embedded sentence, a state of affairs. To say S is necessary is to say that the state of affairs that S can't help but obtain. So the necessitation of 1 and 2's biconditional isn't true, because the states of affairs named by 1 and 2 are different and needn't invariably co-obtain.

The two responses to Kripke may seem to work at cross purposes. If the cognitive significance of "Frege" and "the file's subject" are the same, as the first response has it, then the senses of "Frege writes" and "the file's subject writes" are the same. Since sense determines reference, Forbes would have to say that these sentences determine the same state of affairs. But the response to the modal objection requires that the sentences present different states of affairs.

However, Forbes says that a name and description may have the same cognitive significance while not having the same sense. (The description's sense is then said to *encapsulate* that of the name.) Likewise, sentences may share cognitive significance without having the same sense. Identity of thoughts' cognitive significance is an evidential or epistemological relation: "a reflective thinker who grasps each can [not] take an attitude to one that he doesn't take to the other" (Forbes 1989, 118). The thoughts may still be distinct, since senses with the same cognitive significance may "differ in structure and have different senses as constituents" (Forbes 1989, 118). In the case at hand, the thought that Frege is a student/teacher has the sense of "Frege," which presents Frege, as a constituent; the other thought has constituents corresponding to the quantifier "the" and "is a student of Lotze and teacher of Carnap." This difference in sense accounts for the difference in the state of affairs presented.[3]

On this view we have a trinity—a bearer of necessity, an object of belief, a cognitive significance—where the orthodox Fregean sees but one thing. I will argue that to separate the bearer of necessity and the object of belief as Forbes proposes either leads to grief or to a position that is decidedly unFregean.

Continuing to assume that "Frege"'s sense is encapsulated by that of a description *the F* only contingently true of Frege, consider the sense of "Frege is a mathematician." As a matter of fact, it picks out the state of affairs that Frege is a mathematician. Would it have done so no matter how things might have been? The answer depends on what we say about the sense of "Frege." On a *descriptional* account, the sense presents at w whatever is denoted by the quantifier phrase *the* F at w. On a *referential* account, the sense presents x at w only if x is Frege. On a descriptional account, if it presents anything at w, the sense of "Frege is a mathematician" presents the state of affairs that u is a mathematician, where u is the denotation of *the F* at w. On a referential account, the sense presents at w, if anything, the state of affairs that Frege is a mathematician.

Does Forbes mean to be advancing an account on which the sense of an ordinary proper name is descriptional or referential? Or is he advancing one on which this doesn't matter? It isn't altogether clear, since Forbes doesn't much discuss the modal properties of thoughts. He claims that thoughts obtain their modal status derivatively, with the modal status of p being that of whatever state of affairs p presents (Forbes 1989, 150). But this is consistent with either view of the sense of "Frege."

---

[3] On this view the cognitive significance of a sentence is no longer a candidate for satisfying a principle of compositional determination associated with Frege:
> If the cognitive significance of S is identical with the cognitive significance of S', as each occurs within the context C(...), then the cognitive significance of C(S) is identical with that of C(S').

This principle predicts that the cognitive significance of
> Necessarily, Frege is a student of Lotze and...

and
> Necessarily, the student of Lotze and teacher of Carnap is a student of Lotze and...

will be identical, which they clearly are not. Since the current notion of cognitive significance is very close to the notion of verification conditions, this is not all that surprising.

Several aspects of his discussion suggest that he intends his defense of the Fregean to go through even on the assumption that the senses of names are descriptional. In particular, note that if the sense of "Frege" is referential to begin with, that sense (unlike the sense of the student/teacher description) can only pick out Frege. So *if* the sense is referential, then Kripke's modal objection seems to fail, even if the reference of a sentence is a truth value. So it's not clear what point there would be for a Fregean to take states of affairs to be sentential referents, unless he was trying to keep sense descriptional while avoiding Kripke's modal objection.

Let's suppose that proper names by and large have descriptional senses, and see if the resulting theory is acceptable. If we say this, we must allow that many quotidean thoughts have their modal status contingently. Suppose that the sense of "Twain" is encapsulated by that of "*Huck Finn's* author," that of "Clemens" by that of "Hartford's most famous resident." It is necessarily necessary that Twain is Clemens. So the thought that Twain is Clemens is necessarily necessary.

But it is possible that Hartford's most famous resident be distinct from *Huck Finn's* author. So the proposition that Twain is Clemens could have presented a non-necessary (indeed, impossible) state of affairs. Given that a proposition's modal status is identical with that of what it presents, this implies that it is not necessary that the thought that Twain is Clemens is necessary.

Two types of necessity are at work here, one for states of affairs and one for propositions. If we use "□" as an operator that ascribes necessity to a sentence's referent, and "Nec" as a predicate ascribing necessity to propositions, our observations amount to something like

3. □□ Twain is Clemens, but ¬□ Nec (the proposition that Twain is Clemens).

This is somewhat odd, but perhaps acceptable.

But consider ascriptions of truth to propositions. If we adopt Forbes' account of propositional truth, we will say it is a sort of correspondence: Propositions present states of affairs; true propositions present facts, states of affairs that obtain (Forbes 1989, 46ff). If "p" ranges over propositions, "s" over states of affairs, we say that

P1:   □ ∀p (p is true ↔ ∃s (p presents s & s obtains)).

There are a variety of principles of this ilk, relating the modal status of states of affairs and propositions, such as

P2:   □ ∀p (p is impossible ↔ ∃s (p presents s & □¬ s obtains)).

Given the encapsulations for "Twain" and "Clemens" and their descriptionality, the following principles are correct:

4. □ ∀s(the proposition that Twain is Clemens presents s iff there's an x and a y such that x is the author of *Huck Finn* and y is Hartford's most famous resident and s is the state of affairs that x is y).

5. $\Diamond \exists x(x = $ the author of *Huck Finn* & $\exists y(y = $ Hartford's most famous resident & x is not y))
6. $\Box \forall x \forall y \forall s(x$ is not $y \to (s$ is the state of affairs that x is y $\to \Box \neg s$ obtains)).

Combined with a few uncontroversial claims, all this implies

7. $\Diamond$ (Twain is Clemens & the proposition that Twain is Clemens is not true).[4]

Divorcing propositions from the bearers of necessity in the way in which we have requires rejecting necessitations of (paradox free) instances of

8. The proposition that S is true iff S,

I think this is unacceptable.[5]

Will appeal to referential senses help us? Forbes is sympathetic with the conception of sense advanced by Gareth Evans, invoking what John McDowell calls *de re* sense. s is such sense only if for some x, necessarily, if s *exists*, then so does x, whom it presents. Evans' account (in *The Varieties of Reference*) is perhaps the standard neo-Fregean account of such senses.[6] Evans ties senses to what they present by the way in which they are individuated, which is decidedly "unindividualistic." Evans' idea is that ways of thinking must be individuated in part in terms of contextual factors "outside of the thinker's head", and in part in terms of what they present. In particular, since a correct explanation of why I think of Frege with "Frege" will preforce explain my use as referring to *Frege*, the way of thinking I associate with "Frege" is one that could not present anything but Frege.[7]

---

[4] In the derivation, we must assume that "that Twain is Clemens" can be legitimately instantiated in place of "p." It would be intolerable if this were not so.

[5] It might occur to you that the problem here is not that the bearer of necessity and object of belief are being falsely distinguished, but that we have wrongly separated the bearer of necessity from the bearer of truth. What happens if we say the bearer of truth is a state of affairs, instead of a proposition? Pretty much the same thing, since we must find some way to ascribe truth to beliefs. Presumably, we will do this by extending the inheritance strategy, and say that (necessarily), a proposition is true iff it presents a true state of affairs. This produces the following unsightly bulge in the carpet: We have to allow the truth of claims like

> X: It's possible that: It is true that Twain is Clemens, though the proposition that Twain is Clemens is not true.

This occurs under the following assumptions: *that S* in *it is true that S* names the state of affairs presented by the proposition that S; truth for states of affairs is identified with obtaining. If we don't envision any reference shifting when *true that* S is embedded within the scope of "$\Box$," this validates necessitations of instances of 8. But in X, the first conjunct in the embedded sentence ascribes a property to the state of affairs (Identity, (Twain, Twain)), while the second is concerned with the possession of a (different) property by something else, the proposition that Twain is Clemens. While the state of affairs has its property essentially, the proposition, since it presents different states of affairs in different situations, is only contingently true.

[6] Evans (1982).

[7] The relevant notion of sense is suggested by the following passage from Evans:

> I suggest that the desired notion [*viz.*, Frege's notion of sense] can be explained in terms of the notion of an account of what makes it the case that a subject's thought is a thought about the object in question. Imagine such an account written out. "S is thinking of the object *a* in virtue of the fact that…S…": what follows "that" is an account in which references to the subject and the object thought about appear, possibly at several places. Now I suggest that another subject, S', can be said to be thinking about the object *a* in the same way if and only if we get a true statement when we replace reference to S with reference to S' throughout the account…. (Evans (1982), 20–1).

Presumably Forbes will make use of Evans' account somewhat as follows: The explanation of why I think of Frege when I use "Frege" is: Frege stands in R to my "Frege" file, where "R" is to be replaced with a description of the relations that make something the subject of a file. Arguing with Evans, Forbes will say that nothing could be thought of in the way described unless it was *Frege*. So the sense is *de re*, even though it is encapuslated by a description, *he who stands in R to this file* that only contingently denotes Frege.

I will concede for today the cogency of referential or *de re* senses, and that an account employing them is not thereby unFregean. I will question whether Forbes can use such senses to answer Kripke's modal objection while adhering to basic Fregean principles, such as the principles that sense determines reference, and that sense is a way of thinking of a reference.

Forbes' response to the modal objection requires that

T: the proposition that Frege is a mathematician

in fact presents

s: the state of affairs that Frege is a mathematician

with the latter the reference of "Frege is a mathematician" when it is embedded in "necessarily." To insure the truth of

9. Necessarily, the proposition that Frege is a mathematician is true iff Frege is a mathematician

we must, given the definition of truth for propositions (P1), say that necessarily, T presents a state of affairs that obtains iff Frege is a mathematician. But the idea that "Frege"'s sense is referential is supposed to imply that T can only present s. The upshot is that Forbes' response to Kripke commits him to saying that T present s in every world in which s obtains.

It is this that I think inconsistent with Fregean principles. Consider a world w★, at which Frege is a mathematician (and so at which s obtains), but at which neither I nor my Frege file exist. T must present s at w★, and so

f: the sense of (my use of) "Frege"

presents Frege there. How does it come to be that f presents Frege at w★?
Consider first an easier question: How does it come to be that f presents Frege at the actual world? Well, f is a particular way of thinking of something. Encapsulated by *the subject of this file*, to think of x via f is (or involves, at any rate) thinking of x as the subject of this file. f actually presents what it does because that thing *is* the subject of the file. A plausible answer to the question, What makes f actually present Frege?, is: f, *qua* mode of presentation, presents what satisfies the condition that is (encapsulates, if you perfer) its cognitive significance; and it is actually Frege who satisfies the relevant condition.

The answer we have just arrived at generalizes thus. Sense presents reference via cognitive significance: The cognitive significance is or determines a condition, and in order to be a sense's reference, one must satisfy the condition. There are two ways to formulate the generalization: Satisfying the associated condition can be said to be necessary and sufficient for reference, or it can be said to be merely necessary. Consider the weaker principle:

> FP: If the cognitive significance of a sense s is that of *the F*, then if s presents x, x is the denotation of *the F*.

Such a principle seems to me the heart of Frege's view of sense and its relation to reference. Not only should a Fregean account validate FP; a Fregean account should, I think, validate its necessitation. Given this, and that the cognitive significance of a sense is essential to it, it follows that f does not present Frege at w★, since Frege is not the denotation of *the subject of this file* at w★—the quantifier has no denotation there. So T does not present a state of affairs there. So Fregean principles block Forbes' response to Kripke.

Why is FP's necessitation central to a Fregean view of sense and reference? I will suggest the outline of an argument. For a thought to be true is for it to be a correct way of thinking of the world. This is quasi-definitional for a Fregean, and so necessary. But, necessarily, the cognitive significance of a thought, since it embodies its epistemological and evidential properties, plays a central role in determining whether a situation is correctly thought of via the thought. For example, a thought that has the cognitive significance of the thought *the file's subject is a mathematician* is a thought that involves cognizing the world as one in which a certain file's subject is a mathematician. So it can be a correct way of cognizing a particular situation, actual or counterfactual, only if the situation is one such that, were it actual, there would be one and only one subject of a certain file who would also be a mathematician.

Summarizing: Necessarily, p is true iff it's a correct way of thinking of things. And necessarily, for any p and q, if q encapsualtes p and p is a correct way of thinking of things, then q is a correct way of thinking of things. The premises imply that if p's cognitive significance is encapsulated by q's, then p is true at w only if q is. The premises are clearly Fregean; they have clear Fregen analogues that yield FP's necessitation.

Of the many possible responses, I mention two. (1) The Fregean should concede that sense doesn't determine reference; a causal chain or some such thing does that. *Observation*. This concedes that, unless sense is relevant to the semantics of ascription of attitude, it has no role whatsoever to play in philosophical semantics. On this response, for example, an account of the semantics of "necessarily" need not invoke senses either as semantic values or in the explanation of why a particular expression has a semantic value.

(2) Sense *actually* determines reference, at least in the weak sense given by FP. But FP's necessitation is false; once we have determined an actual reference for a sense, we have determined its only possible reference. *Observation*. This response must give up at least one of the two premises in the argument suggested above for FP's necessitation. So the

response concedes that some of what are plausibly said to be central theses in a Fregean view of reference are mistaken.[8]

To defend Frege as he does, Forbes concedes a good deal to recent criticisms of Fregeanism. But he doesn't thereby concede *everything*. It might be that sense still has a role to play in an account of the semantics of propositional attitude ascriptions, a topic to which I now turn.

II. Sense and semantics

What is the sense of a proper name? Forbes' account begins with a portrait of the thinker as a file clerk. The thinker's organization of information involves a loose segmentation and cross-classification reflecting what he thinks there is and how he thinks it to be. Information is sorted into files, that typically have labels, which often enough come from the ambient natural language.

A file is a way in which an individual is represented in thought; it is with such files that senses are to be identified. When N labels a file, its sense (for the thinker) is encapsulated by the description "the subject of this file." We thus have a criterion for intrasubjective identity of sense: Names will have the same sense provided they label the same file.[9]

Anyone who finds the file metaphor attractive will grant that the Fregean's talk of sense, so understood, has something to it. But even if such talk is sensible, it may not be of much value in an account of natural language semantics. Sense may be psychologically real but semantically irrelevant.

The degree to which sense is semantically relevant is the degree to which appeals to it are necessary in a correct, illuminating account of the truth conditions of natural language sentences (or of their uses, or of whatever has truth conditions). The most obvious way in which a sense of "Frege" could be semantically relevant is by being a semantic value of "Frege," one that directly determines what's named in the "that"-clause of

---

[8] This response also commits Forbes to saying that names are directly referential in (one of) the sense(s) Kaplan introduced. Consider the following passage from Kaplan (1989):

> The semantical feature *I* wish to highlight in calling an expression *directly referential* is not the *fact* that it designates the same object in every circumstance, but the *way* in which it designates an object in any circumstance.... [That something] is a *device of direct reference*... does not imply that it has no conventionally fixed semantic rules which determine its referent in each context of use; quite the opposite. There are semantical rules which determine the referent in each context of use—but that is all. *The rules do not provide a complex which together with a circumstance of evaluation yields an object. They just provide an object.* (Kaplan (1989), 495. Kaplan's emphasis)

Note that if one replaces "conventionally fixed semantic rules" and "complex" with "sense," this is *exactly* the account of the semantics of "Frege" that Forbes seems to be providing, assuming that his account evades Kripke's objection and validates instances of 8.

[9] I gloss over considerable detail here concerning the dynamics of file formation. See in particular Forbes' discussion in Forbes (1990).

10. Michael believes that Frege is a mathematician.

Because of intersubjective variation in sense, accounts of 10 that procede by assigning a sense to "Frege" as semantic value, and taking sentences like 10 to ascribe to Michael a relation to the thought determined under that assignment, can't be made to work. I have so argued elsewhere and won't repeat the details here. Forbes agrees that because of such intersubjective variation, "Frege" in 10 cannot be taken to refer to some sense of Frege.[10]

There are other ways in which sense might be semantically relevant, however. In work extending the account of *Languages of Possibility*, Forbes offers an account of how the senses of "Frege" help determine the truth conditions of a sentence like 10.[11]

Forbes proposes, to a first approximation, that the role of "Frege" in 10 is to direct us to Michael's file (or way of thinking) whose subject is Frege and that is labeled "Frege." To find out whether 10 is true, we "look inside": If we find "is a mathematician," the ascription is true; otherwise it's false. "Frege" in 10 thus directs us to the sense of Frege that *Michael labels* "Frege." It directs us, in Forbes' terminology, to Michael's so-labeled sense.

Obviously it is too restrictive to say that *a believes that N is F* is true only if a has a file *labeled N* which contains the appropriate information. Forbes actually suggests that a name's role in an attitude ascription is to direct us to a file labeled with some *counterpart* of itself. (Forbes' counterpart relation is four placed: N for believer b is a linguistic counterpart of N' for ascriber a. I will surpress the b and the a places whenever possible.) So, for example, if we suppose that N is generally a counterpart of N' if N is N', or N is a conventional translation of N', we can see how "The Babylonian believed that Hesperus rose in the west" could be true, though the Babylonian's files were labeled with Summarian words, not English ones.

Let's use "B" to name the relation one bears to a sense when one has it as belief object. Then the proposal, to a second approximation and mixing use and mention, is that 10 says that Michael bears B to *C is a mathematician*, where C is that sense of Michael's labeled with a counterpart of "Frege." A fairly precise version of the account can be given if we use italicization to form a name of the sense of what's italicized, and "^" to name the operation of "putting senses together to form a thought." The proposal is that 10 is true iff

11. Michael's sense, s, of Frege that is labeled with a counterpart of (my use of) "Frege" is such that B (Michael, s^*is a mathematician*).

It's not hard to generalize this.[12]

---

[10] See Richard (1990), chapter 2; Forbes (1990).

[11] What follows summarizes (and simplifies) parts of Forbes (1990).

[12] Spelled out, a generalization of the proposal might go something like this. Let us say that a sense s corresponds for y to the pair <N, x>, where N is a name and x an individual, if s is (the unique) sense of x determined by a file of y's that has x as subject and is labeled with a linguistic counterpart of N. And we say that a k-termed sequence of senses (s1,...sk) corresponds for y to a k-termed sequence of pairs

Much depends on how the counterpart relation gets elaborated. Forbes gives two sufficient conditions for one name being a counterpart of another, and then suggests that we should "use our intuitions about which belief ascriptions are true and which false to settle what is a counterpart of what." The principles don't appeal to anything at all like a notion of identity or similarity of sense. For example, the first principle is

> P3: If the believer and ascriber each have but one file with x as a subject, then any label of the believer's x file is a counterpart of any label of the ascriber's x file.[13]

It doesn't take very much imagination to come up with cases in which, on Forbes' view, a use of 10 is true, though the only thing Michael's and the speaker's ways of thinking of Frege have in common is that they present Frege. *If* a Fregean account is one in which the truth of a sentence like 10 requires some sort of cognitive similarity between Michael's and the speaker's conception of Frege and mathematicians, this is not a Fregean account.

One response to such complaints is that what we have here is admittedly not an *orthodox* Fregean account, since it doesn't invoke cognitive similarity. What makes the account *Fregean*, however, is that it individuates the (broad) psychological states that realize beliefs in terms of sense.

What would render an account, unFregean, the response goes, would be, for example, identifying the belief realized by "Hesperus rises" with that realized by "Phosphorus rises" no matter what attitude an agent took towards "Hesperus is Phosphorus." Such an account would see but one belief where there were two ways of thinking. Again, the account would be unFregean if it distinguished the belief realized by "Hesperus rises" from that realized by "Phosphorus rises" in a person with a single "Hesperus"/"Phosphorus" file. Such an account would see two beliefs where there

---

<<Nl, xl>,...<Nk, xk>> if each si corresponds for y to si, for i from 1 to k. Then, if S(N1,...Nk) is a sentence with exactly the Ni's as occurring proper names, we might say (suppressing relativizations of the counterpart relation)

> A use of
> a believes that S(Nl,...Nk)
> is true iff, where xl is the referent of Nl on the use, and..., xk is the referent of Nk, there is a sequence s of senses such that s corresponds to <<Nl, x1>,..., <Nk, xk>> for what a names and B(what a names, s + S(...)).

(Here, "+" names an operation that "puts" the senses in a sequence into the "openings" in an incomplete sense.)

[13] The other principle is

> If the ascriber has a file labeled with exactly Nl,..., Nk, and the believer has n distinct files, with file fi labeled uniquely with Ni, then each Ni for the believer is a counterpart of Ni for the ascriber (and generally no other counterpart relation hold).

The principles and material cited in the text are on pages 551–2 of Forbes (1990).

was one way of thinking. What makes the account Fregean is the individuation of the individual's belief states in terms of sense.[14]

Suppose we take this response seriously. Then one important issue on which to focus is whether the (broad) psychological states that constitute beliefs are best individuated in terms of (Forbes' notion of) sense. Perhaps it will help focus the issue to put it somewhat crudely. If we pretend that beliefs are realized by inner sayings, then the issue becomes: Under what conditions do two inner sayings constitute the same belief? For example, under what conditions do two sentences like "Hesperus rises" and "Phosphorus rises" give voice to the same belief? Forbes' answer, once again put crudely to focus the issue, is something like: When the speaker (correctly) takes "Hesperus" and "Phosphorus" name the same thing.

I think Forbes is wrong about this. It seems to me that at least three considerations will lead us to individuate belief states more finely than Forbes would have us individuate them. One is the apparent link between thinking and saying; a second has to do with issues involved in the retention and change of belief; the third has to do with psychological idiosyncracies of believers. I'll review each in turn.

(1) It is clear, I think, that *my saying* that Hesperus rises is not my saying that Phosphorus does, even if I acquired the names "Hesperus" and "Phosphorus" simultaneously as names of Venus. Roughly speaking, uses of sentences that differ by (non-demonstrative) public language word type automatically say different things, no matter what their users know. But it seems that we tend to individuate thoughts in accord with instances of

P4: If to say that A is not to say that B, then to think that A is not to think that B.

Of course, if this is right, then the relation between senses and beliefs, like that between senses and sayings, will typically be one-many, and beliefs aren't individuated in terms of sense.

Evidence for P4 is the evidence of widespread intuition. For instance, the following seems obvious to most of us:

12. Even if you grew up knowing that Twain is Clemens, to think (or say) that (if Twain wrote *Huck Finn*, then, if Twain is Twain, then Clemens wrote *Huck Finn*) is not thereby to think (or say) that (if Twain wrote *Huck Finn*, then if Twain is Clemens, Clemens wrote *Huck Finn*).

But insofar 12's antecedent suggests that you "co-classify" "Twain" and "Clemens," 12, on an account like Forbes', should *not* seem correct to us.

(2) Consider a case in which Smith starts out sure that Hesperus is Phosphorus—he is given the names at the same time as two names of Venus. He *will*, next year, come to

---

[14] To ease exposition, I here and below speak of an individual's attitude towards an identity instead of speaking of the individual's having a single file labeled with the terms flanking the identity.

doubt that they are the same—say, as a result of an article by Carl Sagan in the *National Enquirer*. But he'll continue to believe that Hesperus is itself, Phosphorus itself.

If to have a belief is to be related to a sense, then, presumably, to maintain a belief is to maintain a relation to a sense. So in the story of Smith, a Fregean ought to recognize that there is a sense "realizing" the belief that Hesperus is itself for Smith thoughout the interval, and one realizing the belief that Phosphorus is itself throughout. And *this* implies, I think, that Smith has one way of thinking of Hesperus throughout, and a different way of thinking of Phosphorus throughout.

The problem here is that on Forbes' account, Smith has only one way of thinking of Venus at the beginning, and two distinct ones at the end. The first way of thinking needs to be identified with each of the terminal ways of thinking, but can't, because the terminii are distinct. The solution seems to be to recognize two ways of thinking at the beginning of the story. But then we are committed to seeing different beliefs where Forbes sees but one sense.

(3) What we might call psychological idiosyncracies can also make for a difference of belief where there is no difference of sense. An example is Wanda, who knows that Hesperus is Phosphorus. Like almost every educated non-philosopher and most every philosopher (save Ruth Marcus) who thought about the matter before 1968, Wanda doesn't think it is *necessary* that Hesperus is Phosphorus; she thinks that Hesperus could have been different from Phosphorus (though not that Hesperus could have different from Hesperus, of course).

It's not that she has an elaborate theory of *how* they might have differed. She thinks, perhaps, that Hesperus could have been worshipped by the residents of Belize while Phosphorus wasn't; but she thinks the converse is true, too. There's really nothing she thinks true of Hesperus—save that it's necessarily identical with Hesperus—that she doesn't think of Phosphorus; analagously for Phosphorus.

"Hesperus" and "Phosphorus" are different representations for Wanda, and their difference shows up in the fact that she believes that Hesperus is necessarily Hesperus without believing that Hesperus is necessarily Phosphorus. But she has but one "Venus file": After all, Wanda thinks that there is exactly one object that is Venus, and that object is the same object as Hesperus and as Phosphorus. Her confusion is metaphysical, not empirical. Suppose I say

13. Wanda believes that it is necessary that Hesperus is Phosphorus.

Wanda, like me, has but one file for the planet Venus. By P3, then, each of these names as she uses it is a counterpart of each of the names as I use it. So 13 will be true on Forbes' account just in case the sense Wanda associates with these names—her sense of "Hesperus"—is such that Wanda believes the result of putting that sense into the gaps in the sense *necessarily, . . . is identical with. . . .* This is presumably the sense that Wanda associates with "Necessarily, Hesperus is Hesperus." And that is an object of her belief. So it would seem that 16 must be true on Forbes' account. But it is not.

Some of the examples I have given could conceivably (though I am not sure convincingly) be handled by modifying Forbes' account of sense in order to allow terms which label the same file to nonetheless differ in sense. But it seems to me that, on balance, these examples suggest that beliefs are individuated much more finely than Forbes would have us think. The principle of individuation is at least partially *syntactic*, in some broad sense; even if there is no difference whatsoever in the cognitive significance of two (simple) terms, they may, for any of the reasons outlined above, determine different beliefs.

If this is correct, then sense has little role to play in an account of the semantics of natural language attitude ascriptions. Forbes ought, I think, abandon the idea that a name in attitude ascription goes proxy for one of the believer's *senses*, and instead adopt the idea that it goes proxy for one of the believer's *representations*, where these are individuated much more finely than Forbes' senses.

III. The contingent *a priori*

Forbes allows that if we fix the reference of "Neptune" with "the perturbor of Uranus' orbit," then the *sentence*

14. If some one thing perturbs Uranus' orbit, it's Neptune

will be contingent—in the sense that it presents a contingent state of affairs—and it will be *a priori*—in the sense that it expresses something knowable *a priori* by the reference fixer. The state of affairs presented is pretty much what one would expect, one that obtains at just the worlds at which, if some one thing perturbs Uranus' orbit, it's Neptune. The proposition expressed, however, is not a way of thinking of this state of affairs. It's not the proposition we in fact express with 14, since this proposition does present the state of affairs. Rather, in this case 14 expresses what is expressed by

15. If some one thing perturbs Uranus' orbit, it's the perturbor of Uranus' orbit.

So when reference is fixed via a description, we have a special case in which sense does not present reference.

This approach divorces what a sentence says from the conditions under which it is true, the latter being encoded by the state of affairs referred to. What the reference fixer believes, believing (as he puts it) that if some one thing perturbs Uranus, it is Neptune, is necessary. But it is contingent that if some one thing perturbs Uranus, it's Neptune; and if the reference fixer utters these words, he describes something contingent. The view thus renders consistent sentences of the form

16. Everything Michael believes is necessarily true, and Michael believes that S, and it's contingent that S.

This, I offer, is not a happy result.

In *Languages of Possibility* Forbes responds that "... insisting on this [sort of objection] is just to presuppose that the objects of belief and contingency are the same" [LP 163] (Forbes (1989), 163). He demands an argument for the presupposition. But this, I think, is not quite what's at issue. What is at issue is whether or not claims made by sentences of the form of

17. Necessarily, the proposition that S is true iff S

are true. If they are—and their being so is consistent with one thing being a necessity bearer, another belief object—then things like 16 shouldn't be consistent. Of course, in the case of the reference fixer, Forbes' account requires a failure of 17. I think we need another account of Kripke's examples.

To thus criticize Forbes is not to address the motivation for his view. Forbes is not willing to grant that Kripke's examples are ones of contingent *a priori* knowledge, in which (in Fregean lingo) a thought known *a priori* presents a contingent state of affairs. Like Donnellan, Forbes arrives at his position because he thinks that Kripke's examples, whatever they may be examples of, are not examples of *de re* knowledge. Donnellan argues from roughly these premises:[15]

A1: To know what's expressed by a sentence S(N) containing an ordinary name of x is to have *de re* knowledge of x.

B1: You can't have knowledge *de re* of an object a priori, unless (maybe) the object is yourself.

Forbes seems moved by

A2: To believe a proposition presenting a singular state of affairs is to have *de re* knowledge (Forbes (1989), 161).

B2: Fixing a reference by description is not sufficient for allowing one to have *de re* attitudes (Forbes (1989), 155).

While these claims have force, there are also forceful considerations that make Kripke's account of the example seem correct. Kripke's example seems to be one of an unexceptional use of a sentence by someone who understands the sentence he is using, can identify what the terms in the sentence pick out, and who knows his use true. If we accept a link between understanding a sentence and grasping what it says, we will want to say that in such a case the speaker knows what he says, and thus that the examples are ones of knowing what one says and knowing that it's true. The relevant premises are something along the lines of

C: A speaker who understands a sentence and can identify the referents of the terms in a use of the sentence will, if he takes the use to express something true, in fact believe what the sentence says on the use.

[15] Donnellan (1990).

D: In the Neptune example, the speaker understands his use of 14, can identify the referents of all its terms on that use, and sees *a priori* that what's said is true.

E: In the Neptune example, what 14 expresses is a contingent truth about Neptune.

In thinking about this problem, we might profitably distinguish two senses in which an attitude might be said to be *de re*. On the one hand, an attitude might be *object dependent* in (roughly) the sense that the propositional object o of the attitude "involves" an object x in such a way that o couldn't exist unless x did. The paradigm of object dependent knowledge is knowledge of a Russellian proposition.

I want to distinguish, at least in theory, between a belief's thus depending upon an object x and the belief's involving an epistemic *liaison* with x. A believer B's belief involves a liaison with an object x when (very roughly) part of a correct account of how B comes to "grasp the object of the belief" involves B's standing in an epistemically interesting relation—for example, a perceptual or introspective one—to x.

What determines whether a relation R is "epistemically interesting" enough to qualify as establishing liaison? Perhaps the right answer is that this is a matter of whether or not standing in R to an object puts one in a position to acquire a substantial variety of independent, justified beliefs about the object. This makes perception and introspection paradigm grounds of epistemic liaison, since they are rich avenues of information about the objects to which we have access through them. It does not make dubbing a sort of epistemic liaison, since by dubbing one does not gain a window on the world, nor does one access any other source of information on the dubee. Having an ordinary proper name of an object *in a community with a great deal of information about the object* could, on this account, put one in epistemic liaison with the object, since having the name would allow one to exploit the ambient common store of information.

Object dependence and liaison each give us a notion of *de re* knowledge. If Russell's principle (or a Fregean variation thereon) is correct, the two notions are coextensive, and one has knowledge dependent upon x just in case one has an epistemic liason with x. But if they are not coextensive, it is conceivable that the A's and the B's above are correct, while Kripke's claims—C, D, and E—are too. What would render everything consistent would be taking the A claims as correct claims about object dependent knowledge, while taking the B claims to be correct claims about knowledge involving epistemic liaison, but not about object dependent knowledge.

Does having an object dependent belief require having an epistemic liaison with an object on which the belief depends? I am unaware of a good argument that it does. And we do seem to think that we *understand* (demonstrative free) sentences which express singular propositions, even when neither we nor any we can trace our usage through have had perceptual or otherwise intimate contact with the relevant individuals. There seems to be a strong, quasi-conceptual link between understanding and knowing what is said. We credit each other with a grasp of what is said if we satisfy general standards of linguistic competence—so that we understand the sentence used—and we are able to satisfactorily identify the referents of the terms in a sentence. And neither linguistic competence nor the kind of identificatory ability at issue requires epistemic liaison.[16]

---

[16] This account allows that epistemic liaison—and therefore *de re* knowledge in the "deep" sense—*might* not require any terribly interesting causal relationship between the thinker and the res. On the account being suggested here, the notion of epistemic liaison is explained in terms of having cognitive access to information that is "about" the individual with which one has liaison. Aboutness of information I would identify with something like object dependency.

I would allow that in principle we can have liaison with x without any *very direct* causal contact. So, for example, if we dub x without perception or introspection, *and* we develop a fairly rich, mostly correct, and justified theory of the object so dubbed, we might have liaison with x, in virtue of the dubbing (that makes the information we have about x), having the name used in the dubbing *and* the mostly true, interesting, and justified theory we have of x (the last two establishing liaison). I take it that such is not the case in Kripke's Neptune example, since the dubber doesn't have a rich, mostly correct, justified theory about Neptune. It seems to me unlikely that one could have liaison with a physical object without any causal connection that was epistemically exploitable, since this seems necessary for justification.

Talk of *identifying the referent of term T* can be understood as roughly equivalent to *Knowing the answer to the question, Who is T?* I discuss the latter notion in Richard (1993).

10

Semantic Pretense

Kendall Walton says that talk ostensibly about fictional objects involves pretense.[1] For example, in a typical utterance of

(1) Only Ishmael survived the wreck of the *Pequod*,

we engage in the kind of imaginative pretense involved in reading or appreciating *Moby Dick*, pretending to refer to a man named "Ishmael" and a ship named "the *Pequod*," further pretending to say that the one is related in a certain way to the other. The purpose of engaging in this pretense is to allow us to talk about it; crudely put, to utter (1) is (normally) to say, of the kind of pretense in which we're engaged, that it is one in which readers of *Moby Dick* are supposed to engage. How is it that uttering (1) is making such a claim? According to Walton, the mechanism is of the same kind as that which allows "[a] native of an exotic culture [to] inform his alien guests that the snake livers are to be eaten with the parrot's nest sauce by going ahead and doing so. . . . Doing something is sometimes a way of claiming that it is proper or acceptable to do so" (Walton (1990), 399).

This account allows for the truth of ordinary talk about fiction without implying that what there is includes, not only *Moby Dick*, but Moby Dick. For there doesn't have to be such a thing as Moby Dick in order for me to pretend to refer to such. An additional advantage of the account is its (logico-) syntactic conservativeness. When I utter (1) in pretense, I do not refer to, or pretend to refer to, the novel *Moby Dick*, or to the property of being fictionally true. Rather, I simply pretend to make the references which (1)'s surface syntax suggests its literal utterance would involve. If, as Walton suggests, uttering (1) is (typically) a case of "saying by doing," we do not have to suppose that uses of (1) which say something true are uses of a sentence whose surface or logical form involves a covert operator "it is fictional that"; indeed, we need not suppose that (1)'s apparent syntactic form is in any way misleading as to its logical form.

---

[1] Most notably in Walton (1990).

Mark Crimmins says that talk about propositional attitudes also exploits pretense,[2] though the pretense involved and the mode of exploitation are somewhat different from those invoked by Walton. According to Crimmins, a typical utterance of

(2)   Hammurabi believes that Hesperus is a star,

is embedded in the pretense, that Hesperus and Phosphorus are different things, and that therefore holding a belief "under the Hesperus mode" is believing something about one thing, holding a belief "under the Phosphorus mode" is believing something about another thing. *Relative to such a pretense*, what makes (2) true is that Hammurabi has a belief under the Hesperus mode; *relative to such a pretense*, what makes

(3)   Hammurabi believes that Phosphorus is a star,

true is that Hammurabi has a belief under the Phosphorus mode. Crimmins' idea (very roughly) is that a typical use of (2) says the conditions, which would make (2) true in the pretense, in fact obtain. That is, in uttering (2), we are typically saying (something true if and only if) Hammurabi has a belief, under the Hesperus mode, that what it presents is a star. On this view, we engage in pretense, not to talk about the pretense itself, but (again, roughly put) to talk about the truth conditions which the pretense associates with our utterance.

The payoffs here are kindred to those of Walton's account. Crimmins can be conservative about the logical syntax of (2) and (3). He can deny that they involve reference to modes of presentation or expressions; he can accept that their semantics is Millian through and through. Still, if we are exploiting pretense as Crimmins proposes, then our intuition, that what we say with (2) is different from what we are saying with (3), is not only explained; it is validated. And Crimmins' account can apparently explain how a sentence such as

(4)   Daphne believes that Zeus is a god,

can have robust truth conditions (and ones different from that of "Daphne believes that Ahura Mazda is a god"), even though there is no such thing as the proposition, that Zeus is a god. For we can *pretend* that there is such a proposition, and make it true in our pretense, that someone believes it just in case they are suitably related to the "Zeus mode of presentation."

Walton's original idea about (1) is a clever one, as is Crimmins' variation thereon. But neither, I shall argue, is adequate to the data it sets out to explain. In Section I, I exposit Walton's account of "ordinary" talk about fiction (e.g., typical utterances of (1)). Section II argues that obvious facts about speakers' "low level" semantic beliefs (for example, about when a sentence says something meaningful) imply that speakers will find the mechanism of pretense an unnecessary complication, in assertive uses of sentences like (1); thus, there is no reason to suppose that speakers make use of pretense in using sentences such as (1). Section III exposits Crimmins' view; the following two sections criticize it. Section IV

---

[2] Most notably in Crimmins (1998).

argues that, Crimmins' protests notwithstanding, the pretense account is not able to give a coherent account of the truth conditions of attitude ascriptions whose content sentences contain the identity predicate or the apparatus of quantification. Section V discusses what a pretense theory such as Crimmins' would have to say, about the semantics of expressions like "it is fictionally true." It argues that the sort of problems about logical syntax the pretense account is supposed to solve for sentences such as (2) re-emerge for this operator, and that this fact counts against the pretense account. Finally, Section VI examines Walton's and Crimmins' accounts of denials of existence, such as "Santa doesn't exist." I argue that neither account is acceptable.

I

When we play a game of make believe—Cowboys and Indians, say—we "explicitly pretend" certain things—that I am a cowboy, that you are an Indian, that this orchard is a plain filled with warriors. What is thus pretended true is "true-in-our-game," "fictionally true"—where to say that p is fictionally true in a game is to say that p is something that someone playing the game is supposed to imagine true.[3] Things other than what we explicitly pretend will be true in our game, in virtue of various states of affairs actually obtaining (or in virtue of actually obtaining states of affairs and fictional truths). If, for example, you creep across the orchard and roll under the pear tree, it will be true in the game that an Indian is preparing a surprise attack.

What makes it fictional, that an attack is imminent? Walton speaks of the *principles of generation* associated with a game or fiction. These may be thought of as rules to the effect that if circumstances of kind C in fact obtain, then a proposition of a kind related thus and so to C is fictionally true. For example, in our game it might be a rule that if one points a finger in direction d and says "pkkch," it is fictionally true that one has fired a gun in direction d. Principles of generation may be explicitly laid down, but that would surely be unusual. They are typically implicitly presupposed: "what principles of generation there are [for a particular game of make believe] depends on which ones people accept in various contexts. The principles that are in force are those that are understood, at least implicitly, to be in force" (Walton (1990), 38).

According to Walton, associated with a work of fiction such as *Moby Dick* are various games of make believe, which involve imagining various things explicit and implicit in the fiction to be true. On this picture, a novel or story is a sort of "prop" in the games associated with it; its purpose in these games is to make various propositions fictionally true. Reading a novel or story involves participating in such a game. Thus, associated with *Moby Dick* is a game, the playing of which requires, among other things, imagining

---

[3] This needs to be qualified in certain ways which are irrelevant to present purposes. It should be mentioned in passing that *fictional truth* is something of misnomer. To say it is fictionally true that p sounds a little like saying that there is some world, situation, or such at which p is true. This is not what Walton (or Crimmins) takes fictionality to be; as said in the text, p is fictional in such and such a game just in case (roughly) one is supposed to imagine p in the game.

that the only survivor of certain wreck (that of the ship "the *Pequod*") is the person telling one a story. Part of the games associated with *Moby Dick* involves uttering, or at least thinking, sentences such as

(1)   Only Ishmael survived the wreck of the *Pequod*.

Relative to such games, such an utterance is appropriate, for *Moby Dick* makes it fictionally true that only Ishmael survived the wreck of the *Pequod*. Thus, relative to *Moby Dick*, if one utters (1), one makes it fictionally true that one has spoken truly.

A typical utterance of (1) strikes most of us as saying something true; Walton concurs. What is genuinely asserted is that in a game of the relevant sort, the kind of pretending involved in uttering (1) is OK—engaging in that kind of pretense is making it true of oneself, in the game, that one has spoken truly. Slightly more precisely: Call the games for which *Moby Dick* has the function, of making various claims fictionally true, games that are *authorized for Moby Dick*. In uttering (1), one engages in a certain sort K of pretense, in which one pretends to refer to someone name "Ishmael" and to a boat name "the *Pequod*," and say of the first that only he survived the wreck of the second. What one genuinely asserts, in uttering (1) is

(5)   If you engage in a pretense of kind K in a game authorized for *Moby Dick*, then you make it true of yourself, in the game, that you speak truly.[4]

II

According to Walton, when one utters a sentence such as (1), one is (normally) talking about a certain kind of pretense. Exactly what kind? "When there is no apparent reference to purely fictitious entities... there is a purely descriptive way of specifying the relevant pretense" (see Walton (1990), 401). If there is no such apparent reference—if the sentence uttered is something like

(6)   Only one man lived to tell of how a white whale sank a ship with a one legged captain

—then a proposition (*p* call it) is expressed. In such a case, the relevant kind of pretense is simply: pretending to assert *p*. So, what's said by an utterance of (6) is

(7)   If you pretend to say that only one man lived to tell of how a white whale sank a ship with a one legged captain, in a game authorized for *Moby Dick*, then you make it true of yourself, in the game, that you speak truly.

Now, as Walton observes, there seems to be a much simpler paraphrase of the relevant uses of (6). What, after all, makes (7) true? Well, it's the fact that, according to *Moby Dick*,

---

[4] See Walton (1990), section 10.3, esp. 400. I have not slavishly followed Walton's phrasing of what is said by utterances like that of (1).

only one man lived to tell of how a white whale sank a ship with a one legged captain. So, a gloss of an utterance of (6) "which, although not strictly equivalent, is near enough for many purposes" is

(7.1) It is fictional[ly true] in *Moby Dick* that only one man lived to tell of how a white whale sank a ship with a one legged captain.

"This gives the same result as the familiar suggestion that [in uttering (6) the speaker] has merely omitted, left implicit, some such phrase as 'it is fictional [in *Moby Dick*] that,' or 'it is true [in *Moby Dick*] that.'"[5] Why does Walton resist the claim that (6) is simply an elision of (7.1)? Well, one wants there to be a fairly strong "affinity"[6] between what's said by (1) and what's said by (6) (when each is uttered as a report about *Moby Dick*). If (6) elides (7.1), (1) elides

(1.1) It is fictional in Moby Dick that only Ishmael survived the wreck of the *Pequod*.

More generally, if (6) elides (7.1), then an utterance of sentence S as a report about what happens in a fiction f is an elision of (something of the form) *it is fictional in f that* S. But this "does not solve our problem, of course. [In a case like that of (1) and (1.1)] the longer statement retains the apparent reference to [Ishmael and the *Pequod*] . . ." (Walton (1990), 397). The problem is that a sentence in which a name of a fictional character is used can't *literally* say anything at all, since (on Walton's view) fictional names are empty names (Walton (1990), 385–400), and sentences in which empty names are used don't *literally* say anything. Since "Ishmael" is presumably used in a literal utterance of (1.1), treating (1) as (1.1)'s elision gets us no purchase on the problem of how (1), containing an empty name, can be used to say anything at all.

So far as I can see, Walton's principal reason for resisting the idea that *all* "ordinary" discourse about fiction—all utterances which, like (1) and (6), simply purport to recount what happens in the fiction—is paraphrasable *á la* (7.1) is that many such utterances don't literally say anything, because they involve the use of names of merely fictional characters. I think that if we reflect a little, we will agree that this is really a very bad reason for supposing, either that Walton's account of such sentences is correct, or that an across-the-board paraphrase of ordinary discourse about fiction, *à la* (7.1), would be incorrect. This is so, even if we begin by accepting Walton's account of the role of pretense in the appreciation of fiction.

The problem is that there is no reason to think that the linguistic behavior of normal speakers does or should reflect the (possibly correct but highly theoretical) claim that sentences such as (1) do not literally say anything. The claim, that if there is no such thing as Ahab, then there is no such thing as the claim that Ahab was a sailor, borders on

---

[5] Walton (1990), 401. I have changed the example under discussion.
[6] "affinity" is Walton's term for the relation between the statements made by the relevant uses of sentences related as are (1) and (5); see Walton (1990), 402.

conventional semantic wisdom, in these post-Kripkean times. But this was not always so; what consensus there is has been reached only after a few dozen years of reflection on a variety of arguments and theoretical considerations. The foot soldiers of illocution—the ordinary men and women down in the trenches, doing the dirty work of saying, suggesting, and so forth—would find the idea, that strictly speaking one can't say (or think) that Ahab was a sailor, plainly incredible, perhaps even more incredible than the idea, that to say that Hesperus is Hesperus is to say that Hesperus is Phosphorus.

Suppose that you are such a non-theorist, and are reading *Moby Dick*. How, if you thought about it, would you describe your activity, as you read the Epilogue, whose epigraph is *Job*'s "And I only am escaped alone to tell thee?" Quite probably, you would agree with Walton that you were imagining certain things. You might naturally say something like

> When I read "The drama's done. Why then does any one step forth?—Because one did survive the wreck," I imagine that Ishmael is telling me that he is the only person who escaped the wreck of the *Pequod*.

You would also find it natural to say that according to the novel, Ishmael survived; you would allow that the novel says that he survived. You would recognize no discontinuity among sentences such as

> "Snow is white" says that snow is white.
> Mary said that the rain in Spain falls mainly on the ground.
> In Moby Dick, it says that only Ishmael escaped the wreck of the Pequod.

There will be nothing about your usage or linguistic behavior which would justify thinking that you (or your "language module") perceives the last sentence to differ in some semantically significant way from the first two. There will be nothing that suggests that you see the last sentence as requiring special or exceptional treatment, if its assertive use is to be successful.

Suppose that I am correct about this, and that Walton is correct about the nature of works of fiction and their aesthetic appreciation. That is, suppose that Walton is correct in thinking that: associated with a work of fiction such as *Moby Dick* are various games of make believe, which involve imagining various things true in the fiction to be true; *Moby Dick* is a sort of "prop" in such games, whose purpose is to make various propositions fictionally true; central to reading the novel (and appreciating it) is participating in such a game. What earthly reason could there be, for thinking that when a speaker utters a sentence such as (1) or (6), she performs the quite complex task of engaging in pretense in order to discuss the pretense performed, instead of straightforwardly trying to say, of what's said by (1) or (6), that it's "true in *Moby Dick*?" Why think that "the familiar suggestion," that a fictionality operator is elided, doesn't give a perfectly correct account of how we (are disposed to) think that utterances of (1) and (6) come to say whatever it is that they do say? The theoretical fact, if it is a fact, that (1) doesn't say anything seems perfectly irrelevant. Not only is the fact not in our pre-theoretical ken, it seems to be one which we (obviously) disbelieve. Certainly we can't appeal to it, to explain why the utterer of (1) engages in pretense, for the utterer, as just observed, rejects the theoretical fact. From the speaker's perspective, the suggestion that one needs to engage in pretense, in order to make a claim in uttering (1) or (6), seems an utterly unnecessary complication. After all, if (1) is not semantically defective,[7] then the reason that (5)—Walton's gloss of normal uses of (1)—is true is simply that readers of *Moby Dick* are supposed to imagine that only Ishmael survived the *Pequod's* wreck. So if (1) is not semantically defective, the complex performance—pretending to use (1) assertively and, in doing so, signaling to one's audience that what one is doing is sanctioned by a game associated with the novel—seems little more than a very complicated way of signaling that, according to the novel, only Ishmael survived. And one can signal that, if (1) is not semantically defective, simply by uttering "According to the novel, only Ishmael survived." For to say that relative to *Moby Dick*, *p* is the case, is to say that some of the rules of generation associated with the novel prescribe imaging *p*. So, since, from the perspective of the speaker, (1) non-problematically says that only Ishmael survived, there is no reason, in uttering (1), to depart from what is presumably standard illocutionary practice, of using declarative utterance to assert what is literally expressed—and eliding the (presumably contextually obvious) "according to *Moby Dick*."

But then why think that speakers *do* depart from normal assertive practice in uttering sentences such as (1)? As Walton himself admits, what the speaker means to convey by uttering (1) would be "near enough for many purposes" to what would be literally conveyed by "According to *Moby Dick*, only Ishmael survived the wreck of the *Pequod*," if only sentence (1) said something to begin with. But *we* (normal speakers) think it does say something. There doesn't appear to be anything which we believe, inchoately suspect, or sub-doxastically register which would tend to make us think that an utterance of (1) (involving an elision of "According to *Moby Dick*") would not say exactly the thing which we intend to say, in uttering (1). So we can be expected to believe, of (1) and that which (on all accounts) we are trying to get across with (1)'s utterance, that a literal utterance of the first expresses the second (or something equivalent, for all purposes, thereto). Why would the language module be so inefficient that it invented a novel mechanism for using sentence S to assert *p*, when it already took S to literally say *p* (and so could use S to assert *p* simply by conforming to standard assertive practice)?

III

Among the principles of generation in a game of make believe will (typically) be ones to the effect that uttering a sentence of such and so a kind makes it fictionally true that one has asserted a proposition of such and such a kind. For example, in Cowboys and Indians, we may have a principle of generation along the lines of

---

[7] That is, if its literal, unembedded use makes a truth evaluable claim.

(P1) If one utters "some cowboys are behind that ridge," pointing to a mound of dirt, it is fictionally true that a ridge at which one points is such that one has asserted that some cowboys are behind it.

Suppose I point to a pile of dirt and say "some cowboys are behind that ridge." Whether I have, in the context of the game, spoken truly will depend on (a) what principles of generation besides (P1) operate in the game, and (b) what states of affairs in fact obtain. Suppose, for example, that the *only* other relevant principle of generation is

(P2) If Bill, Tiny, or Jessica is behind a mound of dirt, then it is fictionally true that it [the mound] is a ridge behind which are some cowboys.

Then it will be fictionally true that I spoken truly iff the condition

(C) Bill, Tiny or Jessica is behind the demonstrated dirt,

actually obtains. Let us say that when a game f, an utterance u, and state of affairs s are thus related—s is a situation which must really obtain for u to be a true utterance in f (and whose really obtaining suffices for u to be a true utterance in f)—*that s is a real world truth condition of u, relative to f.*[8]

Suppose we are playing Cowboys and Indians, and it is fictionally true of our belts that they are holsters. Then the real world truth condition of an utterance addressed to you of "your holster is unbuckled" is, of course, that your belt in unbuckled. Now suppose that I notice that your belt is unbuckled and, worried that your pants are headed south, utter "your holster is unbuckled." The point of my utterance is not so much to engage in the pretense that you are a cowboy whose holster is unbuckled and that I am a fellow cowboy saying that this is so, as to convey to you that the real world truth condition of my utterance—that your belt is unbuckled—in fact obtains. My utterance is intended to be construed, and indeed is correctly construed, not merely as part of a game of make believe in which I *pretend* to make an assertion, but as an act which in fact involves making an assertion. When I utter "Your holster is unbuckled," it seems, *I pretend* to say that your holster is unbuckled and *I in fact* say that your belt is unbuckled. Let us call this sort of thing—making an utterance u within a pretense in which u has a real world truth condition c, thereby actually asserting a proposition which is (in fact) true iff c obtains—*piggy backing*.[9]

Crimmins holds that a good deal of discourse is accompanied by one or another sort of pretense, off of which the discourse's assertive utterances piggy back. In particular, he

---

[8] That is: s is a real world truth condition of u relative to f iff (1) it is true in f that u is the assertion of a proposition, and (2) in the context of f, that s obtains is necessary and sufficient, for it to be fictionally true that u is the assertion of a true proposition. The second clause of this is, of course, less than pellucid. Various remarks of Crimmins suggest that we might replace (2) with something like: The principles of generation of f entail that (it is fictionally true in f that u is the assertion of a true proposition) iff s obtains. (See, for example, the discussion of sentences (2) and (3) at Crimmins (1998), 6.) I will generally speak of *the* real world truth condition of an utterance (relative to a fiction), in order to avoid agonizing prolixity.

[9] The term "piggy backing" is mine, not Crimmins' or Walton's.

holds that propositional attitude ascription involves piggy backing. According to Crimmins, when we talk about what someone believes we pretend that different modes of presentation present different objects.[10] In discussing Summarian astronomical beliefs, for example, we pretend that there are two objects, one named "Hesperus" and presented by the mode of presentation [Hesperus] actually associated with that name, the other named "Phosphorus" and presented by the mode [Phosphorus] actually associated therewith. The pretense employs principles of generation along the lines of

(P3) If (and only if) someone has a thought involving [Hesperus], then it is fictionally true that they have a belief about the object named "Hesperus,"

(P4) If (and only if) someone has a thought involving [Phosphorus], then it is fictionally true that they have a belief about the object named "Phosphorus."

Given the game we are playing, when I utter

(2) Hammurabi believed that Hesperus was a star,

it becomes fictionally true that I have said that Hammurabi believed, of the object named "Hesperus," that it was a star. Given the operative principles of generation, the real world truth condition for my utterance—the condition that must actually obtain, in order for it to be fictionally true that I have said something true—is that Hammurabi had a belief involving [Hesperus], which was an ascription to a thing of the property of being a star. (Following Crimmins, we abbreviate this as follows: the real world truth condition of my utterance is that Hammurabi believed <[Hesperus], being a star>.)

Call this sort of pretense—in which modes of presentation associated with different names are pretended to present different things bearing those names, and principles of generation such as (P3) and (P4) are employed—*attitude pretense*. We engage in attitude pretense, Crimmins says, in order to piggy back: My utterance of (2) is the assertion of a claim true iff Hammurabi believed <[Hesperus], being a star>.[11] The general pattern is that, in talking of attitudes, we pretend that different modes of presentation present different objects and adopt the obvious principles of generation. The upshot is that we are able to piggy back an utterance of

So and so believes that...n...,

into the assertion of something that is true iff

So and so believes <[n], the property of being an x such that...x...>.

What work does the postulation of semantic pretense? Well, suppose we have been convinced, by arguments concerning semantic innocence, the coherence of quantifying in, or whatever, that the logical syntax of a belief ascription is what the Millian or neo-

---

[10] Crimmins is non-committal about the nature of modes of presentation; I shall be, too.

[11] It is not supposed to be the assertion of the claim that this condition obtains. As Crimmins is aware, this would assign the wrong modal truth conditions to utterances of (2). See the discussion in Section VI.

Russellian would have us believe. We thus think that (2) literally says, of Hammurabi and the Russellian proposition that Venus is a star, that the one believes the other. We think that the behavior of the words in the complement is, semantically, in no way extraordinary; in particular, "Hesperus" there names Venus, and does nothing else. However powerful the arguments for this view of (2)'s semantics, it seems to sit poorly with truth conditional intuitions: Speakers see the truth of (2) turning on whether Hammurabi conceived of Venus in a particular way.

If, however, utterances of (2) generally involve piggy backing, the view of logical syntax and our intuitions concerning truth conditions can both be correct. Given the view of the logical syntax, uttering (2) makes it true in the pretense that one has said that Hammurabi believed a certain singular proposition, whose constituents are the property of rising in the west and the object named by "Hesperus." The real world truth condition of this utterance is that Hammurabi believed <[Hesperus], being a star>—that is, he believed the proposition that Venus is a star "under the Hesperus mode." So, given that the utterance of (2) involves piggy backing, such an utterance is actually true iff Hammurabi believed the proposition that Venus is a star "under the Hesperus mode." Russellian logical syntax, Fregean truth conditions; the Holy Grail is found, the Fisher King is healed.

IV

Roughly, and to a first approximation, in piggy backing, I play a game g in which it is fictionally true that I say that p, so that I may exploit the fact, that it is c's obtaining which makes p true in g, in order to say that c obtains. This means that when p is something which simply can't be true in the context of the game, there will be little point in trying to piggy back off the fictional truth that I say that p.

Now, on Crimmins' account, when we ascribe an attitude, we begin by pretending that every mode of presentation presents something, and that no two modes of presentation present the same thing.[12] Relative to such a pretense, a sentence such as "Hesperus

---

[12] This seems to be Crimmins' intention. But it is too strong. One thinks that it will be fictionally true that if Hesperus is the heavenly body most discussed by philosophers, then it will be fictionally true that Hesperus is identical with Hesperus, the heavenly body most discussed by philosophers. In many attitude pretenses, the antecedent will be fictional. So, assuming modus ponens in this instance preserves fictionality, we have a case in which distinct modes of presentation fictionally present the same thing. (The modes must be distinct, because they won't present the same thing at a world where no one discusses Hesperus.)

There seems to be serious trouble lurking here. For example, it will presumably often be fictional that an object o is the unique possessor of a property F and the unique possessor a property G, F, and G independent. (This would be so, for example, in a case where we are discussing someone who knows that Twain alone wrote *Tom Sawyer* and *Huck Finn*, but doesn't realize that he alone wrote *The Mysterious Stranger*.) Since we can presumably rely on the fictional truth of principles such as

If o is the F, then what [o] presents is what [o, the F] presents,

as well as modus ponens preserving fictionality, it will be fictional that

What [o] presents is what [o, the F] presents, and what [o] presents is what [o, the G] presents.

is Phosphorus" apparently says something impossible, for it apparently says something true only if the modes of presentation [Hesperus] and [Phosphorus] present different things while also presenting the same thing. So, since "Hesperus is Phosphorus" says something which can't be fictionally true, it says something which, relative to the pretense, can't be known. So there is apparently no (possibly obtaining) condition c which is the real world truth condition for a sentence such as

(8) Hester knows that Hesperus is Phosphorus.

So, apparently, we can't appeal to piggy backing to explain how this sentence can be used to say something possibly true and interestingly different from "Hester knows that Hesperus is Hesperus."

Crimmins is aware of this problem, and suggests a fix. He notes that when we speak of identity, we speak as if it is a relation which can hold between distinct objects ("when two objects are identical, any property of one is a property of the other"). He suggests that such talk involves the pretense that "with certain of our linguistic devices that normally express identity, we can express a relation which can hold between distinct objects" (Crimmins (1998), 35). Call the relation *ickdentity*. Suppose that in attitude pretense we

---

But one would think that we should also be able to rely on the fictionality of principles such as

If o is the F, then what [o, the F] presents is what [the F] presents.

So, again assuming that modus ponens preserves fictionality, it will be fictional that

What [o, the F] presents is what [the F] presents, and
what [o, the G] presents is what [the G] presents.

But as long as banalities such as

If one thing is identical with a second and with a third, then the second is identical with the third

are fictional, and universal specification preserves fictionality, it will be fictional that

what [the F] presents is what [the G] presents.

So if we are thinking apart [the F] and [the G], it will be fictional that what [the F] presents is and is not what [the G] presents.

Generally, attitude pretense will be logically incoherent in this way. I am not completely sure whether this is a problem; fiction is often enough logically incoherent. But this certainly *looks* problematic. Crimmins wants the likes of

Hammurabi believed the planet most discussed by Hammurabi to be a star, but he didn't believe the planet which rises over there to be a star,

to be such that it can be true even when we suppose that Hesperus has both the relevant properties (as we would if, for example, in the discourse as a whole we are discussing two people, one who knows that Hesperus has both properties, one who thinks that different things have them.) Presumably banalities like

If one thing is identical with a second, and Hammurabi believes the first to be F, then Hammurabi believes the second to be F,

will be fictional. But then we have

Hammurabi did and did not believe the star which rises over there to be a star,

being fictional, given that semantic pretense involves principles of generation such as

It is fictional that one believes the star which rises over there to be a star iff one believes <[the star which rises over there], being a star>.

(a) pretend that our use of the "is" of identity expresses ickdentity; (b) pretend that ickdentity holds between the objects presented by modes m and m', if in actuality m and m' present the same thing; (c) assume principles of generation such as

> P5: If (and only if) Hester knowingly believes <[Hesperus], identity, [Phosphorus]>, then it is fictionally true that Hester knowingly ascribes ickdentity to <what is named by "Hesperus," what is named by "Phosphorus">.

Then, when I utter (8), it will be fictionally true that I have said, of what "Hesperus" and "Phosphorus" fictionally name, that Hester knows that they are ickdentical. And this piggy backs into saying something true just in case Hester knows under the relevant modes that Hesperus is Phosphorus.

The fix, then, is that attitude pretense involves re-interpretation of the identity predicate. But this seems to cause problems with sentences in which the apparatus of quantification or counting is used. Recall how an attitude pretense about Venus and the Summarian gets going: We "make believe that Hesperus and Phosphorus are two things... [so that] it is fictionally true that there are two things to which we can refer as 'Hesperus' and 'Phosphorus'" (Crimmins (1998), 9). Consider the most basic fact about the determiner phrase "two things":

> (F1) *two things F is true* if and only if there is an x and a y such that x is not identical with y, x Fs, and y Fs.

Do we carry this fact into the fiction or not? That is, is (F1), as uttered within the fiction, true? Suppose it is. This will certainly force the following to be true, as uttered in the fiction:

> (F2) (There are two things to which we can refer, respectively, as "Hesperus," and "Phosphorus") iff (there is an x and a y such that x is not identical with y, we can refer to x as "Hesperus," and we can refer to y as "Phosphorus"),

Now, assuming that we aren't pretending that "Hesperus" and "Phosphorus" are ambiguous, the following will be fictionally true:

> (F3) (There is an x and a y such that x is not identical with y, we can refer to x as "Hesperus," and we can refer to y as "Phosphorus") iff (Hesperus is not identical with Phosphorus and we can refer to Hesperus with "Hesperus" and we can refer to Phosphorus with "Phosphorus").

But Crimmins' solution to the problem with (8) was to hold that in attitude pretense, we pretended that "is identical to" expressed ickdentity, and so "Hesperus is identical with Phosphorus," within the fiction, says something true! So the right side of (F3)'s biconditional is fictionally *false*; so its left side is too; so, chasing this consequence up the Fs, it is fictionally false that there are two things to which we can refer as "Hesperus" and "Phosphorus." Since it is fictionally true that the names refer, this drags in its wake the fictional equivalence of claims that someone believes Hesperus to be F to claims that she believes that Phosphorus is. And this is something the pretense account cannot allow.

To avoid this one must deny that (Fl) is carried into the fiction. It is not clear that it makes sense to suppose this—(Fl) is, if anything is, analytic. But let us for the moment entertain the idea that attitude pretense involves a sort of uncoupling of "two" (and thus of "one," "three," and the rest of the numerals) from the identity predicate, at least to the extent that both of

(Y)   Hesperus is identical with Phosphorus,
(N)   Hesperus and Phosphorus are two things, not one,

can both be fictionally true—as they would have to be, if we can have an attitude pretense in which it is true that Hester knows that Hesperus is identical with Phosphorus, but in which we begin by "thinking Hesperus and Phosphorus apart"—i.e., making it fictionally true that Hesperus and Phosphorus are two things, not one.[13]

It now becomes quite obscure, what are an attitude pretense's principles of generation—obscure, that is, what principles tell us which real world conditions make which sentences fictionally true. We are told that attitude pretense makes use of principles of generation along the lines of

(F4)   It is fictionally true that Hester believes that Hesperus is a planet iff Hester believes <[Hesperus], being a planet>.

Now, to truly believe *p* is to believe *p* while *p* is true; whatever it is that *Hester truly believes that S* says, it had better not say something which can be true when (what) *S* (actually says in fact) is not. So, given that the likes of (F4) are principles of generation, we are committed to principles of generation on which *Hester truly believes that S* is fictionally true just in case what S says *is actually* true, and it *is fictionally* true that she believes S. In particular, we have

(F5)   It is fictionally true that Hester truly believes that Hesperus and Phosphorus are two things, not one iff (it is true that Hesperus and Phosphorus are two things not one, and Hester believes <[Hesperus], being two things, not one, [Phosphorus]>).

Surely, however, fictional truth is "closed under triviality," so that (all instances of) the schema

(F6)   It is fictionally true that H truly believes that S iff it is fictionally true that S, and it is fictionally true that H believes that S),

---

[13] There is, in fact, a fairly strong argument that Crimmins must say that in an attitude pretense it is fictional that Hesperus is Phosphorus, and it is fictional that Hesperus and Phosphorus are two things, not one. For he holds that the "is" of identity fictionally expresses ickdentity, and this makes it fictional that Hesperus is Phosphorus. And we are supposed to pretend that "Hesperus" and "Phosphorus" name two different things.

are true.[14] All this cannot be. Suppose Hester believes that Hesperus and Phosphorus are two things, not one, and does this "under" the mode of presentation [Hesperus and Phosphorus are two things, not one]. Then she believes <[Hesperus], being two things, not one, [Phosphorus]>. So it is fictionally true that she believes that Hesperus and Phosphorus are two things, not one. And it is fictionally true that Hesperus and Phosphorus are two things, not one. So, by (F6) and (F5), Hesperus and Phosphorus are two things, not one. But this, of course, is not so. I find it hard to believe that a pretense account of attitude ascription can correctly assign truth conditions to claims about knowledge, true belief, or any of the other "factive attitudes."

V

Making believe and pretending would seem to be propositional attitudes: One makes believe *that Hesperus is not Phosphorus*; one pretends *that this is an apple pie*.[15] Making believe and pretending are, furthermore, generators of fictional truth: When we pretend that p, then, relative to our make believe, it is fictionally true that *p*.

Now, fictional truth is presumably a property of the object of pretense and make believe; the latter being a proposition, it follows that fictional truth is a property of propositions. If fictional truth if a property of propositions,[16] what are we saying when we say (for example) that it is fictionally true that Hesperus is a star? The *natural answer* is: We are saying, of the proposition that Hesperus is a star, that it is fictionally true. But much of the point of adopting a pretense account of attitude ascription is to allow us to maintain a broadly Russellian account of propositions, on which the proposition that Hesperus is a star is the proposition that Phosphorus is, given that Hesperus is Phosphorus. So, given the natural answer, if it is fictionally true that...Hesperus..., then it is fictionally true that...Phosphorus.... This, of course, sounds wrong. In an attitude pretense about Hammurabi, it is supposed to be fictional that he sees Hesperus in the evening; it's not supposed to be fictional that he sees Phosphorus in the evening.

In thinking about what is going on here, we need to carefully distinguish

---

[14] Such instances must be true so long as instances of

(T) It is fictionally true that [H truly believes that S iff (S, and H believes that S)]

are true and "fictional truth is closed under biconditional elimination"—i.e., so long as the inference *FT[A iff B], FT [A], so FT[B]* is valid. (Ok, ok, you also need to be able to infer FT[B iff A] from FT [A iff B].) It is difficult to credit the claim that either (T) or closure under biconditional elimination fails.

[15] This is a bit too simple, actually. If I pretend to do something, more than a propositional attitude is involved. Still, a propositional attitude is involved; if I am not imagining that I am serving you a pie, I'm not pretending that I am.

[16] Well, this isn't exactly correct. Fictional truth is relation, between a fiction or game and the bearer of fictional truth: It may be true in one game of capture the flag that this tree is the Pentagon and not the Lincoln Memorial, while in some other game it may be fictional that the tree is the Memorial, not the Pentagon. In what follows, I suppress the relativization, to reduce prolixity.

(a) The proposition in fact expressed by S being fictionally true,
(b) The literal truth of the sentence *it is fictionally true that S*.

Even if fictional truth is a property of propositions, (a) and (b) might come apart: They might, for example, if, for some ("non-homophonic") function *f* from sentences to propositions, *it is fictionally true that S* said, of *f* (S), that it had the property of being fictionally true. In order to facilitate distinguishing (a) and (b), let us write **FT[S]**, where S is replaced by a sentence, to abbreviate *it is fictionally true that S*. (So "FT[Hesperus is a star]" abbreviates "it is fictionally true that Hesperus is a star.") And let us write **FIC[S]**, where S is replaced by a sentence, to say, of the proposition in fact expressed by S, that it is fictionally true.[17]

What we called the natural answer, to the question *What are we saying in saying that it is fictionally true that S?*, must be rejected. That answer—that we are saying of the proposition S expresses, that it is fictional—commits us to instances of

(A) FT[S] iff FIC[S],

at least when S is a sentence which expresses a proposition. But it does not seem likely that we could avoid endorsing instances of

(B) FT[An utterance of "S" is true] iff FT[S],

at least when S is a sentence which expresses a proposition. After all, in pretending that Hesperus isn't Phosphorus, we are not pretending away banalities about meaning. Indeed, our pretense exploits the usual rules for making assertions and surely involves assuming/pretending that, save for the difference in the sense and reference of certain names and other expressions, the language we speak is just as it normally is. And (B) is nothing more than a reflection, within the pretense, of the banality expressed by instances of

(D) An utterance of "S" is true iff S.

(To see this, note that (B) follows from

(D') FT [An utterance of "S" is true iff S],

so long as "fictional truth is closed under biconditional elimination"—see note 14 above.) But since the Russellian proposition that Hammurabi believes that Hesperus is a star is the Russellian proposition that he believes that Phosphorus is, the relevant instances of (A) and (B) imply

(E) FT[An utterance of "Hammurabi believes that Hesperus is a star" is true] iff FT [An utterance of "Hammurabi believes that Phosphorus a star" is true].

But this is disastrous for the pretense account, since the account depends on utterances of the sentences having non-equivalent fictional truth conditions, in order to explain

---

[17] Throughout what follows, I pretend that context sensitivity doesn't exist. Understand me to be speaking of some particular case of semantic pretense, in which someone utters "Hammurabi believes that Hesperus is a star."

how one sentence may be used to say something true without the other sentence being such that its use would be a true one.

We must reject (A), and with it the natural answer to our question about "it is fictionally true." This strikes me as a very odd result. For one thing, it makes the nature of fictional truth opaque: What is it, for it to be fictionally true that Hesperus is a star, if it is not that this—that Hesperus is a star—is fictionally true? Somewhat less question beggingly, the result rings false, if we think about more mundane instances of make believe. In ordinary make believe, the players use various props—cups of mud, their fingers, garbage pail covers—to represent various things—pieces of pie, guns, shields. Such pretense is usually a matter of pretending, of the prop, that it is so and so: a game of mud pies, in which a cup of mud with a leaf on top is pretended to be a slice of apple pie a la mode, is a game in which the participants are pretending, with respect to it, the cup of mud, that it is a piece of pie. And pretending, of x, that it is F, seems to be pretending that x is F. In this case, its being fictional that this [imagine me pointing to a cup of mud] is a piece of pie seems to be a matter of our pretending-true the proposition that this [the mud] is a piece of pie. And this suggests that, in this most basic case, its being fictional that this [the mud] is a piece of pie is simply a matter of the proposition, that this is a piece of a pie, having the property of being pretendedly—i.e., fictionally—true. Why isn't the same thing true in semantic pretense? Hesperus, after all, is just as much a prop of the semantic pretense, involved in pretending to say of Hesperus, that Hammurabi believes that it is a star, as the cup of mud is a prop of the game of mud pies.

One might claim, in defense of rejecting (A), that it couldn't be true across the board, anyway. For, the argument goes,

(F) FT[Zeus is a god] iff FIC[Zeus is a god],

must fail: There will be fictions relative to which its left hand side is true; but, since there is no proposition that Zeus is a god, its right hand side cannot be true.

This strikes me as a disingenuous defense of the pretense account. Recall that the point of the pretense account is to allow us to treat sentences of the form *Hammurabi believes that S*, and of allied forms, as "innocent" constructions, whose logical form is exactly as the neo-Russellian or Millian says it is. The pretense account is supposed to show us how something like

(G) Daphne believes that Zeus is a god iff the proposition that Zeus is a god is such that Daphne believes it,

can be a *consequence* of a correct semantics for English, and its left-hand side can be used to say something true, *even though* there is no such thing as the proposition that Zeus is a god. That is, adopting BT[S] as an abbreviation for *Daphne believes that S*, BEL[S] as a abbreviation for *the proposition that S is such that Daphne believes it*, the pretense account is supposed to reconcile the claims that:

(G') BT[Zeus is a god] iff BEL[Zeus is a god]

is a consequence of a correct semantics of English; its left side can be used to say something true; there is no such thing as the proposition that Zeus is a god.

One would have thought beforehand that, at the level of logical form, the syntactic structures *FT[S]* and *BT[S]* would both pick out relations to (Russellian) propositions if either did. Thus, it is rather dumbfounding to be told that "Daphne believes that" picks out a relation to a proposition, that there is no such thing as the proposition that Zeus is a god *but still* "it is fictionally true that Zeus is a god" may be true. Obviously, if this is so, "it is fictionally true" doesn't pick out a relation to a Russellian proposition. One of course now wants to know exactly what its semantics is—for one suspects that if we understood it, we would be able to validate our intuitions about attitude ascriptions without invoking semantic pretense.

Let us take stock. We began this section wondering what it could be, on the pretense theorist's view, for it to be fictional that (say) Hesperus is a planet. We argued that the pretense theorist could not adopt the natural answer—fictionality is simply a property of a proposition; *it is fictional that S* is true iff the proposition expressed by S is fictional—because of the way the pretense theorist ties what uses of attitude ascriptions convey to fictionality. But, as we just saw, the pretense theorist is under some theoretical pressure to accept the natural answer. At this point, it may occur to one that the pretense theorist might treat fictionality and "it is fictional that" in the way he treats belief and "Daphne believes that": He might claim that while fictionality is a property of propositions, and the literal truth conditions of *it is fictional that S* are simply a matter of the relevant proposition having the property of being fictional, our uses of these sentences involve pretense in more or less the same way that attitude ascriptions do.

How might this go? Consider

(I) It is fictionally true (in pretense p) that [an utterance of "Hammurabi believes that Hesperus is a star" is true iff Hammurabi believes that Hesperus is a star].

One might say that a normal utterance of this involves a rather elaborate pretense: One pretends to refer Hammurabi, Hesperus, and the sentence "Hammurabi believes that Hesperus is a star," while pretending to say that the last is true iff the the first believes that the second is a star. Call this elaborate pretense P; what one normally conveys by uttering (I) is that if one is engaged in P, then performing P makes it the case, in P, that one has spoken truly. The upshot is that when we utter (I), we are not trying to convey the fictionality of the proposition expressed by its embedded sentence; instead we are claiming that certain behavior (engaging in P) will, in certain circumstances (my participating in P), make a certain proposition (namely, the proposition that I say something true) fictionally true.

This is all very well, and it does perhaps explain how, on pretense theoretic terms, "it is fictional that Zeus is a god" can convey a truth. But it is of absolutely no help in dealing with the problem set out at the beginning of the section. That problem was that if the pretense theorist admitted the truth—i.e., the literal truth—of all instances of

(A) FT[S] iff FIC[S],

as well as the truth of

(D') FT [An utterance of "S" is true iff S],

then he was committed to the disastrous

(E) FT[An utterance of "Hammurabi believes that Hesperus is a star" is true] iff FT[An utterance of "Hammurabi believes that Phosphorus a star" is true].

As we observed, rejecting (D') seemed unlikely, given that semantic pretense presumably presupposes banal facts about meaning. And the current proposal just *is* that all instances of (A) *are literally true*. The fact that typical utterances of sentences about fictional truth might be intended to convey something other than what they literally convey is simply irrelevant to the problem on the table.

Perhaps the pretense theorist, given that she is going to assert all instances of (A), must in the end deny that claims such as those made by

"Hesperus is a star" is true iff Hesperus is a star,
  An utterance of "Hammurabi believes that Hesperus is a star" is true iff Hammurabi believes that Hesperus is a star,

are fictionally true in attitude pretense. But how could these fail to be fictionally true? Well, one might suggest that our pretense is not really about Hesperus at all. We pretend that there is *something named "Hesperus,"* but we don't really pretend anything about Hesperus. This would make

(K) "'Hesperus is a star' is true iff Hesperus is a star" is true,

fictional without making

(K') "Hesperus is a star" is true iff Hesperus is a star,

so. And really, all we need to make it fictionally true that I speak truly, when I utter "Hesperus is a star," is (K),

(K') "Hesperus is a star" is true,

and some mundane facts about the biconditional. On this way out, the pretense theorist effectively denies that Hesperus stands to an attitude pretense about Hesperus and Hammurabi, as the mud pie stands to a game of mud pies. In the latter, we pretend that the mud pie is a pie; in the former, however, we do not really pretend anything about Hesperus at all.

This doesn't solve the general problem. So long there *is something* about which we pretend, in attitude pretense, some instances of

(A) FT[S] iff FIC[S],
(D') FT [An utterance of "S" is true iff S],

will jointly generate troubles. For example, notice that in attitude pretense the speaker pretends that *he* is saying something, about the beliefs of others. If Mark Twain were to utter "Dreiser believes that I wrote *Huck Finn*," he would be pretending of himself that he said that Dreiser believes that he wrote *Huck Finn*. Such an utterance would thus make it the case that, literally construed,

  FT(Twain said that Dreiser believes that he wrote *Huck Finn*),

is true. But then, *if* "it is fictionally true" and "Dreiser believes" are innocent, then literally construed, such things as

  FT(Twain said that Dreiser believes that Twain wrote Huck Finn),

and

  FT(Twain said that Dreiser believes that Clemens wrote *Huck Finn*),

will be true. But this seems to show that if the fictional truth condition for an utterance by Twain of "I said that Dreiser believes that I wrote *Huck Finn*" obtains, then the fictional truth condition for "Twain said that Dreiser believes that Clemens wrote Huck Finn," and that for "Twain said that Dreiser believes that Twain wrote Huck Finn" as uttered by anyone obtains. For the fictional truth condition of the latter (presumably) does not vary from attitude pretense to attitude pretense. But since one can say that ... Twain ..., without saying that ... Clemens ..., this is just this sort of thing which the pretense theorist needs to avoid.

VI

Crimmins motivates what he says, of sentences such as "Hester knows that Hesperus is Phosphorus" with a discussion of accounts of statements about non-existence which can be extracted from the work of Walton and Gareth Evans.[18] As Crimmins summarizes these accounts, in uttering

(9) Santa does not exist

  (i) one pretends that every mode of presentation presents something, and further,
  (ii) pretends that all and only those things which *really* exist have the property ascribed by "exists"; thus,
  (iii) the real world truth condition of a sentence of the form *a does not exist* is that the mode of presentation associated with *a* does not present anything (Crimmins (1998), 33).

---

[18] Walton's discussion is in Walton (1990), chapter 11. Evans' is in chapter 10 of Evans (1982). Crimmins characterizes Walton as tentatively suggesting various aspects of the following account; I shall, perhaps a bit misleadingly, simply call the account discussed in this and the next paragraph "Walton's account."

However, Walton and Evans do not appeal to piggy backing in their accounts. According to Walton, in uttering (9) we engage in the sort of pretense just outlined, and pretend to refer to something called "Santa." But the point of this charade is not to piggy back to something true iff our utterance is fictionally true. Instead, the point of the charade is to *disavow* our pretended attempt to refer; according to Walton, what is said in uttering (9) is that an attempt to refer of *this* kind [where the kind in question is exemplified by the pretended reference to Santa] would not be successful.[19]

As Crimmins notes, there is a problem. Crimmins assumes—rightly, I think—that the modes of presentation associated with proper names generally present what they present (or fail to present anything at all) contingently. On many natural ways of understanding the notion of a mode of presentation, this seems guaranteed to be true. For example, the mode [Hesperus] presumably doesn't present anything in a situation in which (on Earth) nothing which looks remotely like Hesperus is visible in the western sky at the times Venus in fact is. Given this assumption—and the assumption that what a sentence says determines its modal truth conditions—Walton's account has the absurd consequence that, if Hesperus could exist without appearing from earth as it in fact does, then what's said by

(10) Hesperus doesn't exist,

could be true even if Hesperus existed. If, furthermore, we understand the notion of a mode of presentation so that it is only a contingent matter that [Santa] doesn't present anything, Walton's suggestion would require us to say, *contra* conventional Kripkean wisdom, that (9) is only contingently false.

Crimmins suggests a correction to Walton's account; to understand it, we need to briefly digress, to discuss the issue of modal content. The pretense account of attitude ascription as thus far presented is not an account of what is said by uses of attitude ascriptions: It does not assign anything like a Russellian proposition, Fregean thought, or even a set of possible worlds or truth supporting situations to such uses. Rather, it is a proposal about utterance truth conditions, purporting to associate, with each possible utterance of an attitude ascription (or, at least, with each such utterance paired with a pretense) a necessary and sufficient condition for the utterance's being true. As it stands, the pretense account, for example, tells us that

(U1) When accompanied by a normal attitude pretense, an utterance in world w of:

(2) Hammurabi believed that Hesperus is a star

says something that is true in w iff in world w Hammurabi believed <[Hesperus], being a star>.

In and of itself this tells us nothing about the conditions under which the utterance correctly describes an arbitrary possible world—it does not tell us how a world $w^\star$ must be,

---

[19] Actually, Walton holds that we may not need to pretend to refer with the utterance of "Santa," but may instead "allude" therewith to a pretense in which such an act of pretended reference occurs. The qualification is for the present purposes irrelevant.

in order that an utterance of (2) *in w* be true at $w^\star$. As Crimmins remarks, "the modal content of an utterance and the utterance's truth conditions (i.e., the rule which tells us the conditions under which the uttered sentence, as uttered in w, is true in w) have to agree about the utterance's truth *value* (they have to "agree at the actual world"), but the truth condition of an utterance need not be equivalent to its modal content" (Crimmins, (1998), 27).

For an actual, piggy backing utterance of (2) to say something which is actually true, the utterance must, actually, be fictionally true. For such an utterance to say something which is counterfactually true, true at a world w, the utterance must be, relative to w, fictionally true. So Crimmins says. He continues

> But what can it mean for an utterance to be fictionally true in relation to another really possible world? I suggest that we need the notion of genuine possibilities generating fictional possibilities. This notion is needed anyway, since even ordinary pretenses... extend modally. [In a game in which you and I pretend that a certain hill is Mount Olympus and that we are gods] it is fictionally true that I *might* have pushed a god and made him fall, and this fact about fictional possibility is generated by the real possibility that I should have pushed you and made you fall. Just as real-world facts about the Hesperus-mode make it fictionally true that there are facts "about Hesperus," so certain genuine possibilities make it fictionally true that there are certain sorts of possibilities "for Hesperus." [An utterance of an] attitude report correctly describes just those possible worlds that generate fictional possibilities that, fictionally, are described truly by the utterance (Crimmins (1998), 30).

It is not altogether clear how we are supposed to determine the conditions under which a really possible world w generates, relative to fiction f, a fictional possibility.[20] But for

---

[20] What is it, for a world w to generate a fictional possibility, relative to a pretense f? Crimmins offers no definition, but there is a

> Very Natural Answer: Relative to a pretense, world w generates p as a fictional possibility iff something happens in w which, according to the rules of the pretense (its principles of generation) is sufficient for p's being fictionally true.

Let me state the answer more precisely. Identify fictional truths with certain propositions (those which are true relative to the fiction). Identify fictional possibilities with those propositions p such that p's possibilization is fictionally true. (This is to say, very roughly, that every instance of

> Relative to f, it is fictionally possible that S just in case, relative to f, it is fictionally true that p could obtain,

is true.) For the actual world to generate, relative to pretense f, a fictional truth p—for the actual world to make p fictional—is for the actual world to contain a state of affairs s and f to contain a principle of generation g such that, according to g, if s obtains, then p is fictionally true. So, presumably, for a counterfactual world to generate, relative to f, a fictional possibility p—for w to make p fictionally possible—is for w to contain a state of affairs s and f to contain a principle of generation g such that, according to g, if s obtains, then p is fictionally true.

If this is what generating a fictionally possibility comes to, then the principle offered in the last sentence of the citation comes to this

> (U2) Relative to pretense f, an utterance u (as it occurs in a world w) is true at $w^\star$ iff there are propositions p and q such that: p is true at $w^\star$; there is a principle of generation g for f such that, according to g, p's truth is sufficient for q's being fictionally true (relative to f), and it is fictionally true (relative to f) that if q is true, then p is true.

present purposes we can ignore most of the details. All we need to remark is that the proposal Crimmins makes involves the claim

(a) If an utterance u involves piggy backing relative to a pretense f, the modal content of u is the set of possible worlds w such that, relative to f, u is fictionally true at w.

Notice that (a) apparently implies what Crimmins observes, about utterance truth conditions constraining modal content:

(b) If an actual utterance u involves piggy backing relative to fiction f, and it is fictional relative to f that u is true, then the actual world is a member of the modal content of u.

And this, in turn, means that if a pretense involves pretending that a sentence S's utterance would be the utterance of something true, then one cannot piggy back, using the pretense and an utterance of S, to the saying of something necessarily false. For in this case, whatever is said must be, in actuality, true.

Now, let us return to the issue of denials of existence. How, exactly, are we to understand them, if we are not to understand them as Walton would have us? Well, we could understand them as involving piggy backing. Relative to the pretense (i)–(iii), an

---

Recall that one of the principles of generation in our pretense about Hammurabi is that

(P3) If (and only if) someone has a thought involving [Hesperus], then it is fictionally true that they have a belief about the object named "Hesperus."

According to (P3), it is necessary and sufficient, for its being fictionally true that Hammurabi believed that Hesperus is a star, that he believed <[Hesperus], being a star>. So, given the Very Natural Answer, it would seem that

(U4) An utterance in world w of "Hammurabi believed that Hesperus is a star," is true in w^* iff in world w^* Hammurabi believed <[Hesperus], being a star>.

But, as Crimmins acknowledges, this gets the truth conditions wrong, at least given the assumption that [Hesperus] could have presented something other than Hesperus.

> ...which real possibilities generate fictional possibilities in which there are attitudes "about Hesperus"...? [That is, which are ones which a sentence such as (1), as used in semantic pretense, correctly describes, relative to the pretense?] The argument from
>
> (2) Hammurabi believed that Hesperus is visible in the evening,
>
> to
>
> (3) There's a real thing such that Hammurabi had a belief attributing evening visibility to it,
>
> fails to exhibit an entailment in modal content if we answer this question in a particular way: by deciding that *all* possibilities in which there are attitudes involving the Hesperus-mode generate fictional possibilities involving attitudes "about Hesperus".... But clearly this cannot be the right answer. Instead, the contours of our pretense seem normally to be such that only possibilities that both involve the Hesperus-mode *and are about Venus* generate fictional possibilities concerning attitudes "about Hesperus." Plausibly, this is a reflection within the pretense of the rigidity of names (Crimmins (1998), 30–1), numbering altered).

It is not altogether clear what the methodology is here. It seems as if the proposal is that we simply look at our modal intuitions about utterances of sentence (2), in order to determine what worlds would be, from the perspective of semantic pretense, correctly described by (2)'s utterance. That is, we consult our modal intuitions about the conditions under which what (2) says is true, and identify (2)'s modal content with what they yield. The disadvantage of this methodology is that it is painfully *ad hoc*.

utterance of (9) piggy backs to a claim true just in case [Santa] doesn't present anything. So, as a mater of fact, what (9) says on a piggy backing account is true. What about counterfactually?

...we need to ask which real possibilities make it fictionally true that there are possibilities in which "Santa exists." I believe that the following... [is] defensible: normally,... no possible world makes it fictionally true that there is a possible world in which "Santa exists" (so that (9) normally expresses a necessary content despite having a contingent truth condition)... (Crimmins (1998), 34–5, numbering altered).

Let's just grant that, relative to the pretense (i) through (iii), there is no situation which makes it fictional that Santa exists. There is still a problem: (9) is not the only way we might say that there is no such thing as Santa; we might also utter

(11) There is no such thing as Santa,

to get this across. Indeed, if we are arguing with someone with more or less Meinongian tendencies, the best, and perhaps only, way for us to express our disagreement is to utter (11), for she who "distinguishes existence from being" may well agree with (9).

If the general strategy of piggy backing is to apply not just to (9) but to (11), it must be possible for (11) to be fictionally true. But relative to the pretense framed by (i) through (iii) (11) cannot be fictionally true: *The point* of the pretense is to set things up so that sentences like (11) are guaranteed to be fictionally false. As Crimmins puts it

[In the context of such a pretense] when the speaker says "There are some things that do not exist," I would say, she is relying both on the genuine universal property of existence (which informs "there are") and the pretended discriminating property (which informs "do not exist"). Within the pretense, this might be described as the distinction between *being* and *really existing* (Crimmins (1998), 34).

To indulge in the pretense outlined by (i) though (iii) is to pretend that an extreme form of Meinongianism is correct, and thus to pretend that any denial of being is false. Relative to the pretense, "there is [no]" serves to (fictionally) ascribe the universal property of being something or other (so that if a has a sense, *there is no such thing as a* is fictionally false); "[does not] exist" serves to (fictionally) ascribe the pretense's pretend property of existing (so that if a presents nothing, *a does not exist* is fictionally true). So (11) is false relative to the pretense outlined by (i) through (iii). The current account, then, seems to be unable to explain how a sentence such as (11) can be used to convey something true. Indeed, this account has the incredible implication that what we normally intend to get across with the sentence "There is no such thing as Santa" is not only *false* but *trivially and obviously false*. For, if the account is correct, then our normal use of this sentence is a piggy backing use of the sentence within a pretense whose rules of generation (i.e., whose rules for fictional truth) make the sentence false provided the name "Santa" has some mode of presentation or other associated with it. But it is a trivial, obvious fact that the name is senseful.

There is a response which needs be considered, namely that idioms such as "there is" and "exists" have multiple uses within the sort of pretense we are considering.[21] On this response, "there is [no]" may be "informed" by either the genuine property of existence or the pretend discriminating property; likewise for "[does not] exist"; thus, there is a use of (11) on which it is true in the pretense if (and only if) [Santa] presents nothing, as well as the use on which the just lodged objection capitalizes. Thus, it is perfectly possible to use (11) to express a truth.

Suppose we grant that there is *a* pretense bound use of (11) on which what is said is true. This doesn't erase the incredible implication that (11) has a use on which it says something trivially and obviously false. Neither does it erase the incredible implication that the dominant, default use of (11) is one on which it says something trivially and obviously false.[22] Indeed, the problem is exacerbated, since it now turns out that there is a use of "Santa *exists*" (the one on which "exists" is "informed" by genuine, not pretend, existence) on which it says something trivial and obviously true.[23] It seems absolutely incredible to think that any linguistic practice in which we routinely engage is one on which this sentence can (naturally!) be used to say something *trivially and obviously* true.

Interestingly, Walton's view is not liable to the objection just lodged, for on it the truth condition of—indeed, the proposition expressed by—an utterance of (9) does not turn on the fictional truth conditions of its utterance. In fact, Walton's account does not even require the pretense that there is a property of existing possessed by some but not all of what there is: Since the point of the utterance of (9) is simply to disavow that a certain kind of pretended reference could actually succeed, all one has to do is to pretend that such a reference is possible. One could do this within the scope of a pretense that every mode of presentation presents something which exists. And there seems to be no reason one could not, within the scope of such a pretense, also utter (11) in order to disavow that the relevant sort of attempt to refer could be successfully carried off. Walton's account gets the truth conditions of (11) right, but it gets the modal content wrong. A piggy backing account of (11) doesn't even get the truth conditions right.

In my opinion, it is a serious objection, to a piggy backing account of sentences such as (9), that it cannot be extended to sentences such as (11), for surely the ways in which these sentences come, on normal uses, to say what they do are pretty much the same. Of

---

[21] Crimmins made the following response in correspondence.

[22] The implication is a result of the fact that the principles of generation for the fiction framed by (i) through (iii)—i.e., the principles which determine truth in that fiction—explicitly make it fictionally true that every senseful name names something, and thus (since it will be fictionally true that "Santa" is senseful and "Santa" names something iff a use of (11) is true) make it fictionally true that a use of (11) is true.

[23] This is the use on which "exists" is functioning as "there is" normally does, so that *a* exists says something which agrees in truth value with (a normal use of) *there is such a thing as a*.

course, that it gets the modal content wrong is a devastating objection to Walton's account. And it is not at all clear, given that piggy backing and disavowal fail to account for the semantics of denials of existence, that pretense has anything to do with those semantics.[24]

---

[24] Thanks to Mark Crimmins for comments on an earlier draft and thanks to Harry Deutsch for telling me to re-write it.

11

Intensional Transitives and Empty Terms

I

The sentence

1. Mary seeks a tattooed dog

is ambiguous. It has a reading, brought out by adding "but no dog in particular," on which

A. The position of "a tattooed dog" is not extensional (she might not seek a three-legged dog, even if the tattooed dogs are the three-legged dogs);
B. The sentence does not say something which entails
2. There is a tattooed dog which Mary seeks.

Call this, for future reference, (1)'s *D-reading*. The sentence also has a reading on which the position of "a tatooed dog" is extensional and on which the argument from (1) to (2) is valid. Call this (1)'s *R-reading*. When a verb V is like this—that is, sentences of the form

3. a Vs an F

have both a D- and an R-reading—V is an *intensional transitive*.[1]

Intensional transitives are very common. Here are some examples:

seek, look for, hunt (for), imagine, dream of, owe, want, desire, describe, talk about, refer to [in its colloquial sense], need, ask for, demand, worship, blaspheme, curse, buy, sell, trade, bet, fear, love, loathe, hate, wait for, expect, build (in the progressive), write (in the progressive), bake (in the progressive), plan, see, is (ontologically) committed to, believe in, resemble, sound like.

---

[1] Whence the D/R terminology? "D" is supposed to evoke "de dicto"; "R" is supposed to evoke "raised" (since, in an R-reading, the quantifier is understood as raised above the verb). Quine's use of *notional* versus *relational* readings of sentences such as "he seeks a sloop" draws, I think, a distinction kindred to that I wish to draw in distinguishing D from R readings. But "de dicto" suggests sentence embedding (which I do not think occurs on D-readings), and "relational" contrasts with non-relational (and I think a D-reading can be every bit as relational as an R-reading). So I have thought it best to adopt novel terminology, in order to discourage misleading assumptions about what is to follow.

It's controversial that all of these fit my definition. I don't want to argue about every case, but I will pause to address one sort of objection, concerning verbs such as "loathes" and "worships." Someone might wonder whether sentences such as

4. Cara loathes a horse
5. Lenny worships a god

are really ambiguous: Isn't, for example, the only understanding of (5) one on which it entails

6. There's a god Lenny worships?

After all, it seems that if Lenny worships a god, there must be some god in particular—Zeus or Allah or another—that Lenny worships. But then (6) is true, right?

No. (5) of course can be understood along the lines of (6), for (6) limns the R-reading of (5). However, while (5) can be true (it will be true, if Lenny is, say, a devout Catholic), (6) cannot. After all, there are no gods, save (perhaps) fictional and mythical ones. And even if there are fictional and mythological gods, they are not gods. For in general, a fictional F is not an F—a fictional horse, for example, is no horse. Since there are no gods save fictional and mythical ones, (6) is false, since it entails that there are gods. So the possibly true reading of (5) is not one that entails (6). And this reading is one on which "a god" is not in extensional position, since (5)'s truth does not guarantee that Lenny worships a unicorn. So (5) has a D-reading as well as an R-reading.

Whence the intuition, then, that (5) does not have the sort of ambiguity that (1) has? When I hunt, expect, worship, fear, or loathe, I am focused on some representation of mine that "is the object of my activity." Now, there is a difference, between what can be an object of a fear, worshipping, or loathing, and what can be an object of a search or expectation. While I can look for or expect a rabbit, but no rabbit in particular, it does not seem to make sense to say that I fear/worship/loathe/a rabbit, but no rabbit in particular. If I fear/worship/loathe, there is always an answer to the question, What thing in particular is it that you fear/worship/loathe? Not so with hunting and expecting. The objects of a worshipping or loathing will, so far as I can see, invariably be "singular" expressions or representations. That is, they must be representations with the semantics of an expression—such as a proper name, demonstrative, visual representation, or definite description—which purports to pick out a single individual. Not so with the goals of searches and expectations, which can be any noun phrase whatsoever.

It is this fact that is, in my opinion, responsible for the intuition, that "worships," "loathes," and so on do not induce a D/R ambiguity. Part of what is involved in knowing what it is to worship (and so part of what is involved in a normal understanding of "worship") is recognizing that worshiping must be directed toward what the worshiper takes to be an individual. If so, then "he worships a god" can be true only if "he worships α" is true, for some "identifying" expression (name, demonstrative, definite description) α. And I think it's plain that, even when we know better, we are prone to infer *there's something he Vs* from *he Vs* α.

II

The metaphysician finds intensional transitives—ITs, for short—interesting, because the states and events of which they are true *seem* to involve relations to non-existents. It seems undeniable that someone can think about the golden mountain or seek seven dogs that can square dance. Such a person is thinking about or seeking *something*. So there must be such things.

Semanticists should be interested in ITs for at least four reasons. (i) They make the question, Do sentences with "empty vocabulary" such as "Hera" and "Pegasus" say anything? an especially pressing question. For it can hardly be denied that people have worshiped Hera or sought Pegasus. (ii) They raise interesting issues about logical form. When a sentence displays the sort of ambiguity that (1) does, we typically assume that the sentence contains two sentence operators, with the ambiguity being one of scope. This is what we say, for example, about

7. Mary believes she owns a talking dog.

In (7) "believes" embeds a sentence; in logical forms of (7), the quantifier "a talking dog" can govern or be governed by "believes." But this explanation is apparently not available for intensional transitives—where, after all, is the second sentence operator in (1) or (5)? (iii) ITs present many of the same puzzling "hyper-intensional" behaviors that propositional attitude ascriptions do: it seems obvious, for example, that there is a use of

8. Jane is June, and Jim seeks all June's old flames

from which

9. Jim seeks all Jane's old flames

does not follow. (iv) Obviously, the ambiguity intensional transitives induce is not limited to sentences with objects of the form *an F*. Perfectly parallel ambiguities arise for sentences such as

10. a. Mary expects 17 football players.
    b. Mary dreamt of exactly four hurricanes.
    c. Mary sought every survivor of the plane crash.

Now the behavior of quantifiers in D-readings of sentences like these is just plain puzzling. On the one hand, even in D-readings these quantifiers seem to have something like quantificational force. This is witnessed by the apparently obvious validity of indefinitely many inferences; here is a small sample[2]:

Mary expected at least four expensive presents from Bloomie's
So, Mary expected something from Bloomie's.

---

[2] In the following litany, only D-readings are at issue. It may help, in evaluating validity under the intended readings, to tack "but none in particular" at the end of each sentence in which an IT occurs.

Buddy wants exactly seven tattooed dogs
So, Buddy wants an odd number of tattooed dogs.

Sam hunts at least one talking chicken
Sam hunts at most one talking chicken
So, Sam hunts exactly one talking chicken.

Sam seeks a dog
Sam seeks a cat
So, since dogs aren't cats, Sam seeks two things.

Jane described at least six dancing pigs
So, Jane described at least four dancing pigs.

Michael bought exactly seven flying pigs
So, Michael did not buy exactly forty-two flying pigs.

Henry planned no more than six surprise parties
So, Henry planned no more than ten surprise parties.

Mary dreamt of many golden mountains
So, Mary dreamt of at least two golden mountains.

Sidney waited for more than ten accidents
So, Sidney waited for no less than six accidents.

Henry is hunting for thirteen horses
So, Henry is hunting for a baker's dozen horses.

These apparent validities cry out to be explained quantificationally.[3]

Now, I want to admit at the outset that not all of these arguments and their close cousins are *exactly* valid. People can have some pretty wild beliefs—that a dozen is 13, that dogs are the same thing as cats, and so on. If someone has wild enough beliefs, then they may make the premises of some of the arguments true without making the conclusions true too. But all of these arguments, I think, are *near valid*, where to say that an argument is (relative to a population) near valid is to say that, by supplementing its premises with (sentences which express) things that would almost invariably be presupposed by anyone who accepted those premises, we get a valid argument.

---

[3] As Terry Parsons pointed out to me, multi-premise arguments such as the third and fourth in the list cannot really be valid, since their premises might be made true by different events. (The point is that, for example, from

Some hunt of Sam's is for at least one talking chicken

Some hunt of Sam's is for at most one talking chicken

it does not follow that

Some hunt of Sam's is for exactly one talking chicken.)

But a minor complication evades this sort of point. Consider, for example, the result of adding

Sam isn't engaged in more than one hunt

to the third argument as a premise.

I think it is a reasonable demand to make upon a semantic theory that it should give us the tools to explain, not just why it is that valid arguments are valid, invalid ones invalid, but that it should take us pretty far in explaining why near valid arguments are near valid. And so one thing an account of intensional transitives should explain is how it comes to be the case that their quantifier objects (on D-readings) behave enough like quantifiers that arguments like those in our litany are valid or nearly so.

However, while the quantifier objects of intensional transitives often behave very much like conventional quantifiers, there are cases in which those objects decidedly do not behave as quantifiers normally do. The sentences

11. a. I kicked at least two men.   b. I kicked at most one man.

can't both be false and they can't both be true. Not so, the sentences

12. a. I sought at least two men.   b. I sought at most one man.

For consider

> **The Literary Example:** I sought a man who had read Proust and also sought a man who had read Gide, but was indifferent as to whether I ended up with a single reader or one for each author.

In this example, (12a) is false, for my search would be over if I found a suitably well-read man. And (12b) is false, for, in adverse situations, my search may require finding two readers.

III

If we approach intensional transitives with the idea that we need to explain the (near) validity of the arguments in the litany, Montague's account in PTQ is a natural starting point.[4] Simplifying in inessential ways, Montague held the following: (1) all noun phrases, including quantifier phrases, are semantically significant units whose extensions are sets of sets. For example, the extensions of phrases of the forms

F1. an/at least two/at most three/most/every horse

are the sets that contain exactly those sets containing

F2. an/at least two/at most three/most/every horse.

(Wanting all noun phrases to have the same semantics, Montague makes the extension of a proper name the set of all those sets containing the name's bearer.) (2) The *in*tension of a noun phrase is the function which takes a possible world to the phrase's extension there at. It is in terms of the intensions of expressions embedded within propositional attitude verbs that the truth conditions of a propositional attitude ascription is to be

---

[4] Montague (1974a).

given. (3) Verbs such as "seeks" and "owes" name a relation between individuals and things of the type of noun phrase intensions.[5] For example, the D-reading of "Mary seeks a tattooed dog" says that Mary is related by a relation **seek** to the intension of "a tattooed dog"; its R-reading says that, for some tattooed dog u, Mary is related by **seek** to the intension a variable assumes, when it is assigned u.

And that was really *all* Montague told us. To my knowledge, he said practically nothing about the nature of the relations these verbs pick out beyond this austere formal characterization. In particular, he had nothing substantive to say about how the extension of such verbs is determined. This makes Montague's view, in my opinion, at best unacceptably incomplete. As it stands, it gives no account of the indefinitely large class of validities that Section II's litany exemplifies. Montague's view offers no explanation of why, in a D-reading, quantifier objects of intensional transitives seem to be doing something very much like quantifying (witness all the validities), but yet are not aping the behavior of conventional quantifiers, as witnessed by the odd fact that (12a) and (12b) can both be false. And of course Montague's view is of no help in explaining the hyper-intensionality of D-readings, or how a sentence such as "Mary seeks a unicorn" can be true, given that "unicorn," and therefore "a unicorn," altogether lack an intension—which, according to conventional Kripkean wisdom, they do.

I do think Montague was on the right track. Of course, to deal with hyper-intensionality and the "unicorn" problem, we will have to avail ourselves, at some point, of semantic values more finely grained than (structured) possible worlds intensions. Still, the ideas—that intensional transitives name relations to semantic values of the sort to which propositional attitude verbs are sensitive (call these *embedded semantic values*); that intensional transitives are not covertly clausal, but name relations to the embedded semantic values of noun phrases; that the D/R contrast is (roughly) the contrast between ascribing a relation to the embedded value of a quantifier and the embedded value of variable under assignment—seem to me exactly right. Indeed, the idea that the core of the semantics for intensional transitives is a possible worlds semantics seems to me, understood in a certain way, to be exactly right.

In what follows, I will sketch what I think is a promising line on the semantics of intensional transitives which embodies these ideas. It will not apply to every intensional transitive—in particular, it will not help with "verbs of resemblance" ("looks like," "smells like"); but it will, I think, apply to a lot. What I present is, I think, in the general spirit of Montague's approach, though it hardly follows his letters.

I will pretty much ignore the hyper-intensionality of ITs, other than its manifestation with empty vocabulary items such as "unicorn." I suppose a discussion of intensional transitives without one of hyper-intensionality sounds a little like a redaction of *Paradise Lost* that eliminates the Prince of Darkness. But my primary interest here is in explaining the behavior of quantifier objects of ITs in D-readings. Such objects are doing

---

[5] Actually, in "On the Nature of Certain Philosophical Entities" (in Thomason (ed.), 1974) Montague (1974b), Montague suggests adopting a clausal analysis of verbs like "seeks;" the view here outlined is found in PTQ.

something very much *like* quantifying (as witnessed by the validities in the litany). I want to explain exactly what they are doing, explaining in particular: (a) how empty expressions such as "two unicorns" can make a non-vacuous quantificational contribution when governed by "seeks," while they do not when governed by "shakes," and (b) how it comes to be that many, but not all, classical quantifier transitions remain valid when we exchange "shakes" for "seeks"—to explain, that is, not only the litany but the literary example. As it makes the going much easier if I just ignore most substitution issues, that is what I shall do. This also allows me to remain in a (more or less) conventional possible worlds framework. And, indeed, a subsidiary goal of this discussion is to show that the data concerning intensional transitives can be explained without invoking (to my mind) obscure semantic values such as properties and relations that are not reducible to constructions from possible worlds.

I will talk mostly about "hunts," "seeks," "looks for," and "searches," slurring any semantic differences among them, though I will now and again discuss how what I say generalizes to other verbs.

IV

Consider, not the verbs "hunts" and so on, but the events of which they are true. A hunt is guided by a hunter's intentions, that her hunt should bring it about that she find so and so. I shall be ruthlessly sentential about intentions, assuming that for each intention there is a "syntactic object" of the intention; I call these objects the *goals* of a hunt. The assumption is, of course, relatively unproblematic if intentions are sententially realized states, for then the goals of my hunt are just those noun phrases α at the terminus of the sentences (*I shall find* α) that realize my guiding intentions.

Ignore for now the possibility that I hunt (say) with the intention of finding a unicorn, and so my hunt has a goal ("a unicorn") without a conventional semantic value. My goals determine possible worlds intensions; I assume a Montogvian account of them.[6] So, in the literary example, where I hunt with the intentions that I find a man who has read Proust, and that I find a man who has read Gide (but no particular readers), the goals of my hunt are

G: "a man who read Proust," "a man who read Gide."

Given a possible world, one goal returns the set of sets containing at least one man from the world who's read Proust, the other the set of sets containing at least one Gide reading man there from.

The goals of my hunt impose requirements on what counts as a successful hunt. If I hunt with goals G, my hunt is a success just if I find a Proust reading man and a Gide reading man; that is, just if the set s of things I find is in the extension of each member of

---

[6] In particular, for consistency, I take the intension of n, where n is a proper name or variable under assignment, to be that of *the x such that x is n*.

G. A hunt's goals thus determine a collection of pairs <w, s>, where w is a possible world and s a subset of w's domain, such that, for each goal g of the hunt, s is in the extension of g at w. Such structures—I call them *success structures* or *success stories* (*ss*'s, for short)—are abstract representations of (the domain of) the sorts of situations in which the goals of my hunt are satisfied, s representing the set of things found.

There are analogs to success structures for hunts among many of the events and states picked out by intensional transitives. A few examples:

1. Suppose I am in a state of expectation. That state will be realized by my having an attitude to one or more mental sentences of roughly the form *NP will so and so*. For example, I expect "two hurricanes will occur next week, and no tornadoes will occur." The NP subjects—"two hurricanes," "no tornadoes"—are, let us say, the *themes* of my state of expectation. A structure <w, s> such that, for each theme t of my expectation s is in the extension of t at w, provides an abstract representation of (the domain of) a situation in which my expectations are fulfilled. If, for example, <w, s> is a success structure for my weather expectation, s will contain two hurricanes (from w) and no tornadoes.

2. If I have an occurrent fear or loathing, that state is evoked by some sensory or linguistic representations. For example, my current visual representation of Marvin the mugger may evoke my fear.[7] Such representations are the themes of my fear; "success structures" for such—models of situations in which my fear is actually targeted on some individual or individuals—are pairs <w, s> such that s is included in the extension of each of the themes of my fear at w; that is, such that s "contains the objects which I fear." (I take the semantics of a visual representation to be that of a demonstrative, so that, for instance, the extension at any w of my visual representation of Marvin is the collection of sets containing Marvin.)

I said that the goals of my hunt impose certain demands or requirements on what counts as a successful hunt, and something analagous is true of expectations, wagers, fears, and the rest. We can model various notions of requirement using success structures. Let h be a hunt, G the set of its goals. Let us use **demand** so that *hunt h demands NP* is true just in case every ss <w, s> for h is such that s is in the extension of (the intension of) NP at w. In the literary example, my hunt demands at least one man, for in any success story for my hunt—in any model <w, s> of a successful terminus of the hunt—s, the set of things found, is in the extension of "at least one man" at w. My hunt does not demand at least two men, for, if Foucault is an omnireader at w, <w, {Foucault}> is a success story for my hunt, but {Foucault}—not containing at least two men—is not in the extension of "at least two men." And my hunt does not demand (finding) at most one man, for if you

---

[7] One might object that I may fear a nuclear war or thundershower, but none in particular. I am inclined to ascribe this to an ambiguity in "fear." I will suppose this sort of thing to be true of "fears" in what follows.

read Proust and not Gide, Marvin reads Gide and not Proust, there is a success story whose s, being {you, Marvin} does not contain at most one man. Obviously, we can apply the notion of the demands of an event or state to the other event and state types mentioned above. My meterological expectation, for example, demands at least one storm and no tornadoes.

As I see it, a sentence of the form α *hunts* β make a claim about what is required by one of α's hunts—that is, by the goals of some such hunt. On a first, evocative pass, α *hunts* β says that there is a hunt, its agent is α, and it (its goals) require(s) β; analagously for sentences about expectations, fears and loathings, bets and worshipings, and so forth. Formally, the proposal is that verbs such as "hunts," "loathes," and so forth name relations between events or states and possible worlds intensions of noun phrases (or something determined in a straightforward way by such intensions). Perhaps the simplest account is one that has verbs such as "hunts" naming the sort of relation we have implicitly assigned to "demand." Let us henceforth use "**demand**" to name a relation between token events and states (for which the notion of success and minimal success structures are defined) and intensions. Use "^" to form a name of an expression's intension from the expression; ruthlessly ignore contextual sensitivity. Our initial hypothesis is

H1:α *hunts* β is true iff for some hunt e, what α names is the agent of e, and e **demands** ^β.[8]

Ignoring a problem which I will raise (and eventually solve) below, H1 gives an extremely plausible account of the truth conditions of sentences (like those) of the form α *hunts* β, for monotone upwards β.[9] It is, for example, very plausible that a person who hunts with the intentions G in the literary example hunts for at least one man and does not hunt for at least two men. H1 squares with this, as we just saw.

However, all is not rosy. Consider

14. She expects no visitors.
15. He wants no mistakes.

These seem most naturally understood as claiming that the individual has the "corresponding" propositional attitude (expectation, desire) to a state of affairs picked out by a clause in which the quantifier object is used (e.g., that no visitors arrive, that no mistakes

---

[8] This is sloppy in (at least) four ways. First, it supresses relativization of truth to an assignment to the variables and to a context (or some parameters representing contextual contributions). Second, it doesn't bother to observe that α must be a name, variable, or demonstrative, but β can be any NP. Third, it doesn't bother to note that the relation between what α names and the Ving will probably vary across Vs—I am the agent of my hunts, the experiencer of my fears. Fourth, it doesn't bother to take into account the fact that I speak of the themes, not goals, of certain sorts of events and states (e.g., the themes of expectations and fears). For the most part, anyone who notices this sort of sloppiness ought to be able to remove it, if she desires. Since it makes it much easier to follow an already mildly technical discussion, I ruthlessly (and Boazlessly) suppress such details.

[9] A quantifier QA is monotone upwards when any inference of the form *QAs are Bs, All As are Cs, so QCs are Bs* is valid. It is monotone down when any inference of the form *QAs are Bs, All Cs are As, so QCs are Bs* is valid.

occur). If we take the theme of an expectation expressed by *I expect α to come/arrive/appear* to be α, and the theme of a desire expressed by *I want α to occur* to be α, H1 assigns truth to these sentences when the relevant agent has the relevant propositional attitude.

It is, however, possible to hear the sentences as making somewhat weaker claims, ones equivalent to those made by

16. She doesn't expect any visitors
17. He doesn't want any mistakes.

Suppose, for example, Mary has not thought about whether anyone will call; consider the colloquy:

Sam: Someone's at the door; do you know who it is?
Mary: Nope; I expected no visitors today.

Mary's response *is* a bit arch, compared to "Nope; I didn't expect any visitors today." But it seems perfectly acceptable. Furthermore, sentences such as

18. I sought no Samoans
19. [Whatdya mean I owe you a buck?] I bet no money.

simply do not say anything like

20. I sought with the intention of finding no Samoans
21. I made a bet whose object was no money.

Rather, they seem to say something more or less equivalent to the claims made by

22. I didn't seek a Samoan
23. I didn't make a bet whose object was some money.

If we suppose that these intuitions reflect truth conditions, and we eschew the hypothesis that sentences like "she expects no visitors" are (their R-readings set to the side) ambiguous, all this speaks against H1. For H1, given natural assumptions about the themes of seekings and bets, does not square with the just mentioned intuitions about truth conditions. H1 implies, speaking incredibly crudely, that the only thing *she expects/ hunts/bet no Fs* could mean is something like *her expectation/hunt/bet has "no Fs" as theme*. This just isn't what the relevant "hunts" and "bets" sentences mean.

As noted, (14) and (18) are somewhat arch, just as

24. I kicked no Samoans

is. (24) cries out to be parsed by one of

24'. I didn't kick any Samoans.
24". I didn't kick a Samoan.

One might suspect that the truth conditions (24') or (24") can carry are precisely those (24) can. One hypothesis to consider is that the same sort of thing is true of (18): While it has a D-reading—that is, a reading on which it contains a quantifier phrase that is not raised above its verb—that reading is given by (22).

But what would justify such a story about (18)? One might suppose that, quite generally, sentences containing monotone down quantifiers "decompose" into negations of sentences with the corresponding "positive" quantifier. For montone down quantifiers seem to be, in some sense, "definable" as negations of other (monotone up) quantifiers, as is suggested informally by the equivalences

no Fs G = not an F Gs
few Fs G = not many Fs G
at most n Fs G = not more than n Fs G

One version of the decompositional hypothesis about monotone down quantifiers is that the logical forms of a sentence in which such occurs are those of sentences obtained by replacing the monotone down quantifier with the corresponding monotone up quantifier and appropriately positioning a negation operator. If such a view is correct, our embarrassment over (18) is at an end; and since (H1), combined with the decompositional hypothesis, accounts for all the data reviewed in the last few paragraphs, it would seem that we could adopt (H1).

However, the decompositional hypothesis is refuted by the literary example. In it

12a.   I sought at least two men

is false, and thus

12c.   I didn't seek at least two men

is true. Now the decompositional hypothesis tells us that

12d.   I sought at most one man

is equivalent to

12e.   I didn't seek more than one man.

Since (12d) is false in the case, if the decompositional hypothesis is true, (12e) is false, too. But (12e) cannot differ in truth value from (12c).

Before considering ways in which we might modify our hypothesis to account for the data thus far assembled, it is worth looking briefly at some judgments concerning sentences of the form α *seeks* β, when β is non-monotone. Consider

> **The Political Example.** I seek a chaste politician. I am not adverse to finding two, but one would do; I will stop should I run across even one.

There is, so to speak, a lower bound on my search, for I seek at least one chaste politician. But is there an upper bound? Do I seek at most one chaste politician? For that matter, do I seek exactly one such politician? I find that most people have pretty pronounced intuitions about this example, thinking that it is false that I seek either at most or exactly one chaste politician. It is interesting to compare the intuitions about the political example and

> **The Scientific Example.** I am told that John Wheeler is on campus. Having always wanted to meet him, I search with the intention that I should find Wheeler.

I think it is obvious that in this case I am looking for exactly one person. Indeed, I think it is obvious that there is no sense in which the sentence "I am looking for exactly one person" is false in the scientific example. (H1) squares with the first intution, but not with the second.

Can we make sense out all of the data? I think so. Why is it that I am looking for exactly one thing in the scientific example, but not in the political example? I think the answer is something like this. Imagine yourself searching for Wheeler, or searching for a chaste politician. If your search drags on for more than a second or two, you will "find" an incredibly large number of things—that is, an incredibly large number of things will be salient to you. Searching for Wheeler by going from one room to another will involve finding the door, the floor, your shoes (if you look down), etc. Of course, this stuff you find is simply *irrelevant* to your goal, for none of it is/has the property of being identical with Wheeler. Suppose now that your search has come to an end, successfully or otherwise. Consider the collection of things you have found that are *relevant* to your search—that is, the set of things found that have the property of being Wheeler. This set, if your search was successful, is of course a singleton. It is because the set of *relevant* things found in any successful completion to your search will be a singleton that you are, in the scientific example, looking for exactly one thing.

Likewise, though you will assuredly "find" ever so many things (your legs, the floor, etc.) as you hunt for a chaste politician, most of what you find is just irrelevant, given your goals. What *is* relevant is what has the property—being a chaste politician—which is determined by your goal. There are successful completions to your search where the collection of *relevant* things found contains more than one chaste politician. Thus, you are not looking for at most, or exactly, one chaste politician in the political example.

We can amend (H1) to implement this idea so: Suppose that the intensions of quantifier phrases are structured, containing as constituents the intension of their determiner and the intension of their noun. We call the latter the property determined by the quantifier. We now restrict the success stories for a hunt to *relevant success stories:* to those pairs <w, s> such for each u in s there is a monotone up or non-monotone goal g of h such that u, at w, has the property determined by g. That takes care of the scientific example. Now let's attend to the monotone down quantifiers.

Why, in the literary example, *doesn't* the fact that circumstances might require me to locate a Samoan in order to complete my search show that

18. I sought no Samoans

is false?

Well, suppose I was so forced by circumstances, and I successfully completed my search by finding (the members of) a set consisting of a Proust reading angry Samoan and a Gide reading happy Egyptian. For each object in this set, it will be possible to explain, by referring to the goals of my search, why it is there. I explain the presence of each man by noting that one read Proust, one Gide; their nationalities and temperaments are irrelevant. Even though I was forced by circumstance to put a Samoan in the set, he is not there *because* he is such. Perhaps the operative notion of requirement is to be understood in terms of such explanations. The proper gloss to put on *I seek so and so many Fs* is then something like *I seek, and an adequate explanation of why my seeking ends successfully (should it do so) will make reference to [something which requires] my finding so and so many Fs*.

The idea is that "I seek no Samoan" is false in the literary example because we never explain why some object is to be found among the things collected in a successful hunt by saying that it is there *because* it is Samoan. What we need to do now is find a way to formalize away the "because." Consider a (relevant) success story m = <w, s> for a hunt h. Since m is relevant, each thing in s is in s *because* it has one or more of the properties determined by a (monotone up or non-monotone) goal of h. Is a thing ever in s because it has a property P not determined by any of the goals of h? Well, of course: If u is in the s of a success story for the literary hunt, he is there either because he is a Gide reading man or because he is a Proust reading man. And since being either *entails* being a man, he is there (in part) because he is a man.

In general: u is in s because it has P, provided that there is some (monotone up or non-monotone) goal g of h such that h determines property Q, having Q entails having P, and u has Q. That is: u is in s because it has P if u was admitted to s in virtue of helping to satisfy some goal g of the hunt, and helping to satisfy that goal necessitates being a P.

Call the set of things in s because they are P's the P-census of the success story <w, s>. That is,

The **P-census for <w, s> relative to hunt h** is the set of those things u in s such that, for some (monotone up or non-monotone) goal g of h, g determines the property Q, having Q entails having P, and u has Q.

Now, change the definition of "demands" in the obvious way:

Hunt h **demands*** an intension i provided: i determines the property Q, and for every *relevant* success story m = <w, s> for h, the Q-census of m relative to h is in the extension of i at w.

Let's look at a few examples. Go back to the Proust/Gide example, whose goals were

G: "a man who has read Proust," "a man who has read Gide."

There is a relevant success story a = <w, s> for this hunt, whose s is a singleton of a Proust/Gide reader, and there is one a' = <w', s'> with s' a doubleton, of a Proust not Gide reader and a Gide not Proust reader. In each case, whatever is in s is there because it has the property of being a man who read Gide or the property of being a man who read

Proust. So the **man**-census will be s itself for each success story. Thus, the **man**-census is not invariably in the extension of "at least two men" at w, and is not invariably in the extension of "at most one man" at w. Thus, both "I seek at least two men" and "I seek at most one man" are false. Since neither the property of being a Proust reading man nor the property of being a Gide reading man entails the property of being a Samoan, the **Samoan**-census of any relevant mss for the literary hunt will be empty, even though there are plenty of ss's whose s contains Samoans. Thus,

18. I seek no Samoan

is true in the literary example.

Amending (H1) in the way we have also removes the objection that it does not allow

14. She expects no visitors

to be true in cases in which the woman simply does not expect a visitor. For if (mixing use and mention) for any n and F, Mary does not expect at least n Fs, where n is greater than zero and being an F entails being a visitor, then the **visitor**-census for all the ss's for Mary's expectation will be empty, and thus it will be true that she expects no visitors. It is clear, I hope, that moving from (H1') to (H1*) doesn't affect what we say about the political or the scientific example. And it is easy to verify that (H1*) validates all of the arguments in Section I's litany.[10]

V

I suggested above that the semantics of the verbs "fear," "worship," and "loathe" run in parallel to that of "seeks." Let's recap the details. An occurrent state of fear f will have a set T_f of themes. These determine what we might call *relevant fear structures* (rfs's), pairs $<w, s>$ such that (a) u is in s only if for some t in T_f, u has at w the property determined by t,[11] and (b) s at w is in the extension of each t in T_f. Where P is a property, the P-census of an rfs $<w, s>$ relative to a fear f is defined exactly in parallel with the P-census of an rss for a hunt h, so that it is the collection of members of s which have a property Q which entails P and which is determined by a theme of f. We extend the definition of **demands*** to fears, with f demanding intension i just in case i determines Q and for any rfs a = $<w, s>$ for f, the Q-census for a (relative to f) is in the extension of i at w. α *fears* β is true just in case there's a fear which is experienced by what α names, and that fear **demands*** the intension of β.

A single state of fear, or loathing, or worship may be evoked by or focused upon a number of representations. I may see Marvin the mugger and be caused to feel fear, both

---

[10] Assuming that (in any context) a set contains many Fs only if contains at least two, and that, of necessity, thirteen is a baker's dozen.

[11] Since the themes of fears are always things with the semantics of singular terms and definite descriptions, we do not have to qualify the definition so that only monotone up and non-monotone themes satisfy this condition.

because he is presented to me as someone about to harm me, and because I recognize him as "Marvin," someone of whom I am afraid. There are two representations that evoke my fear, my visual representation and the name "Marvin"; each is a theme of my fear. Given that we treat the visual representation as something with the semantics of a directly referential expression,[12] and that the visual representation is one *of* Marvin, the situation is like a situation in which, say, both the names "Bill Clinton" and "William Jefferson Clinton" are terror triggers.

Let <w, s> be an rfs for this state of my fearing Marvin, the fear whose themes are "Marvin" and his visual representation. s (which represents the set of things on which my fear is directed) will be a singleton. For <w, s>, being relevant, can only contain things that have a property determined by some theme of my fear; each theme, however, determines the property of being identical with Marvin. Thus, in the present situation, there is exactly one man whom I fear, Marvin; "I fear exactly one man" is true, on both its D- and R-readings.

If I misidentify the object of my fear—I misidentify object X as Y, using a name or demonstrative presentation of Y, there are two objects I fear. What if I misconceptualize the object of my fear? I see *that man* and am thereby made to be afraid; I conceptualize what I see as "the man who mugged June." But no one mugged June. (Perhaps in my wretched deafness I misunderstood her when she said "this guy really bugged me.") "The man who mugged June" will be a theme of the fear in this case, as well as "that man." This means that on the story I am pushing it is true that I fear the man who mugged June. Some may find this a bit odd, since we naturally hear *X is afraid of the F* as implying *there is an F.*

I agree that the implication is there, but I think it is purely pragmatic. When a city is thrown into a panic by a string of grisly killings represented by the media as the work of a single man, it is natural and, I think, correct to say that the populace fears/is afraid of the man responsible for the murders, even if every murder was committed by a different person. Alone in rebel territory, I believe that there is a leader of the rebels; since I think any rebel leader would be cruel to foreigners, I am particularly afraid of the rebels' leader. But there is no such person, as the rebels are committed anarchists.

The example raises an issue. I claimed in the case in which I misconceptualize *that man*—Marvin, let us suppose—as the man who mugged June, my fear has two themes, "*that man*" and "the man who mugged June." Now, I think it is clear that, in this sort of situation, there is no sense in which I fear two men. There certainly are not two men such that I fear each. And it is not the case that it seems to me, "from the inside," as it were, that there are two men I fear. In fact, it would seem that it ought to be true in *some sense*—the D-sense—that I fear exactly one man. This, after all, is how my state of fear is structured by my beliefs. But if "that man" and "the man who mugged June" are themes of my fear, then if <w, s> is an rfs for my fear, s will contain Marvin and the object that,

---

[12] Thus, a visual representation of u is to be assimilated to the description *the thing identical with that*, "that" used therein to pick out u.

at w, is the mugger of June. Some such s's will be doubletons. So it will not be true that I fear just one man.

This is easily enough solved by imposing a bit of extra structure on rfs's (and their analogs for hunts and so forth). What one wants is something in the structure that corresponds to the subject's accepting an identity between themes or goals. So, instead of taking the set of themes of a state of fear to be a set of noun phrases and representations, we take it to be a set consisting of noun phrases, representations, and (possibly) sets thereof. The themes of f include the set $t = \{t1, t2, \ldots, tn\}$ if the subject of the fear "accepts the identity *ti is tj*," for any ti and tj in t. And if such a set t is a theme of my fear, we require that in any rfs <w, s> for my fear that the members of t have the same extension at w.

Thus, in the current example, not only does my fear have the themes

"that man," "the man who mugged June";

it has the theme

{"that man," "the man who mugged June"}.

Thus, each rfs for my fear has a single individual in its s, who is the extension (at the rfs' world) of "that man" and is (at the world) June's mugger. Thus, the D-reading of "I fear exactly one man" is true.

We are not yet out of the woods, though. Suppose I misidentify the object of my fear: I see "that [man]," *mis*identify him as the dangerous "Marvin," and as a result feel fear. Since I think the man is Marvin, among the themes of my fear are {*"that man,"* "Marvin"}. So <w, s> is an rfs for my fear only if the extension of "that man" and "Marvin" are the same at w. But since these are rigid designators of distinct objects, there are no such worlds. So my fear has no rfs, and, in this situation, I fear nothing. Whoops.

The solution to this problem, surprisingly enough, drops out of the solution to the problem of explaining how "He seeks a unicorn" can be true and have different truth conditions from "He seeks a centaur."

VI

I shall assume that expressions like "unicorn," "centaur," "Zeus," and "Hera" either have no intensions or have completely vacuous ones, and so, as it stands, we cannot assign intuitively correct truth conditions to sentences such as

27. Mory seeks a unicorn and two phoenixes.
28. Manny worships Zeus.

But I assume that such sentences can be true, and that the empty vocabulary in these sentences plays some semantically significant role (since, for example, (28) is not equivalent to "Manny worships Hera").

I think it is obvious that speakers see no interesting difference in kind between the sorts of conditions under which (27) and (28) are assertable—or true, for that matter—and those in which the relatively non-problematic

27.1   Mory seeks a unicycle and two photographs.
28.1   Manny worships Zasu Pitts.

are assertable or true. When, for example, can you assert (27) or (27.1)? Well, it turns on what sort of intentions you are licensed to ascribe to Mory. If, for example, you are licensed to ascribe to him an intention to find three phoenixes and a unicorn, you are going to be licensed to assert (27). Why? Well, putting the matter crudely, if Mory has such intentions, then the sort of computations that our little story about success stories formalizes would, if performed by Mory, lead him to the conclusion that he needs to find two phoenixes and a unicorn. For he would (if he didn't make silly mistakes) reason that a set with two phoenixes and a unicorn would be a set with three things in it, two being phoenixes, one being a unicorn. For—given that Mory is a ordinary guy—it will go without saying (to Mory) that the unicorns and phoenixes are different sorts of things. So the set would contain two phoenixes and a unicorn. So from Mory's perspective "I gotta find two phoenixes and a unicorn" checks out. And it is quite acceptable for *us* to interpret his use of "unicorn" and "phoenix" with our terms "unicorn" and "phoenix." So (27) can be asserted. A perfectly parallel story goes for (27.1).

We can distinguish two moments in what entitles us to assert a sentence like (27) or (27.1). First of all, we must be entitled to think certain things about Mory's mentality: that he has certain intentions which are suitably related to one of his ongoing seekings, and that certain simple computations "performed from Mory's perspective"—performed (accurately) by Mory in his language—would lead to a certain result R in that language. Second of all, we must be entitled to think that we can acceptably interpret result R—and, in particular, acceptably interpret R's noun phrases—using the embedded vocabulary in the (27)'s. As I see it, the (27)'s are true when and only when all of this in fact obtains—that is, when and only when Mory is in a mental state of the appropriate sort, which has, "from his perspective," an output R, and R is interpretable using the (27)'s vocabulary.

The (outcome of the) computations in question are represented by rss's and the associated notion of **demand★**. What is it, though, to "perform these computations from Mory's perspective"? It is, roughly speaking, to go through the computations Mory goes through using a language whose semantics *is* as Mory *thinks* the semantics of his language to be. But what would it be for Mory's language to have such a semantics?

Well, Mory makes certain broad ontological presuppositions. He thinks that there are, or could be, unicorns and phoenixes. It goes without saying for him that they are of different sorts, and that they both fall under the sort *animal*. Such presuppositions are mirrored by claims about the intensions of kind terms and names in Mory's language. For example, the presupposition that unicorns are a sort of animal is mirrored by the claim that the intension of "animal" includes that of "unicorn" (i.e., at any world, the former's extension includes the latter's); the presupposition that unicorns are of a kind different from ducks is mirrored by the claim that the extension of "unicorn" excludes that of "duck" (at no world do their extensions overlap). And the presupposition that unicorns could exist is mirrored by the claim that the intension of "unicorn" is non-vacuous.

Mory's presuppositions generate, through their meta-linguistic mirrors, a *taxonomic profile* for his language, something that is encoded by a collection of sentences of the forms

> k is non-vacuous
> k excludes t
> k includes t,

k and t kind terms of the language, and by sentences of the forms

> n excludes m
> n includes m
> n excludes k
> k includes n,

n and m names of the language, k a kind term. To capture the way Mory would apply the machinery of rss's—to "apply the machinery of rss's from Mory's perspective"—we should apply it to languages that reflect Mory's ontological presuppositions—languages that conform to the taxonomic profile his presuppositions generate for his language. That is, we should apply the machinery to (minimal) re-interpretations of his language, ones in which (a) each simple vocabulary item of Mory's language is assigned a (non-vacuous) intension, and (possibly) the intensions of other simple expressions are changed; (b) these re-assignments of intensions to atomics bring the language into accord with Mory's taxonomic profile; and (c) no more changes are made in the intensions assigned to simple vocabulary items than are necessary to satisfy (a) and (b).[13]

---

[13] More precisely: Where L′ is a language with the syntax of L, say that the overlap of L and L′ is the set of those atomic expressions e such that the intension of e in L is that of e in L′. (Obviously, I am, for simplicity, ignoring the existence of contextual sensitivity in L and L′.) Let L★ be someone's language of thought, P her taxonomic profile for L★. We say that a language L$ is a minimal re-interpretation of L★ generated by P provided: (1) L★ and L$ have the same syntax; (2) P is true of L$; (3) there is no difference, between L★ and L$, in the way the semantic values of complex expressions are determined on the basis of those of their constituents and their syntax; (4) there is no language L$$ satisfying (1) through (3) whose overlap with L★ is a proper superset of the overlap of L$ and L★. (The intention behind clause (3) is that "the" rules that spell out the semantic values of complexes for L$ and L★ be the same. Given that one could quite reasonably be skeptical about there being anything like a unique set of rules, clause (3) of course needs some spelling out. I will not try to do that here.)

I suspect that this definition could use some sharpening. For example, we might want to require that, after maximizing the sort of overlap just characterized, minimal re-interpretations of L★ should maximize overlap of extensions of simple predicates with those of L★'s. I will not pursue such complications here.

What would such a re-interpretation look like? Well, suppose Mory's language is English, that Mory makes the natural presuppositions about unicorns and phoenixes, and that he makes no erroneous presuppositions about objects and kinds other than these. And for simplicity suppose that "phoenix" and "unicorn" are the only (simple) empty terms in his language. Then a minimal re-interpretation for his language—an MRI—will be something with a syntax just like that of his language, and semantics just like it, too—save that (I) "unicorn" and "phoenix" are assigned non-vacuous intensions, ones that exclude each other (and those of other animal terms in the language) and that are included by "animal," and (II) as a consequence of these assignments, complex terms of Mory's language involving "unicorn" and "phoenix" (e.g., "two unicorns and a phoenix") receive intensions, too.

Minimal re-interpretations give us the means to model what it is to apply the machinery of ss's from a particular individual's perspective, by relativizing that machinery to an MRI. Let h be a hunt of Mory's, G_h its goals. Let us henceforth use *success story for h* so that such a success story is a pair $<L, <w, s>>$, where: (1) L is an MRI for the language of h's agent; (2) w is a world, s a subset of its domain; (3) for each u in s there is a (monotone up or non-monotone) g in G_h, such that u has at w the property determined by g *when g is interpreted relative to L*; and (4) for each g in G_h, s is in the extension of g *interpreted relative to L* at w. If a = $<L, <w, s>>$ is such a success story for Mory's hunt, and expression α's extension at w *when α is interpreted relative to L* includes s, then a corresponds to a situation in which, "looking at things from Mory's perspective, he finds α."

Let the P-census of an ss = $<L, <w, s>>$ for Mory's hunt h be the set of things in s which have a property Q, determined (relative to L) by a goal of h, which entails P. Imagine now we run through all the ss's for Mory's hunt h. We will find that for certain predicates P of Mory's language and quantities q, the P-census in an ss $<L, <w, s>>$ (P the property determined in L by P) invariably contains q many objects. When this is so, then "from Mory's perspective" a successful hunt requires that Mory find q many Ps.

For example, suppose Mory's hunt has the goals

g′. "two phoenixes," "a unicorn."

Assume that the taxonomic profile of Mory's language is as above. If a = $<L, <w, s>>$ is any ss for the hunt based on an MRI L of Mory's language, then the extensions at w of "two phoenixes" and "a unicorn" (interpreted as L-expressions) include s. Since the intensions of "unicorn" and "phoenix" must exclude each other and be included by the intension of "animal," s contains at least three objects which fall under "animal"; at least two of these fall under "phoenix," and at least one under "unicorn." Given that g′ gives the goals of Mory's hunt, the "unicorn" census of a (the members of s which are, in L, in the extension of "unicorn" at w) will be the "unicorn" in s; the "phoenix" census will be the "phoenixes"'s in s; the "animal" census will be s itself. So, speaking from Mory's perspective "my hunt requires that I find two phoenixes and a unicorn; it requires that I find at least three animals."

How, exactly, does this relate to the truth conditions of (17)? Crudely put, as follows. When a quantifier *d Ns*—for example, "two unicorns," "at least three animals"—always includes the "N"-census of an ss for his hunt, that means that *Mory's* use of *I'm hunting d Ns* is true. *We* can truly say *Mory is hunting* β when we can properly interpret—translate, if you like—Mory's use of *d Ns* with our use of β.

The picture, then, is this. A hunter will frame his intentions in some (not necessarily public) language. His ontological presuppositions generate a taxonomic profile for the language. The profile, in turn, determines a collection of minimal re-interpretations of the hunter's language; in these, every expression receives an intension. Such re-interpretations reflect the hunter's ontological take on the world. Given the re-interpretations, the machinery of ss's can be used to isolate a collection of expressions of Mory's language, those expressions which the hunt, as we shall say, **requires**. Reverting to the form of our original definition, we say that

> Where P is a property, the **P-census for <L, <w, s>>** relative to hunt h is the set of those things u in s such that, for some (monotone up or non-monotone) goal g of h, g determines, relative to L, the property Q, having Q entails having P, and u has P.

And requirement is then defined:

> Hunt h **requires** expression α: for every success story A = <L, <w, s>> for h, if Q is the property determined by α relative to L, then the Q-census for A relative to h is in the extension of α at w.

Taking the notion of translation for granted, the proposal is then that

> When *t* is a name or variable, α a noun phrase, then (relative to an assignment f to the variables) the sentence *t hunts* α is true just in case: for some hunt h of which f(*t*) is the agent, there is a β of f(*t*)'s language such that h requires β, and α translates β (relative to f).[14]

Let's review how this applies to the running example. Mory's language is, supposely, English. His taxonomic profile for English has "unicorn" and "phoenix" excluding each other, and both being included by "animal," as he thinks that unicorns and phoenixes are different sorts of animals. He hunts with the goals "two phoenixes" and "a unicorn." So, in an ss for Mory's hunt, the set s will contain, so to speak, two "phoenixes" and a "unicorn," all different and all "animals." So Mory's hunt requires "at least three animals." Given that we can interpret him homophonically, it follows that our use of "Mory hunts at least three animals" is, on its D-reading, true.

I want for today to take the notion of translation for granted. But I do need to point out that whether α in our language translates β in Mory's language is a matter of α and β's properties in our language and Mory's, *not* of their properties in various re-

---

[14] This, of course, makes the semantic value of an expression embedded under an IT the expression itself. In a fuller treatment, I would make this semantic value a more complex entity, roughly a pairing of the expression with its unembedded semantic value (or as much of such as value as it has). Nothing would be gained here from complicating matters in this way.

interpretations of these languages. I can render or translate Mory's use of "unicorn" with my use of "unicorn" because of the broadly semantic (and social) relations possessed by these words, as Mory and I in fact use them. Such translation has nothing to do with any similarity between minimal re-interpretations of our languages. Minimal re-interpretations are a device for modeling "the world as the hunter sees it," thereby creating an environment in which the hunter's quantifier phrases behave like quantifiers, even if they are, as he uses them, semantically defective.

The proposal I've just made changes truth conditions assigned to sentences in cases in which no empty vocabulary is involved. Indeed, it changes them in such a way that the problem left hanging at the end Section V is solved.

Suppose Manny is confused. He thinks Twain is Melville and is searching with the intention "I shall find Twain"; he is thus also searching with the intention "I shall find Melville." Suppose Manny has no other search-relevant intentions, and he knows that Twain/Melville is a man. Exactly what is Manny looking for? Well, he's looking for Twain. And he's looking for Melville. And so he's looking for two men. Clearly enough, it's also the case that, in some sense, he's looking for exactly one man.

Suppose Manny thinks in English. The only presently relevant expressions of his language are "Twain," "Melville," and "man." Since minimal re-interpretations have to do minimal damage to the actual interpretation of Manny's language, such re-interpretations will always leave the intension of "man" as it is. Each such re-interpretation will re-interpret exactly one of "Twain" and "Melville," so that the names are co-referential. SS's for Manny's hunt based on such re-interpretations will always have a singleton s, whose occupant will be either Twain or Melville, and which will always be in the extension of "man." The upshot is that Manny's hunt will require "Twain," "Melville," and "exactly one man."

Let us make the simple, natural assumption concerning translation, that co-referential names translate one another. We also need to be able to speak of variables under assignment as translating names; the natural continuation of the natural assumption is that when "v" is assigned u, "v" translates a name n just in case n names u. Then name to name translation from Manny's language to ours is homophonic. And a variable assigned Twain will translate Manny's "Twain" (not his "Melville"), a variable assigned Melville will translate his "Melville," not his "Twain." Our "exactly one man" translates his. The upshot is that

29. Manny seeks Twain, and Manny seeks Melville

is true, as "Twain" and "Melville" are required for his hunt and translate homophonically. True as well is the D-reading of

30. Manny seeks exactly one man.

But its R-reading is false, for there are two men, Twain and Melville, such that assigning each of them to "v" in

31. Manny seeks v

makes the sentence true.[15]

VII

Before wrapping up, we need to discuss an issue having to do with monotone down quantifiers and D-readings of intensional transitives. Consider once again

18. I seek no Samoan.

Suppose I am asleep, in a coma, or otherwise engaged, and participate in no seeking whatsoever. The R-reading of this sentence is obviously then true. But what of the D-reading? There are two issues here. The first is whether (18) on its D-reading implies that I am engaged in a seeking; the second is whether (18) has a use on which it is false in the envisioned situation.

Though the preceding has been relatively informal, it should be clear that I envision embedding the account I have been sketching within a semantical framework that takes English verbs to involve quantification over events and states. If the account is to be so embedded, then it might appear that (18)'s D-reading must imply that I am seeking. For on such a view, it would seem, the D-reading of *I seek* α will be regimented so

18.1 There is an s: s is a seeking; I am its agent; for some β, such that s requires β, "no Samoan" translates β.

Now this is not necessarily a bad thing, so long as there is an understanding of (18) on which it entails that I am seeking. I am not altogether clear whether there is such an understanding. It is true that we naturally take the sentence not to have such an entailment. But this is a function of the fact, I think, that we tend to interpret (18) as an arch version of "I'm not seeking any Samoans." And, as we argued in Section IV, this is a misinterpretation. In (somewhat weak) defense of the idea that even when α is monotone down, there is a reading of *I seek a* which entails that I am hunting, we might note that a sentence like "he sought few, if any, tattooed dogs" would be automatically understood

---

[15] The proposal sketched in this section presupposes the notion of a kind term. But what exactly is a kind term? For present purposes, I am inclined to take a quite liberal view of such, allowing any noun, whether simple or complex, to count as a kind term. Presuppositions that give rise to meta-linguistic claims about intension inclusion and exclusion continue to be identified with presuppositions and beliefs about the necessity of extensional overlap or the necessity of its absence. Thinking of matters in this way means that the taxonomic profile of a language (for a thinker) is liable to be a fairly unwieldy affair, though in practice most of it is irrelevant to evaluating the truth of a claim involving an intensional transitive.

It should perhaps be stressed that even though taxonomic profiles constrain how intensions are to be assigned to complex expressions, minimal re-interpretations proceed by (minimally) re-interpreting lexical items. In particular, a minimal re-interpretation may not alter, in a systematic or ad hoc way, the way in which the semantic values of complexes are determined by the semantic values of their parts and by syntax.

Thanks to Paul Teller for questions that prompted this note.

as implying that he had been seeking something, even by those who know that there are no tattooed dogs.

But suppose that there is no reading of (18) on which it entails that I seek something. Does that show that the account we have been developing is untenable, or at least inconsistent with the view that English verbs import quantification over events? Not at all. It is only an impediment to that quantification's being *first order*. That I do not seek does not mean that there is not such a thing as the set of those current seekings of which I am an agent, for that set can be empty. If indeed no reading of (18) entails that I seek something, then (18) is not to be understood as regimented as (18.1) but by something along the lines of

18.2 For some X, X the collection of my current seekings, there is a β such that X REQUIRES β, and "no Samoan" translates β.

where REQUIRE is a relation of sets of seekings to expressions constructed out of the resources from which we constructed the original relation of REQUIREment. It is not hard to define the appropriate relation, preserving the truth conditions the account I have been sketching assigns to the likes of "I sought three Samoans" and other "seeks" sentences with other than monotone down objects. The easiest way to do this is simply to treat the case, in which the set of a hunter's hunts is empty, as if it were a case in which the hunter was engaged in a hunt whose goal to find a ★ and nothing but a ★ (where ★ is an expression whose extension and anti-extension are null at every world):

18.3 If H is a set, all of whose members are hunts, then H **REQUIRES** α just in case: (1) H is not empty, and for some h in H, h requires α, or (2) H is empty, and, where L is any minimal re-interpretation of the language of the hunter, w a possible world, and Q the property determined by α relative to L, the Q-census of <L, <w, ϕ>> is in the extension of α at w.

The effect of the second clause is roughly that, when H is empty, it requires a phrase <d, N> just when ϕ is in the extension of the phrase at every world. Pretty clearly, this will be the case (for N that isn't necessarily non-empty) just in case d is monotone down. And so, in the case that interests us, once we add (18.2) to our regimentation, and adopt (18.3) as our definition of truth, we have the result that, if I do not hunt, then I hunt no Samoan. Just as clearly, these alterations have no effect on what "hunts" sentences come out true when I am engaged in some hunts.[16]

---

[16] What reason is there, independent of our current need to understand (18) as involving quantification which involves collections of events, for thinking that English event quantification is sometimes collection quantification?

A fair question. Schein (1993) makes a nice case for the view that many sentences of English are best understood as involving second order event quantification. Schein points out that a sentence such as

(7) Twenty composers collaborated on seven operas

has a natural interpretation on which it is silent as to how many collaborations, among the twenty composers on a total of seven operas, occurred. For it could be true if the composers have rivalries, so that (say) three

VIII

I have painted in broad strokes, and some refinements are necessary. Let me say what needs adjusting, without making the adjustments:

1. Something needs to be said about whether the D-reading of

    Benny seeks d Fs

can be true (a) if Benny lacks the conceptual resources to formulate a determiner with d's meaning; (b) if he lacks the conceptual resources to form the concept of an F. The first issue is whether it can be true that Benny is looking for finitely many ducks, if he is looking for exactly two ducks, but doesn't have the concept of (in)finitude; the second issue is whether it can be true that Benny is looking for a reptile if he is looking for a snake but doesn't have the concept of a reptile. The machinery I have set up validates both inferences. Either the implications need to be defended, or the machinery needs adjusting. One implication, I think, is acceptable; the other is not, but adjustments can be made.

2. A lot needs to be said about searches, describings, and so on with impossible themes—for example, about a search for a disproof of Godel's first incompleteness theorem, or Martin's describing a duck that was never a duck (but always a crow). By generalizing the approach I have sketched—imposing a construction of

collaborated on one opera, two collaborated on another, another four (including one of the first three) collaborated on a third, and so on through (various ways of dividing up) the twenty and the seven. We do not want to say here that there must be twenty collaborations. Neither does it seem, as Schein points out, that we can be certain that there is a single event, which is a collaboration, which has the twenty as its agents and the seven as its objects. Presumably, the semantics of English is neutral as to whether there are such "sum collaborations." The proper regimentation of (7), for the reading in question, is something like

(7′) (Some X: (Some Y: Y is a collection of 20 composers) (X is a collection of collaborations whose agents are all and only the members of Y)) (Some Z: Z is a collection of 7 operas) (each member of X has a member of Z as its object and each member of Z is the object of some member of Y).

(This is a simplification of Schein's proposal.) A second example Schein discusses is

(8) No more than two detectives solved no more than three crimes.

It should be clear that this has a reading on which it is silent as to how many if any crime solutions occurred. It is difficult to see how to capture this reading other than by quantifying over sets of events, understanding the sentence as saying something like: The (contextually relevant) collection of all crime solutions has no more than two detectives as agents, and no more than three crimes are objects of those solutions. It certainly will not do to understand (8) as saying:

(8′) ¬∃X∃Y(X is a set of more than two detectives and Y is a set of more than three crimes and ∀y(y is in Y→∃e (e's agents are in X and e is a solution and z is e's object)),

for this, unlike (8), is consistent with one detective having solved 10 crimes (Schein (1993), 119–22, and Chapter 9, passim). Schein's argument that, given that we see English as involving event quantification, sentences such as (8) must be taken to contain second order event quantifiers is complex; I pass over many relevant details.)

The upshot is that there is evidence for the view that some English sentences involve "essentially second order" quantification over events. And if this is so, it cannot be a cogent objection to the current account that it invokes devices, such as implicit second order event quantifiers, for the use of which in natural languages we have no independent evidence.

"impossible worlds" on top of the possible ones, and adopting a standard "truth value glut" approach to defining the relation of requiring—one can, I think, not only say something adequate to this case, but actually simplify the way the apparatus of taxonomic profiles and minimal re-interpretations gets deployed, in characterizing the extensions of intensional transitives.

But all of this is a long story, too long to recount here.[17]

---

[17] This is an expanded version of "How to Seek a Unicorn: Remarks on Intensional Transitives," the third Weatherhead Lecture in the Philosophy of Language. That lecture was given at Tulane University in October 2000. I am grateful to the Weatherhead family for making the lecture possible and to the audience at Tulane for their stimulating comments.

I am also indebted to audiences at UC Davis, UC Irvine, Rutgers University, and Ohio State University for discussion and objections. Among those I am particularly indebted to are Peter Ludlow, Terry Parsons, Rich Larson, and Cara Spencer, some of whom disagree with much of the above. Graeme Forbes, Jeff King, and Kathrin Koslicki gave me very helpful written comments.

This chapter is a descendent of Richard (1998); its account of intensional transitives supersedes the account given there.

12
Objects of Relief

The beliefs expressed by tensed sentences such as "Smith was sad" or "My plane is leaving" obviously have a cognitive role quite different from those expressed by untensed sentences such as "The time of my plane's departure is 7:00." A familiar sort of example: given that I do not know that it is 7:00, I will run if I think my airplane is leaving, but not if I think it is leaving at 7:00.[1] A closely allied point is that whether an emotional reaction like relief or anticipation is sensible seems to depend on belief's being tensed. The point is famously made by Prior: "One says, e.g., 'Thank goodness that's over!', and ... says something which it is impossible that any use of a tenseless copula with a date should convey. It certainly doesn't mean the same as, e.g., 'Thank goodness the date of the conclusion of that thing is Friday, June 15, 1954', even if it be said then. (Nor, for that matter, does it mean 'Thank goodness the conclusion of that thing is contemporaneous with this utterance'. Why should anyone thank goodness for that?)" (Prior (1959), 17).

That tensed belief—that is, belief expressed by tensed sentences—has such properties can seem puzzling. After all, believing that the airplane is leaving is presumably believing that it is leaving now; and if it is now 7 a.m., that is, on a broadly Russellian conception of belief, believing that it is leaving at 7 a.m. Some explanation of the distinctive properties of tensed beliefs seems called for.

Some would give such an explanation in terms of the states of affairs that are the objects of tensed thoughts: they involve, it is said, *temporal transients,* properties like *being present* and *being past,* which attach to states of affairs, events, or propositions at some times and not others; that tensed belief has such an object explains its distinctive properties. This view seems to imply that (in some motivationally important sense of "state of mind") the states of mind that realize tensed beliefs are ones we can be in only if we are thinking about temporally transient properties.

I'm grateful for the comments of participants at the conference "Time, Tense, and Reference" held at Santa Barbara City College in April 1997, especially those of my commentator, Mark Balanguer. Thanks also to Jason Stanley and Jeff King for comments on temporal parts hereof.

[1] Perry (1979) is the classic development of such examples.

Reasons to be suspicious about this claim arise, once we notice that thinking about a temporal transient *in and of itself* cannot be what is responsible for the motivational properties of tensed belief. Suppose I am introduced to a property of events, being serp, by being told the following:

(D1) Let midnight, January 1, 2001, be called t_m; call the present time t_i. At t_i, a claim p is serp iff p is true at t_m. In general, a claim p is serp at a time t_e iff p is true at t_e plus the difference between t_m and t_i.

(In notation familiar from Kaplan (1989), this cashes out so:

(C) For any t_j and t_e: $t_j[\text{Serp}(A)]t_e$ iff $t_j[A]t_e + (t_m - t_i)$.)

If, as it happens, t_i is t_m, then being serp is (at least from a tense-logical perspective) the temporal transient being present. If I understand the way in which "serp" is introduced, I understand such sentences as "The millennium is serp" and thus can think that the millennium is serp. This is so, even if I did not realize that the time I learned the term "serp" was the millennium. So thinking of the millennium and the property of being present, that the first has the second, does not in and of itself have the motivational powers of the tensed thought that the millennium is present.

The way in which one thinks of a (putative) state of affairs has as much to do with the motivational powers of one's thought as does the state of affairs of which one thinks. Given this, it is unclear why we should think that invoking temporal transients would have any special explanatory power. After all, we will have to invoke ways of thinking of the transients, as well as the transients themselves. And since it is the way of thinking, not the referent, that does the psychological heavy lifting, the temporal transient will tend to drop out of the explanation.[2]

This suggests looking for a more or less Fregean explanation of the cognitive role of tensed beliefs, claiming that tensed belief's distinctive cognitive role flows from the ways of apprehending states of affairs that we deploy in such belief. For example, some say the state of affairs that my plane is leaving (i.e., leaving now) obtains (or not) timelessly. When I believe that my plane is leaving, that state of affairs is apprehended under an

---

[2] One might deny that temporal transients, qua constituents of tensed thoughts, are to be identified with temporal intensions—functions from times, or worlds and times, to extensions. But, one might continue, (D1) "acquaints" us only with a temporal intension, not with the property of being present that is a constituent of the thought that my plane is leaving at present. Alternatively, one might concede that (D1) "acquaints" us with a property (in a sense of property other than that in which temporal intensions are properties), but say that the property it acquaints us with is but (necessarily) coextensive with presentness, and is not presentness itself.

This does not by itself meet the general point behind the argument in the text. It would seem that we can be "acquainted" with or "grasp" a property in a number of ways, just as we can be acquainted with an individual in a number of ways. Given this, and failing an argument that one can only be acquainted with presentness in ways that guarantee that we ascribe it to what "seems present," appeal to temporal transients alone has no explanatory utility in the present context.

These issues are pursued further in Section II.

"indexical mode of presentation"; the latter is responsible for tensed belief's motivational role.[3]

This essay examines two attempts to explain the motivational role of tensed belief in a more or less Fregean manner. I will suggest that neither of these explanations is quite right. Section I takes up an interesting proposal about the nature of tensed thought and the semantics of its ascription due to James Higginbotham. Higginbotham's view is (not unfairly understood as) one that attempts to explain tensed belief's distinctive role as resulting, not from the propositional object of a tensed belief, but from the "way it is apprehended." Higginbotham's proposal can be construed in two ways; neither, I argue, accounts for the facts. Section II discusses the idea, familiar from the works of David Kaplan, that the character of a sentence (or of a belief state realized by tokening a sentence) both determines the semantic properties of the sentence (state) and is responsible for its cognitive role. I argue that while there is a regular connection, in the case of indexicals, between character and cognitive role, character cannot be seen as *explaining* cognitive role. Section III sketches my own views of the matter; Section IV discusses the relations between ascriptions of tensed beliefs and ascriptions of the motivational properties of such beliefs.

I Higginbotham on tensed thought

If right now I think that I am flying home today, I think of a day—today—in a certain way. In order to think of the day in this way, I must stand in a certain relation to it— I must be "located in it" at the time of the thinking. If I demonstrate Maggie and say with understanding, "She's a Jungian," there is (arguably) a way I think of Maggie, associated with the sentence's demonstrative use; to think of Maggie in this way requires that I stand in a particular relation to Maggie—I must, *inter alia*, perceive her.

One feels a generalization hovering: to apprehend a proposition under a particular mode of apprehension is, *inter alia*, to bear a certain relation to what the mode presents. For Frege, the relation seems to have been invariably conceptual. But one can certainly broaden Frege's idea to allow for non-conceptual relations to help constitute sense. One might hope that by finding the right "sense-making" relations, be they conceptual or non-conceptual, one could give an account of the distinctive role of tensed thought.

James Higginbotham has made a proposal about tensed thought that can be seen as an implementation of this strategy. According to Higginbotham, a state of having a tensed thought is "reflexive": it is a state of thought whose object contains that very state as a constituent. Specifically, such a state involves temporally locating an event or situation (that which the thought is intuitively about) as simultaneous with, before, or after that very state. For example, when I am relieved that my root canal is over, "the thought that I think is indicated in (1):

---

[3] I am, of course, departing from Frege in making the reference of a sentence a state of affairs or Russellian proposition.

(1) (∃s) s is the situation of my root canal's being over & (the time of) s includes (the time of) e." (Higginbotham (1995) 228; numbering altered here and for subsequent examples)

Here, s includes s' if all the times at which s' obtains are ones at which s does; "e" names my thinking the thought in question.

Higginbotham grants that one might in principle think this thought at any time one exists, and that thinking it is not "intrinsically relieving." One might anticipate that there would be a first time one would be relieved that the impending root canal was over, christen that state of relief "Anton," and think to oneself,

(2) (∃s) s is the situation of my root canal's being over & (the time of) s includes (the time of) Anton.[4]

But in such a case, of course, the thought state one was in would not be Anton himself, but some other thought state. But things are different, Higginbotham tells us, if (2) is the object of Anton himself:

The point of reflexivity emerges when we consider that the thought that I would express by saying (3) essentially involves cross-reference between (the time of) my state and (the time of) the presence of a situation:

(3) I think that my root canal is over.

We thus distinguish between

(4) the thought that e is a state of my thinking that my root canal is over as of e

and

(5) the thought that e is a state of my thinking that my root canal is over as of e'

which is not cross-referential, even when e = e'. When I am relieved that my root canal is over, I think (4). (Higginbotham (1995) 229)[5]

---

[4] The example is mine, not Higginbotham's, though I imagine he would approve.

[5] A natural objection to this proposal is that it makes false predictions about the truth conditions of embeddings of tensed sentences. For example, one might observe that on Higginbotham's view, the thought that I think, if I think that my root canal is over, is the thought that a certain state of thinking postcedes the end of my root canal. Modal arguments, however, suggest that this identification is incorrect. Here is Higginbotham's version of such an argument:

Consider the utterance

(C1) My root canal might not have been over (now)

This utterance should be capable of expressing the thought

(C2) Possibly: not: (∃s) (over (my root canal, s) & s includes s').

... [But] whether I ever happen to think anything again... Is irrelevant to (C1)
... [Not so, for]

(C3) My root canal might not have been over as of my so thinking.

There are two questions one could raise: Is thinking that s is present thinking that s is simultaneous with one's so thinking? If so, will this help us to explain the distinctive cognitive role of tensed thought? Here, I will pursue only the first question, for I think its answer is negative.

We need to get a bit clearer about the sort of cross-reference that is supposed to lie at the bottom of tensed thought. According to Higginbotham, tenses encode temporal relations, thereby making possible the temporal cross-reference that occurs in belief reports; it is this sort of cross-reference that occurs in the tensed thoughts such reports report. Higginbotham's account of this cross-reference is set in a broadly Davidsonian framework, in which predicates have implicit argument places for situations (i.e., events or states). Tensed utterances are taken as token reflexive, so that an utterance u of "Smith's sad" says, roughly, that the sadness is simultaneous with u.

Ignore the Davidsonian embedding and token reflexivity for a moment, and replace the implicit argument places for situations with ones for temporal intervals. Then the proposal assigns

> ... [These] familiar observations constitute a demonstration that when I say "My root canal is over," I cannot express the thought [that my root canal is over as of my so thinking]. (Higginbotham (1995), 241–2, with inessential notational changes)

Higginbotham responds:

> [An argument such as that involving (C1–3)] evidently depends upon the assumption that embedding under modality does not discard information. But it may be that it does, and even necessarily so, though of course we would want to know why. (ibid., 242)

> Many of our thoughts, and... Virtually all of the contents of our utterances, are reflexive... Their reflexivity is often suppressed, however, when these thoughts are viewed as the objects of other thoughts or utterances; for thoughts that are common knowledge, or thoughts that one can carry through time, will not in general be reflexive. It is perfectly in order to consider a thought denuded of reflexivity. (ibid., 245–6)

As I understand the proposal, it is that sentences like

> (C4)   My root canal is over (now)

and

> (C5)   My root canal is over as of this thinking

express the same thought if uttered by me in isolation, but embed differently in modal and (sometimes) belief contexts. No mechanism for how embedding proceeds is suggested, but, as observed, there may be perfectly good reasons for a language to work in this way. I do not see why one could not work out the details more or less systematically. Most simply, one could assign a pair of objects, a thought and a "modal proposition," to a sentence. The latter would be controlled by the material explicitly occurring within a sentence, so that (C5)'s modal proposition contained a mental state while (C4)'s did not. I do not think such a proposal incoherent. I propose, therefore, not to press objections like the above.

One might also object that the proposal, taken to apply quite generally to tensed thoughts, implies that (1) the argument

> (i)   I am relieved that my root canal is over. You are relieved that my root canal is over. So, there is something about which we are both relieved

must be invalid; (2) a sentence like

> (ii)   You and I are both relieved that my root canal is over

cannot be true.

I think Higginbotham is simply stuck with implication (1), at least on natural construals of the prepositional quantifier. Note 7 suggests a way to evade implication (2).

(6) Smith is sad

and

(7) Smith was sad

the forms

(6′) $(\exists t)(\text{includes }(t, \text{now}) \ \& \ \text{Sad}(\text{Smith}, t))$

and

(7′) $(\exists t)(t < \text{now} \ \& \ \text{Sad}(\text{Smith}, t))$.

Here, inclusion is the relation an interval t bears to an interval t' if all of t' is in t; "<" names the precedence relation, which t bears to t' if all times of t are before all in t'. The proposal assigns the ambiguous

(8) Mary said that Smith was sad

the logical forms

(8′) a. $(\exists t)(t < \text{now} \ \& \ \text{Say}(\text{Mary}, t, \text{that }(\exists t')(\text{Sad}(\text{Smith}, t') \ \& \ t' < t)))$
 b. $(\exists t)(t < \text{now} \ \& \ \text{Say}(\text{Mary}, t, \text{that }(\exists t')(\text{Sad}(\text{Smith}, t') \ \& \ t' \text{ includes } t)))$.

Replacing the temporal reference of "now" with a reference to one's utterance (use "u" for this), replacing the quantification over and predication of times with quantification over and predication of events, and taking inclusion and precedence as relations between situations, we obtain the forms Higginbotham in fact assigns (8):

(8″) a. $(\exists e)(e < u \ \& \ \text{Say}(\text{Mary}, e, \text{that }(\exists e')(\text{Sad}(\text{Smith}, e') \ \& \ e' < e)))$
 b. $(\exists e)(e < \text{now} \ \& \ \text{Say}(\text{Mary}, e, \text{that }(\exists e')(\text{Sad}(\text{Smith}, e') \ \& \ e' \text{ includes } e)))$.[6]

Here, "Say (a, b, c)" says that b is a's making an assertive utterance whose content is c.

Cast in this format, Higginbotham's idea is that an utterance U of

(9) I am relieved that my root canal is over

has the logical form

(10) $(\exists s')(s' \text{ includes } u \ \& \ \text{Relieved}(I, s', \text{that }(\exists s)(\text{over}(\text{my root canal}, s) \ \& \ s \text{ includes } s')))$,

where "u" picks out U. That is, to put it crudely, an utterance of (9) says that I have a state of relief whose object is that that very state of relief is contemporaneous with the root canal's being over.

One understanding of Higginbotham's proposal is that there is something "intrinsically relieving" about being in such a state, at least given a strong distaste for root canals. That is, (a) where U is an utterance of (3) (named by "u"), the logical form of (3) is

---

[6] I have departed from Higginbotham, in ways irrelevant here, in the form of the content-specifying clause.

(11) $(\exists s')(s'$ includes u & Believe (I, s', that $(\exists s)$(over (my root canal, s) & s includes s')));

(b) if I am in the state described by (11) and dislike root canals, I will be relieved. That is, given that (11) or

(11′) $(\exists s')$ (Believe (I, s', that $(\exists s)$(over (my root canal, s) & s includes s')))

is true ((11′), since I might have the belief without speaking) and that I have a strong distaste for root canals, (9) will be true.

Suppose that I anticipate that my root canal will be over at 4:00 p.m., and that I anticipate that I will then think, with relief, that it is over. Suppose, being the christening kind, I introduce "Glenn" as a name of the first (occurrent) state of belief I have, concerning my root canal, after 4:00 p.m. Later, in the dentist's chair, I suddenly think to myself,

(12) There is a state of affairs s such that my root canal is over by s and s includes Glenn.

I am, sadly, *in medias rootcanalis,* and the thought causes me no relief.

But if the time of my thought was just after 4:00 p.m. and there was no other thought of root canals occurrent when I had it, then the state of believing I was then in was Glenn. And so it would seem that

(12′) Believe (I, Glenn, that there is a state of affairs s such that my root canal is over by s and s includes Glenn)

must be true at the time of my thinking. But existentially generalizing on "Glenn" here yields (11). So, it would seem, on the current construal of Higginbotham's proposal I must be relieved. The problem is that a state of believing can apparently be a constituent of its propositional object in virtue of two kinds of relations: either in virtue of "direct" relations—as when, as it were, I think to myself, "This very thinking I am currently doing is some thinking about the government"; or in virtue of "indirect" ones, as when I have a name that picks out a token judgment j, and that name figures in j itself.

One response—I do not think it would be Higginbotham's—would be to simply deny that a mental state could think about itself indirectly. This is tantamount, it seems to me, to denying that we can name our mental states, and seems most implausible.

A more interesting response holds that I have subtly misdescribed what occurs in the dentist's chair at 4:00 p.m. My objection, in essence, was that one might reflexively think one's root canal over but in an "untensed way." The response is that if I am thinking anything at all when I mentally rehearse (12), I am having a tensed thought: (12)'s first "is" is in the present tense. So what I am thinking is something conveyable so:

(12′) Consider the state of affairs: there being a state of affairs s such that my root canal is over by s and s includes Glenn. *That* state of affairs includes (and is thus temporally simultaneous with) my current state of thinking.

Call the state of affairs that is the subject of this thought (the one picked out by "that") "Ed." Ed is tenseless in the sense that he either always obtains or always fails to do so, depending upon whether Glenn occurs after the ending of my root canal. (12″) is the thought that this state of affairs obtains—speaking as I might at the time of the thought—*right now*. Since Ed is tenseless, it is no wonder that thinking (12″)—that is, (12)—yields no relief. But since the thought in question is not the one that would be expressed by "My root canal is over," this is not a problem for Higginbotham's account.

To give this response is, in effect, to deny that one can *have* untensed thoughts; if it is to be seriously advanced, one must be ready to say, for example, that to think that $2 + 2 = 4$ is to think that $2 + 2$ is presently 4, or that the state of affairs that $2 + 2 = 4$ is something that obtains *right now*. For the response is to insist that the main verb of (12) is tensed and thus involves, when I think (12), reference to my thought; if this is true of (12), it surely is true across the board.

I think this view is implausible. Here are two reasons. (a) Surely there can be languages that make claims that are untensed. Arguably, interpreted versions of first-order logic, which have sentences that are naturally read as is

(13) Smith is tired at time *t*,

are such. We understand such languages. Understanding them requires being able to think the thoughts their sentences express. But on the current response we cannot think them, as they are untensed. (b) Surely it is *possible* for you and me to literally think the same thought. Not so, on the current response. For example, no matter what we might try, we will end up, if we try to think what (13) says, thinking things that are not even metaphysically, much less logically, equivalent. For when you try to think what (13) says, you will think something that involves reference to your mental states, and I will think something involving reference to mine. Since one of us could have existed without the other, one thought could be true without the other's being so. While there is no formal incoherence in any of this, it is, well, strange.[7]

There is another interpretation of Higginbotham's account. It identifies tensed beliefs with states of believing that are reflexive "in the right way." We posit a relation—let us call it *awareness*—that a state *s* realizing a propositional attitude of an agent *x* can bear to a mental state *s'* of *x*. One stipulates that one can be aware of one's mental states only when they occur; it is to be understood that awareness of a state involves "taking it as

---

[7] I am not here objecting that Higginbotham, if he adopts the response, makes it impossible for both of us to have the same thought—that is, that he make sentences of the form

(i) You and I both think that *S*

invariably false. Higginbotham would say that whether

(ii) You believe that *S*

is true or not depends upon whether you have a belief with a content similar to that of the complement as uttered; he can say that similarity is usually computed by adjusting for the mental state component. My objection here is not to this, but to the idea that it is in principle impossible for us to literally think the very same thing.

present." Strictly, we should speak of a state of belief s being aware of a mental state s' as it occurs (at a particular locus) in an object of a propositional attitude. Write

$Ref(s\star, s, p)$

for

$s\star$ is a state of s bearing the awareness relation to the state that occupies the tense position of the thought p,

it being understood, for example, that the tense position of the thought

(14) $(\exists s)$(over (my root canal, s) & s includes s')

is that occupied by s'. We say that tensed belief involves "reflexive awareness" and that there is a "subatomic" reference to the relation Ref in a belief ascription; sentence (3) is to be ascribed the logical form, or is at least necessarily equivalent to,

(11★) $(\exists s')$(s' includes u & Believe (I, s' that $(\exists s)$(over (my root canal, s) & s includes s')) and $(\exists s\star)$(s' includes $s\star$ & Ref ($s\star$, s', that $(\exists s)$(over (my root canal, s) & s includes s')))).

Roughly put, this says that there is a state s' of my believing, its object is that it itself includes my root canal's being over, and s' bears the Ref relation to itself, as it occurs in that object.[8]

I will express two reservations about this proposal.

Reservation 1. As I see it, states of thinking, like other states, can endure through time. For example, I may spend a few minutes thinking, "Eventually the millennium will come"; if so, there is a single state of my thinking that lasts several minutes. But now consider what I am supposed to think when I think, say, that Smith was sad. On Higginbotham's view, I think,

(15) $(\exists s)(s < s'$ & Sad (Smith, s)),

where s' is my state of thinking this. But given that s' might commence before the onset of Smith's sadness, (15) can be false, even though it is true that Smith was sad.

It may be felt that we need only to tinker with the logical form. Why not say that the content of my belief is not (15) but

(16) $(\exists s)(s <$ the current moment of s' & Sad (Smith, s)),

with, again, s' being my very thought thereof? But this seems to finesse all the interesting questions, with its insertion of "current" into the specification of my belief. To meet the objection, one must do one of three things: (a) find a way to specify the relevant time of s' without introducing either a tensed expression such as "now" or an untensed one such as "the moment of s that is identical with my 45th birthday"; (b) say that the constituent of my thought that Smith is sad is not my state of thinking it, but a minimal temporal slice thereof; (c) deny that states of thought can endure. Since it is *states* of

---

[8] Some of Higginbotham's remarks suggest he intends to be understood in some such way. See especially Higginbotham (1995), 247–8.

thought that are under discussion, I do not see how we cogently take the third route; the first appears hopeless.

I am not sure we should rest happy with the second option. Suppose I think (15) at t, with the value of "s'" being some previous temporal slice of the state of thinking I am in at t. Then (15) may still be false, though "Smith was sad" is true. (Suppose as before that I started thinking, "Smith was sad," a bit before Smith began to be sad and that I continued in that state of mind as he became sad; and take s' to be the slice at which my thinking commenced.)

Perhaps we should say that at a time t a state of thinking can only be aware of its current temporal slice, ascribing to (3) a logical form along the lines of

(11★★) ($\exists s'$)(s' includes u & ($\exists s''$)(s'' is a temporal slice of s' & Believe (I, s', that ($\exists s$) (over (my root canal, s) & s includes s''))) and ($\exists s$★)(s' includes s★ & Ref (s★, s', that ($\exists s$)(over (my root canal, s) & s includes s'')))).

We might gloss this so: some state s' of my thinking has as object that s''—which is in fact a temporal slice s'—is after my root canal, and s' Refs s'' as it occurs in that object. Given that necessarily, if s' is aware of s'' at t, then s is a momentary temporal slice of a mental event that occurs at t, this seems to solve the problem of getting the truth conditions of tensed thoughts right.

I see no formal problem with this proposal. But I think we should be uncomfortable with it. It builds into tensed belief and the semantics of its ascription a very restrictive notion of acquaintance, since the proposal will succeed only if we insist that we cannot be aware of (non-instantaneous) mental states and that we cannot be aware of the temporal parts of mental states we remember. It is simply not obvious that there is a relation that will do the work that needs doing here. Furthermore, we would apparently have to ascribe to thinkers to whom the proposal applies the ability to discriminate (momentary) temporal parts of states from those states themselves. For the idea here is that the content of my thought at t that Smith was sad is given by

(17) ($\exists s$)($s < s''$ & Sad (Smith, s)),

where the value of "s''" is the temporal slice of that state of thought which is my thinking this content. *Something* has to make it the case that when I think that Smith is sad, I am picking out just the momentary slice of my thinking, and not the temporally whole enchilada. I am not sure what would make it the case that it was plausible to ascribe this sort of ability to an ordinary thinker. When I think to myself, "This very thinking has taken a few seconds," I don't sense that I am caught up in necessary falsehood, or that I make sub-sentential reference to some function from temporal parts to wholes.

Reservation 2. If it is the reflexivity of tensed belief that accounts for its distinctive cognitive properties, this is because of the truth of something like

(18) I must be aware, if I think reflexively of a state s of mind, that s is presently occurring.

One can think of a relatively straightforward argument for (18): Whenever I am thinking, I know that I am thinking—that is, presently thinking. Thus, if I think reflexively of my thinking, I know that what I think of is simultaneous with something presently occurring. Thus, a reflexive state "knows" that it is present. Thus, the reflexivity of tensed thought guarantees that it is thought that locates an event, for the thinker, relative to her present, since it locates the event relative to something the believer knows is occurring in the present.

An obvious upshot is that Higginbotham's account fails on its own terms, if it is possible for someone to reflexively think that her thinking is simultaneous with an event e, but not believe that her so thinking is presently occurring. That is, the account requires that it be impossible that there be a state of thinking s (a) whose object is that s is simultaneous with some event e, (b) that is reflexive, but (c) that is such that s "as it is presented in s" is not presented as present.

Now, "think" and allied expressions are ambiguous between something like "believe" and "entertain." Conditions (a) through (c) are possible, if "think" is understood as "entertain;" for it is possible to "reflexively entertain" the claim that event e is simultaneous with one's so thinking without thereby taking one's entertaining the claim to be presently occurring.

Suppose that I am given to particularly vivid recall of things that have happened in the past. For example, I at times recall (without trying to recall) the tolling of the midnight bells so vividly that I need to reflect in order to determine that my experience is a memory, not a present event. Not only do I on occasion so recall external events, but on occasion I have, or at least believe that I have, such recollections of my internal reactions to them. For example, I at times recall (without trying) hearing the tolling of the midnight bells and occurrently thinking, "This [the bells' tolling] marks midnight." On some such occasions, I take the entire episode to be a memory, of my experience of the bells and my mental reaction thereto; on others, I am unsure whether I am recalling something past or not.

Suppose that I know that a certain sound is characteristic of the dog's clawing at the door to gain entrance. Suppose the dog claws, I hear it, and that causes me to think,

(19) The dog's wanting entrance is simultaneous with my hearing this [I intend the clawing] and with my so thinking.

I know how I often vividly recall the past. And so, at the same time I think (19), I take myself (mistakenly) only to be recalling (quite accurately) something that happened several weeks ago; consequently, I don't go to the door to let the dog in, which I would if I thought the dog was *now* clawing.[9]

---

[9] One might deny that I can "vividly recall" internal occurrent thinkings. Even if that were so, which I doubt, it suffices for the present case simply that I be disposed to take some occurrent thinkings as memories of such.

Let t be the state that is my thinking (19) to myself on hearing the dog. t is a state with propositional content. Its content is that of (19) when tokened therein. So t is a state in which I entertain (what's said by t's tokening of) (19). And t seems reflexive, given that my tokening of (19) is my thinking, "The dog wants entrance *while this (i.e., t) happens*." But I do not take the reference of "my so thinking" in my tokening of (19) to be present, since I (mistakenly) take myself to be recalling something that happened in the past. Thus, s is a reflexive state of thinking, but in s, s is *not* presented as presently occurring. In s, s is simply presented as simultaneous with some other events, events that I also take to be past. So here we have an example of a state that satisfies conditions (a) through (c) above. This seems to show that what makes a propositional attitude tensed is not its being reflexive.

It might be objected that t itself is not a propositional attitude. My propositional attitude, it might be said, is a state that takes t, or constituents thereof, as objects. After all, what I *believe* is that *that thinking* (i.e., t) *was* simultaneous with the noise, not that *this thinking* (i.e., t) *is* so simultaneous. In response: to grant the point about belief is not to grant the objection. Note that if t occurred "in a different mental environment"—one in which I did not take myself to be merely recalling something—t would obviously be an entertaining of the content (19). The fact that t is embedded as it is does not rob its constituents of their semantic values. And t, in its actual mental setting, involves "apprehending" the content (19). So it would seem to be a propositional attitude.

It might be objected that *in t itself* I take my thinking (i.e., t) to be present; it is just that I have another mental state that "overrides" this apprehension. After all, t is a state "engaged" in the activity of thinking. How, then, can t not "recognize" the fact that what it "is doing" (i.e., thinking) it is presently doing?

In a sense, this objection just reiterates Higginbotham's position: to think reflexively, we are told, just is to take one's thinking as present. But as I see it, we have no very strong reason to think that this is so. In thinking that *this very thought* is such and such, I focus on a thought. I do not conceptualize or pick it out by its temporal location. Rather, I "mentally demonstrate" it. The default assumption, about such demonstration, is that what's demonstrated is present, for how else could I demonstrate it? But that assumption is quite separable from the act of demonstrating itself. I don't need to make the assumption to demonstrate; I just need, so to speak, to point. And of course the point of the example is that the demonstrating can occur without the assumption's coming into play.[10]

Finally, one might respond that the example does not show that Higginbotham's account fails for attitudes that involve belief: If I believe (what I express when I token) (19), it might be said, then my belief is realized, not by the tokening t of (19), but by some other occurrent mental state. After all, I am reflecting upon t. I take it to be a veridical memory of something that once happened. It is my so taking it (call the token state of my so taking it t') that makes it the case that I believe what (19), when I token it, says.

---

[10] I am indebted in the last two paragraphs to comments from Jason Stanley.

But then the belief I have whose object is what (19) says when I token it is not a reflexive belief, since the state that realizes the belief is not t, but t'.

The observation about the non-reflexivity of the belief in (19) (as opposed to the entertaining of (19)) is perhaps correct. However, it raises another question: why is t, my tokening of (19), not itself a state of my believing what (19)-as-tokened-by-me says? It would seem, after all, that if I didn't have an erroneous belief about t's causal history, t would be a present tense belief.

It seems to me that what keeps t from itself being a present tense belief is that in so tokening (19) (i.e., in t), I do not take the state of mind I represent with the words "my so thinking"—t itself—to be present. In order that t realize a present tense belief, I must take the state of mind I am representing in t (t itself) to be one presently occurring. And what the example shows is that it does not follow from the sort of reflexivity t exhibits that I so take it.

What makes Higginbotham's account plausible is the fact that a reflexive state indeed is *normally* one that presents itself as present. But, as I hope the argument has made clear, thinking reflexively of a state is only normally, not necessarily, thinking of it as present.

II Character and cognitive significance

David Kaplan's and John Perry's work suggests accounting for the cognitive role of tensed thoughts in terms of "indexical modes of thinking," modes indexical because (unlike traditional Fregean senses) they present different things in different contexts. Such views often distinguish between two "objects of belief." One, a proposition, is identified with the object of assertion and bearer of truth. The other, which provides a "way of grasping" the first, is held to (contextually) determine the first, and to determine the cognitive properties of a state of belief.

A Kaplanesque version of this view identifies modes of grasping with Kaplan's characters, functions from contexts to propositional constituents. It encourages us to think of "using" a mode m of grasping a proposition as having a belief in virtue of accepting a sentence with m as its character. It claims that the special motivational role of my belief that I am flying home today is to be explained in terms of my accepting a sentence with the character of "I am flying home today"; analogously for the explanation of why I might be relieved when I think, "I am flying home today," as opposed to "I am flying home on February 9, 1997."[11]

As with Higginbotham's account, we can pose two questions. Is the identification of thinking that e is present with thought held under a certain character plausible? If so, can the psychological properties of tensed thought be explained in terms of its semantic ones? I shall eventually allow that the first question can (probably) be answered yes, but the second cannot.

---

[11] In fact, Kaplan *identifies* the cognitive significance of a thought with the character under which it is held.

Whether the first question *can* be answered affirmatively depends upon the exact nature of character. If the picture sketched a paragraph ago is correct, then my accepting any sentence with the character of "I am flying home today," and thereby having a belief, should have, all else being equal, the same motivational upshot as the belief realized by "I am flying home today." But doesn't this idea trip over the problem raised at the beginning of this essay, concerning temporal transients and being serp? Suppose I am taught a word "yadot" on a day *d*, being told,

(D2) Today, "yadot" names Sunday, February 9, 1997. And each day, "yadot" names the day immediately succeeding (immediately preceding) the day it named the day before (it names on the next day).

So long as I understand these instructions, I understand "yadot." And so when I accept "I am flying home yadot," I will be in a belief state in virtue of that acceptance. Suppose I was told the above on Sunday, February 9, 1997, but I didn't know that the day was Sunday. Then in accepting "I am flying home yadot," I am accepting a sentence with the character of "I am flying home today" and am in a belief state individuated by its character. But of course the belief state does not have the motivational properties of the belief state that I am flying home today.

In a way, the preceding misinterprets Kaplan.[12] Kaplan *represents* the character of an expression as a function from contexts to propositional constituents. But he explicitly says that character is a *rule* and observes that representing characters as functions will result in the identification of distinct characters (Kaplan (1989) 505). Isn't that what is going on in the preceding argument? There are (at least) two *rules* one might associate with "yadot," (D2) and something like

(D3) In any context, "yadot" names the day of the context.

Given that the rules are different and that it is (D3) that corresponds to the character of "today," the above is no counter-example to the claim that the distinctive properties of tensed belief can be explained by reference to the character of (the sentence that realizes) the belief.

In what sense do (D2) and (D3) determine different rules? Well, one might say, to give a rule is to write out a sentence that refers to some functions, individuals, properties, and relations, and that determines a "procedure" (via the sentence's syntax); to follow the rule is to apply the procedure to the functions, and so on. (D3)'s rule is thus something like this: Find the context; apply the *day-of* function thereto; the result is the referent (in the context) of "yadot." (D2)'s rule is quite different, requiring a computation on, among other things, February 9, 1997. Call the picture of rules and rule following suggested in these sketchy remarks the *procedural* picture of rules.

The picture does not meet the problem we are considering. Consider the yad function, which maps contexts to days. It is defined as follows:

---

[12] Kaplan has emphasized this point in conversation.

(D4) For any context c,
   a. yad(c) is February 9, 1997, if the day of c of today;
   b. if the day of c postcedes today, yad(c) is one day later than yad($c^\star$), for any context $c^\star$ whose day is one day earlier than c's;
   c. if the day of c precedes today, yad(c) is one day earlier than yad($c^\star$), for any context $c^\star$ whose day is one day earlier than c's.

What function (D4) defines is a matter of when it is introduced; if it is introduced on February 9, 1997, it of course defines the function *the day of context c*. Suppose (D4) is introduced on February 9, 1997, and subsequent to that introduction, the following rule is introduced:

(D5) In any context, "yadot" names the yad of the context.

On the procedural sense of rules, it would seem, (D3) and (D5) encode the same rule, namely: To discover what "yadot" names, figure out what the day of the context is.

If the suggestion that character determines cognitive significance is to succeed, the requisite sense of procedure must be more fine grained than that introduced above, in which the rule encoded by a sentence is something one follows if one, understanding the sentence and applying the procedure straightforwardly determined by its syntax, arrives at a result. For no matter what set of instructions we might write down, there will be various ways of implementing those instructions, as there will be various ways of "grasping" the functions, properties, and individuals mentioned therein. Different ways of implementing the instructions will (or at least can) correspond to (or determine) different motivational properties. So, no matter what instructions we write down, there will be a straightforward sense in which one can understand the instructions, but not know how to follow the rule (i.e., the character) that the instructions are supposed to give—*at least given that motivational properties are to supervene on character*. If it determines motivational properties, character is, in a certain sense, ineffable.

How, then, are we to explain the requisite notion of rule? One account—we might call it the *evidentiary*—proposes that such rules are (sometimes, and in part) individuated in terms of an epistemic notion like that of evidence. Consider, for example, Gareth Evans's suggestion that to give an account of a way of thinking of something "is to explain how [its possessor] knows what object" the sense presents. In the case of the sense of "today," "this knowledge at least partly consists in a disposition to judge the thoughts [involving the sense] as true or false according to how things observably are upon" the day in which the thought is had: "we can test very easily whether someone, in this interpretation of a sentence, is thinking of the day in the right way be seeing if he is disposed to judge the sentence as true or false according to how things observably are on that day" (Evans (1990), 81).

Adapting the idea for Kaplan's purpose, we might propose that there is a way C of thinking of contexts such that, for any context c, an expression as used by the agent of c expresses that way of thinking of c if and only if (in part), where w expresses the way of thinking in question, the person is disposed to accept ... w ... as true or false depending upon how things observably are (to the person) in c. We might go on to give an account, in terms of evidence, of what it is to grasp the day-of function. We would then have identified an indexical way of thinking of contexts, C, and a way D of thinking of the day-of function. Fusing all this with the idea that (D3) gives the (form of the) rule for the character of "today," we might say that the character of "today" is the rule that someone follows when, thinking of the day-of function in way D and thinking of the context she occupies in way C, she applies the function to the context and thereby identifies a day. Arguably, this account is immune to the sort of objection raised above.

Character is a semantic notion; according to Kaplan, the character of a sentence is its meaning:

The character of an expression is set by linguistic conventions and, in turn, determines the content [i.e., propositional contribution] of the expression in every context. Because character is set by linguistic conventions, it is natural to think of it as meaning in the sense of what is known by the competent language user. (Kaplan (1989), 505)

Given this, there are two worries one might have about the evidentiary account of character we are considering.

First of all, one might well question whether evidential criteria ought be built into a semantic notion. The character of an expression is the rule that determines its contribution to what's said. If we think of such contributions in the way Kaplan counsels us to—in a broadly Russellian fashion—the addition of an epistemic layer to character seems completely gratuitous. Isn't the rule that determines the contribution to what's said for "today" simply the *procedural* rule (D6)?

(D6)   For any context c, "today" in c contributes the day of c to what's said.

Someone who has mastered that rule, however she understands the day-of function and so forth, will associate the same Russellian assertion with a use of "Today is sunny" as do we. Building the notion of evidence into the notion of character may help save the thesis that the semantic properties of tensed language determine its cognitive properties. But one feels that this thesis is being saved by fiat, by simply *calling* an epistemic phenomenon—which has nothing to do with the determination of a sentence's truth conditions or assertoric content—a semantic one.

A related worry is that on the evidentiary account, character is not plausibly identified with meaning, at least given fairly natural assumptions concerning meaning. People who (apparently) are able to understand one another's tensed utterances—indeed, who very obviously *mean* the same thing by their tensed utterances—need not associate the same evidentiary rules with tensed sentences. Sentence meaning is less fine grained than such things as evidentiary role.

I elaborate. On the current account, for an expression to have (say) the character of "now" for a certain person would be (in part) for that person to take perceptual evidence as especially relevant to (certain) sentences in which the expression occurs. Understanding "Someone is now in the room" of necessity involves being disposed to take one's current perceptions as evidence for or against its truth. But a person could believe that at any time t her experiences—at least her experiences of external objects—were experiences, not of those objects at t, but of those objects as they are at some other time—say, k seconds in the future: she thinks that her perceptions are consistently of how things will be in just a little while. When you ask her a question, she consistently waits k seconds before answering; if she hears the telephone ring, she waits k seconds before answering it; and so on. She in fact complains about her cursed luck, of being perceptually out of touch with the present, saying things like, "I know that you are in the room now, because I saw that you were k seconds ago."

As I understand Evans's suggestion, for a person to use an expression α with the normal sense of "now," it must be true of the person that, at least so far as an "observation sentence" $F\alpha$ is concerned, at each time t, the person is normally disposed to take the perceptual evidence she has at t to be (potentially) conclusive, as to whether *it is now the case that $F\alpha$* is true or false. But while I think the person I have just described could use "now" and "in k seconds" with the semantics we do, this person would not take her perceptual evidence at t as potentially conclusive for the truth of *it is now the case that $F\alpha$*; she would take it as potentially conclusive for *in k seconds it will be the case that $F\alpha$*.

Indeed, I am inclined to think that such a person could *mean* what we do with "now." We would understand the person, the person would understand us. We would not think the person to suffer from any *linguistic* deficit. If, as Kaplan suggests, character is meaning, it follows that the person, since she has beliefs realized by sentences synonymous with "now"-sentences, has beliefs under the character of "now"-sentences. But those sentences do not have the distinctive evidentiary role of present tense beliefs. Such a person would obviously have present tense beliefs—beliefs realized and expressed by sentences that mean what present tense sentences mean—but those beliefs would not have the evidentiary role that a belief expressed by a present tense sentence would have to have, on an account like Evans's. It follows that it is in no sense necessary that if a sentence has the character of a present tense sentence as I use it, the sentence will have the (ordinary) cognitive role of that sentence. So cognitive role is not determined by character; it does not "supervene" thereon, in that it is in some interesting sense necessary that if an expression α has the character of "now" or of the present tense as I use it, then it has what is ordinarily the cognitive role of "now" or the present tense.

As I see it, attempts to "thicken" the notion of character-as-a-procedural-rule, by adding one or another epistemic overlay to the notion, make it implausible that character is a semantic notion—at least given the widespread and natural assumption that speakers who understand one another and appear, to themselves and others, to share a language, normally do share a language, in the sense of using forms with the same meanings. But it is implausible that one could in any interesting sense explain the cognitive significance of present tense belief merely in terms of the character-as-a-procedural-rule under which such beliefs are held. I conclude that, insofar as character is a semantic notion, it will not be of much help in explaining the cognitive role of present tense beliefs.

III Cognitive role and tensed thoughts

In speaking of the cognitive significance of a (type of) belief, I intend—as I think are usually intended—salient and typical aspects of the belief's evidential and motivational role, as well as salient and typical aspects of its inferential role. Somewhat more precisely: The cognitive significance of a type of belief is given by a set of salient properties, having to do with evidence, inference, and action, which are typically possessed by belief states of the type. The typicality is typicality relative to a (presupposed) way of individuating the states and within a (presupposed) population. Suppose that we identify present tense beliefs with those beliefs that are realized (in us) by present tense sentences. Then to say that a token state s has the cognitive significance of a present tense thought is to say that there is a cognitive role (i.e., a family of evidential, inferential, and motivational properties) R that is typically possessed by the thoughts expressed (in a certain class—say, adult humans) by present tense sentences, and s has (enough of) R. I think it is tolerably clear what the properties in question are. They are imputed by banalities such as

(P1) If at t one has an experience as of rain, then one normally accepts "It is (now) raining" and thereby believes at t that it's (then) raining

and

(P2) If at t one believes that one's plane is (then) leaving (and one wants to catch it), then one normally moves toward where one takes the plane to be located.

Now, what would it be to explain the fact that present tense beliefs have the role they have by reference to their character—that is, by reference to the character of the sentences that realize them? The most obvious way in which one would explain the other is for the latter to be in some straightforward sense a result or consequence of the former, with consequence being understood in some sense of necessity: in some sense of "necessary," it is necessary that, normally, if something has a rainy experience (and it understands a sentence with the character of "It's raining"), it will accept it; necessarily, it is normally the case that if one believes (under the right character) that one's plane is leaving, one will move toward where one takes the plane to be located.

I have argued that the ordinary cognitive role of tensed thoughts is not, in this sense, explained by the character (cum procedural rule)[13] of the sentences that realize those thoughts: that is, character does not determine (normal) cognitive role. It could be the case that everyone knew that "yadot" named the yad of the context, but no one knew that yadot is today. It is not normally the case that the woman who believes she perceives the future thinks, on having a rainy experience, that it is raining.

I do not deny that semantic properties like character can be said to be the "bearers" of cognitive role, if by this is meant only that there is a regular or normal connection between the semantic and the cognitive roles of beliefs and other attitudes. But to say

---

[13] Henceforth, it goes without saying that it is this notion of character that is at issue.

this is not to say that there is a way to explain the cognitive properties of beliefs in terms of their semantic properties: there is, after all, a regular connection (in English speakers) between the present tense syntactically conceived and its cognitive role; but no one, I hope, will be tempted to explain the latter by reference to the former.

To say that character is the bearer of cognitive role in this sense is to assimilate the relation between the semantic and cognitive role of temporal expressions to that between such roles of non-indexical expressions. There is, for example, a cluster of evidential and motivational properties normally associated with (sentences in which) "fire" (occurs). It borders on the cognitively pathological to understand "fire" (and thus "have the concept of fire") but not take fiery experiences as evidence of the presence of fire; it borders on the behaviorally pathological to understand and think true "There is a fire in the house" (and thereby think that there is a fire in the house) but not be moved to put it out. But presumably both are straightforwardly possible; we cannot explain the cognitive properties of someone's belief that there is a fire in the house by pointing to its semantic properties.

If the semantics of a tensed belief do not explain its cognitive role, what does? Well, what we have learned and the way in which we are constituted seem good starting places. In learning to speak (and thus developing our ability to think), we acquire the disposition to form present tense beliefs upon appropriate visual stimulation: upon seeing a dog running at me, I think, "A dog is running at me," not "A dog runs at me on Sunday," even if I know it's Sunday. We acquire dispositions to act in certain ways when we have present tense beliefs and desires. And so on, for other familiar aspects of the cognitive role of tensed belief. Given that these dispositions serve us well and involve no particular irrationality, why should any more explanation be called for?

The distinctive role tensed thoughts play in our psychology is best characterized in terms of a large collection of principles such as (P1) and (P2). For "constructions" (or aspects of belief states) to have the conceptual role of the tenses in someone's mental economy is for "sentences" (belief states) in which the constructions "occur" (to which the aspects attach) to satisfy enough of the principles about tensed attitudes that have as humdrum a status as (P1) and (P2). That a construction has such a role for someone is an important fact, but it is not to be explained by reference to truth conditions, or a mode of presentation thereof. If we choose to call what determines the role "sense," we should be clear that it is a sort of sense that has nothing to do with reference.

IV Cognitive role and attitude ascription

I will suppose that one way in which we can individuate states of belief and the other attitudes is sententially. I also suppose that for each character C there is a more or less mundanely determined collection S of principles that determine a conceptual role regularly but not of necessity associated with C, CR_C. Using bracketing to form a name of a sentence's character, examples of such principles for "It is raining" might include

(P3) If someone has an experience as of rain, she normally accepts a sentence with [it is raining]

and

(P4) If someone accepts a sentence with [it is raining] and desires to keep dry, she normally seeks shelter.

Such principles determine a cognitive role for sentence types in a straightforward manner. For instance, the two just mentioned determine a role that a sentence S plays for x just in case (1) if x has an experience as of rain, she normally accepts S; and (2) if x accepts S and desires to keep dry, she normally seeks shelter.

Since we would not require, in order that a state have the conceptual role for you that "It is raining" has for me, that our states satisfy *exactly* the same platitudes, we might best understand talk of conceptual role in terms of satisfying "enough" of the platitudes. Continuing to suppose that for each character C, there is a set $C^\star$ of mundane principles like the above that determines a conceptual role, we then say that a sentence S plays the conceptual role CR_c for x provided S plays for x a role defined (in the way just indicated) by enough of the members of $C^\star$. I leave it open for today as to when enough is enough.

If what I have said thus far is correct, there are at least three accounts possible of the connection between an ascription of a tensed belief, such as

(20) Mary believes that Smith is sad

and the ascription of the typical cognitive role of a tensed belief. Each has (20) entail that Mary is in a state of belief whose content is that Smith is sad.[14] But the stories differ so:

(S1) It is sufficient for (20)'s truth in a context c that Mary be in a state with the content that Smith is sad at t, where t is the time of c.

(S2) It is necessary for (20)'s truth in c that Mary be in such a state *and* that, for some a that refers to Smith and some predicate F that refers to the property of sleeping, the state have [a is F].[15]

(S3) It is necessary for (20)'s truth in c that Mary be in a state with the content that Smith is sad and that has for Mary $CR_{[a\ is\ F]}$, for some a and F as in (S2).

(S3) has (20) entail that Mary is disposed to behave in certain ways characteristic of having a present tense belief. On (S2), (20) does not entail this, but it does imply that she is in a state that is normally accompanied by a disposition to behave in these ways, at least given that beliefs realized by sentences with a character of a sentence of the form a *is* F are normally accompanied by such dispositions. (S1) has neither of these implications.

---

[14] By this I mean something like: The content of Mary's belief state is the Russellian proposition that Smith is sad.

[15] I will henceforth not be prissy about distinguishing character as a property of sentences from character as a property of belief states.

If the argument above was correct, (S3) is to be rejected because one could have a belief realized by (a sentence with the character of) "Smith is sad" but, because of a disruption of the normal relations between such beliefs and action and evidence, not be disposed to act in ways characteristic of a present tense belief. Since someone who has a belief expressed by the English "Smith is sad" can be ascribed that belief using "Smith is sad", (S3) must be rejected.

(S1), in my opinion, must be rejected as well. For it certainly seems to be true that, for example,

> (21) Normally—that is, in all but the most exceptional cases—if someone believes (at a time) that Smith is (then) sad and has a standing desire to comfort those who are sad, that person will try to comfort Smith.

But the truth of this does not seem to be consistent with (S1), as it is not, or at least need not be, at all exceptional for someone to believe at a particular time t that Smith is sad at t by accepting *Smith is sad at T*, where T names t, while not realizing that T names the time of belief.

This leaves us with (S2).[16] If we accept (S2), we will say that when we ascribe a belief using tensed language, what we say (semantically) implies something about "how" the belief is realized—we say that the belief is realized by a tensed construction with a particular kind of character. And given the facts about those to whom we normally ascribe beliefs—in particular, that for us these characters normally carry a particular conceptual role—what we say will have certain implications about the behavior of the believer. But these implications can only be extracted by invoking background assumptions—in particular, that the believer is, like most of us, someone in whom the tenses are associated with a particular conceptual role.

If something like (S2) is true, what shall we say about the semantics of ascriptions of tensed beliefs? I shall sketch an answer. It piggy backs upon Higginbotham's account of the tenses as involving quantificational cross-reference, one that I find attractive. I think the account to be sketched could be embedded in other syntactic proposals about tense, but I shall not investigate that here.

I have assumed that beliefs and other attitudes are realized sententially, and I will continue to do this. Under this assumption, it makes sense to speak of a natural language sentence "translating" someone's belief. I am going to simply assume that we should say that

> (22) Mary believes that S

is true or false depending upon whether or not S adequately translates one of Mary's beliefs. I have argued for this view elsewhere (see Richard (1990)). I think that in ade-

---

[16] Of course, one might look for an option other than (S1), (S2), or (S3). I will not explore this possibility here.

quate translation referential structure is always preserved, so that (R1) is a requirement on adequate translation in belief ascription:

(R1) If *q* in *a believes that q* is, relative to context *c*, an adequate translation of a belief *p* of the agent of a context *c★*, then the syntactic structures of *p* and *q* are isomorphic, and their constituents have, pointwise and in their respective contexts, the same semantic values.

I have made much in the past of the idea that what counts as an adequate translation may vary with context. This would explain why in some contexts we allow substitution of "Hesperus" for "Phosphorus" within "She believes that Phosphorus is rising," but in others we do not, even if the contexts do not differ in whose beliefs are being discussed or in what the conversants know about the subject's belief states. Here, I want to observe that by adopting this picture of attitude ascription, but holding that the translation of tenses is *not* variable across contexts in this way, one can account for tensed ascriptions of belief.

Recall Higinbotham's proposal. It regiments utterances of

(22) Smith is sad

and

(23) Smith was sad

as

(23′) $(\exists t)(\text{includes}\,(t, t\star)\,\&\,\text{Sad}\,(\text{Smith}, t))$

and

(24′) $(\exists t)(t < t\star\,\&\,\text{Sad}\,(\text{Smith}, t))$.

For Higginbotham, the *t*-variables range over events and states, "includes" and "<" pick out temporal relations between events and states, and "$t\star$" picks out the utterance. I propose to adopt the regimentation's form, but to understand the variables as ranging over intervals. Let us call the first arguments in "includes (t, $t\star$)" and "t < $t\star$" the *locating* arguments (since variables co-bound with them serve to locate an event or state of affairs in time); call the second arguments in these predicates *anchoring* arguments (since, when unembedded, these arguments will in one way or another be assigned, or replaced with, something that picks out a time, thus "anchoring" the sentence as a whole in time). Higginbotham's idea is that when embedded as in an ascription of belief, the anchoring variables in (23′) and (24′) are (appropriately replaced with new variables and) bound to the locating variables of the superordinate tense, as in the regimentations of

(25) Mary believes that Smith is sad

and

(26) Mary believed that Smith was sad

as

(25′) (∃t)(includes (t, t*) & Believe (Mary, t, that (∃t′)(includes (t', t) & Sad (Smith, t'))))

and

(26′) (∃t) (t < t* & Believe(Mary, t, that (∃t′)(t' < t & Sad (Smith, t')))).

(26') gives the "past over past" reading of (26); to achieve the reading, on which Mary is said to have believed something she would have voiced in the present tense at the time of belief, Higginbotham invokes a principle according to which presents embedded within pasts may be realized phonetically by the past tense, yielding

(26″) (∃t) (t < t* & Believe (Mary, t, that (∃t′)(t' includes t & Sad (Smith, t')))).

Let us accept this syntactic proposal. Note that on this proposal, *all* beliefs realized by a tensed sentence contain a "present tense constituent." For example, to think, "Smith was sad," is to think, "(∃t) (t< t* & Sad (Smith, t))," with "t*" picking out the present time. If we take the latter sentence to give the "logical form" of the former, then we will say that "t*," as it occurs in an unembedded occurrence of (23′), has the character of "now," since (when (23′) is unembedded) "t*" therein will, taken relative to any context, rigidly denote the time of the context. Thus, all belief realized by a tensed sentence will, in a certain sense, be present tense belief with the "present tensing" realized by a constituent with the character of "now."

How, given this much, should the embeddings of tensed sentences be understood? If we accept what I said above about belief ascription, we will say that (25′), (26′), and (26″) are true, taken in context, provided that, in context, the sentences following "that" are acceptable translations of one or another of Mary's beliefs at the appropriate time. If we accept story (S2), we will say that (25′) implies that Mary's belief is realized by something with the character (of a sentence of the form) α *is* F; (26)'s two readings require, respectively, that in the past, Mary had beliefs realized with the character α *was* F and α *is* F. (25) and (26) have such truth conditions, given that the following is involved in specifying the translation relation invoked by verbs like "believes":

(R2) If q, taken relative to a belief ascription B = *a believes that q,* is, in context c, an adequate translation of a belief p of the agent of a context c*, and the anchoring argument of q's (main) tense is in B bound with the locating argument of the immediately superordinate tense, then the expression in p that occupies the position of the anchoring argument of q's main tense has [now].

More simply: If the tense of q in *a believes (believed, will believe) that q* is bound to the tense of "believes" ("did believe," "will believe"), then the bound element translates something that is present tense.

How does this work? Well, consider (26)'s two readings, given by (26′) and (26″). Take (26′) first. For my present use of this to be true, there must be some past time, T call it, and some belief b Mary had at T, such that when T is assigned to "t" in

(26'*)   (∃t) (t' < t & Sad (Smith, t'))

(*26'**) adequately translates b. Suppose belief b is indeed so translated by (*26'**). By (R1), this means that b is "referentially isomorphic" with (26'*)—b must look something like

(26'**)   (∃u') (u' R u & Sad (s, u')),

with the parts of (26'**), in their context, having the same references as those of (26'*) in its context. So, in particular, "R" in (26'**) picks out the earlier-than relation, and u picks out the time T. And by (R2) and the fact that (26'*)'s "t" is bound to the superordinate tense, "u" as it occurs in (26'**) must for Mary have the character [now]. So if, on the current proposal, (26) construed as (26') is true, then at some time in the past, T, Mary had a belief, the referential content of which was that at some time before T, Smith was sad, and this belief was realized by something whose tense position was present tense—that is, occupied by something with [now]. Given that Mary is like the rest of us, it follows that the sentence realizing the belief had, for Mary at T, the motivational powers of a sentence like "Smith was sad before now." And this is exactly the result we are looking for. An analogous argument establishes that (26") gets assigned the right truth conditions and had the right motivational implications.[17]

Summing up: I have found fault with two broadly Fregean accounts of tensed thought. Against Higginbotham, I have argued that tensed thoughts cannot be identified with certain reflexive thoughts; against the followers of Kaplan, that plausible accounts of meaning cum character cannot support the idea that the semantics of a tensed sentence secures its cognitive properties.

More positively, I have suggested that to have a present tense belief is to have a belief whose realization has a certain sort of semantics. Sentences with such semantics typically (in us) have a certain sort of cognitive role. To ascribe a tensed belief is to say that someone has a belief that has a realization of a certain semantic sort; the sort in question typically has (in us, as a matter of contingent fact) a certain kind of cognitive role. There is this much connection between the semantics and psychology of tensed thought. But this much does not imply that there is an interesting explanatory connection between the two. So far as I can see, there is not.

---

[17] As I have spun story (S2), it is part of the semantics of claims like (26) that they imply something about the character of Mary's belief. I remark that it is possible to slightly weaken (S2). One might hold that *normally* in ascribing tensed beliefs to others, (R2) is one of the constraints on the translation relation. This would allow one to say that sentences like (20) normally imply that a belief is held in a certain way, while allowing that in certain cases (e.g., ascriptions of beliefs to animals), the implication is absent. Whether this is to be preferred to the account just sketched is a matter I shall not pursue here.

13

Meaning and Attitude Ascriptions

There is much to admire in Soames (2002) (henceforth BR). It's must reading for anyone with even a passing interest in the last 30 years of debate over meaning, modality, the status of the necessary *a posteriori*, "Millian" accounts of names, the semantics of propositional attitude ascriptions, or how one is to balance semantics and pragmatics in one's account of natural language.

That said, I come to critically discuss Soames' book, not just to praise it. In Section I, I discuss Soames' view of sentence meaning in BR and later works. In Section II, I discuss propositional attitude ascriptions. In particular, I respond to Soames' objections in BR to my own proposals about the semantics of such constructions.

I

1. Soames distinguishes two conceptions of sentence meaning. On the first, a (non-indexical, non-ambiguous) sentence's meaning is what "the sentence 'says', which ...is closely related to what speakers say, and convey, when they assertively utter [it]" (55).[1] This he calls a sentence's *semantic content*. On the second, "the meaning of an expression is information grasp of which explains speakers' ability to understand it, and to be able to use it competently" (56). It is semantic content which is being discussed when, for example, a Millian says or a Fregean denies that sentences in which names are used express singular propositions; it is on meaning in this sense which I will focus upon.

Soames' lead idea concerning sentence meaning *cum* semantic content is simple and intuitively compelling. Central to linguistic activity is the use of (declarative) sentences to convey information; a (non-indexical, non-ambiguous) sentence's meaning can be identified with that piece of information which its literal use always asserts and conveys. A (non-indexical, non-ambiguous) sub-sentential expression's meaning, in turn, may be

---

[1] All parenthetical references are to Soames (2002).

identified with what it invariably contributes to the meaning of a sentence in which it occurs.² There being no plausible candidate for what is invariably conveyed by a use of *Scott Soames wrote Beyond Rigidity*, other than the Russellian claim that Soames wrote *Beyond Rigidity*, Soames concludes that this is the meaning of the sentence, and that he himself is the meaning *cum* content of the name *Scott Soames* (63–7).³

One expects meaning to be compositionally determined. One expects meaning to determine truth: holding the context fixed, same meaninged sentences cannot diverge in truth value. Given these expectations and the conclusion just drawn, we arrive at the result that substitution of one of a person's names for another within the scope of a verb of propositional attitude is meaning and truth preserving. And, at first glance, this conclusion seems warranted by Soames' lead idea. Even if one thinks that occasionally, or even often, a speaker conveys, or even asserts, something about the "way" in which Stanley thinks about Soames with an utterance of *Stanley believes that Soames wrote Beyond Rigidity*, there doesn't seem to be a plausible candidate for what is invariably conveyed by the sentence's use, beyond the claim that Stanley believes the Russellian claim that Soames wrote *Beyond Rigidity*.

But first glances sometimes lead us astray. Consider the sentence

(1) Stanley doesn't think that Soames wrote *Beyond Rigidity*.

It is perfectly possible to use this literally without intending to assert, or indeed asserting, that Stanley does not believe, of Soames, that he wrote the book. Suppose, for example, that I know that you introduced Soames to Stanley as the author of the book. I also know that Stanley is somewhat confused; he thought he was introduced to Nathan

---

² There are various caveats. For example, in assessing whether a sentence means p, we are to ignore uses in which pragmatic factors such as conversational implicature defeat the presumption that the use commits the user to p. (See BR, 60ff.)

³ Here and below I use "content" as an abbreviation of Soames' "semantic content."

It occurs to one that this is not the only candidate for something the sentence invariably conveys. Surely any literal use of the sentence commits one to the claim that the author of *Beyond Rigidity*, which is named "*Beyond Rigidity*," is Scott Soames, who is named "Scott Soames;" surely this is among the things always conveyed by its literal utterance. Soames tells us that this isn't (part of) the content of the sentence because "someone who assertively uttered [it] would not commonly intend to communicate, or assert, any metalinguistic claim" (BR 332, n. 9; example altered).

It is not obvious why Soames thinks this. That we do not always *consciously* intend to assert such a claim doesn't show that we don't always intend to assert it. I suspect that Soames would agree that, should he walk up to a stranger he wants to meet at the gym and say "Hi, I'm Scott Soames," part of what he asserts is that he is named "Scott Soames." But there isn't normally a conscious intention in such cases to convey information about language.

More significantly: A common (quasi) Fregean view is that part, or even all, of the sense of a name n is the property *being named n* (see, for example, Katz (1994)). If that view were correct, then someone who intended to assert that Soames is a philosopher—i.e., who intended to assert what is said by "Soames is a philosopher"—would intend to assert that Soames, who is named "Soames," is a philosopher. For on such a view, to assert the one just is to assert the other. It is not clear why a Fregean, or other descriptivist about names, needs to hold that the descriptive information which the name's use conveys is immediately present to consciousness when the name is used; that it is mutual knowledge among speakers that the information is conveyed by the name's use seems all that is necessary. A view of meaning such as Soames', if anything, makes such a view of sense quite plausible.

Salmon. If you ask me why Stanley is talking as if Salmon wrote the book, I might well say *Well, when you introduced Soames as the book's author, Stanley thought you were introducing him to Nathan Salmon.* Stanley doesn't think that Soames wrote *Beyond Rigidity*. There is nothing bizarre about such an utterance. Such an utterance would be accompanied by the knowledge that it's obvious to all that Stanley believes of the man to whom he was introduced—Soames—that he wrote the book. Given that the utterance is in no way bizarre, it seems correct to conclude that the utterer does not mean to, and indeed does not, commit himself to denying what he recognizes to be obvious. So he does not assert, of Soames, that Stanley does not believe that he wrote *Beyond Rigidity*.

In a way, the point here is simply that names can't always be exported across negations of attitude verbs. That they cannot implies that if the meaning of a sentence is to be identified with what it is invariably used to assert, meaning is not determined compositionally.

2. In work done after BR (Soames (2005)), Soames recognizes this. He suggests that the meaning of a sentence is a "propositional matrix"—something like a proposition containing some "gaps" waiting to be filled by constituents. When a speaker assertively utters a sentence, something about her intentions and the context (typically) "enriches" the sentence's meaning, filling in its gaps with propositional constituents. The resulting proposition is asserted by the speaker. For example, the meaning of "Twain is Clemens" is something like the singular proposition involving the identity relation, Twain, Clemens, and two "gaps" which can be filled with descriptive material which "presents" Twain and Clemens. In a context in which it is mutual knowledge that Twain wrote *Huck Finn* and that Clemens was a newspaperman, an utterance of "Twain is Clemens" might be enriched with the properties *being Huck Finn's author, being a newspaper man*. If so, the utterance would express the proposition that the x such that x = Twain and x wrote *Huck Finn* and the y such that y = Clemens and y was a newspaperman are such that x = y.

This view allows for the meaning of a sentence to be compositionally determined, while also allowing that the content of a name is simply its referent. It allows this by allowing one to deny (to put it dramatically) that an assertive, literal use of a sentence is always an assertion of what the sentence means. The propositional matrix determined by (1) will have the matrix determined by *Soames wrote Beyond Rigidity* as a constituent. In Section I's example, my utterance of (1) will be enriched with something like the property of being named "Soames." This results in my utterance being an assertion of the claim that Stanley does not think, of Soames, that he is named "Soames" and wrote *Beyond Rigidity*. While I assert this, I do not assert the "unenriched" claim which is, in Soames' current view, the meaning of (1).

There are well-known objections to views which read descriptive material into the claims made by sentences in which names are used, most notably Kripke's objections in *Naming and Necessity*. Is Soames' view liable to these?

Begin with Kripke's modal objections. Soames summarizes these objections as follows:

To say that *Aristotle* is a rigid designator is to say that it denotes the same thing in (or at, or with respect to) all possible worlds. The reason we think it does this is that we think the truth-values, at different worlds, of sentences containing the name depend on the properties of one and the same individual at those worlds. For example, we take the sentence *Aristotle was a philosopher* to be true at a world w iff a certain individual—the person who was actually Aristotle—was a philosopher in w. Since a sentence α *is F* is true at an arbitrary world w iff the denotation of α at w is in the extension of F at w, we conclude that for any arbitrary world w, *Aristotle* denotes in w the individual who was Aristotle in the actual world. (23–4, with omissions)

One might well wonder how Soames can accept these claims and hold that what is said with sentences such as *Twain was a newspaperman* may involve pragmatic enrichment. The passage apparently endorses the idea that this sentence as (actually) used by me is true at w iff at w Twain—"our Twain"—is a newspaperman. But presumably the sentence as (actually) used by me is true at w iff what I say in (actually) using the sentence is true at w. So what I say, when I use the sentence, must be something true at a world iff Twain is a newspaperman there. But then the sentence, as used by me, cannot be used to say that there is something which is identical with Twain and which wrote *Huck Finn* and was a newspaperman. But if I can "pragmatically enrich" the meaning of the sentence with the property of having written *Huck Finn* as Soames suggests, then I can use the sentence to assert this claim.

There is, however, a complicating factor. Soames' view in BR is that background information and speaker intentions can bring it about that an utterance is an assertion, not only of what the sentence means, but of other claims as well. To adapt one of Soames' examples: Suppose A asks "Where is Twain?" and B utters *Twain is wearing a red shirt,* gesturing towards a group including Twain in a red shirt. We can report what was said thus: *B said that Twain was wearing a red shirt.* We surely also speak truly if we utter *B said that the man A was looking for was wearing a red shirt.* Now, though it contains gaps, a propositional matrix itself can be asserted. The matrix determined by *Twain was a newspaperman,* after all, has determinate truth conditions, being true at w iff at w Twain was a newspaperman. One might naturally propose that whenever a sentence s determines a matrix m and is used, via enrichment, to assert a proposition p, m itself is also asserted, so long as p entails m. If this is so, then it is plausible that when we think about what is said by *Twain was a newspaperman,* we tend to focus on what it is invariably used to assert. This would account for our intuition, that it says something true at a world just in case there Twain was a newspaperman.

Suppose we were to take this line. What should we say is wrong with the argument two paragraphs back? Let us use *what was said in uttering S* so that it picks out what was said on a particular utterance in uttering S—sometimes a single claim, sometimes a plurality of claims. If we want to continue, with Kripke, to say that a use of *Aristotle was a philosopher* is true at a world iff at the world Aristotle was a philosopher, we will then say one of the following:

(a) A use of a sentence may be true at a world even if not all of what was said in uttering the sentence is true there.
(b) A use of a sentence may be the assertion of a claim p even if the sentence, on that use, does not express p.

In defense of the first, it might be pointed out that we do often say things in using sentences, in virtue of pragmatic mechanisms such as implicature, which seem irrelevant to the question—would the sentence, as just used, be true if the world were thus and so? In defense of the second, it might be pointed out that when something is said in virtue of pragmatic mechanisms, we are comfortable enough with the idea that it was the speaker who said the thing, not the sentence.

So it is not clear that Soames' current view is liable to objections such as Kripke's modal objection. It seems, however, likely to be liable to objections which are, in effect, epicycles on Kripke's semantic argument. This, it will be recalled, is simply the point that speakers are often unable to correctly identify the referents of their uses of names; thus, a view which holds either that a name is generally synonymous with a description determined by the speaker's cognitive state, or one which holds that the name's reference is fixed by such a description, cannot be correct.

Now, such a point doesn't apply directly to Soames' view. Soames doesn't hold that *Twain*, when used in an utterance enriched with the property of having written *Huck Finn*, is synonymous with *Twain, the author of Huck Finn;* neither does he hold that the reference of the name, on such an occasion, is determined by the descriptive material. However, Soames' general strategy is one on which intuitions, that different thoughts are expressed or ascribed by uses of sentences differing only by co-referential names, are explained by reading different descriptive conditions into the propositional matrices associated with the sentences. What descriptive condition is involved in the thought expressed or ascribed by a use of a sentence ... **N** ... will depend upon what descriptive conditions the user associates with the name **N**. Thus, we can expect that there will be cases in which, on a view like Soames', a speaker will utter a sentence like *Aristotle was a philosopher* and say something false, because the "descriptive enrichment" of (the matrix associated with) his utterance is a condition not true of Aristotle. And in many of these cases, I think, it is extremely implausible that a false belief is expressed or ascribed.

Let me try to make these abstract worries concrete. Suppose that Bertrand is innocent of the identity *Twain is Clemens,* and would, if asked to identify Clemens, misidentify him as the author of *The Adventures of Augie March*. If Bertrand is party to a conversation in which 19th-century fiction is being discussed, he will become puzzled if he recognizes that the conversants presuppose that Twain and Clemens are one. If he knows the others to be more knowledgeable than he, he will take this presupposition to be correct. He will thereby realize that Twain is Clemens.[4] Suppose this happens, but Bertrand continues to identify Clemens as *Augie March's* author. What exactly did Bertrand realize? Not the Russellian claim *cum* propositional matrix, that Twain is Clemens. He already knew that to be true, knowing that Twain was Twain. Neither did he realize the enriched claim, that Clemens, the author of *The Adventures of Augie March,* is Twain, the author of *Huck Finn. Realize* is factive, and thus Bertrand cannot realize this.

---

[4] It is, in fact, this sort of case—in which we report someone as realizing or learning something, the Russellian content of which they already know to be true—which moved Soames to adopt the view about pragmatic enrichment.

Did he, perhaps, realize that Twain, who is named "Twain," is identical with Clemens, who is named "Clemens"? I doubt that this is what we are trying to convey, when we say that he realized that Twain was Clemens. To see why, consider a case just like the above, save that Bertrand learned some time ago of a man (Mark Twain, in fact) that he was named both "Twain" and "Clemens." Bertrand can do this in such a way that he believed, and continues to believe, of Twain that he has the two names, while not taking this two-named man to be identical with either Twain, the author of *Huck Finn* or Clemens, the (as he sees it) author of *Augie March*. In this case, it cannot be that Bertrand *realizes* that Twain, who is named "Twain," is identical with Clemens, who is named "Clemens." He *already* knew that. And I do not see why we would want to say that what Bertrand realizes in the new case is any different from what he realizes in the old one.

There is something which in both cases Bertrand realizes. Since he *realizes* it, it is true. It is not, however, clear that this thing need be, or even could be, an enrichment of the matrix that Twain is Clemens.[5] What this thing might be is an issue to which I will return below.

3. In BR, Soames proposes that use of the attitude ascription

(2)   Bertrand believes that Twain was a newspaperman

may ascribe to Bertrand belief, not simply in the Millian claim, that Twain was a newspaperman, but in a more complex claim in which Twain is "presented" as having certain properties. Roughly put, Soames' idea is that if (i) in a context to utter *Twain was a newspaperman* would be to assert that Twain, the author of *Huck Finn*, was a newspaperman, and (ii) conversants would take an utterance of the attitude ascription to be true only if Bertrand believed this last claim, then uttering (2) asserts that Bertrand believes this claim. The view discussed in the last section has the same upshot. The propositional matrix associated with (2) contains a gap in the position associated with the name *Twain* which can be enriched by descriptive material. If I utter the sentence and suitably enrich it, I will thereby assert that Bertrand believes that Twain, the author of *Huck Finn*, was a newspaperman.

Each view promises to reconcile the Millian idea that a name's meaning is in some important sense exhausted by its referent, with the Fregean idea that attitude ascriptions tell us something about how a person conceptualizes the objects of her attitudes. I think both ideas are correct. So there must be some way of reconciling them. But I don't think Soames' general strategy for reconciliation works.

Let us concentrate on pragmatic enrichment. As I understand Soames' view, assertive utterance proceeds as follows. A speaker "produces" a propositional matrix by uttering a sentence which has the matrix as its meaning. Sometimes she simply asserts this matrix. Sometimes her intentions and beliefs about conversants make a certain way of "adding" material to the matrix appropriate, and this makes the use of the sentence assert the enriched proposition. Thus, if I utter *Donald knew that Jones was in jail*, I assert either that

---

[5] There are various other things one might say Bertrand realizes in a case like this. Arguments that there is no satisfactory answer, on a view like Soames', can be found in Richard (2006).

Donald knew the matrix that Jones was in jail, or that he knew some enrichment of this matrix. If I utter *Drummond didn't know that Jones was in jail*, I assert either that Donald didn't know the matrix, or that he didn't know some enrichment thereof. If I utter *Just one of Donald and Drummond knew that Jones was in jail* either I assert that just one of them knew the matrix, or, for some enrichment thereof, that just one of them knew that enrichment.

Consider, now, the following story.

Donald wants to break Jones' finger, for Jones has welched on a debt. Sgt. Drummond wants to arrest Jones, for Drummond suspects him of robbing a store. Both Drummond and Donald are searching the South Side for Jones. Jones decides he will be safe from both injury and arrest for robbery if he has himself arrested under an alias for a petty crime. So he loiters in front of the 7/11. Drummond sees him there but doesn't, for some reason, recognize him as the man he is looking for. He does recognize him, however, as the man Donald is looking for. Being in a bad mood, Drummond runs Jones in for loitering. Donald, who has no idea that Drummond was looking for Jones, sees this happen. He arranges for a henchman to be arrested, so that the henchman can break Jones' finger. Drummond continues to search the South Side for Jones; Donald, of course, stops doing so.

Question: Why is just one of Drummond and Donald continuing to search the South Side for Jones? Answer: Because just one of them knows that Jones is in jail.

The ascription at the end of this story is perfectly natural; it is plausible to think that, if the story's other details were true, it would be true. Indeed, it would correctly explain why only one of the men continues to search. We cannot explain the truth of this ascription, however, in terms of pragmatic enrichment. Is it, after all, true that just one of Donald and Drummond know the Russellian matrix, that Jones is in jail? No, both of them know, of Jones, that he is in jail. Is it the case that just one of them knows the enrichment of this matrix, that Jones, the man Donald was looking for, is in jail? No, both of them know this. Is it the case that just one of them knows the enrichment of this matrix, that Jones, the man Drummond was looking for, is in jail? No, neither of them knows this. So far as I can see, there is no plausible candidate for a single descriptively enriched proposition which only one of them knows which can be appealed to, in explaining why just one of them stops looking for Jones.[6]

4. In uttering

(3) Donald, but not Drummond, knows that Jones is in jail,

we seem to ascribe one piece of knowledge to Donald while denying, not that Drummond has that piece of knowledge, but some other one. We also, of course, seem to say that there is a single piece of knowledge—that Jones is in jail—which Donald has and Drummond lacks. What gives?

---

[6] As with the argument in Section 2, one might insist that there will be *some* enrichment of a propositional matrix which will do the job. Again, I refer to the reader to Richard (2006), which argues that this will not in general be true.

The answer I favor goes something like this. Think of utterances of a sentence of the form *a believes/knows/says that S* as attempts to represent the beliefs/knowledge/sayings of a in the idiom of the utterer. Then a use of (3) has something like the force of *Donald's, but not Drummond's, knowledge is well represented as knowledge that Jones is in jail.* Think further of attempts at representing the attitudes of others as piecemeal, *ad hoc* affairs: how we represent one person's knowledge may differ from how we represent another's, given our interests in and knowledge of how the others represent the world. We may in a particular conversation use sentences with "Jones" to represent knowledge of Drummond's associated with a particular way of thinking of Jones (as the liquor store robber), while also using such sentences to represent knowledge of Donald's associated with some *other* way of thinking of Jones (as the debt welcher). If that is what we are doing, then Donald's, but not Drummond's, knowledge may be represented as knowledge that Jones is in jail. And if that is so, then it will be true to say that Donald, but not Drummond, knows that Jones is in jail. And saying this ascribes one bit of knowledge to Donald, while denying some *other* bit of knowledge to Drummond. Of course, there is a superficial sense in which in uttering (3) we are talking about a single bit of putative knowledge. For the clausal complement in (3) has a single referent—the claim that Jones is in jail. But we use this claim to represent two different bits of knowledge.

II

5. BR gives a penetrating and useful discussion of my development (in Richard (1990), (1995)) of this view. What follows is the briefest sketch of that development, along with responses to Soames' three most significant criticisms.
Imagine that I utter

(4) Marsha thinks that Twain is older than Clemens!

because I hear Marsha say "Twain is older than Clemens" and want to convey her state of mind. I am focused on how she expresses what she thinks; my use of "Twain" represents her tokenings thereof; analogously for "Clemens." For the purposes of ascribing beliefs to Marsha, I have adopted a partial "translation manual":

(T) Marsha: "Twain" → "Twain"
               "Clemens" → "Clemens"

How is (T) to be interpreted? Translation—that is, the sort of translation or representation of a person's thoughts which is involved in attitude ascription—should preserve (the sort of thing with which Soames identifies) content. The first line of our little manual is thus short for: In rendering Marsha's representations, my "Twain" used as a name of Twain can translate only Marsha's uses of "Twain" as a name of Twain.[7]

---

[7] In somewhat more detail: Think of a word, used with a particular semantic content, as a pairing of a linguistic item and a semantic value: "Twain," used as a name of Twain, is thought of as <"Twain," Twain>. The rules in (T) are to be understood along these lines: in speaking of X, translate <word, value> only via representations having property P. (In the first rule in (T), P is something like: being associated by Marsha with

(T) says nothing, as to how to translate Marsha's "is older than," or her uses of "is cleverer than," or the woman in the corner's perceptual representations of objects other than Twain, or ... When no such rules are in effect, we can translate the idiom of another in any way we please—so long as we preserve content.

Call what realizes a propositional attitude in a person's mind a *representation*. Let us suppose that the representations which realize attitudes have enough structure so that given a representation and what its constituent representations represent, a Russellian proposition is determined. Indeed, let us assume that when one has a proposition p as an object of an attitude and p has x as a constituent, there is a (complex) representation r which realizes the attitude in question which has a constituent representation r' which is "responsible" for x. We can then, for the purposes of semantics, identify the complex representations which realize attitudes, with what one gets, if one takes the Russellian proposition the representation determines and pairs each of the proposition's constituents with that part of the representation which determines the propositional constituent. An example: Pretend that representations are mental tokens of English sentences. Then the representation that determines Marsha's belief, that Twain is older than Clemens, is the English sentence "Twain is older than Clemens," whose (relevant) parts are "Twain," "is older than," and "Clemens." This sentence determines a Russellian content which, let us assume, is the tuple <the being older than relation, <Twain, Clemens>>. The suggestion is that, for simplicity in semantics, we identify Marsha's representation with the fusion of this Russellian content and the parts of "Twain is older than Clemens" which contribute the parts of the proposition—i.e., we identify the representation with <<"being older than," the being older than relation>, << "Twain," Twain>, <"Clemens," Clemens>>.

Call these sorts of things *sentential propositions*, their representation/value pairs *words*.[8] Clearly, natural language sentences determine sentential propositions. Attitude ascription, as I see it, involves producing a sentential proposition which purports to translate a (sentential proposition which corresponds to a) representation realizing one of the ascribee's attitudes. The translation rules introduced above are rules which restrict how

---

<"Twain," Twain>.) Formalizing, the rules in a translation manual can be represented as triples <X, <w, v>, P>, which tell us that in rendering X, the word w (with value v) translates only representations with P.

This way of putting matters represents an improvement on the way I put them in Richard (1990), where instead of a property P of representations, the third element of a translation rule was a set of representations. (One reason that this is an improvement is that it results in a better account of the modal profile of a sentence such as (4).) The improvement is a result of suggestions in Soames (1995) and Soames (2002), chapter 7. Soames also suggests—correctly—that for a fully general account, we should replace the first member of such trios with a property, so that translation rules end up being represented by things such as

<being identical with Marsha, <"Twain," Twain>, being expressed by Marsha with <"Twain," Twain>

<being an ordinary citizen of Metropolis, <"Clark Kent," Clark Kent>, representing Clark Kent as a mild mannered reporter).

[8] This is a terminological change from Richard (1990) (where these things were called Russellian annotated matrices, and what I am here calling words were called annotations) and Richard (1995) (where sentential propositions were called articulated propositions).

such translation may proceed. A belief ascription *X believes that S* is true in a context c provided that, given the translation rules operative in c, (the sentential proposition determined in c by) S is an acceptable translation of some belief making representation of X's. Analogously for other propositional attitude verbs.⁹

6. According to Soames, the "most revealing...problem" with this proposal is that it "misidentifies the basis of our reluctance to substitute coreferential names...in belief ascriptions"; that basis, says, Soames, is that "the relevant ascriptions would naturally be taken to attribute descriptively different" beliefs (171). Now Soames concedes that on the account just sketched a belief ascription can convey information about descriptive beliefs. For example, if I utter (4) when the translation rules

(T★) Marsha: "Twain" → representations of Twain Marsha associates with the property of having authored *Huck Finn*
"Clemens" → representations of Twain Marsha associates with the property of being a newspaperman

are in place, then I say something which is (roughly put) true iff Marsha believes that Twain, who authored *Huck Finn,* is not identical with Clemens, who was a newspaperman. But, Soames says, the idea that this is how a use of (4) might convey that Marsha has such a belief is

indirect, complicated, and theoretically contentious. Do ordinary speakers really intend to commit themselves to claims about the languages or internal mental representations used by agents to which they typically ascribe beliefs? Are the descriptive contents of the beliefs that ordinary speakers attribute to agents when assertively uttering [attitude] ascriptions really mediated by complicated assumptions (sufficient to account for Pederweski-type cases) about the expressions or mental representations used by agents? (Soames (2002), 170)

The questions get their rhetorical force from their suggestion that on the view in question speakers *commit* themselves to claims about internal representations, that they make *assumptions* about such. And this is worrisome, insofar as it suggests a heavy intentional commitment on the part of speakers to a theory about such.

Consider the hoary example of Hesperus and Phosphorus. Is it really theoretically contentious that ordinary people discussing the beliefs of the ancients about the night-time sky will mutually presuppose that the ancients had two ways of representing Venus: one (which the ancients associated with one position in the sky) that we translate with "Hesperus," another (which the ancients associated with another celestial position) that we translate

---

⁹ Here are the technical details. Let a translation function be a mapping from English words (i.e., expression/value pairs) to the words of someone X's internal idiom. When q is the result of replacing each of the words in p with their image under a translation function f, say that f(p) = q. Say that a translation function f is acceptable for an individual u in a context c provided it preserves Russellian content (f(<a, b>) = <a', b'> only when b is b'), and it obeys all the translation rules in effect in c concerning u. Then the ascription *X believes that S* is true in context c iff where p is the sentential proposition determined by S in c, there's a translation function f, acceptable for X in c, such that for some belief making representation q of X's f(p) = q.

with "Phosphorus"? Surely not. Speakers who know enough to use "Hesperus" and "Phosphorus" know these things. They know that other speakers who understand the words know them. Does the idea—that a speaker's words in attitude ascriptions serve as proxies for the presupposed representations—make attitude ascription an "indirect and complicated" affair? Frankly, the "complexity" here seems to me about on the order of what is involved in getting from Pierre's utterance of "you drank domestic wine yesterday" to the content sentence of "Pierre said that I drank French wine Thursday." Humdrum interpretation of context sensitive speech obviously involves a "translation" or mapping of one idiom into another. Such translation is, of course, largely unconscious, but that doesn't mean that it doesn't occur. The difference between this sort of "translation" and that involved in attitude ascription is simply this: while the former is mediated by our knowledge of how word content varies across contexts in virtue of its linguistic meaning, the latter is mediated by our (by and large correct) beliefs that our audience will recognize what (if any) ways of representing objects we have in mind as we utter a clausal complement.

My own view is that it is uncontroversial that conversants routinely make presuppositions about how others represent the world, and that they use their words, in ascribing attitudes, to more or less systematically track such representations. It is, in my opinion, hardly more controversial that speakers routinely and correctly expect their audience to be cognizant of these presuppositions and how their words are tracking representations, in much the way that the audience is routinely and correctly cognizant of other presuppositions. Speakers expect the audience to extract from attitude ascriptions, on this basis, information about how the subjects of attitude ascriptions represent the world. It seems to me that these facts have considerable explanatory power concerning our intuitions about the truth conditions of attitude ascriptions. For example, they explain how in the Donald/Drummond case (3) conveys that Donald knows that the man *he* was looking for is in jail, while Drummond doesn't know that the man *he* was looking for is in jail. I don't see that taking these facts as determining the truth conditions of attitude ascriptions makes their semantics any more arcane or baroque than, say, building facts about contextual common ground into the semantics of conditionals makes their semantics baroque.

A more significant objection, occuring in BR, Soames (1995), and Sider (1995), turns on the observation that just as a believer may be confused or ignorant about the identity of someone about whom she has beliefs, so a belief ascriber may be confused or ignorant about the identity of someone to whom he ascribes beliefs. Suppose that I don't realize that Superman is Clark Kent, that I wish to convey both that Superman believes Twain (under a "Twain" representation) boring, and that Clark Kent believes Twain (under a demonstrative representation) tired. My context might contain the translation rules

(R1) Superman: "Twain" → "Twain"
(R2) Clark Kent: "Twain" → "that man over there."

For each of

(S) Superman believes that Twain is boring
(C) Clark Kent believes that Twain is tired,

to be true, the clausal complement must translate some sentential proposition which realizes a belief of the subject. The translation cannot violate any of my context's translation rules. But these rules can't all be followed at once: one rule mandates that "Twain" translate "Twain" when we speak of Superman, the other that "Twain" translate "that man over there" when we speak of Clark Kent—i.e., Superman. So neither of (S) and (C) are true. This is so, even if the information I am trying to covey—that Superman believes Twain boring, using a "Twain" representation, and that Clark Kent believes Twain tired using a "that man over there" representation—is completely accurate. Insofar as a translational account of attitude ascriptions is supposed to capture the idea that ascriptions such as (S) and (C) have as their truth conditional point to convey exactly this sort of information, this is a genuine problem.

A beginning of a response is to observe that a translation manual is a contextual parameter determined (in good part) by the intentions and dispositions of speakers. When speakers are confused, their attempts to supply such parameters may turn out to be defective. Suppose in uttering "Nancy is tall," I intend to compare Nancy Kerrigan's height with that of the grandchildren of, as I put it to myself, "that man, Grandpa Kerrigan." Suppose the gentleman is her maternal, not her paternal, grandfather. Then there will be two candidates for the reference class contextually associated with "tall," the maternal grandchildren and the paternal ones. There may be no non-arbitrary way to decide between these candidates. Thus, it seems that no reference class is associated with "tall," and thus—since the adjective needs such, if "Nancy is tall" is to be assigned a truth value—my utterance will be without truth value, even if Nancy towers over all the grandchildren, maternal and paternal.

When there are multiple "best candidates" for a contextual parameter which a word requires, truth value is determined by looking to see whether the choice among them makes any difference. If I utter "Nancy is tall" and context provides $S1, S2, \ldots$, and Sk as "best candidates" for the reference class associated with my use of "tall," then my utterance is: true if it comes out true under any choice of $S1, \ldots, Sk$ as reference class; false, if it comes out false under any such choice; and without truth value, otherwise. Surely we can say the same sort of thing for attitude ascriptions and translation manuals. I think Superman is not Clark Kent. I try to use "Twain" to represent Superman's tokenings of "Twain," while trying to use "Twain" to represent Clark Kent's—i.e., Superman's—tokenings of "that man there." This can't be done; the context's translation manual is defective. What can be done is to correct the context's translation manual in various ways, by removing one or more of the manual's rules for translation until (and only until) we have a manual which can be used. Call such corrections *resolutions* of the manual. When a context's translation manual is defective, whether an attitude ascription is true or false depends upon how it fares under all of the resolutions of that manual: If it would be true under all resolutions, it is true simpliciter; if false under all resolutions, it is false simpliciter; otherwise, it is just indeterminate, whether it is true or false.[10]

---

[10] The last few paragraphs summarize material in Richard (1995).

In BR, Soames observes that this response apparently makes both (S) and (C) truth valueless in a case where: My intentions put rules (R1) and (R2) into play; Superman has no opinion whether Twain is Clemens; he accepts both "Twain is boring" and "that man over there [referring to Twain] is tired," but fails to accept "Twain is tired" or "that man over there is boring." And this may seem to show that we have made no headway on the problem. After all, when I utter (S), the relevant translation rule is (R1); (R2) is an unfortunate contextual hanger-on. The information that (S) is intended to convey—and should convey, if anything like a translational account is correct—is the (correct) claim that Superman believes that Twain is boring under a "Twain" representation. If the account does not make (S) true in this case, it fails to validate the intuitions it was designed to validate.

Now, I agree that in such a case there is a strong intuition that if I utter (S) focused on Superman's uses of "Twain," then I convey correct information if Superman accepts "Twain is boring." Indeed, I think it is clear that I do convey this information. And I think a proper explanation of this should advert to the semantics of (S). Parallel claims are true of (C). But I think we can explain these facts by adverting to a translational semantics for (S) and (C).

The contexts of semantics are abstractions from actual and possible "concrete speech situations." In constructing the context of an utterance it is often possible to construct it in different ways; in some cases, there need not be any (interest independent) reason to prefer one account of "the" context of an utterance to another. An example: Suppose we accept the view of David Lewis (1979), on which "moves" in a conversation effect the "standards of precision" associated with vague predicates such as "hexagonal." On Lewis' picture, if one applies "hexagonal" in such a way that one's application will be true only if the relevant standards shift, then—all else being equal—if no one objects to the application, the standards shift so as to make the application true. Suppose that Tom utters "France is not hexagonal," and conversants let him get away with it. So the standards for something's being hexagonal shift so that his utterance is true. Several conversational moves later, Jerry takes exception to Tom's claim, and Tom concedes to Jerry, saying "You're right—France is hexagonal, and I shouldn't have said it wasn't."

In what context does Tom's original utterance u of "France is not hexagonal" occur? Is it a context in which standards have shifted so that u is true—that is, "the" context which results from his utterance going unchallenged? Or is it a context in which the standards are as they are after Tom has accepted Jerry's correction? I see no reason to suppose that we have to choose once and for all between these; surely it can make sense to evaluate u either way. u occurs in at least two contexts, one "local" (determined by what happens in the situation "immediately surrounding" u), the other "global" (determined by the overall history of the conversation). Interpreted locally, as one would naturally interpret it as it is uttered, u is a true utterance; interpreted globally, as one would interpret it after Jerry has had his say, it is not.

Suppose that I utter (S) and later (C). My focus and dispositions during the first utterance would bring rule (R1) into play. Focus and dispositions will normally have shifted by the time I utter (C); (R1) is no longer relevant, (R2) has become relevant. It is not unreasonable to think that, just as Tom's utterance u occurs in two contexts, so these utterances occur in multiple contexts. Each utterance has its own "local" context—(S)'s contains only (R1), if my focus as I speak is "on Superman", (C)'s contains only (R2), if my focus as I speak is "on Clark Kent." And each utterance can be taken globally, taking into account all of the intentions and dispositions operative in my conversation. Interpreting each utterance locally—and such interpretation is quite natural—a translational semantics will make each utterance true. Thus, a translational semantics *does* validate our intuitions about (natural fleshings out of) the case under discussion: Interpreting (S) and (C) in natural ways, given natural fleshings out of the case, assigns them truth values in accord with our intuitions.

Of course, a conjunctive utterance, of say

Superman thinks that Twain is boring and Clark thinks that that man is tired

or of

Superman, but not Clark, thinks that Twain is boring

will most naturally be interpreted against a background involving both (R1) and (R2). (Actually, the first sentence can be interpreted, not unnaturally, as involving a "context switch" somewhere around the "and.") That a sentence such as the last will, given the facts we have been presupposing about my intentions and Superman's beliefs, come out truth valueless does not seem counter-intuitive.

It will, perhaps, be said that in saying all of this, I have jettisoned our logical intuitions. Consider the argument

Superman thinks that Twain is boring.
Clark does not think that Twain is boring.
So, Superman, but not Clark, thinks that Twain is boring.

Haven't I backed myself into the position of having to say that someone might utter the premises truly, the conclusion falsely? If so, then (absurdly) I must say that this argument is not valid.

The validity of the argument is a matter of the truth of its premises in any context guaranteeing the truth of its conclusion *in that context*. True utterances of all three of the argument's parts must occur in different contexts (given that "Superman" and "Clark" co-refer), if contexts are individuated in part in terms of the translation manual they provide. It is hardly surprising that uttering a valid argument form involving context sensitive expressions in both premise and conclusion may not be the giving of a valid argument, since contextual parameters, and thus context, can shift as one gives the argument.

I turn to a last objection. Consider indirect speech reports of utterances in which a context sensitive expression e is used. In such a report one usually *must* replace e with another expression in order to accurately convey what was said. If Mary utters "I am hot," I cannot report her utterance with "Mary said that I am hot;" I must say something like "Mary said that she [Mary] is hot." The explanation for this is that typically a sentence containing a context sensitive expression has different contents in different contexts; but a report *a said that S* is correct only if S, as used in the report, has the content of a sentence used assertively by *a*.

On the account of attitude ascriptions which I defend and Soames opposes, attitude verbs like "thinks" are treated as context sensitive: The relation-*cum*-function from worlds to extensions which "thinks" expresses on a particular use depends upon the rules for translation operative in the context of use. But then how, one wonders, is it that we can always report what one person says using "thinks" by using the verb itself? Suppose, for example, that John utters

(5) Ham thinks that Hes is hot.

Suppose that in John's context some translation rules (having nothing to do with Ham) are operative, rules not operative in my context. The content-*cum*-function from worlds to extensions of "thinks" in John's context will then be different from its content in my context. But *of course* I can use

(6) John said that Ham thinks that Hes is hot

to correctly report John's utterance of (5).

My explanation of this is that what "thinks" and other attitude verbs contribute to what is said by sentences in which they are used is *not* a relation-*cum*-function from worlds to extensions, but something which determines this. For present purposes, we can think of this latter thing as the Kaplanian character of the verb—the function which maps each context to the relation which the verb picks out in the context. Character does not vary across contexts. So if this character is what "thinks" contributes (in *any context*) to what's said by sentences in which it is used, then the claim expressed by John's use of (5) will be the same as that expressed by my use of (5) in (6).[11] So we have the basis of an explanation of why (6) can be used to correctly report John's utterance of (5), even though "thinks" determines different relations in my context and in John's. An upshot of the explanation is that the claim which John expresses with (5)—the *claim,* not just sentence (5) itself—is something which does not have an absolute truth value; rather, it has a truth value only relative to a context. (After all, the claim which (5) expresses doesn't contain a *relation* between thinkers and claims; rather, it contains something (a Kaplanian character) which only determines such a relation relative to a context.)

Soames objects to all this; he has two principle worries. One is simply that it makes the attitude verbs "special exceptions to an otherwise conceptually unified treatment of indexicality" (197). The complaint is that every other context-sensitive expression is one "the interpretation [*cum* what it contributes to what is said] of which is provided by elements of the context—such as the time, place, agent, and world of the context. When

[11] Strictly speaking, what "thinks" contributes to what is said by a sentence in which it occurs is the pair <"thinks," m>, where m is the character of the verb "thinks."

[a sentence containing such an expression] is placed in a context, it determines a proposition, which may be evaluated for truth or falsity at different possible worlds" (196). But on the view I just sketched, placing a sentence like (5) in a context, while it does determine a proposition, does not determine something which can be evaluated for truth at a world. Instead, the proposition (5) expresses has a truth value only relative to a world *and* a context. Furthermore, it is not the case that the interpretation *cum* content of the context-sensitive "thinks," on my view, is determined by the context in which (5) set; rather, the content of "thinks" is fixed prior to its being set in a context.

I agree with Soames that if the account I defend really did require that attitude verbs display a kind of semantic behavior which no other (context-sensitive) expression displays, that would be a reason to wonder about its cogency. But the fact is that many context-sensitive expressions are most naturally understood as behaving in the way I say attitude verbs do: That is, as picking out different properties or relations in different contexts even though they make the same contribution to what is said across contexts. This is true, I think, of many—perhaps most—gradable adjectives. Take "rich" as an example. The extension of (and thus the property expressed by) "rich" varies across contexts depending upon the interests and focus of conversants. One group of people may take an individual to be (clearly) rich, another may take the same individual to be (clearly) not rich. If we are sympathetic with David Lewis (1979), we will allow that within each group the use of "rich" may be accommodated in such a way that its application, in that group, is correct. If the applications of each group are correct, the extension of "rich" differs across the groups. And if the extensions of uses of a predicate differ, so do the properties they pick out.

But we typically report the members of two such groups as *disagreeing* about the individual in question. Suppose, to take an example, that Mary wins a million dollar lottery. Didi is impressed, and remarks to a friend "Mary's rich." Naomi, for whom a million dollars is not really all that much, remarks in a conversation disjoint from Didi's, "Mary is not rich at all." Suppose the salient comparison class is the same in both cases. (Both are taking New Yorkers to be the relevant field of comparison.) Suppose that there is no difference between the two conversations in the point of assessing people as rich or otherwise. (Each conversation began with the observation that some wealthy person doesn't deserve to be rich, and each of the women is now idly assessing people as rich or otherwise, and then assessing whether the rich ones deserve their wealth.) It seems to most of us that Naomi is contradicting Didi. But, especially if each remark is part of a longer conversation (with Namoi assessing various people she and her friend know for wealth, Didi doing the same), it is very plausible that the truth of their claims about wealth turns on whatever standards prevail within their conversations.

Didi and Naomi disagree. So there is something which Didi says and Naomi denies. Within the confines of each woman's conversation, each use of "is rich" is correct. So Didi says something true when she utters "Mary is rich," Naomi also states something true when she utters the sentence's denial. This is consistent with the two disagreeing over the truth of a single claim, if the truth of the claim may be relative, so that it may be "true for Didi, but not for Naomi." We can make sense of the example, that is, if we relativize not what is said by sentences such as "Mary is rich," but the truth of what is said. I conclude that what I say about the context sensitivity of attitude verbs does not make them special cases. A vast collection of context-sensitive expressions—"rich," "expensive," "dirty," etc., etc.—are plausibly thought to behave in just the way I suggested "thinks" and "knows" do.[12]

Soames' second objection is that relativizing truth has "strongly counter-intuitive" consequences. Suppose sentence S expresses p in your context and in mine; suppose further that p is "true for me but false for you." Then it seems that I should be able to say correctly the following:

> When you uttered "S" what you said was false in your context, though it is the case that S, and when you uttered "S" what you said was that S.[13]

Soames, as I said, thinks this counter-intuitive.

What of this objection? I agree that many philosophers find this way of speaking "strongly counter-intuitive." But it seems to me that this is not an expression of pretheoretic intuitions shared by normal speakers, but of a theoretical commitment to the idea that a claim's truth can't be relative to a context, discourse, world view, or whatever. For better or for worse, non-philosophers don't balk at claims like the claim that

> The claim that there's such a thing as absolute motion was true for Newtonians but isn't true for us.

That normal speakers don't have a problem with this way of talking does not, of course, show that a claim might be true for Newton but not us. But it does, I think, show that those who think it counter-intuitive to say that a claim might be true, but not true for you, are not expressing intuitions to which a semantic theory need (obviously) be responsive.[14]

---

[12] Obviously a great deal more needs to be said concerning the issues here. I have tried to say some of it, in the context of a discussion of contextualism in epistemology, in Richard (2004).

[13] This is a simplification of the objection in Soames (2002), 202. The objection there is, roughly, that it is counter-intuitive to say things like: it's false in John's context that Hes Ham believed that p, although John said that Hes Ham believed that p, and everything John said is true.

[14] This chapter was a contribution to a symposium on Scott Soames' *Beyond Rigidity* (Oxford University Press, 2002). Some of the material in this chapter appears in a somewhat different form in Richard (1995, 2006).

14

Kripke's Puzzle

I

You are, of course, familiar with the story of Pierre. Raised in France, he acquires the name "Londres" as a name of London. He accepts, in French of course, many claims about the city—elle est grande, jolie, dans Angleterre, and so on, and so forth.[1] Spirited away to England, confined to an unpleasant part of London, forced to learn the language by speaking to the natives, he acquires "London" as a name of London. He accepts, in English of course, many claims about the city—it is large, not at all pretty, in England, and so on, and so forth. He does not recognize that the city he is in is the city, Londres, of which he learned in France. He remembers, and continues to accept in French, all the claims he learned in France about Londres—qu'elle est grande, jolie, dans Angleterre, and so on.

Pierre's experience in France warrants our saying that he believed that London is pretty. That, and the fact that he doesn't seem to have changed his mind about what he learned in France, warrants our saying that he still believes that. Pierre's experience in England warrants our saying that he believes that London is not pretty. This, Kripke claims, leads to a puzzle: "Does Pierre, or does he not believe that London is pretty? It is clear that our normal criteria for the attribution of belief lead, when applied to *this* question, to paradoxes and contradictions."[2]

---

[1] When I say that someone x accepts the claim that p in a particular language, I mean roughly that: there's a sentence S of the language that, used by x, says that p; x is related to S in a way that warrants saying that he understands it; and (because x takes the sentence to be true) he has a belief that he could express by uttering S. Thus, for example, the text tells us that Pierre's relations to his language warrant us in thinking that he understands the French sentence "Londres est grande, jolie, et dans Angleterre" and, because he accepts this sentence as true, believes what he would say by uttering it.

This usage means that the inference *Pierre accepts the claim that London is pretty; so, Pierre believes that London is pretty* is not trivial. Obviously, the validity of the inference is closely related to the validity of the disquotational principle discussed herein.

[2] Kripke (1979).

How so? Why not say that poor Pierre has contradictory beliefs—that he believes that London is pretty and that London is not pretty? The short answer is that Pierre is (to be supposed to be) rational and reflective. So if Pierre has these beliefs, we have a case of a rational and reflective person who has contradictory beliefs. But this is impossible: "surely anyone... is in principle in a position to notice and correct contradictory beliefs if he has them. Precisely for this reason, we regard individuals who contradict themselves as subject to greater censure than those who merely have false beliefs" (122).

It does indeed seem that we cannot imagine a sane person understanding and sincerely uttering a sentence of the form

(A)   b is such and such, although b (the very same b) is also not such and such.

No sane person would think of the world in this way. And this suggests that we cannot imagine a sane person having beliefs that he would ascribe to himself with a sentence such as (A). Call such a situation—in which someone *does* have such beliefs, and has them because he thinks of the world in the way in which someone who would sincerely utter (A) thinks of it—a case of contradictory belief.[3]

Call a use of a sentence of the form

(B)   a believes that b is such and such, and a believes that b is not such and such

in which we do not capitalize on any ambiguity or contextual shiftiness in *b* or *such and such* a case of ascribing inconsistent beliefs.[4] One thinks that to ascribe inconsistent beliefs is to imply that the ascribee has contradictory beliefs. And if this is so—if saying that Pierre believes that London is pretty and he believes that it is not pretty implies that Pierre has contradictory beliefs—then Kripke is right: our normal criteria for ascribing belief lead to trouble in the case of Pierre. For a rational person could be in a situation like Pierre's. Indeed, rational people often *are* in such situations.[5] So there are possible—indeed actual—situations in which our normal criteria for ascribing belief lead us to say (things that imply) that there are cases in which rational people have contradictory beliefs. But we think it's impossible that a rational person should have such beliefs.

II

Why should we care about Pierre? Kripke suggests that the way the puzzle about Pierre arises casts doubt on a standard argument against "Millianism," the view that the semantic role of a proper name is exhausted by its being a name of whatever it names.

---

[3] Perhaps you are wondering what exactly is meant by saying that someone thinks of things in *the* way in which someone who would sincerely utter (A) thinks of them; if you are, try to go with the flow until Section III.

[4] Note that here and in the following, "a has contradictory beliefs" and "[in uttering (B) we are saying that] a has inconsistent beliefs" are used in the quasi-technical senses just assigned to them.

[5] David Sosa, for example, tells us (Sosa (1996), 384) that for some time he didn't realize that John Glenn the astronaut was the same person as John Glenn the senator.

Here and below I assume that (B) ascribes inconsistent beliefs iff the result of replacing the second occurrence of "b" therein with a pronoun anaphoric on the first "b" does; I also assume that if (B) implies that someone has contradictory beliefs, such a variant does as well.

Millianism seems to imply that names of one thing have the same semantic role; thus, it seems that (setting aside quotation and other contexts where a name's shape or sound is invoked) if we accept Millianism, we must accept a principle of substitutivity:

(S) If one sentence comes from another by replacing a proper name with a co-referential one, then (provided the sentences are relativized to the same context, and the names are not being quoted or the like) the sentences don't differ in truth value.

A familiar objection to Millianism seizes on this apparent consequence of the view: Surely, the objection goes, someone rational could believe that, say, Twain wrote *Huck Finn* and that Clemens did not. If so, and (S) is true, a rational person could believe that Twain wrote the book and believe that Twain didn't.[6] So a rational person could have contradictory beliefs. But a rational person can't have such beliefs. So Millianism is false.

What's the connection with the puzzle about Pierre? Kripke's idea is that what justifies us in thinking that someone might believe that Twain wrote the book and that Clemens did not is *au fond* the same set of principles—those which govern our ascriptions of belief and other propositional attitudes—that justify us in thinking that Pierre believes that London is pretty and that London is not pretty. So those principles all by themselves—quite apart from appeal to Millianism or a principle such as (S)—lead to the conclusion that a rational person might have contradictory beliefs. So it seems somewhat precipitate to object to Millianism in the way just rehearsed. For either we must reject the principles that underwrite the claim that someone might think Twain wrote a book but Clemens did not, or we must renounce our conviction that rational people can't have contradictory beliefs.[7] Either way, the objection to Millianism is undermined.

III

As we are using "contradictory beliefs," one has them when one believes of something that it is so and so, believes of it that it is not so and so, and has these beliefs because one thinks of the world in the way in which someone who accepts a sentence of the form *a is F and a (the very same a) is not F* thinks of it. I know that you would like an account of what I mean by "thinks of the world in the way in which someone who accepts sentence S does." I know that I would like to give you an account. Sadly, I can't find one. At least I can't find one that will be neutral among all the views of belief and its objects which you, gentle readers, hold.

---

[6] Of course the argument here relies on going back and forth, from an ascription of belief to an ascription of truth to such an ascription; such back and forth is taken to be justified by the obviousness of things like *Pierre believes that London is pretty* iff *"Pierre believes that London is pretty" is true in English* ("English" here understood as naming the language of the sentence in which it occurs).

[7] Or we must say that the truth of a sentence like (B)—that is, the truth of an ascription of inconsistent beliefs—doesn't imply that anyone has contradictory beliefs. See the next section.

We could, of course, make things somewhat clearer if we adopted one or another of these views. A Fregean can cash out the notion of contradictory belief in terms of the "constituent senses" in the objects of the contradictory beliefs. Russell could have done something similar in terms of "propositional constituents." Someone who thinks that propositional attitudes are realized by "representations," and that such representations can be typed both semantically and in terms of properties that the thinker is sensitive to (so that we can speak of different token representations as being of "computationally identical" types), can cash the notion out in those terms. It is noteworthy that Frege, Russell, and the representationalist would all say that a thinker is sensitive to the identity and distinctness of the ways of thinking involved in her beliefs. Frege seemed to think that when names have the same sense for a speaker, he accepts an identity involving them; Russell's idea that we are acquainted with propositional constituents of our thoughts is apparently supposed to guarantee something like this; something similar is true of "synonymy in the language of thought."

Probably no particular precisification of the notion of a way of thinking is uniquely determined by our pretheoretic commitments about belief and other attitudes. But there *is* a commonsense notion of contradictory belief; there *is* commonsense talk of people thinking of objects in similar and dissimilar ways. And it is, I think, plausible to think that the first notion is to be explicated, as I have tried to explicate it, in terms of the second. If we take Kripke to have something like this notion in mind when he writes "surely anyone...is in principle in a position to notice and correct contradictory beliefs if he has them," then I think we must agree with him; and, I think, we must agree that such beliefs are a mark of irrationality. For having contradictory beliefs is a matter of being (relevantly like) someone who is disposed to sincerely think to himself "this is F and this (very same thing) is not F." Since we can become aware of and evaluate such occurrent mental states, since a rational person is disposed to retract beliefs when he is aware of their impossibility, and since those who understand something with a meaning like that of the form *a is F and (the very same) a is not F* are aware of its impossibility, someone who has contradictory beliefs is indeed in a position to become aware of them and correct them.

Do all who believe that Paris is pretty and that Paris is not pretty have contradictory beliefs?

One wants to tie belief in language users fairly closely to assent. Suppose that Jones understands the sentences he utters, that he is not given to deceiving others, and that he is not suffering from self-deception or kindred pathology. Then if he or we ask him "S?," and after reflection he assents, surely he believes what he or we say, when we utter the sentence S. Kripke's version of this principle—one of the above-mentioned principles governing attitude ascription—is the principle of disquotation

(D) If a normal English speaker, on reflection, sincerely assents to "p," then he believes that p.

This is a schema, "p" to be replaced inside and outside of quotes with a sentence which "is to lack indexical or pronominal devices or ambiguities" (113). If we accept (D), we will also accept its analogues in other languages.[8]

Now, tense and the contextual shiftiness of "pretty" set to the side as irrelevant, neither "London is not pretty" nor "Londres est jolie" appears ambiguous or context-sensitive in their languages. So given (D), it would appear that

(C$_1$) Pierre believes that London is not pretty
(C$_2$) Pierre croit que Londres est jolie

are true in their respective languages. The truth of (C$_1$) in English implies that, indeed, Pierre believes that London is not pretty. And even a C+ student in second-semester French can tell you what (C$_2$) means—it means what "Pierre believes that London is pretty" means—that is, that Pierre believes that London is pretty. But sentences that, in their respective languages, mean the same thing can't differ in truth value in those languages. As Kripke puts it, we accept a principle of translation:

(T) If a sentence of one language expresses a truth in that language, then any translation of it into any other language also expresses a truth (in that language). (114)

So, by appeal to what every mediocre student of French knows, Pierre believes that London is pretty.

So the answer to our question seems to be "no": Someone like Pierre who believes that London is pretty and that London is not pretty need not have contradictory beliefs. Pierre, after all, does *not* have contradictory beliefs. He has, after all, no disposition whatsoever to assent to a sentence of the form *a is F, and a—the very same a—is not F*. He does not think of the world in the way that someone who has such dispositions thinks of it. Though he is French, he is not crazy.

IV

One feels something has gone seriously awry. If we accept the argument just given, we will conclude that Pierre believes that London is pretty and (that he believes that) London is not pretty. How can we then *not* say that Pierre has contradictory beliefs? Commonsense tells us that someone who believes that London is pretty and (that it) is not

---

[8] Kripke also discusses a strengthened version of (D), in which assent to "p" is said to imply and be implied by belief that p. Relatively little is made of this principle in Kripke's essay and very little will be made of it here. It will be clear by the end of this discussion that I think that the stronger principle is false. Anyone who thinks that we may believe what a sentence says although our understanding of the sentence is "imperfect" (in the way that, for example, the understanding of the sentence "I have arthritis" in Tyler Burge's well-known example is imperfect) will be inclined to dismiss Kripke's strengthened principle. (This is because (a) one can believe what is said by sentences one only imperfectly understands, and (b) one could apparently have imperfect understanding of synonymous sentences which led one to reject one but not the other.) The example by Burge appears in Burge (1979).

pretty is deranged. Surely Pierre's irrationality is implied by saying that he so believes. Since he is not irrational, there must be something wrong with (D) or (T), or our translations from Pierre's idiom into ours, or in some unmentioned bridge principle carrying us from the story of Pierre and these premises to the contrary conclusion.

It will help, in trying to determine whether we have gone off the rails, if we return to speaking of "the way in which someone thinks of the world" when they believe this or that. However we choose to make sense of this notion, we will surely take ways of thinking of the world to be "made up" of ways of thinking of the things that make the world up, as well as ways of thinking of the properties and relations these things have and bear. We will thus be able to talk about constituent relations amongst ways of thinking, as well as saying such things as: When a thinks that b is F and c thinks that b is G, they think of b in the same way, though when d thinks that b is F, he thinks of b in some other way. In particular, we will be able to say things like:

(E_1) In thinking that London is pretty (as he does when he says "Londres est jolie"), Pierre thinks of London in the same way as he does when (saying "London is not pretty") he thinks that London is not pretty.

(E_2) In thinking that London is pretty (as he does when he says "Londres est jolie"), Pierre thinks of London in a different way than he does when (saying "London is not pretty") he thinks that London is not pretty.

Presumably, Pierre is irrational only if something along the lines of (E_1) is true.

The suggestion is that our notion of contradictory belief as something irrational (irrational, in part, because it is something that a responsible and reflective thinker can be aware of as a matter of course) presupposes that when one has a belief (or other propositional attitude) with a particular content, associated with the belief are "ways of thinking" of the objects and properties the belief is about; these ways of thinking determine, or at least reflect, the thinker's "access to the content of the belief." By this I mean (for example) that if A's beliefs that b is F and that b is G involve the same way of thinking about b, then A takes those beliefs to present a single individual as being F and G. If all this is so, then whether a belief is irrational will be (in large part) determined by the ways of thinking it involves. After all, if (E_1) were true, then given what we just said about ways of thinking, Pierre takes those beliefs to present a single individual as both pretty and not pretty. But part of rationality is being disposed to withdraw at least some of any set of beliefs with this property.

The suggestion, then, is that the irrationality of a belief is a matter of relations among the ways of thinking involved in the belief. In particular, the irrationality of a belief one would self-ascribe with a sentence of the form of (A) is a matter of its involving thinking of an individual *with a single way of thinking* as both having and lacking a property. Suppose that the suggestion is correct. And now suppose further that when we ascribe beliefs and use an expression e several times, reoccurrence of e in the ascription implies identity of ways of thinking involved in the attitudes ascribed. Suppose, for example, that if we say *Pierre believes that London is blah blah, and that London is blee blee,* we imply that there is a way of thinking of London such that, thinking of London in that way, Pierre thinks that it is both blah blah and blee blee. Then an ascription of inconsistent beliefs *does* indeed imply that the ascribee has contradictory beliefs.

We began this section wondering how to reconcile our feeling—that to say that Pierre believes that London is pretty and that it is not pretty *is* to imply that he has contradictory beliefs—with the observations that belief ascription seems to be governed by (D) and (T), and that if a practice is so governed then to say that Pierre believes that London is pretty and that it is not pretty is *not* to imply that he has contradictory beliefs. We have in effect offered an explanation of the first mentioned feeling, by linking the notion of contradictory belief to the notion of a way of thinking, and by saying that our practice of ascribing beliefs is governed by a principle along the lines of

(R) Multiple occurrences of an expression within ascriptions of attitude to a single person indicate that the attitudes involve multiple occurrences of a single way of thinking in the attitudes ascribed.

Given that (D), (T), our ordinary practices of translation, and (R) govern our practices of ascribing attitudes, and given that our notion of contradictory belief reflects the ideas about ways of thinking and irrationality just sketched, we have an explanation of both our feeling that Pierre must have contradictory beliefs, and our feeling that obviously he does not.

The explanation is, of course, only as good as our evidence for (R). It seems to me that it is not hard to garner evidence for this principle. Consider, for example, explanations of behavior by ascription of attitudes, such as

(F) Mary hit Twain because she wanted to humiliate him, and she thought that if she hit him, she would humiliate him.

We take these to be potentially explanatory. Notably, we do not have the same attitude towards ascriptions in which different names of a single individual occur. While, for example, we find (F) or

(F') Mary hit Twain because she wanted to humiliate Twain, and she thought that if she hit Twain, she would humiliate Twain

to be explanatory without supplement, we do not feel that way about

(F") Mary hit Twain because she wanted to humiliate Twain, and she thought that if she hit Clemens, she would humiliate Clemens.

What, after all, if Mary didn't know that Twain was Clemens? (F") as an explanation is just bizarre without supplement. (R) provides the basis of an explanation of both why (F') should be explanatory, as well as why (F") needs supplementation before it is explanatory.[9]

---

[9] For further discussion of these issues, see Richard (2006).

V

With studied vagueness, I have said that (D), (T), and (R) "govern" our practices of ascribing attitudes. But what does that mean? Are (D) and (T) supposed to be true, full stop, so that it is true, full stop, that Pierre believes that London is pretty and that it is not? Or are they rules which tell us something about when we are, *ceteris paribus*, warranted in saying that someone has a certain belief? For that matter, what exactly is (R) supposed to mean? Is "indicate" in (R) to be understood as involving some semantical rule, or some defeasible pragmatic signal?

What can be said in favor of the thought that (D) and (T) (with (T) informed by our normal practices of translation) are true, full stop? Well, they do have the air of trivialities. One way to come to believe something is by considering its verbal expression and, understanding what one is doing, assenting to it. If Pierre asks himself, having been in England for three years, "Is this place ugly?" and looking around, says with disgust, "Sure is," what good reason can be given for saying that he is not expressing what he thinks? And how, if he understands what he is saying, can he not be expressing the claim that London is ugly? As for (T), it apparently follows from the absolutely trivial claims that (a) translation preserves meaning, and (b) meaning determines truth (that is, sentences which mean the same thing must have the same truth values).[10]

What can be said against (D)? The most likely objection to (D) is that it combines a relatively benign idea about belief with controversial—some would say obnoxious—ideas about language identity. What, it might be asked, is the import of the phrase "normal English speaker" in (D)? Are we to suppose that there is some one language all of us "English speakers" speak? That is, are we to suppose that there is some one set of syntactic, phonetic, and semantic principles that correctly describe "the" language being spoken by everyone who has (say) received passing grades in American high school English? Chomsky tells us that to think this is to confuse politics and linguistics.[11]

Certainly it is true that the syntactic and phonetic description of my language will be different from the description of the language of others, assuming that such description is supposed to generate the sentences I produce when I am not tired, misspeaking, being linguistically creative, and so on. After all, you say toe-may-toe, and I say toe-ma-toe. Suppose we allow that this shows that language is idiosyncratic, so that strictly speaking no two people speak the same language. Once we allow that when Pierre is "speaking English" he may not be speaking a language with the same semantics as the language in which we speak when we formulate (D), (D) seems either implausible or too weak to

---

[10] Of course meaning doesn't determine truth simpliciter. "I am sad" in English means the same as "je suis triste" in French, but while the first is false when I use it, the second is true when Pierre uses it. The correct principle is *something* along the lines of *sentences with the same meaning taken relative to the same (or relevantly similar) context(s) have the same truth value*. Since we are supposed to be concerned only with expressions that aren't context-sensitive, such as "London," Kripke presumably thought it was acceptable to simplify the principle of translation.

I return to the issues raised in this note in the last sections of this essay.

[11] This claim appears repeatedly in Chomsky's writings. See, for example, Chomsky(1980).

yield the conclusions it is supposed to yield. For suppose that Pierre's spoken language—PL, call it—is not the same as my spoken language—call it ML. How are we to understand an instance of (D) such as

(D$_1$) If Pierre, on reflection, sincerely assents to "London is not pretty," then he believes that London is not pretty?

If I utter (D$_1$), my utterance is an utterance of a sentence of my language, ML. But both ML and PL contain a sentence that looks like "London is not pretty." Which one does (D$_1$)'s quotation name name? That is, should we understand (D$_1$) as

(D$_{1.1}$) If Pierre, on reflection, sincerely assents to the PL sentence "London is not pretty," then he believes that London is not pretty,

or as

(D$_{1.2}$) If Pierre, on reflection, sincerely assents to the ML sentence "London is not pretty," then he believes that London is not pretty?

We have, it might be argued, no reason to think that (D$_{1.1}$) is true. Since ML and PL are different languages, "London is not pretty" may mean different things in them. When Pierre sincerely assents to "London is pretty" he is, we may assume, expressing a belief in what this string says in PL. But since the string may mean one thing in PL and another in ML, this fact doesn't give us reason to think that Pierre believes that London is not pretty—that is, it doesn't give us reason to think that the ML predicate "believes that London is not pretty" is true of Pierre. On the other hand, it is not clear what to make of Pierre's assent to the ML sentence "London is not pretty." Presumably he has not made the theoretical judgment that his language and my language are distinct, so it has not even occurred to him that he is assenting to something that is not a sentence of his language. He may, when he assents, be indicating belief, but there is no reason to think that he is indicating belief in what the relevant string says in *my* language. After all, he understands the utterance as he understands his own utterances. So once again, we have no reason to think that the principle is true.

So I imagine someone objecting to (D). Note that someone who so objects to (D) need not be objecting to the idea that assent indicates belief. Indeed, we can imagine someone who objects to (D) in this way allowing that certain "first-person variants" of (D) are perfectly acceptable. What I have in mind is something along the lines of

(D$_2$) Pierre's uses (in the language he speaks in London) of "If I, Pierre, on reflection, sincerely assent to 'p' where 'p' is a sentence of my language, then I, Pierre, believe that p" are true in the language Pierre speaks in London.

This, like (D), is a schema in which "p" is to be replaced by a non-ambiguous, non-contextually sensitive sentence. Given that Pierre's language has a disquotational truth predicate and a normal logic, it follows that if Pierre assents, on reflection, to "London is not pretty," then Pierre can, speaking his London language, say truthfully

(P) I, Pierre, believe that London is not pretty.

French analogues of (D_2) establish that Pierre can, speaking his Parisian language, say truthfully

(P') Je, Pierre, crois que Londres est jolie.

We can use (T) and our normal practices of translation to go on to derive the conclusions that Kripke finds so puzzling.

Whether we accept the Chomskyan objection to (D) or not—I will take that objection up in the next section—the derivation of Kripke's puzzle just sketched is worth contemplating. For instances of schemata like (D2) certainly do seem plausible. What (D2) captures is the idea that *whatever it is that Pierre is saying, when he sincerely assents to a sentence of his language, it is something he believes.* It is hard to see how this idea could fail to be correct. And as just indicated, it seems that we need only it, our usual practices of translation (including our practice of homophonic "translation"), and (T) to generate the conclusion that Pierre believes that London is pretty and that it is not pretty. If we think this conclusion cannot be correct, it seems, we must lay the blame at the feet of (T) or our practices of translation.

VI

It is easy to see why someone might be moved to say that phonetics and syntax differ enough to make it implausible that we English speakers all speak a single language. That doesn't imply that our normal practices of translation (including our practice of homophonic translation) don't preserve meaning.

We think we all *mean* the same by "London is pretty"; we think that the way to *translate* any normal French speaker's use of "Londres est jolie" is with "London is pretty." Why? Well, the fact is that we understand one another, and our translating the French in the conventional way allows us to understand them. By saying that we understand each other, I mean (roughly) that we are able to make sense of each other's verbal behavior (in the context of each other's behavior as a whole), and we do this in a non-accidental way (that is, if interpreter and interpretee proceed in the ways they have been proceeding, our understanding will continue). It is hard to see this understanding as not based in the presupposition that (ambiguity and context sensitivity to the side and speaking—now schematically and for myself) when you utter "p." you are saying p. These facts—that we undeniably understand one another, and that our understanding seems to be grounded in the assumption that we say the same things with our sentences—provide one route to the idea that we mean the same thing with these sentences. And of course this idea underwrites the idea that our sentences homophonically translate each other.[12]

---

[12] Some of a Davidsonian bent would say that the facts—that we make sense of each other, that we do this by translating homophonically—simply entail that we mean the same thing by our sentences; there is, they would say, nothing more to same-meaning. Others who yet like to visit the museum on a Sunday afternoon see no entailment here. We can sidestep this dispute. For only a jejune skeptic would say, in the face of our ability to make sense of each other, that we do not understand each other.

One might respond by pointing out—correctly—that we have very different concepts of the things to which we refer. Often, our concepts are different enough that—save for the fact that we label them with the same public language word—we would never think that they were concepts of the same thing or property. And this, the response concludes, shows that we can't really mean the same thing by our words.

It is hard—for me, at least—to take this response seriously. If successful linguistic interpretation can (and often does) proceed despite the fact that very different mental structures are associated with our words, that simply shows that those mental structures do not have to be identical (or even very much the same) in order for us to successfully interpret. And since we understand one another when we successfully (and non-accidently) interpret each other, this shows that the mental structures in question need not be very much the same in order for us to understand each other. As I see it, non-accidental homophonic interpretation is a sign that interpreter and interpretee mean the same things by their words. What more evidence could we possibly demand?

Now, the argument I have been giving could well be taken as an argument for an analogue of Kripke's disquotational principle (D):

(N) If a normal English speaker, on reflection, sincerely (and without irony) utters "p," then he (sincerely) says that p.[13]

The argument is, put simply, that using (N) allows us to make sense of each other; it wouldn't do so if it weren't true. It is noteworthy that a perfectly similar argument seems to be possible for (D). After all, to make sense of one another requires knowing not just what we say, but what we think. And we determine this, in good part, by interpreting one another's speech and (assuming that the speech is sincere) ascribing belief in what is said. That is, we assume

(O) If a normal English speaker sincerely says p, he believes that p.

(N) and (O), nearly enough, entail (D).

I will return, at the end of this essay, to the status of principles such as (N), (O), and (D).

VII

Let us take stock. We have isolated a sense of "contradictory belief" in which no rational person has contradictory beliefs. We have observed that we have reason to think that our ordinary practices of translation preserve meaning. We have noted that the principle (T) Kripke invokes, to the effect that translation preserves truth, seems absolutely banal. And we have observed that (a) our reasons for thinking that our ordinary practices of translation preserve meaning are in fact reasons for accepting Kripke's disquotation principle (D), and (b) even if we reject (D), far weaker and

---

[13] (N) is, of course, subject to the same sort of caveats concerning substitutends for "p" as is (D). It requires other caveats for cases in which sincere, non-ironic speech is not assertive, which I won't try to formulate.

seemingly undeniable principles are sufficient, once the other things just mentioned are in place, for deriving the conclusion that Pierre believes that London is pretty and that it is not pretty.

It is beginning to look as if what we should do is understand (R) in such a way that while

(G) Pierre believes that London is pretty and that it is not pretty

implies that Pierre has contradictory beliefs, the implication falls short of entailment. We are familiar enough with the idea that we may imply something without actually saying it. One conclusion to draw from Kripke's essay is that (G) does not entail that Pierre is irrational. If we do draw this conclusion, we may well go on to conclude that the semantics of attitude ascription is Millian through and through.

Some have drawn these conclusions; some have contested them.[14] I don't propose to rehearse past arguments. I will observe that the last conclusion—implying as it does that if Mary believes that Twain wrote *1609*, she believes that Clemens wrote it—is somewhat fantastic. It is fantastic because it is so at variance with our understanding of our talk about our attitudes. We presuppose that the syntax of the content sentences of attitude ascriptions reflects properties of the mental states ascribed. We assume, for example, that if Mary believes that if p, then q, and she wants q, she has some inclination to make it the case that p; it goes without saying that if Marty thinks that if p, then q, but is pretty sure that it's not the case that q, he will be pretty sure that it isn't the case that p, either.[15] We not only assume that the attitudes are (Freudian and such forces set to the side) under rational control and are motivational; we also assume that our way of ascribing them invokes the properties that make the attitudes subject to rational review and motivational. The properties we are invoking in such ascriptions, if the semantics of those ascriptions are Millian through and through, are *not* properties in virtue of which the attitudes are motivational or transparent to reason.[16] What is in my opinion completely fantastic in the thought that attitude ascriptions have a Millian semantics is the idea that the meaning of talk about the attitudes could be this far out of whack with its purpose and use. Only someone in the grip of a philosophical theory could think that what we mean and what we do with our words was *this* disconnected.

This leaves us with the intermediate conclusion, that (R) is to be understood so that (G) does not *entail* that Pierre's beliefs are contradictory. If we accept this conclusion—and by the end of the essay, we shall—we need some explanation of how we can draw this conclusion but avoid drawing a Millian conclusion from the puzzle about Pierre.

---

[14] Keith Donnellan is an example of someone who reads Kripke as providing a good argument for Millianism; see Donnellan (1989). Sosa (1996) resists the conclusion.

[15] Kripke emphasizes this in discussing the puzzle at p. 122.

[16] Argument for this claim can be found in Richard (2006).

VIII

One reaction to Kripke's essay—a reaction that the last few sections may tend to reinforce—is that Kripke has uncovered a genuine puzzle; but it is really a puzzle about belief *ascription*, not a puzzle about *belief*. The puzzle just posed—how can (G) be true if Pierre doesn't have contradictory beliefs?—is a puzzle about our talk about Pierre. And, in any case, it might be said, it is clear enough what Pierre believes: He believes that London—that is, the city of which he heard in France, called "Londres"—is pretty, and that London—that is, the city in which he currently finds himself, whose inhabitants call it "London"—is not pretty. What is puzzling is not what Pierre believes (which is perfectly consistent), but how to say what he believes in the idiom for belief ascription provided by English, if we limit ourselves to identifying the object of his beliefs with the name "London."[17]

Kripke anticipates this reaction towards the end of "A Puzzle about Belief." According to Kripke, one can't get rid of the puzzle simply by saying that Pierre associates different identifying properties with "London" and "Londres" (and thus his beliefs are "really" consistent), since "the puzzle can arise even if Pierre associates exactly the same identifying properties with both names" (125). After all, Pierre might "define" "Londres" as "la capitale d'Angleterre" and "define" "London" as "the capital of England." If he did, and we individuate his beliefs in terms of the objects, properties, and relations they are about, we will conclude that he expresses exactly the same belief with "London is pretty" as he does with "Londres est jolie."

One way to put Kripke's point is this. If Pierre "associates the same identifying properties" with the names, then the way he thinks of London when he speaks French is *the same* as the way he thinks of it when he speaks English. And this is quite puzzling apart from any issue about how we might ascribe Pierre's beliefs: How can Pierre be rational, if thinking of London in one way (as England's capital) he thinks it pretty, while thinking of it in the *same way* he thinks it not pretty?

It will be objected that if Pierre "defines" the names in this way, he must associate different properties with the English and French names of Britain.[18] But why is this? We come to know individuals "under guises," and can fail to recognize an individual from

---

[17] There is a family of proposals along these lines. The simplest ones insist that all belief (or all belief save that about the self, or save that about the self and the present moment) is descriptive. Others take the modal profile of all beliefs (or all beliefs save those about the self, or save those about the self and the present moment) to be explained in terms of David Lewis's counterpart relations. Natural ways of fleshing *this* out render Pierre's "French beliefs" consistent with his "English beliefs" because different counterpart relations are used to interpret Pierre's "French thought" and his "English thought." (Something like this is suggested in Lewis (1999). Lewis's own proposal is complicated by the suggestion that there are two ways to interpret someone, "narrowly" (using a counterpart relation) and "widely.")

What follows is meant to be responsive to all such proposals. (In the case of Lewis's proposal, let me add somewhat cryptically that the primary problem with it is that it is inconsistent with the idea that what motivates us has the semantics of the language in which we report what motivates us—it is, if you like, inconsistent with the idea that what we say is what we think.)

[18] Thus Sosa (1996), 397.

encounter to encounter because we do not take the guises under which he appears to be guises of one individual. Why shouldn't this be true of properties and relations as well? One might respond that properties and relations are different: if being F just is being G, one just *can't* know what it is to be F, know what it is to be G, but mistakenly think that being F isn't being G.

This seems desperate. It requires us to find meanings for "capital of England" and "capitale d'Angleterre" as used by Pierre that characterize the city in terms of different properties. Are we to suppose that Pierre's utterance of "Londres est jolie" means something along the lines of *the capital of the country the French call "Angleterre" is pretty* or *the capital of the country my countymen call "Angleterre," is pretty*? Then we are being asked to simply reject all the lessons about the modal profile of a sentence involving names that we learned on reading *Naming and Necessity*. Are we supposed to divorce what our sentences mean from the beliefs we express with them, saying with Russell that (since we must have an intimate epistemic relation to something before we can have a belief about it) there is a judgment about London that we should like to make (one which is expressed by our sentence "London is pretty"!), but cannot, because when we try to make it, we are "necessarily defeated, since the actual [London] is unknown to us"?[19] As Kripke observes, saying this leads to saying that no two people (or person at different times) mean the same thing—at least, express the same beliefs—with their sentences.[20] As Stephen Schiffer once said, "believe it if you can."

If one thinks of a way of thinking as something to be identified with, or at least individuated in terms of, a collection of objects, properties, and relations, the puzzles Kripke presents us with are indeed difficult to solve. If one thinks of thought in the way that Russell did, it is hard to know how else to think of a way of thinking. A—perhaps the—standard way of thinking of Frege's notion of the sense of a name thinks of senses in this way.[21] The proper conclusion to draw, it seems to me, is that what I have been calling ways of thinking are not to be individuated (simply) in terms of objects, properties, and relations. Whether two expressions (as used by a particular individual) are associated with the same way of thinking is not a matter of their semantic properties (where these are individuated in terms of the expressions' conventional potentials for referring or applying to objects). It is a matter of their cognitive properties, properties reflected by such facts as whether (if the expressions are terms) the user accepts or is disposed to accept the relevant identity. This sort of fact is (of course) relevant to whether the person has contradictory beliefs, and to the issues raised by Kripke's puzzle.

---

[19] "Knowledge by Acquaintance and Knowledge by Description," reprinted in Salmon and Soames (1988), 22.

[20] Sosa, who thinks that Pierre's uses of "Londres" and "London" must have different meanings, seems prepared to endorse this conclusion in Sosa (1996), 398.

[21] This understanding arises, I think, because of Frege's habit of using different codesignating descriptions to provide examples of different senses that present the same object, along with the assumption that predicate senses, as public but platonic entities, must be the sort of thing Russell had in mind in speaking of universals. I am frankly uncertain whether this is the proper way to understand Frege.

IX

Kripke's puzzle is a puzzle about belief. But it turns into a puzzle about translation: Can we, or can we not, translate Pierre's use of "Londres est jolie" with our use (or Pierre's, for that matter) of "London is pretty"?

There are at least two projects we may undertake which could be called "interpretation" or "translation." One is finding a projectable way of going from someone's utterances (inscriptions and even occurrent linguistic mental events) to (potential) utterances (inscriptions and occurrent mental events) of our own, a way of doing this which allows us to understand the other's language. Armed with such, we would be in a position to say things like "Pierre's utterance of "London is pretty" means that London is pretty," or "Pierre's use of 'je ne pense pas que Roubaix est au sud de Lille,' meant that he doesn't think that Roubaix is south of Lille." A second project is finding a way of getting from the other's utterances (inscriptions, occurrent mental events), behavior, and general position in the world to a characterization of what he thinks, wants, says, and so forth—and thus, to a position in which we can say things like "Pierre thinks that London is pretty," or "Pierre wishes that Roubaix were south of Lille." Call the first project *linguistic interpretation,* the second *individual interpretation.*

These are not completely separate projects, of course. But it is worth insisting that they *are* separate projects, and are typically subject to differing constraints.[22] Linguistic interpretation is, and must be, done at the wholesale (not the retail) level: it is impossible to start anew with each individual and puzzle out what their words mean. What we do—do because we have learned to do it and expect one another to do it—is impose a single scheme of interpretation on those around us, tinkering at the edges when it seems advisable. The scheme we impose, of course, is usually the scheme we were *taught* to impose, when we were "taught the ambient language." Wholesale imposition of such a scheme on one another allows us to understand one another in large part because our wholesale mutual imposition of (and acquiescence in) a uniform scheme of interpretation helps make it the case that we all mean the same thing with our words. The *point* of our all behaving as if we speak the same language is that our behaving in this way pretty much guarantees that (niceties about morphophonetic and small syntactic variation to the side) we *do* have a common language. Our so behaving thus helps to ensure that linguistic interpretation can pretty much proceed on automatic pilot.

Linguistic interpretation is not exactly Millian, but it is, or at least is usually, pretty close. How, after all, could it help but be? Our talk is about objects, their properties, and their relations; we care very much what others say and think about them. We care enough about this that we demand that interpretation preserve reference and satisfaction conditions. And beyond reference and satisfaction conditions, there just isn't that much that linguistic interpretation can preserve. It is, as Kripke notes, pretty rare for a word like a

---

[22] Davidson's use of the idea of radical interpretation as an account of linguistic interpretation is unfortunate in that it blurs the fact that linguistic interpretation and individual interpretation are quite different projects.

name to have a community-wide connotation (108), and so it is for the most part impossible for translation to preserve such. Ways of thinking are so idiosyncratic, for the most part, that requiring translation to preserve them would bring the enterprise to a grinding halt.[23] A (more or less) Millian scheme of linguistic interpretation seems like a good place—pretty much the only place—to start, if we are looking for a way to interpret those in the environs.

But when I want to know what someone thinks, wants, and hopes—when I want to interpret an individual—something more than this is called for. To know the attitudes of another is to be in a position to understand how those attitudes motivate him, to know "how the world seems" to him. If I am to come to know these things by interpreting the other's utterances and behavior in my own idiom, that interpretation needs to reflect more than just what objects, properties, and relations he refers to or thinks about. After all, if only that were reflected in individual interpretation, such interpretation could not distinguish between someone who had contradictory beliefs (believing that, say, Twain is dead and Twain—the very same Twain—is not dead), and someone whose beliefs were inconsistent but not contradictory (as are those of one who thinks that Twain, but not Clemens, is dead).

Over and above correctly capturing the reference of another's words, what seems necessary (and in practice seems to be all we can reasonably be expected to achieve) for individual interpretation is that we capture the overall structure of the way in which they think about the world—capture the identity and difference of their ways of thinking of things and properties, as those ways of thinking are deployed in their hopes, knowledge, desires, and dreams. If, for example, the other's use of sentences S and S' involve the same (different) way(s) of thinking of an individual, that is to be reflected in our interpretation of those uses. Of course, the natural way to achieve this is for our account, of what another believes, wants, and so on, to satisfy a principle like (R). It is easy enough to see how one attempts to satisfy such a principle: One surmises when utterances (or actions expressive of an attitude) involve the same way of thinking of an individual, and when they involve different ways of thinking thereof; one tries to preserve such sameness and difference in interpretation, assigning to each way of thinking its own linguistic representation. Of course, that may not always be possible, at least not without introduction of neologisms—as when one says, of a person who thinks that Paderewski the politician and Paderewski the musician are distinct, that they do not realize that Paderewski the politician is Paderewski the musician.[24]

---

[23] Our ways of thinking are, of course, also typically unknown to others, so that even if they were shared, our ignorance of them would—if we need to preserve them to linguistically interpret—bring linguistic interpretation to a standstill.

[24] David Braun suggested to me that Kripke's example of Peter (who accepts "Pederewski was a musician" and "Pederewski wasn't a musician") casts doubt on the claim at the beginning of this section that Kripke's puzzle turns on a puzzle about translation. I disagree. What is puzzling about the man who doesn't realize that Pederewski the musician is Pederewski the politician is—I would say—that the meaning of "Pederewski was a musician, but Pederewski wasn't a musician"—the linguistic meaning of the

Linguistic interpretation is something one does (so far as is possible) in advance. Individual interpretation is much more a one-off affair. This is, of course, partly a matter of its being (more nearly) possible to know in advance, and independently of much interaction with another, what her words and gestures mean, than it is to know how those words or gestures express beliefs. But individual interpretation is also one-off simply because there is no one way to do it. This is not (or not just) because (for Quinean reasons) there is semantic indeterminancy. Rather, it is because there will be, when others are confused or ignorant, more than one way to limit the structure of their picture of the world, which is determined by the ways they think of its objects.

Linguistic intepretation is something we can (almost) always pull off, if only because we work so hard (all of us going to school and "learning the same language") to be in a position to be able to (effortlessly) pull it off. Individual interpretation is something we cannot always do—or cannot always do limited to the resources at hand. In the case of Pierre, for example, we are hamstrung: His way of looking at the world has a structure not reflected in the vocabulary we have to describe it. He has two ways of thinking of a thing for which we have but one name.

This section began with a question about translation: Can we, or can we not, translate Pierre's use of "Londres est jolie" with our use (or Pierre's, for that matter) of "London is pretty"? The suggestion just made is that the question can be taken in two ways, as a question about linguistic interpretation, or as one about individual interpretation. We can give a linguistic translation of Pierre's utterances. We can also give a piecemeal individual interpretation of Pierre's utterances as expressive of what he believes. We can, after all, focus simply on his "French beliefs," ignoring his English ones. And then we can pretty much preserve what needs preserving, in the way the world looks to Pierre, by using a linguistic translation of those utterances. We can do the same thing should we focus solely on his "English beliefs." What we can't do—at least not without making use of an idiom whose syntactic resources reflect the structure of Pierre's conceptual system—is give an interpretation of all of his beliefs at once.

---

sentence—as he uses it is the same as the meaning—the linguistic meaning—of the sentence as we use it. Ditto for "Peter believes that Paderewski is a pianist, but Paderewski is not a pianist." But when the confused man (sincerely) utters the first sentence, he doesn't express a contradictory belief, while we would do so if we uttered it. And while it is no big thing for the man to use the second sentence in a way that doesn't imply that Peter has contradictory beliefs, it is difficult indeed for us to do this. What is puzzling, is how these sentences could mean the same as Peter and we use them—how one could translate the other—but have such different properties when it comes to what mental states they express and what the implications of using them in ascribing such states are.

The problem here, as in the case of Pierre, is one that arises because identity of linguistic meaning is not a reliable guide to identity of belief expressed, even given that we are looking at someone who understands the sentences in question (and so "knows what they mean"). That is, the problem arises because (given the identity of linguistic meaning) we can translate the other's idiom into ours, but that translation doesn't allow us to interpret (in the sense of the text) the other.

X

The linguistic interpretation—the translation, if you will—of Pierre's sentence "Londres est jolie" is "London is pretty." We do not have to know very much about Pierre, beyond the fact that he speaks French, to know that. The linguistic interpretation of "Pierre croit que Londres est jolie" is "Pierre believes that London is pretty." This we know, as it were, once and for all, and not on a one-off basis.

When Pierre sincerely says "Londres est jolie," *he* knows that he is expressing a belief; *he* knows how to interpret himself: je crois que Londres est jolie. Can *I* interpret him by saying that he believes that London is pretty? That all depends. It depends, in particular, on what I have already done in the way of interpreting him. If I have been discussing the beliefs he is wont to express in English about London, I will most probably have been using sentences in which the word "London" occurs, saying that Pierre is convinced that London is not pretty. I cannot then just turn around and say that he believes that London is pretty; at the very least, some contextualization of such a claim is needed.

This may seem weird. Given the facts about linguistic interpretation—about translation—how can there be any doubt about whether I can interpret Pierre's "je crois que Londres est jolie" with "Pierre believes that London is pretty"? The two sentences mean the same thing, for goodness sake.

Indeed. But whether I can describe another's beliefs in a particular way very much depends upon the context of description. My descriptions of others' beliefs—my ascriptions thereof—are sensitive to the context in which they are made. And as we all know, when a sentence is context-sensitive, its truth in one context does not assure its truth in others. Likewise, there is no guarantee that the translation of a context-sensitive sentence will, in the context of translation, have the truth value of the translated sentence in the context from which it is translated. The two sentences "Pierre croit que Londres est jolie" and "Pierre believes that London is pretty" mean the same thing. So do the sentences "je suis fatigué" and "I'm tired." But one wouldn't infer from this synonymy that when Pierre says "[je crois que] je suis fatigué," I can interpret him as saying "[Pierre thinks that] I'm tired."

The banal principle (T) is *of course* subject to qualification: If S translates as T from your language to mine, and S is true as you use it, T will be true as I use it *if* S (and T) are free of context-sensitive vocabulary. I suspect that Kripke, in framing (T), thought that such qualification was unnecessary. He was, after all, concerned with sentences like "Pierre believes that London is pretty" and its French translatation; tense aside, he probably thought, there is nothing context-sensitive in such sentences. As I see it, Kripke's puzzle arises, in part, because such sentences *are* contextually sensitive in the way I have been suggesting. Given the sort of contextual sensitivity I am suggesting they have, given someone suffering from the sort of confusion from which poor, poor Pierre suffers, *and* given the lack of multiple words for London in English, we are in a bit of a pickle, when we try to answer the question, Does he, or does he not, believe that London is pretty?[25]

Let us take stock. Schematic principles such as

(D$_2$)   Pierre's uses (in the language he speaks in London) of instances of "If I, Pierre, on reflection, sincerely assent to 'p', where 'p' is a sentence of my language, then I, Pierre, believe that p" are true in the language Pierre speaks in London

are surely true. Uses of instances of (D), the schematic, third-person ancestor of (D$_2$), are perhaps invariably true when taken relative to contexts in which no substantive interpretation has already occurred. We can reliably *begin* interpreting another by using the linguistic interpretation of his speech. If, however, he suffers from some sort of confusion (which may become manifest when we look at linguistic translations of his speech), we may not be able to completely interpret him via linguistic translation.

Construed as principles about linguistic interpretation and suitably qualified, principles such as (T) are banal truths. But they do not yield puzzling or paradoxical consequences about Pierre's beliefs. Indeed, given the ubiquity of context dependence in natural language—is there, for example, a comparative adjective which is *not* context-dependent?—there is very little which a suitably qualified version of (T) tells us. The principle

(R)   Multiple occurrences of an expression within ascriptions of attitude to a single person indicate that the attitudes involve multiple occurrences of a single way of thinking in the attitudes ascribed

seems (to me) to tell us something important about how we ascribe attitudes to others. It is, in my opinion, in part because something along the lines of (R) is true that we find Kripke's puzzle genuinely puzzling. (R) is craftily phrased ("indicate") so that it can be taken as a principle about the semantics of attitude ascription, or as one about its pragmatics; only those who take it to be a semantic principle are likely to be moved by the argument of the last two sections, that what Kripke's puzzle shows us is that interpreting others by assigning them beliefs is a contextually sensitive affair. I hope that even those who reject this will at least assent to the pragmatic version of (R), and the diagnosis of Kripke's puzzle that I've offered.

Do we say, when we say "Pierre believes that London is pretty, and Pierre believes that London is not pretty" that Pierre's beliefs are contradictory? Since the language we use to ascribe belief is context-sensitive, there need be no unequivocal answer to this question.

---

[25] At this point, one wants to hear a story about the precise nature of the context sensitivity I allege for sentences like "Pierre believes that Paris is pretty." Different authors will tell different stories here, and an essay on Kripke's essay is not the place for that literature review. A reader interested in my own views of the matter might look at the close of Richard (2005).

It would not be surprising, I think, to discover that the answer was that it depends: a *normal* use of this would entail that he had contradictory beliefs, but unusual uses of this—ones in a special context in which our interests are simply to convey the truth conditions of various pieces of Pierre's unfortunate mental landscape—may not have such an entailment.[26]

"Does Pierre, or does he not, believe that London is pretty?" If there were a Pierre, and someone asked such a question about him—in the course of an everyday, "nonphilosophical" conversation, with interests of a more or less normal sort—the question might well have a straightforward answer. What that answer would be would depend on the situation in which the question was asked, the interests and focus of conversants, what had been said already, and what was presupposed. If the question were asked when our philosophical noses were being rubbed in the sordid details of Pierre's intellectual history, the question probably wouldn't have a straightforward answer. That doesn't seem terribly problematic to me—lots of questions don't have a straightforward answer.[27]

---

[26] This is my own view of the matter. I take (R) to be a rule of thumb about the truth conditions of ascriptions of attitude. Normally, ascriptions of attitude to an individual will be *true* only if the identity and difference of vocabulary in the ascriptions faithfully reflects identity and difference among ways of thinking involved in the attitudes ascribed. But (R) is a rule of thumb, and when pressure is put upon it, by a case like that of Pierre's, it may be broken. Again, the interested (or puzzled) reader can look at "Propositional Attitude Ascriptions." Richard (2006).

[27] Thanks to David Braun for comments. And thanks to Saul Kripke for providing a model of how philosophy can be rigorous and accessible, genuinely significant and still fun.

This essay was finished almost six years ago (2006). I have resisted the urge to revise to discuss recent work—especially that of Kit Fine and Scott Soames—that bears on the essay's topic.

References

Almog, J., Perry J., and Wettstein, H. (1989) (eds), *Themes from Kaplan* (Oxford University Press).
Azcel, P. (1988), *Non-Well-Founded Sets* (University of Chicago Press).
Burge, T. (1979), "Individualism and the Mental," *Midwest Studies in Philosophy* 4(1), 73–121.
Chisholm, R. (1981), *The First Person* (University of Minnesota Press).
Chomsky, N. (1980), *Rules and Representations* (Columbia University Press).
Church, A. (1950), "On Carnap's Analysis of Statements of Assertion and Belief," *Analysis* 10(5), 97–9.
Crimmins, M. (1992a), *Talk about Beliefs* (MIT Press).
Crimmins, M. (1992b), "Context in the Attitudes," *Linguistics and Philosophy* 15, 185–98.
Crimmins, M. (1998), "Hesperus and Phosphorus: Sense, Pretense, and Reference," *Philosophical Review* 107, 1–48.
Crimmins, M. and Perry, J. (1989), "The Prince and the Phone Booth," *Journal of Philosophy* 86, 685–711.
Dennett, D. (1978), "A Cure for the Common Code?," in D. Dennett, *Brainstorms* (Bradford Books).
Devitt, M. (1981), *Designation* (Columbia University Press).
Donnellan, K. (1979), "The Contingent A Priori and Rigid Designation," in P. French et al. (eds), *Contemporary Perspectives in the Philosophy of Language* (Minnesota University Press).
Donnellan, K. (1989), "Belief and the Identity of Reference," *Midwest Studies in Philosophy* 14, 275–88.
Evans, G. (1982), *The Varieties of Reference* (Oxford University Press).
Evans, G. (1990), "Understanding Demonstratives," in P. Yourgrau (ed.), *Demonstratives* (Oxford University Press), pp. 71–96.
Fine, K. (2007), *Semantic Relationism* (Blackwell).
Forbes, G. (1987), "Indexicals and Intensionality: A Fregean Perspective," *The Philosophical Review* 96, 3–31.
Forbes, G. (1989), *Languages of Possibility* (Blackwell).
Forbes, G. (1990), "The Indispensibility of Sinn," *The Philosophical Review* 99, 535–63.
Forbes, G. (2011), "The Problem of Factives for Sense Theories," *Analysis* 71, 654–62.
Grandy, R. (1986), "Some Misconceptions about Belief," in R. Grandy and R. Warner (eds), *Philosophical Grounds of Rationality* (Oxford University Press), pp. 317–32.
Gupta, A. (1982), "Truth and Paradox," *Journal of Philosophical Logic* 11(1), 1–60.
Higginbotham, J. (1995), "Tensed Thoughts", in *Mind and Language* 10, 226–49.
Kaplan, D. (1964), *Foundations of Intensional Logic* (University Microfilms).
Kaplan, D. (1975), "What is Russell's Theory of Descriptions?," in D. Davidson and G. Harman (eds), *The Logic of Grammar (Dickenson Publishing Co.)*, pp. 210–17.
Kaplan, D. (1979), "On the Logic of Demonstratives," in P. French et al. (eds), *Contemporary Perspectives in the Philosophy of Language* (University of Minnesota Press), pp. 401–14.

Kaplan, D. (1986), "Opacity," in L.E. Hahn and P.A. Schilpp (eds), *The Philosophy of W.V. Quine* (Open Court), pp. 229–89.
Kaplan, D. (1989), "Demonstratives," in Almog, Perry, and Wettstein (eds), pp. 481–564.
Kaplan, D. (1990), "Words," in *Proceedings of the Aristotelian Society*, supp. vol. 64, 93–119.
Katz, J. (1994), "Names without Bearers," *The Philosophical Review* 103, 1–39.
Kripke, S. (1976), "Is there are a Problem about Substitutional Quantification?," in G. Evans and C. McGinn (eds), *Meaning and Truth* (Oxford University Press), pp. 325–419.
Kripke, S. (1979), "A Puzzle About Belief," in A. Margalit (ed.), *Meaning and Use* (Reidel), pp. 239–83. Reprinted in Salmon, N. and Soames, S. (eds), (1988).
Kripke, S. (1980), *Naming and Necessity* (Harvard University Press).
LaPorte, J. (2004), *Natural Kinds and Conceptual Change* (Cambridge University Press).
Levin, H. (1982), *Categorical Grammar and the Logical Form of Quantification* (Bibliopolis).
Lewis, D. (1979), "Attitudes *De Dicto* and *De Se*," in *The Philosophical Review* 88, 513–43.
Lewis, D. (1979a), "Scorekeeping in a Language Game," in *Journal of Philosophical Logic* 8, 339–59.
Lewis, D. (1983), *Collected Papers, Vol. 1* (Oxford University Press).
Lewis, D. (1999), "What Puzzling Pierre Does Not Believe," in *Papers in Metaphysics and Epistemology, Vol. II* (Cambridge University Press), pp. 408–17.
Montague, R. (1974a), "The Proper Treatment of Quantification in Ordinary English," in Thomason (1974).
Montague, R. (1974b), "On the Nature of Certain Philosophical Entities," in Thomason (1974).
Perry, J. (1979), "The Problem of the Essential Indexical," *Noûs* 13, 3–21.
Perry, J. (1980), "Belief and Acceptance," in P. French et al. (eds), *Midwestern Studies in Philosophy*, Vol. V (University of Minnesota Press), pp. 533–42.
Prior, A.N. (1959), "Thank Goodness That's Over", *Philosophy* 34, 12–17.
Prior, A.N. (1971), *Objects of Thought* (Oxford University Press).
Putnam, H. (1975), "The Meaning of 'Meaning,'" in H. Putnam (1975), *Mind, Language, and Reality* (Cambridge University Press).
Quine, W.V. (1956), "Quantifiers and Propositional Attitudes," *The Journal of Philosophy* 53, 177–87.
Quine, W.V. (1960), *Word and Object* (MIT Press).
Quine, W.V. (1960), "Variables Explained Away," in *Proceedings of the American Philosophical Society* 104, 343–7.
Quine, W.V. (1966), *The Ways of Paradox* (Random House).
Richard, M. (1982), "Tense, Propositions, and Meanings," *Philosophical Studies* 41, 337–51.
Richard, M. (1988), "Taking the Fregean Seriously," in D. Austin (ed.), *Philosophical Analysis: A Defense by Example* (Kluwer Academic Publishers), pp. 219–40.
Richard, M. (1990), *Propositional Attitudes: An Essay on Thoughts and How We Ascribe Them* (Cambridge University Press).
Richard, M. (1993), "Critical study of Boer and Lycan, *Knowing Who* (MIT Press)," *Nous* 27, 235–43.
Richard, M. (1998), "Commitment," *Philosophical Perspectives* 12, 255–81.
Richard, M. (2004), "Contextualism and Relativism," *Philosophical Studies* 119, 215–42.

Richard, M. (2006), "Propositional Attitude Ascription," in M. Devitt and R. Healy (eds), *The Blackwell Handbook of Semantics* (Blackwell), pp. 186–211.

Richard, M. (2006a), "Opacity," in E. LePore and B. Smith (eds), *The Oxford Handbook of Philosophy of Language* (Oxford University Press), pp. 667–88.

Russell, B. (1911), "Knowledge by Acquaintance and Knowledge by Description," in N. Salmon and S. Soames (eds), (1988).

Russell, B. (1912), *The Problems of Philosophy* (H. Holt and Co.).

Sainsbury, M. (1977), "Semantics by Proxy," *Analysis* 37, 86–96.

Salmon, N. (1981), *Reference and Essence* (Princeton University Press).

Salmon, N. (1986), *Frege's Puzzle* (MIT Press).

Salmon, N. and Soames, S. (eds) (1988), *Propositions and Attitudes* (Oxford University Press).

Saul, J. (1999), "The Road to Hell: Intentions and Propositional Attitude Ascription," *Mind and Language* 14, 356–75.

Schein, B. (1993), *Plurals and Events* (MIT Press).

Schiffer, S. (1990), "The Relational Theory of Belief," *Pacific Philosophical Quarterly* 71, 240–5.

Sider, T. (1995), "Three Problems for Richard's Theory of Belief Ascription," *Canadian Journal of Philosophy* 25, 487–513.

Soames, S. (1987), "Substitutivity," in J.J. Thompson (ed.), *On Being and Saying* (MIT Press), pp. 99–132.

Soames, S. (1995), "Beyond Singular Propositions?," *Canadian Journal of Philosophy* 25, 515–49.

Soames, S. (2002), *Beyond Rigidity* (Oxford University Press).

Soames, S. (2005), "Naming and Asserting," in Z. Szabo (ed.) (2005), pp. 356–82.

Sosa, D. (1996), "The Import of the Puzzle About Belief", *Philosophical Review* 105, 373–402.

Stalnaker, R. (1984), *Inquiry* (MIT Press).

Sazbo, Z. (ed.) (2005), *Semantics vs. Pragmatics* (Oxford University Press).

Thomason, R. (ed.) (1974), *Formal Philosophy: Selected Papers of Richard Montague* (Yale University Press), pp. 247–70.

Walton, K. (1990), *Mimesis as Make Believe* (Harvard University Press).

Index

Acceptance 29–30
Accommodation 20, 130–4, 261
Acquaintance 2, 223 fn2, 231
Aczel, P. 91 fn8
Adjectives, gradable 261
Almog J. 156 fn1
Annotations 21–2, 85–6
  see also restrictions on translation
Attitude ascriptions
  cognitive models (CM's) 70, 74–6
  and content 20, 21
  de dicto 34
  de re 27–39, 42–4, 45 fn18
  de se 7 fn10, 27, 31, 32–5, 37–9, 43, 47 fn21
  and explanation of behavior 65–6, 69, 72–3, 75–6, 78
  Fregean approach to 3, 65–7, 69–70, 73, 76, 79, 82–3, 88, 89, 115, 156, 266
  implicit quantifier account 68, 70, 74–5, 78
  and principle of disquotation (D) 266–73, 281
  Russellian approach to 65–6, 68–9, 72–3, 76–7, 79, 81, 84–6, 89, 91 fn10, 94 fn10, 156, 266
  and sentential propositions 254–7
  substitutivity 65–6, 73, 77–8
  tensed beliefs
    see also tense; translation

Belief
  belief text 113–15
  contradictory 264–9, 273–81
  de dicto 34, 38–9
  de re 27, 31–9, 42–4
  de se 27, 31–4, 37–9, 43
  individuation of 166–8
  manner of 30, 46–7
  mediators of 81–3, 85, 86
  object dependent 170
  objects of 27, 29–31, 33 fn12, 34, 36, 97, 101, 141, 143 149, 155, 157–8, 160 fn5, 167–70, 230–4
  realizing state 18, 165–7
  and representational system (RS) 85–6, 88–90, 95
  Russell's multiple relation theory 138
  tensed 222–6, 228–35, 239–43, 245
  triadic view of 26–7, 29–32, 41
  and ways of thinking 266, 268–9

Belleaubois, D. 190–6
  see also Roquelaure, Duc de
Burge, T. 1, 267 fn8

Carnap, R. 81, 89–91, 149, 152
Character 28, 29, 30 fn8, 103 fn3, 224, 234–45, 260
Chisholm, R. 32 fn11, 33 fn12, 39
Chomsky, N. 270, 272
Church, A. 81, 87 fn5, 89, 91, 139, 152
Cognitive significance 157, 158, 162, 168, 224–5, 234, 236, 238, 239–41, 254
Compositional semantics 140
Concept 14, 16, 18, 20, 220, 240, 273
Conceptual role 82, 89, 240–2
Conditions 51–60, 62 fn17
Content
  referential and non-referential 14, 16–7, 24–5, 82, 88–90
  structured and unstructured 18–20
Context
  defective 124–6, 128, 133 fn14
  donut contexts 117
  global 130 fn11, 132, 133 fn15, 258–9
  local 130 fn11, 132, 258–9
  normalization 132–4
  saying potential 152–3
Context sensitivity 101, 103, 108–9 121, 130–4, 205, 256, 259–61, 267, 270, 280–1
  adjectives 121, 257, 261, 281
  attitude verbs 24–5, 121, 134, 260–2
  and restrictions on translation 22, 24, 86–90, 92–4, 97–8, 102–3, 105–8, 114–15, 122, 125–30, 134–6, 150–2
Contingent a priori knowledge 156, 168–9
Correlation 85–7, 93
  see also translation
Counterpart relation 164, 165, 167
Crimmins, M. 100–8, 111, 114–20, 173–4, 179, 180–4, 190–4

Davidson, D. 62, 226, 272 fn12, 277 fn22
Demonstratives 26–35, 39–44 78, 81, 83, 89, 96, 142, 144–7
Dennett, D. 17
Devitt, M. 145 fn7
Direct reference 26–32, 33 fn12, 39–41, 47, 89, 156, 163 fn8, 211
Dispositions and belief 18–19
Donnellan, K. 169, 274 fn14

E-isomorphism 144–5, 147, 150, 154
Evans, G. 160–1, 191, 236, 238
Explanation of behavior 65–6, 69, 72–3, 75–6, 78
Extensions 51–7, 62, 201–4, 209–10, 212, 214–19, 260–1

Fiction
　discourse about 172, 176–9, 181, 184, 186
　objects from 172, 180–5
　truth in 172–4, 181, 184–96
Forbes, G. 13, 67 fn2, 156, 157–8, 160–2, 164–9
Frege, G. 2–6, 11–14, 65–79, 82–9, 115, 143–5, 156–67, 170, 223–4, 245, 246, 251, 266, 276
　see also sense

Godel, K. 220
Grandy, R. 149 fn9
Gupta, A. 63 fn19

Higginbotham, J. 224–34, 242–5

Indeterminacy 15 fn25, 24 fn37, 279
Indexicals 26–7, 32 fn11, 78, 80, 83, 87 fn5, 90–1, 102, 103 fn3, 106, 108, 224
　indexical modes of thinking 234
Indiscernibility of identicals 48 fn1
Intensional entities 137
Intensionality 138–41
　hypter-intensionality 199, 202
Intensional transitives (IT's) 197, 199, 201–4, 218, 221
　D-reading 197–9, 201–2, 207, 211–12, 216–18, 220
　R-reading 197–8, 202, 206, 211, 217–18
Intensions 58, 60, 63 fn17, 130, 137–41, 148, 151, 153, 201–5, 208–10, 216

Kaplan, D. 1, 26, 27 fn4, 28–9, 30 fn8, 33 fn12, 35 fn14, 41 fn17, 56 fn11, 59 fn13, 62, 81 fn2, 87 fn5, 90, 96 fn12, 101, 103 fn3, 108–9, 116–18, 133 fn18, 143, 145 fn7, 155–6, 163 fn8, 223–4, 234–8, 245
Kerrigan example 123–5, 136
Kripke, S. 1, 66 fn1, 81, 105 fn7, 141, 156–7, 159–62, 169–70, 248–50
　puzzle about belief 92–4, 263–81

Leibniz's Law (L) 48–64
Levin, H. 52 fn6
Lewis, D. 33 fn12, 39, 130–2, 258, 261, 275 fn17
　conversational score 130–2, 258

McDowell, J. 160
Meaning 1, 4–5, 13–15, 26, 29–38, 42–5, 47, 270
　as character 29, 30 fn8, 90
　i-reduced meaning 36–7
　propositional matrix 248–52
　reduced meaning 33–6
　Soames on 246–62
Millianism 156, 180, 187, 246, 251, 264–5, 274, 277–8
Modality 157–61, 191–6, 248–50
　and sentential accounts of propositions 153–5
Mode of demonstrating and mode of addressing 30 fn8
Modes of presentation 140, 162, 172–3, 180–2, 185, 190–1, 194–6, 224
Montague, R. 155, 201–3

Names, empty 199, 202, 212, 215, 217
　in fiction 172, 175–86, 189, 194
　and intensional transitives 197, 199, 201–4, 218, 221
　and pretense 172–5, 189
Negative existentials 174, 190–6

Perry, J. 26, 100–1, 105, 107 fn8, 115–20, 222 fn1, 234
Piggy backing 179–82, 191–6
Possible worlds semantics 13, 19, 51, 191, 201–5
Pragmatics
　Pragmatic enrichment 249–52
　Pragmatic explanations of intuitions 65, 77–8, 103, 211, 281
Pretense
　and attitude ascriptions 180–5, 188–91
　and fictional discourse 172, 176–86
　fictional truth 185–96
　and negative existentials 190–6
　principles of generation for 174, 178–80, 192 fn20, 192–4, 195 fn25
Principle of substitutivity 265
Prior, A. N. 137–41, 143, 146, 153, 155 fn13, 222
Proper names 81, 95–6, 157–9, 163, 170, 198, 201, 203 fn6, 264–5
　descriptional account of sense 158–9
　referential account of sense 158–61
Propositions
　annotated 21–5
　articulated 125, 136, 254
　individuation of 98
　mode of apprehension 224
　propositional quantification 67, 96
　sentences and 84
　sentential 254
　structured 3, 14, 21, 23, 66, 68, 72–3, 81, 84–5, 97, 101, 116, 119, 138, 181, 185–6, 188, 224 fn3, 241 fn14, 254
　and truth predicate 91 fn8, 97, 271

INDEX 289

unstructured 13, 19, 51, 191, 201–5
  see also sense, RAMs
Proto-properties 43–4
Putnam, H. 15
Puzzles about attitudes and attitude ascription
  Hesperus / Phosphorus 8, 48–9, 56, 63, 67,
    70–1, 76–8, 81–8, 96–7, 164–7, 173, 177,
    180–93, 243, 255–6
  Peter / Pederweski 81, 92–6, 110, 278 fn24
  Pierre / London 81, 92–6, 100–20, 150–2, 256,
    263–82

Quantification
  decomposition hypothesis 207
  higher order 220 fn16
  and intensional transitives 199, 200–8,
    216–20
  monotone down quantifiers 207–8, 218
  monotone up quantifiers 207, 210 fn11
  nominal 138–41, 147 fn8
  objectual 21, 48–57, 62, 67, 137–40, 151, 155
  over propositions 137–8, 141, 147–8
  propositional quantifiers (PQ's) 138–42, 144,
    148–9, 151
  Quine on 49–52, 56–63, 137–41
  sentential 138–42
  see also variables
  substitutional 137–42, 146–8, 155
Quine, W.V.O. 49, 50, 52, 56, 58–60, 63, 134–43,
    197 fn1

RAM
  see Russellian Articulated Matrix
Reference 1, 5, 12–17, 24–5, 26–34, 39–42, 47, 48,
    65–70, 73, 77–8, 80–5, 88–90, 95, 98,
    100–1, 113–16, 119–20, 140–8, 152–3,
    156–64, 168–70, 211, 217, 225–30, 233, 235,
    239–45, 248, 250–9, 277–8
  tacit reference 100, 116, 119–20
Reflexive attitudes 8–9, 104–5, 224–34, 245
Relativism 21–5, 262
Representations 1–25, 95–6, 100–20, 105–13, 198,
    204, 210–12, 253–8, 266
  linked representations 7–9, 11
  representational identity 5–7
  representational paths 113–16
  representational types 5–7, 21, 101 109–13
  ways of representing 4–8, 14, 109, 115
  Restrictions on translation 98, 102–8, 114–15,
    122, 124–31, 134–6, 150–1
Rigid designators 13, 28, 155 fn13, 212, 249
Roquelaure, Duc de 212–18
  see also Belleaubois, D.
Russell, Bertrand 1–4, 11–14, 21–3, 50, 65–9,
    76–9, 81–6, 89, 101–3, 129 fn11, 138, 156,
    170, 181, 185–7, 222, 237, 247, 250,
    266, 276

  on acquaintance 2, 266
  on definite descriptions 50, 62
  multiple relation theory of belief 138
  on proper names 65
  R-structures 73–7, 79
  Russellian entities 65–6, 72–3, 81
  Russellian proposition 1, 14, 21, 23, 66, 68,
    72–3, 81, 84–5, 97, 101, 116, 119, 138, 170,
    181–8, 191, 224 fn3, 241 fn14, 254
  Russellian Articulated Matrix (RAM) 84–92,
    95–8, 101–2, 103 fn3, 105–6, 108, 113–14,
    115 fn14, 119, 125 fn7
  supplemented RAM 97
  see also proposition, articulated; proposition,
    sentential

Sainsbury, M 63 fn17
Salmon, N. 27 fn3, 63 fn18, 77 fn8, 81 fn2, 156 fn1
Schein, B. 219 fn16
Schiffer, S. 155 fn13, 276
Sense 2, 5–6, 27–8, 50 fn3, 65–73, 79, 82–3, 88–9,
    115, 137–8, 143, 145, 148, 151, 156–68, 224,
    234, 240, 276
  de re 160–1
  and propositional attitude ascription 65–73,
    79, 266
Sententialism 148–55
Sentential meaning 26, 29, 47
Sequence 51–8
Sider, T. 121–2, 124–5, 256
Sinn 26
  see also sense
Soames, S. 77 fn8, 79 fn10, 89 fn6, 121–2, 124–7,
    129 fn11, 134, 246–52, 255–62, 276 fn19,
    282 fn27
Sosa, D. 264 fn5, 275 fn18
Substitutionalism 141–55

Tarski, A. 50, 51 fn4, 53–7, 91 fn8, 139
Taxonomic profile 214–16, 218 fn15, 221
Tense
  and belief 222–4, 226, 228–35, 238–45
  temporal transients 222–3, 235
Translation
  agglomerative account 128–30, 134–5
  attitude ascription as involving 12–3, 17–8,
    21–5, 67, 80–1, 83, 90, 92, 99 fn14,
    100–3, 105–6, 115, 121–3, 126–7, 130–1,
    135–6, 147, 150–3, 243–5, 253,
    256–9, 272
  Kripke's principle of (T) 267–70, 272–3,
    280–1
  linguistic interpretation and 23–5, 270–3,
    277–81
  manuals and attitude ascription 12, 22–5, 90,
    102, 105, 122, 125, 135–6, 152, 252–4,
    257, 259

Translation (*cont.*)
  translation rules 12–13, 23, 125, 254–8, 260
Truth
  definition of 36–7, 43, 51 fn4, 54, 57, 61, 70, 219
  fictional truth 185–90, 192 fn20, 196
  Tarski-style definition 53, 55, 91
  truth bearers 97, 157, 234
  truth intuitions 103–4, 129
  truth operator/predicate 91, 144, 271
  truth value glut 221
Twin Earth experiments 15–23
Two-dimensionalism 13

Utterances and semantics 5–6, 15, 18, 40–1, 78, 107, 111, 116–20, 123–33, 143–51, 172–96, 226–9, 237, 243, 246–62, 264–6, 271–3, 276–9

Variables
  in objectual quantification 48–61, 138–42
  in RAMs 88, 96
  variable identification problem 71, 78

Walton, K. 172, 174–8, 190 fn18, 191, 193, 195–6
Ways of apprehending 81 fn2, 223–4
Words
  as constituents of propositions 6, 14, 84, 87, 101–2, 114, 254–7
  identity conditions 142–9

The manufacturer's authorised representative in the EU for product safety is
Oxford University Press España S.A. of el Parque Empresarial San Fernando de
Henares, Avenida de Castilla, 2 – 28830 Madrid (www.oup.es/en or product.
safety@oup.com). OUP España S.A. also acts as importer into Spain of products
made by the manufacturer.

www.ingramcontent.com/pod-product-compliance
Lightning Source LLC
LaVergne TN
LVHW010337260326
834688LV00036B/757